LE CORBUSIER

AN ANALYSIS OF FORM

To my parents

LE CORBUSIER
AN ANALYSIS OF FORM

Geoffrey H. Baker
School of Architecture,
Tulane University, New Orleans

third edition

Spon Press
Taylor & Francis Group
LONDON AND NEW YORK

Published by Spon Press,11 New Fetter Lane, London, EC4P, 4EE
29 West 35th Street, New York, NY 1001

First published in 1984 by Van Nostrand Reinhold (International) Co. Ltd

Reprinted 1985, 1986, 1987

Second edition 1989

Reprinted 1991

Third edition 1996

Reprinted 2001 by Spon Press, 2004.

Spon Press is an imprint of the Taylor & Francis Group

© 1984, 1989 Van Nostrand Reinhold (International) Co. Ltd

© 1996 Geoffrey Baker

Printed and bound in Hong Kong

ISBN 0 419 16120 1

CONTENTS

Colour plates appear between pages 178 and 179

v

ACKNOWLEDGEMENTS

The main inspiration for this study came from Peter Eisenman's unpublished doctoral dissertation The Formal basis of Modern Architecture (University of Cambridge 1963) and I must acknowledge a considerable debt to Dr. Eisenman's analytical technique. During my research into Le Corbusier's approach to design I have been encouraged by many people in the places where I have taught and must mention those students at the University of Newcastle upon Tyne who were receptive to the ideas formulated in this book. In particular I must thank Leon von Schaik for his support during the early stages and David Walters for his continued interest over the years.

I must also thank Mme. Françoise de Franclieu for providing access to archive material at the Le Corbusier Fondation in Paris, and M. Fernand Donze for allowing me to examine the Jeanneret archive in the Art School Library at La Chaux-de-Fonds. I am grateful to Mme. Stotzer, M. and Mme. Cornu, Mme. Rahm and M. and Mme. Jaoul for allowing me to invade the privacy of their homes. Thanks are also due to the monastic community of Ste Marie de la Tourette for their kind hospitality during my stay with them. I would like to thank Margaret Hudson and Jean Middleton for their ever-willing help and all my colleagues at the University of Newcastle and Brighton Polytechnic who have offered advice during preparation of the study.

Especial thanks are due to Frank Lyons, for helpful comments on the manuscript, for encouragement throughout and for vital assistance in the closing stages without which the book could not have been completed. I must also thank Lesley Ward, whose commissioning of the book provided the vital spur towards its completion.

art always serves beauty, and beauty is the joy of possessing form, and form is the key to organic life since no living thing can exist without it, so that every work of art including tragedy, witnesses to the joy of existence.

Boris Pasternak, _Doctor Zhivago_, London 1958 p. 444.

... the idea of the artist is form. His emotional life turns likewise to form : tenderness, nostalgia, desire, anger are in him, and so many other impulses, more fluid, more secret, oftentimes more rich, colourful and subtle than those of other men, but not necessarily so. He is immersed in the whole of life ; he steeps himself in it. He is human, he is not a machine. Because he is a man, I grant him everything. But his special privilege is to imagine, to recollect, to think, and to feel in forms... I do not say that form is the allegory or symbol of feeling, but rather its innermost activity. Form activates feeling... Between nature and man form intervenes. The man in question, the artist that is, forms this nature ; before taking possession of it, he thinks it, sees it, and feels it as form.

Henri Focillon, _The life of Forms in Art_, trans. by Beecher and Kubler, New York 2nd ed. 1948, p. 47. by permission of Wittenborn Art Books Inc.

PREFACE

Architecture receives expression through the medium of form and this study focuses on architectural organisation by examining Le Corbusier's manipulation of form. In order to do this a diagrammatic method of analysis is used which dissects the form in order to show how the various elements are related to each other and to particular site conditions. This kind of dissection highlights certain underlying aspects of the organisation, seeking to discover the theme of a work and how this is developed.

The intention is to allow an ordered discussion of design and perhaps in the process to externalise those intuitive processes which inform the final work. This analytical approach does not attempt to suggest how Le Corbusier actually designed his buildings, and although inevitably subjective the analyses discuss relationships which do exist.

In this study an attempt will be made to reveal certain principles of design which can be discerned in Le Corbusier's work. Although used in specific ways by Le Corbusier it is hoped that these principles and techniques may have a wider application so that the study can contribute to our present knowledge of architectural theory.

Geoffrey H. Baker

PREFACE TO THE THIRD EDITION

When this book was first published in 1984, my work on Le Corbusier was about half completed. Missing from the first edition were significant works such as the La Roche-Jeanneret houses and the Villa Stein-de-Monzie (included in the second edition) and the Pavillon Suisse and Villa Shodhan (included in this volume).

But the analytical studies that comprise this book only tell half the story. Over three decades, in parallel with the studies of buildings, I have been drawing together the painstaking research carried out by Charles-Edouard Jeanneret during his formative years, concentrating in particular on those sketches done in La Chaux-de-Fonds and on the study tours to Italy and Asia Minor that form the core of this work. I concluded this survey with an investigation of the way he composed the Purist paintings, and these studies will have been published as <u>Le Corbusier: The Creative Search</u> before this book is in print.

Publication of these complementary investigations points up the connections that can be made between the two strands of Le Corbusier's output. The Ruskinian reverence for nature, so innocently depicted in his youth, re-emerges as part of a majestic synthesis in works such as the monastery of La Tourette or the chapel at Ronchamp. The visit to Italy, where he recorded great frescos and sculpture, imbued his work with a profound respect for the integrity of the artist, and experiences in the eastern Mediterranean informed his understanding of the emotional power of forms seen in light. Compositional moves apparent in the conceptual evolution of major works such as the Pavillon Suisse can be directly related to the way Le Corbusier manipulated the guitars, books and bottles of his Purist paintings.

This body of work has sought to relate the sources of knowledge that informed Le Corbusier's intuition to his theoretical proposals and built work. To do this it has been necessary to identify what he believed to be important, and then to show how this was made manifest in the act of creation. In fact, the close correlation between the way the brain receives information and the way his is processed as the 'raw material' of creativity, have each lent themselves to analysis as a means to reveal the two sides of this single coin.

Geoffrey H. Baker, New Orleans 1995.

PROLOGUE

Like other creative artists architects become familiar with certain workable strategies which they use time and again in various combinations. They learn by experience, absorbing fresh lessons with each successive design so that everything they do is affected by what has gone before. In this way are they fashioned by their works as much as they fashion them.

The extent to which architects design intuitively varies; some more than others rely on a philosophical base as a guide to making decisions. Of the great twentieth century architects Le Corbusier is recognised for his forthright proclamation of architectural theories and his work relates closely to those principles which he advocated.

In this study an attempt will be made to identify key propositions which Le Corbusier advanced and to examine these in terms of buildings which explain them. An exhaustive survey would defeat this objective, so for clarity and convenience his output is divided into four phases, each of which is discussed in outline only in order to show main trends in his work. Many important buildings are omitted from the survey, choice of examples being determined by their capacity to demonstrate key issues.

The book should therefore be seen as a stage-by-stage charting of the way Le Corbusier's design strategies evolved. Each phase has a different kind of importance and despite the apparent simplicity of both buildings and analyses, the section dealing with his formative years outlines how foundations were laid for everything which followed.

As his work grows in sophistication so the analyses become more complex, earlier chapters being seen as preparatory to an understanding of his later buildings. Because this analytical approach will be unfamiliar to many, an introductory section deals with those aspects of form most relevant to the analytical studies which follow, using modern and historical examples to illustrate the various points. Finally various themes in Le Corbusier's work are brought together in order to elucidate those strategies and tactics which have emerged in the study.

1

INTRODUCTION

ASPECTS OF FORM

SITE FORCES

Professor Rudolph Arnheim argues that it is by the controlled application of forces that visual phenomena may be communicated to us as an expression of the forces which govern our lives, indicating either balance or discord, growth, movement, tension or interactions of these phenomena. Discussing the forces which underlie artistic expression he explains that

> the work of art is far from being merely an image of balance
> ... Just as the emphasis of living is on directed activity and
> not on empty repose, so the emphasis of the work of art is
> not on balance, harmony, unity, but on a pattern of forces
> that are being balanced, ordered, unified. [1]

Concluding a discussion of the deployment of cells within organisms D'Arcy Wentworth Thompson describes the behaviour of cells in the growing point as 'determined not by any specific character or properties of their own, but by the position of the forces to which they are subject in the system of which they are a part.' [2]

This growth principle, in which organisms take their form in accordance with those forces which surround them, has a similarity to the way architectural form results partly from the resolution of a particular problem but also from the force characteristics of the context in which this is situated. Buildings relate to their surroundings in the most positive way, taking account of such factors as a view, the position of the sun or the proximity of a route. Site factors such as a hill or a valley, a river or a road may be considered as forces, and as forces they act directly or indirectly on the form.

1 Rudolph Arnheim, Art and Visual Perception, London 1954, p.360
2 D'Arcy Wentworth Thompson, On Growth and Form, Cambridge 1961, p.102

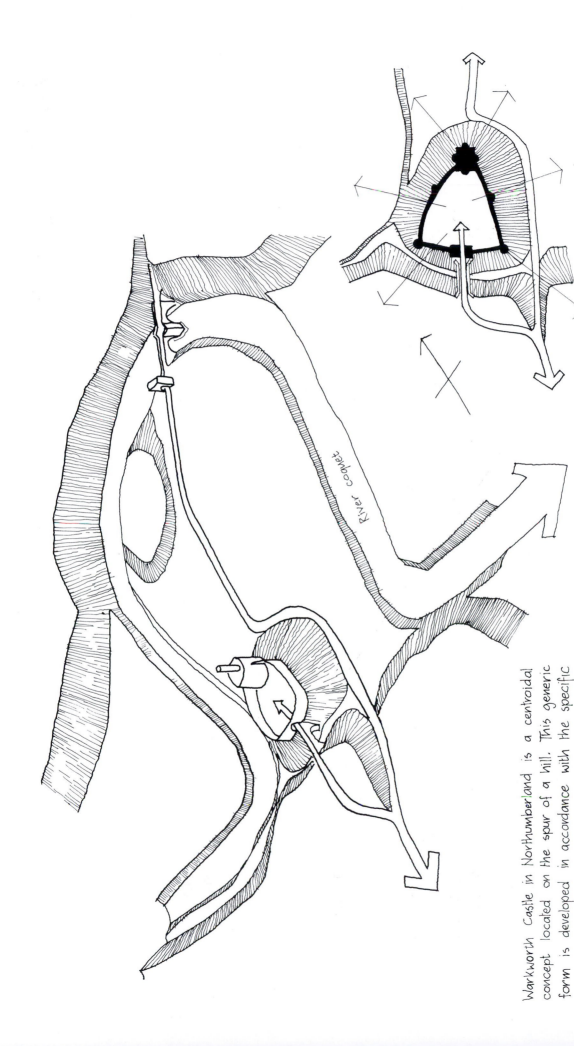

Warkworth Castle in Northumberland is a centroidal concept located on the spur of a hill. This generic form is developed in accordance with the specific requirements of the architectural programme and the characteristics of the particular site. These two sets of conditions may be regarded as forces – a defensive force governing the shape of the castle, this being affected by the centroidal force of the hill and the linear force of the river.

River coquet

In specific terms the form becomes radial and proclamatory.

after a drawing by Simon Buckley

Centroidal configurations such as the sphere and the cube maintain a balance of forces as distinct from linear configurations in which the predominant force has a particular energy and direction.

Centroidal bodies suggest repose and stability whereas linear forms imply activity.

Frank Lloyd Wright's Robie house deploys two linear forms in a potentially shifting relationship.

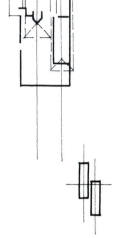

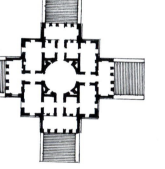

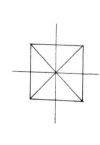

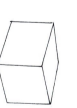

Andrea Palladio's Villa Capra is an almost symmetrical centroid.

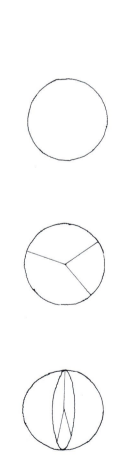

DYNAMICS OF FORM

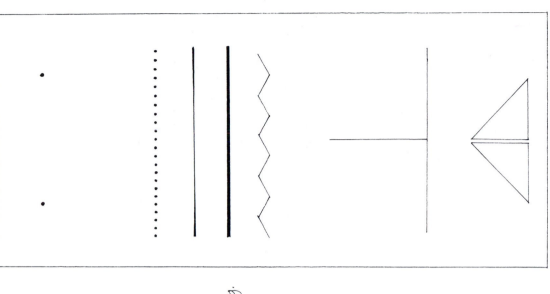

About the dynamics of form Maurice de Sausmarez has written

The simplest unit, a spot, not only indicates location but is felt to have within itself potential energies of expansion and contraction which activate the surrounding area. When two spots occur there is a statement of measurement and implied direction and the 'inner' energies create a specific tension between them which directly affects the intervening space.

A line can be thought of as a chain of spots joined together. It indicates position and direction and has within itself a certain energy, the energy to travel along its length and to be intensified at either end, speed is implied and the space around it is activated. In a limited way it is capable of expressing emotions, e.g. a thick line is associated with boldness, a straight line with strength and stability, a zig-zag with excitement.

Horizontals and verticals operating together introduce the principle of balanced oppositions of tensions. The vertical expresses a force which is of primary significance – gravitational pull, the horizontal again contributes a primary sensation – a supporting flatness ; the two together produce a deeply satisfying resolved feeling, perhaps because they symbolise the human experience of absolute balance, of standing erect on level ground.

Diagonals introduce powerful directional impulses, a dynamism which is the outcome of unresolved tendencies towards vertical and horizontal which are held in balanced suspension.

Maurice de Sausmarez, Basic Design: The Dynamics of Visual Form, Studio Vista London 1964 pp 20-22. by permission of The Herbert Press Ltd.

CORE SYSTEMS

Architectonic arrangements may be described as systems in which the various parts are organised in relation to a thematic idea. The inherent structural nature of architecture implies a geometric organisation and the systemic ordering of architectonic form is therefore geometrical.

Centroidal core systems include the spiral — often expressed as a pinwheel — cluster and cruciform systems.

Systems provide a discipline rather than a limit. They allow for growth, they accommodate the scherzo: They can be elaborated to encompass infinite variations and complexities.

Peter Eisenman

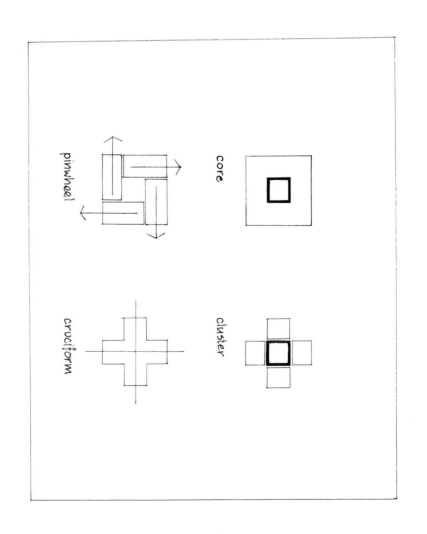

core

cluster

pinwheel

cruciform

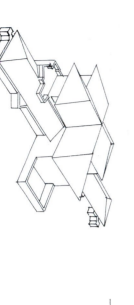

cruciform system   Ward Willitts house : Frank Lloyd Wright.

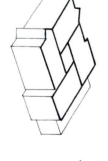

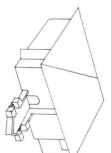

pinwheel system   Arthur Heurtley house : Frank Lloyd Wright.

LINEAR SYSTEMS

Linear systems afford additive opportunities along axes.
This allows for repetition and the development of rhythms.
Movement becomes an important component of the form.

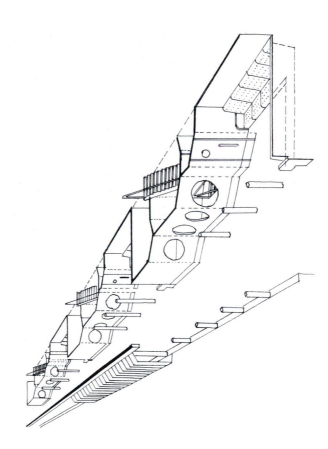

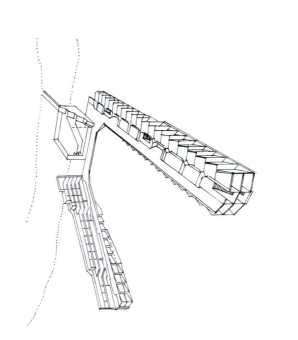

James Stirling   Residential expansion for St. Andrews University 1964

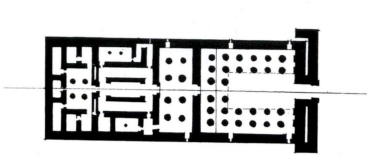

AXIAL SYSTEMS

Axial ordering has formed the basis of monumental architecture since ancient times. Bi lateral symmetry with a hierarchical volumetric arrangement was the main organisational system prior to the twentieth century. During the present century axes have also played a key role in the design strategies of many architects.

Temple of Khons Karnak B.C. 1200

Frank Lloyd Wright Darwin D. Martin house 1904

ECHELON AND RADIAL SYSTEMS

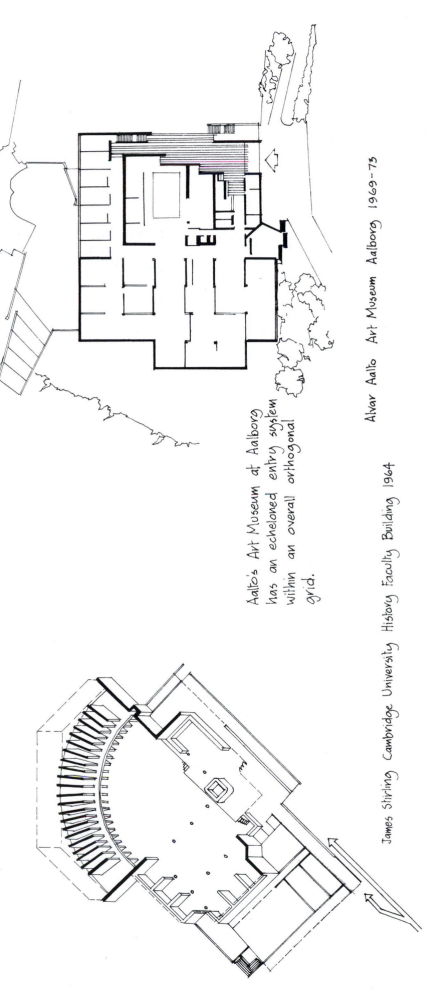

James Stirling's History Faculty Library at Cambridge has a radial plan for the main reading room. This becomes polygonal at the perimeter and entry to the reading room is by an echelon system.

Aalto's Art Museum at Aalborg has an echeloned entry system within an overall orthogonal grid.

Alvar Aalto   Art Museum Aalborg 1969~73

James Stirling Cambridge University History Faculty Building 1964

Unity Church posed a problem for Frank Lloyd Wright in the way to relate the square church to the rectilinear ancillary accommodation. The architect resolves this by locking the two forms together by extending the side walls to the terraces. In his elemental organisation Wright observes the geometric properties of the generic forms.

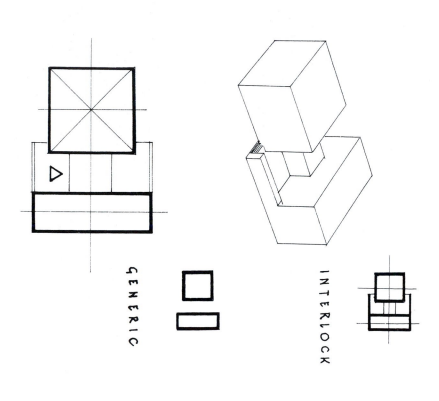

INTERLOCK

GENERIC

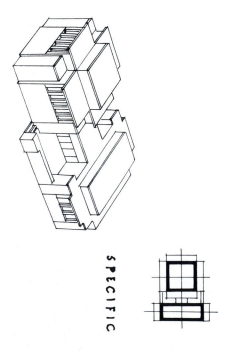

SPECIFIC

Frank Lloyd Wright   Unity Church   Oak Park   Illinois   1906

FORM DISTORTION

Alvar Aalto's Cultural Centre at Wolfsburg is concerned with a centroidal problem on a linear site. The generic core form is distorted by the site to become rectilinear and in specific terms the form responds radially to the piazza by the arrangement of lecture theatres.

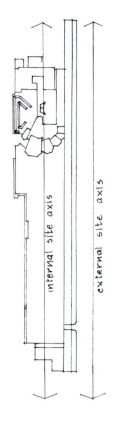

internal site axis

external site axis

SPECIFIC FORM

internal site axis

external site axis

LINEAR SITE

GENERIC FORM   DISTORTION

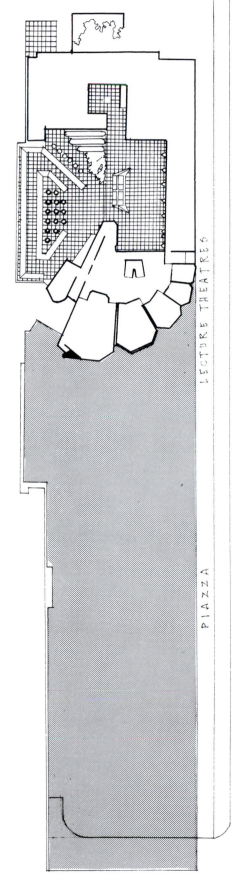

PIAZZA

LECTURE THEATRES

Alvar Aalto Cultural Centre Wolfsburg West Germany 1958-63

Le Corbusier once wrote that 'Nature is order and law, unity and diversity without end, subtlety harmony and strength.'[1]

This attitude towards nature began when he attended the Art School in La Chaux-de-Fonds in Switzerland. During his formative years nature was an important source of decorative ornament and contemporary theorists had formulated a series of principles which acted as a basis for design.

Le Corbusier studied the underlying structure and patterns of growth in plants and shells, and his realisation that efficient growth produced a recognisable sense of equilibrium convinced him that this force was present not only in nature but throughout the Universe.

In this chapter Le Corbusier's attitude towards nature is explained in terms of his designs for three houses, each of which attempts to translate theoretical maxims into architectural form.

1 Le Corbusier The Modulor London 1954 p. 25

2

CHARLES-EDOUARD JEANNERET

THE FORMATIVE YEARS

LA CHAUX-DE-FONDS

Charles-Edouard Jeanneret-Gris, later to adopt the pseudonym Le Corbusier, was born in the Swiss watchmaking town of La Chaux-de-Fonds on October 6th 1887. At a height of 3000 feet La Chaux is reputedly the highest town in Europe and its central location in relation to the main cultural centres became of considerable importance in Jeanneret's development.

After its destruction by fire in 1794 the town was rebuilt on the same hillside in the form of a grid plan with a series of roads parallel with the hillside joined by others at right angles leading directly up the hill. Without the spectacular scenic quality of alpine regions this 'roof' of the Neuchâtel Jura' has its own grandeur, situated amid pine forests, rivers and lakes, with sweeping views towards distant mountains.

Nature's presence is deeply felt in La Chaux, not only topographically but in the sharp contrast between summer warmth and heavy winter snow due to its altitude and latitude. Jeanneret, whose father was a President of the local mountaineering club later wrote of his years spent in La Chaux:

My childhood years were spent with my friends among nature. My father moreover was a fervent worshipper of the mountains and river which formed our landscape. We were constantly among the mountain tops ; we were always in contact with the immense horizon. When mists stretched out on a limitless sea it was like the true sea - that which I had never seen. It was the ultimate spectacle. This period of adolescence is a period of insatiable curiosity, I knew what flowers were like inside and out, the shape and colour of birds, I understood how a tree grows and why it keeps its balance, even in the middle of a storm. [1]

[1] Le Corbusier, L'Art Decoratif d'Aujourd'hui, Paris 1925 p. 198 unpublished translation by permission of Judith Hayward

NEUCHÂTEL LAKE

NEUCHÂTEL

LE LOCLE

RIVER DOUBS

LA CHAUX-DE-FONDS

POUILLEREL

NORTH

JEANNERET'S FIRST HOUSES ARE BUILT ON THE SLOPE OF THE POUILLEREL OVERLOOKING LA CHAUX-DE-FONDS

17

THE ART SCHOOL

When he was fifteen years old Jeanneret took the engraving course at the Art School in La Chaux-de-Fonds. It was here that he encountered Charles L'Eplattenier, his teacher and mentor during the most formative period of his life. L'Eplattenier saw nature as the key source for the decorative artist at a time when decoration in the form of ornament was a vital part of any designer's equipment.

L'Eplattenier's views owed a great deal to the writings of Ruskin and he used Owen Jones' _Grammar of Ornament_ as a source book in the classroom. He persuaded Jeanneret to train as an architect and taught him to use drawing as his main observational tool. It was under L'Eplattenier's guidance that Jeanneret began the series of sketchbooks which he used throughout his life to document the visual world.

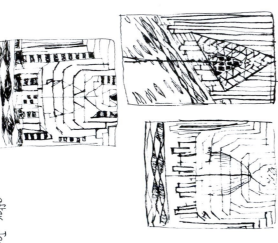

Many of Jeanneret's sketches capture the changing moods of nature, showing landscapes under varying conditions ; trees, plants and flowers were drawn as seen and then progressively abstracted to form decorative patterns. It was also important to understand the structure of natural phenomena.

In these typical studies of a tree on a slope, Jeanneret explores the pattern possibilities of its triangular shape and the play of light and shadow on the hillside.

after Jeanneret, from one of the earliest sketchbooks while he was studying at the Art School

EARLY SKETCHES

after Jeanneret

He varied his approach in accordance with the subject matter. In a series of studies for a watch case he employs an Art Nouveau mode translating free sketches of foliage into the actual watch case design.

after Jeanneret from an early sketchbook

Jeanneret's analytical technique used a kind of visual shorthand whereby the essentials of a sketch would be reduced to a small diagrammatic summary.

JOHN RUSKIN

L'Eplattenier's high regard for Ruskin was shared by Jeanneret whose attitude towards nature and architecture seem to have been profoundly affected by Ruskin's writings:

THE FUNCTION OF ARCHITECTURE   IN THE CONTEXT OF HAVING TO LIVE IN CITIES

The function of our architecture is .... to tell us about nature; to possess us with memories of her quietness; to be solemn and full of tenderness, like her, and rich in portraitures of her; full of the delicate imagery of the flowers we can no more gather, and of the living creatures now far away from us in their own solitude.

The Stones of Venice

for whatever is in architecture fair or beautiful, is imitated from natural forms.

The Seven Lamps of Architecture

THE PINE

The pine, placed nearly always among scenes disordered and desolate, brings into them all possible elements of order and precision... these two great characters of the pine, it's straightness and rounded perfectness; both wonderful, and in their issue lovely... when the sun rises behind a ridge crested with pine... all the trees, for about three or four degrees on each side of the sun, become trees of light, seen in clear flame against the darker sky, and dazzling as the sun itself... It seemed almost as if these trees, living always among the clouds, had caught part of their glory from them; and themselves the darkest of vegetation, could add yet splendour to the sun itself.

Modern Painters

THE ROOF

The very soul of the cottage, the essence and meaning of it, are in its roof; it is that wherein consists it's shelter... the best and most natural form of roof in the North is... the steep gable.

Lectures on Architecture and Painting

NOBLE ORNAMENT

Then the proper material for ornament will be whatever God has created; and its proper treatment that which seems in accordance with or symbolical of His laws. And for material, we shall therefore have, first the abstract lines which are most frequent in nature; and then, from lower to higher, the whole range of systematised inorganic and organic forms.

The Stones of Venice

MAJESTY OF BUILDINGS

The relative majesty of buildings depends more on the weight and vigour of their masses, than on any other attribute of their design: mass of everything, of bulk, of light, of darkness, of colour, not mere sum of any of these but breadth of them; not broken light, nor scattered darkness, nor divided weight, but solid stone, broad sunshine, starless shade.

The Seven Lamps of Architecture

WEIGHT AND SHADOW

It matters not how clumsy, how common the means are, that get weight and shadow — sloping roof, jutting porch, projecting balcony, hollow niche, massy gargoyle, frowning parapet; get but gloom and simplicity and all good things will follow in their place and time.

The Seven Lamps of Architecture

MASONRY

The very noble character obtained by the opposition of large stones to divided masonry, as by the shafts and columns of one piece or massy lintels and architraves to wall work of bricks or smaller stones; ... I hold therefore that for this and other reasons, the masonry of a building is to be shown: and also that ... the smaller the building the more necessary that its masonry should be bold.

The Seven Lamps of Architecture

21

FIRST HOUSE

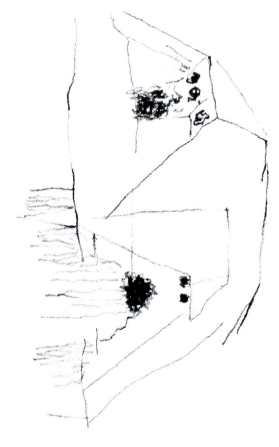

sketch of the Villa Fallet, after *Jeanneret*

Louis Fallet, a well known local jeweller and member of the Commission of the School of Art entrusted L'Eplattenier with the design of his own house opposite the one which he had built on the Pouillerel hillside overlooking La Chaux-de-Fonds. L'Eplattenier gave the task to Jeanneret, who designed the house when he was only seventeen and a half. The final drawings and site supervision were executed by *René* Chapalaz, a local architect who had helped L'Eplattenier build his own house.

VILLA FALLET 1905–1906

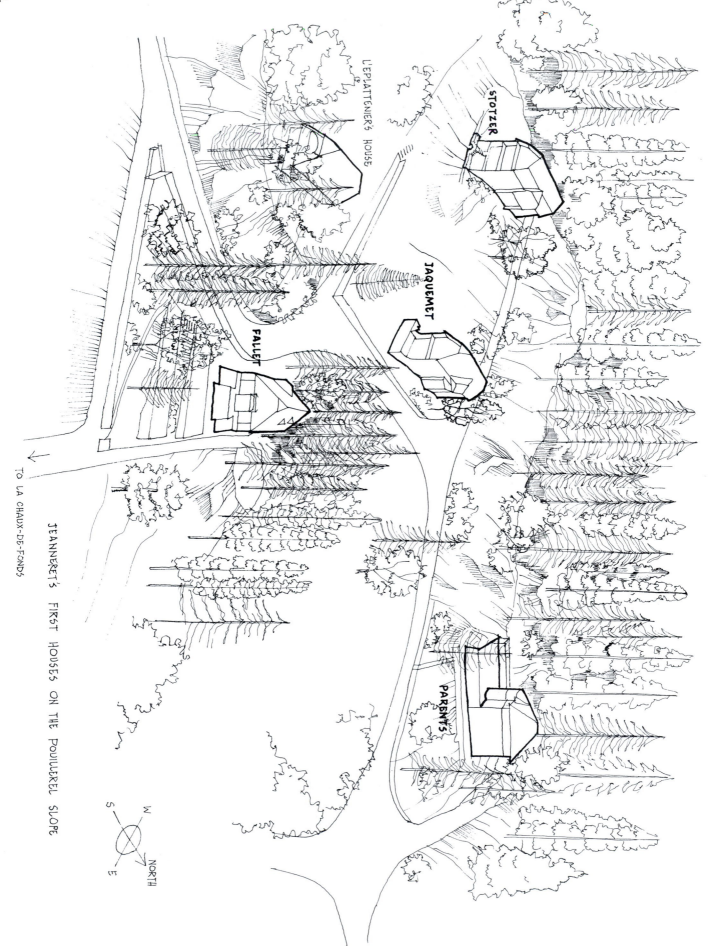

L'EPLATTENIER'S HOUSE

STOTZER

JAQUEMET

FALLET

44

PARENTS

TO LA CHAUX-DE-FONDS

JEANNERET'S FIRST HOUSES ON THE POUILLEREL SLOPE

S

W

NORTH

E

SITE FORCES

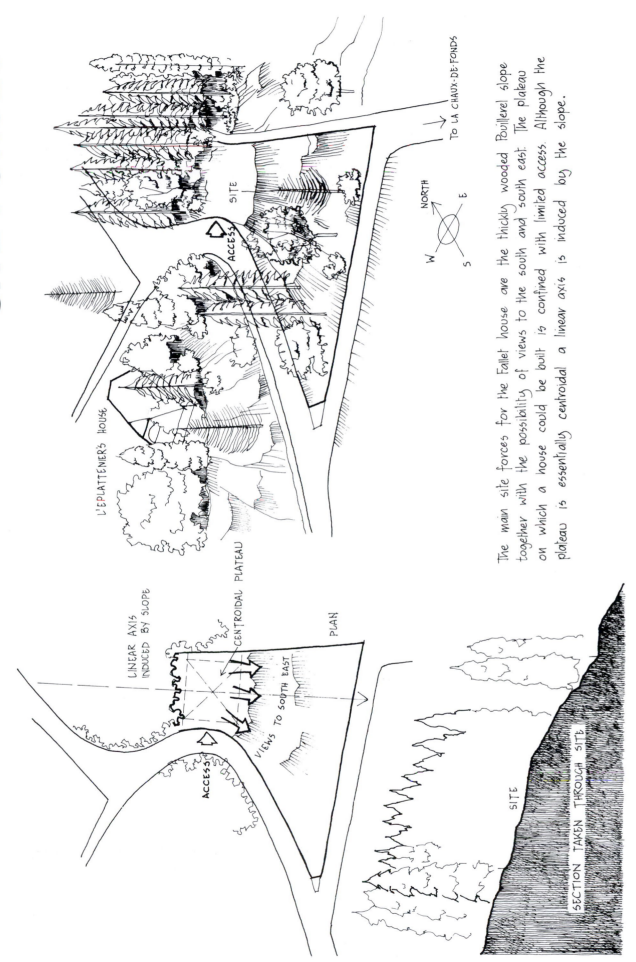

L'EPLATTENIER'S HOUSE

ACCESS

SITE

TO LA CHAUX-DE-FONDS

NORTH

W
E
S

The main site forces for the Fallet house are the thickly wooded Pouillerel slope together with the possibility of views to the south and south east. The plateau on which a house could be built is confined with limited access. Although the plateau is essentially centroidal a linear axis is induced by the slope.

LINEAR AXIS INDUCED BY SLOPE

CENTROIDAL PLATEAU

PLAN

ACCESS

VIEWS TO SOUTH EAST

SITE

SECTION TAKEN THROUGH SITE

ALTERNATIVE IDEAS

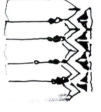

There are several drawings in an early sketchbook which try out a number of alternative house designs. Although they may not be for the Fallet house they all could be, as each is about the right size and appears to fit the conditions of the Fallet site.

One of these schemes has its ridge line along what could well be the linear axis of the Fallet site, with a pronounced side entrance, while the other two designs are pyramidal with corner entry on the diagonal.

after Jeanneret from an early sketchbook

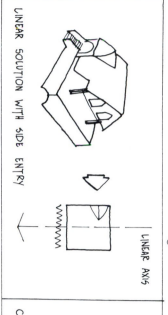

LINEAR SOLUTION WITH SIDE ENTRY

LINEAR AXIS

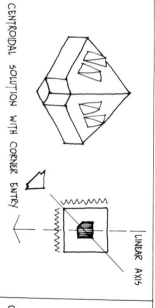

CENTROIDAL SOLUTION WITH CORNER ENTRY

LINEAR AXIS

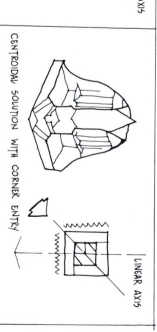

CENTROIDAL SOLUTION WITH CORNER ENTRY

LINEAR AXIS

DESIGN STUDIES

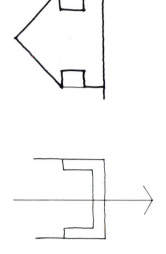

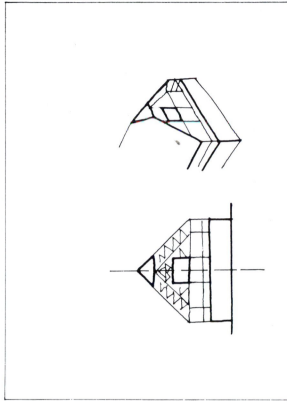

Jeanneret shifts the emphasis from the flanks to the centre with a hooded roof overhang. Now on a podium a terrace extends along each side.

The south elevation has a tree-like silhouette.

after Jeanneret

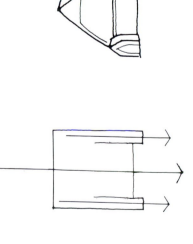

In a solution close to the final design Jeanneret provides twin side loggias which reinforce the linear theme.

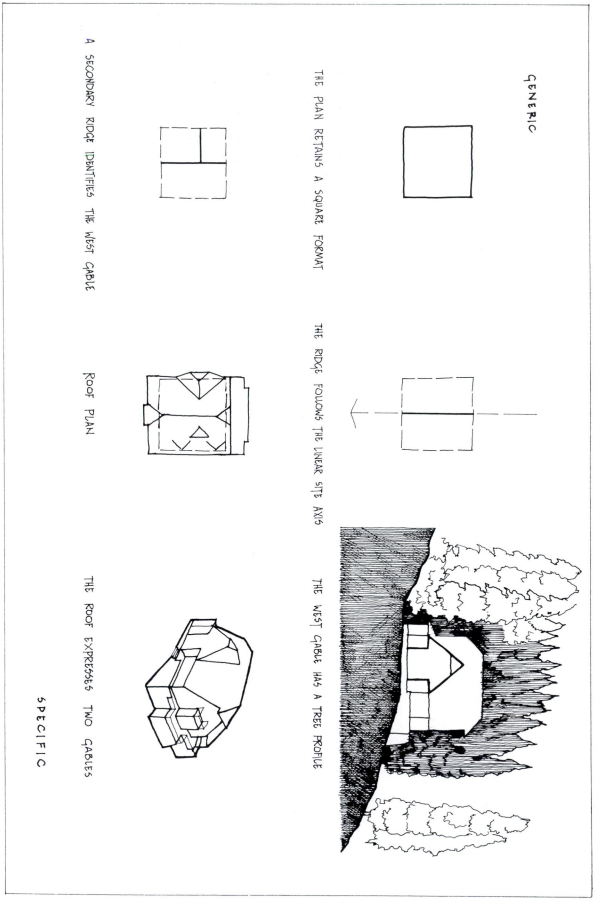

GENERIC

THE PLAN RETAINS A SQUARE FORMAT

THE RIDGE FOLLOWS THE LINEAR SITE AXIS

THE WEST GABLE HAS A TREE PROFILE

A SECONDARY RIDGE IDENTIFIES THE WEST GABLE

ROOF PLAN

THE ROOF EXPRESSES TWO GABLES

SPECIFIC

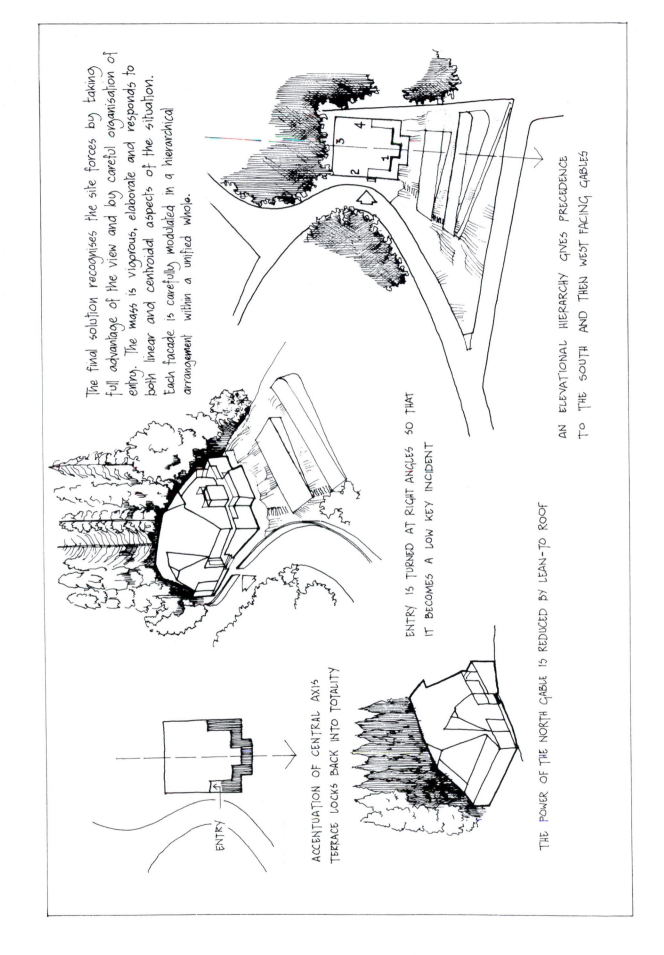

The final solution recognises the site forces by taking full advantage of the view and by careful organisation of entry. The mass is vigorous, elaborate and responds to both linear and centroidal aspects of the situation. Each facade is carefully modulated in a hierarchical arrangement within a unified whole.

ENTRY IS TURNED AT RIGHT ANGLES SO THAT IT BECOMES A LOW KEY INCIDENT

AN ELEVATIONAL HIERARCHY GIVES PRECEDENCE TO THE SOUTH AND THEN WEST FACING GABLES

ACCENTUATION OF CENTRAL AXIS TERRACE LOCKS BACK INTO TOTALITY

THE POWER OF THE NORTH GABLE IS REDUCED BY LEAN-TO ROOF

ENTRY

DESIGN THEME

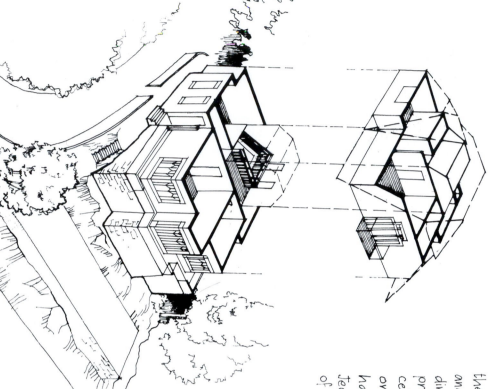

JUNCTION WHERE BALCONY PROJECTS ON SOUTH FACADE

The Fallet theme is concerned with the modelling of form and the richness of surface treatment. Each material, stone, timber, stucco and wrought iron, is exploited fully in terms of pattern and texture directly inspired by Jeanneret's studies of nature. The pine tree provides the main source for a design in which every detail celebrates Jeanneret's capacity to translate natural form into decorative ornament. The planning is unremarkable with only the hall having impact as an important space, the concept reflecting Jeanneret's concern with the decoration of form at this early stage of his architectural career.

SKETCH OF CRYSTALLINE FORMATION
after Jeanneret

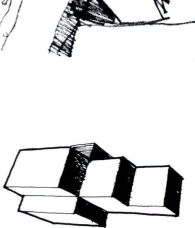

STONE SUPPORT BRACKET

SUPPORT TIMBERS ON SOUTH GABLE

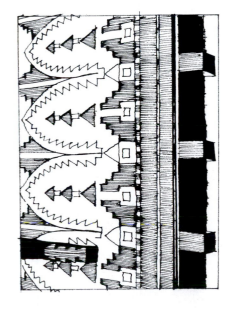

LOW RELIEF STUCCO ON SOUTH FACADE

Sketches of geological formations added to Jeanneret's repertoire of forms inspiring the treatment of support members in stone and timber. These sketches are typically elaborate and three-dimensional and the resultant cubic forms provide a contrasting rhythmic component to that of the stucco patterns on the south and west gables.

The theme is developed by a series of complementary contrasts; between smooth and rough textures; rectangles, curves, pyramids and zig zags; between the flat, the cubic and the inclined plane (of the roof); between massive support (stone) and lighter support (timber). The entire design is charged with a most literal, nature-inspired symbolism.

In 1907 Jeanneret visited Italy on a study tour, following this by spending the winter in Vienna. The Stotzer and Jaquemet houses were largely designed during the period in Vienna, and as with the Villa Fallet, René Chapallaz was responsible for the working drawings. Letters written by Jeanneret suggest that he found designing these houses far from easy, and that he was worried about his lack of constructional knowledge, having been taught little on this subject at the Art School.

The two villas are almost identical in plan, similar in general disposition to the Villa Fallet, with a central hall, south-facing main rooms and imposing south elevation. And as with the earlier villa, Jeanneret concentrates on the modelling and surface treatment of the form while responding to particular site characteristics in each case.

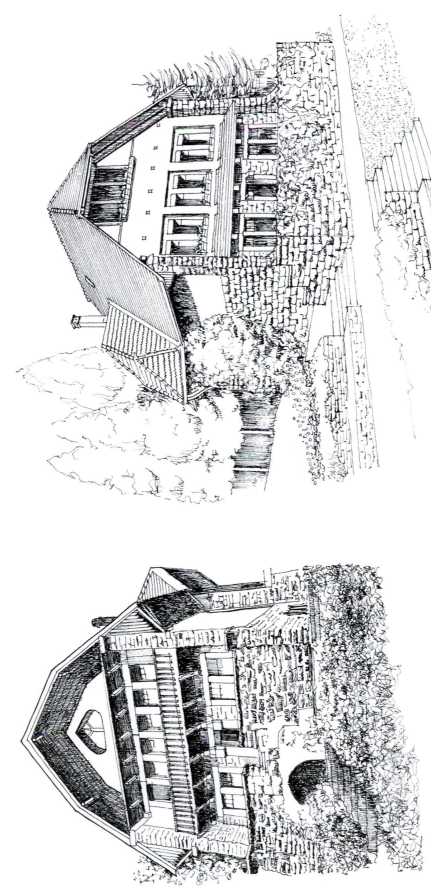

VILLAS STOTZER AND JAQUEMET 1908

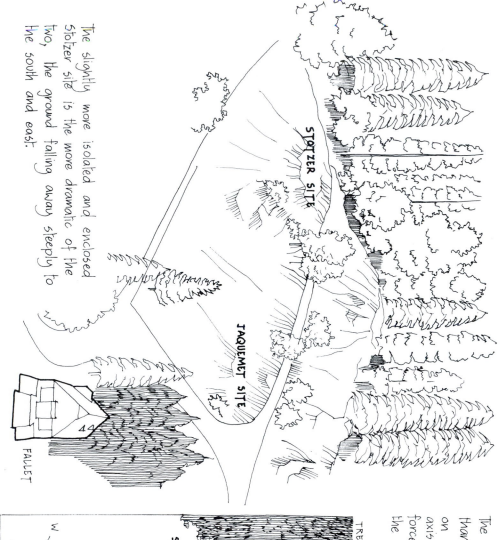

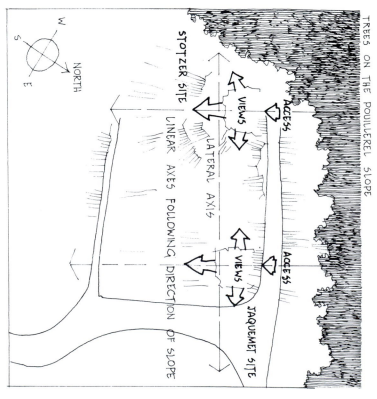

The Villa Stotzer is placed on a steeper part of the slope than its neighbour the Villa Jaquemet, which is lower and on more gently sloping terrain. The site has a lateral axis running across the slope with a pronounced directional force running down the hill. Access to each site is from the north with the best views to the south.

The slightly more isolated Stotzer site is the more dramatic and enclosed of the two, the ground falling away steeply to the south and east.

SITE RESPONSE

The villas are almost identical in plan and in each the ground and first floors are virtually the same with a basement and an attic storey in the roof.

Jeanneret responds to the site by adopting a linear solution for each villa while establishing a lateral axis which is pulled back in acknowledgement of the slope.

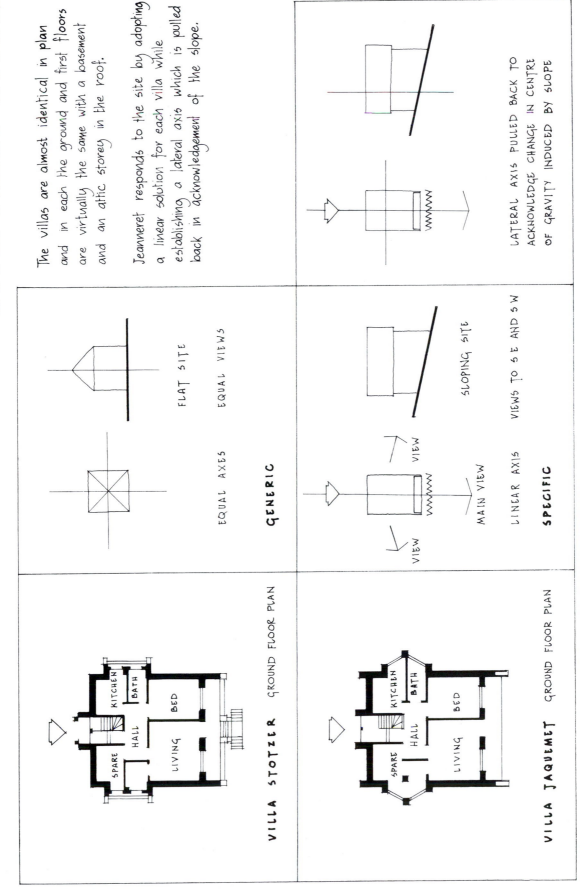

FLAT SITE

EQUAL VIEWS

EQUAL AXES

GENERIC

VILLA **STOTZER** GROUND FLOOR PLAN

KITCHEN

BATH

SPARE

HALL

BED

LIVING

LATERAL AXIS PULLED BACK TO ACKNOWLEDGE CHANGE IN CENTRE OF GRAVITY INDUCED BY SLOPE

SLOPING SITE

VIEWS TO S E AND S W

VIEW

MAIN VIEW

VIEW

LINEAR AXIS

SPECIFIC

VILLA **JAQUEMET** GROUND FLOOR PLAN

KITCHEN

BATH

SPARE

HALL

BED

LIVING

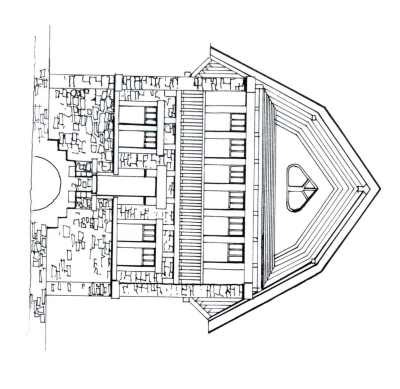

BOLD SYMMETRY OF SOUTH FACADE

POWER THEME

Jeanneret exploits the dramatic site by cranking the roof and projecting it beyond the south facade. A balcony is stretched taut between the flank walls.

LINEARITY INTENSIFIED
BY ROOF TREATMENT

The lateral axis is played down in support of the dominant linearity. Heavily rusticated masonry and an insistent rhythm of windows on the south facade contribute towards the dramatic theme.

BALCONY AND TERRACE INCREASE TAUTNESS OF SOUTH FACADE

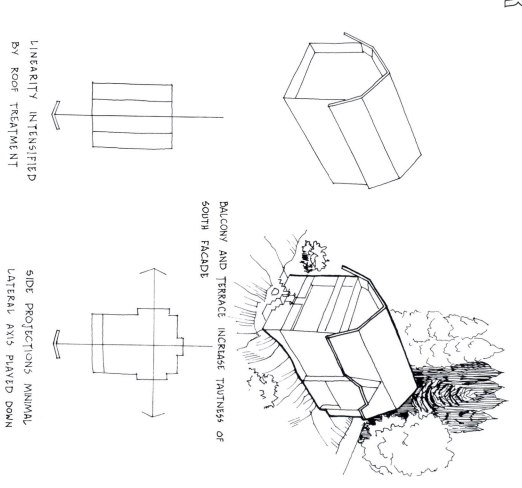

SIDE PROJECTIONS MINIMAL
LATERAL AXIS PLAYED DOWN

BENIGN JAQUEMET

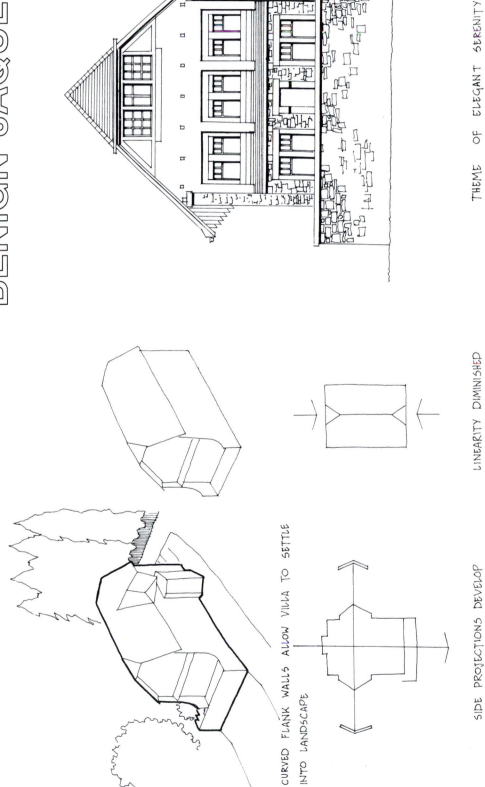

CURVED FLANK WALLS ALLOW VILLA TO SETTLE
INTO LANDSCAPE

SIDE PROJECTIONS DEVELOP
LATERAL AXIS

LINEARITY DIMINISHED
BY ROOF TREATMENT

THEME OF ELEGANT SERENITY

Jeanneret responds to the gentle slope and benign
site with a correspondingly serene theme.

In direct contrast to the Villa Stotzer Jeanneret develops the centroidal
characteristics of the form by diminishing the linear axis and by
intensifying the lateral axis.

ELABORATE GABLES

JAQUEMET

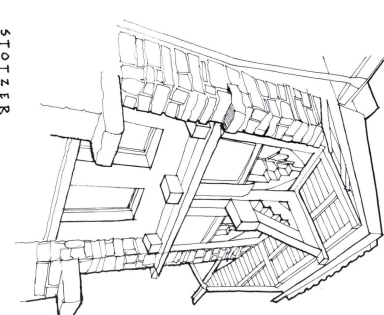

STOTZER

As with the Villa Fallet, each gable is elaborate with the roof overhang supported by timber brackets onto which a timber framework rests. Stone piers help to clarify the composition, a statement of structure which contrasts with the stucco-faced panels which they frame. This deployment is punctuated by corbelled stone brackets. Windows are placed within the overall framework in compositions which are vigorous but controlled.

DESIGN STRATEGY

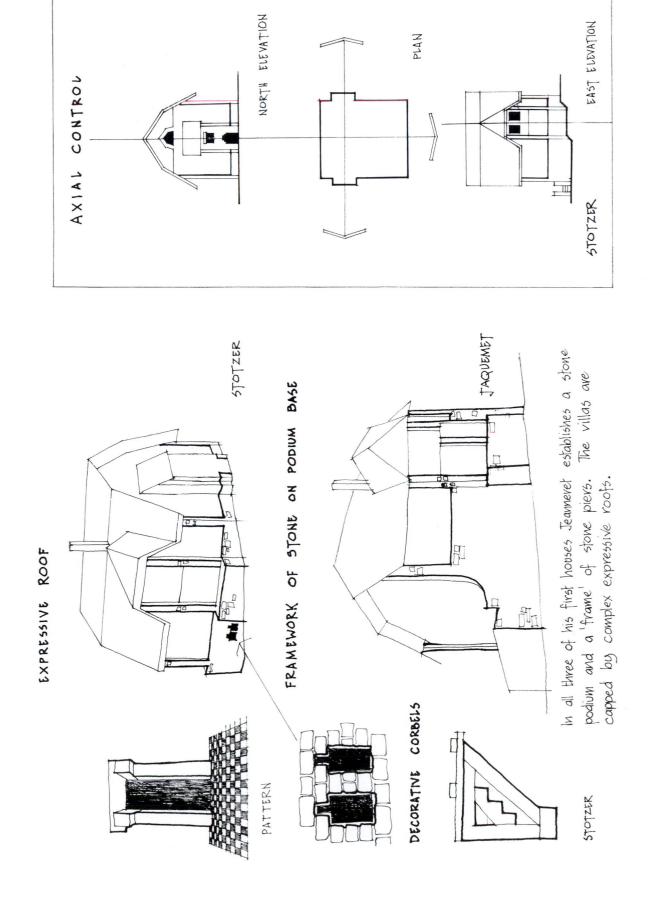

AXIAL CONTROL

NORTH ELEVATION

PLAN

EAST ELEVATION

STOTZER

STOTZER

EXPRESSIVE ROOF

PATTERN

FRAMEWORK OF STONE ON PODIUM BASE

DECORATIVE CORBELS

STOTZER

JAQUEMET

In all three of his first houses Jeanneret establishes a stone podium and a 'frame' of stone piers. The villas are capped by complex expressive roofs.

SUMMARY

Although the first houses are in the Swiss vernacular tradition, resembling many similar chalets in the region, they nevertheless employ basic principles to be retained in his later work.

S I T E

The character of each house is determined substantially by its particular location with a response to such natural forces as the slope, the best views and the position of the sun.

G E O M E T R Y

Axes are used as the basic ordering discipline in each case exploiting the contrast potential between the linear and transverse axes.

F O R M

Each villa has a compact 'closed' form which does not extend into the landscape. Pitched roofs contrast with rectilinear configurations with the roof becoming an expressive element. The mass is sculpted in a positive way with a tendency towards complexity.

S U R F A C E

Surfaces are enriched by pattern and texture which exploits the characteristics of the materials used. Surfaces are ordered by a system of framing which may represent structure as with window jambs and lintels, or be aesthetic as with stone 'piers' at extremities. Surfaces respond to each particular theme.

S T R U C T U R E

The inherent properties of stone and timber form the basis of their structural expression, the heavy limited span characteristic of stone contrasting with the lighter broader spanning timber.

40

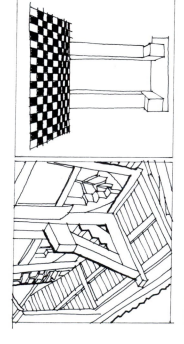
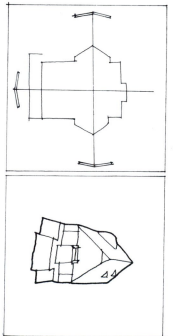

T H E M E

In his thematic interpretation Jeanneret attempts to transmit principles evident in nature into architectural form. The resultant special character in each house may be likened to the way natural organisms have a special character because all their parts contribute towards a common intention. A fish, for example, has a shape, structure and skin which have evolved in relation to such functional needs as where it will swim and how it will acquire food. Similarly a tree, its branches and leaves are all part of one growth requirement which relates directly to those conditions in which growth takes place.

Jeanneret follows this principle in each of his first three houses, starting with the function in which a protective roof covers enclosing walls. The roof may be likened to a shell in the way it expresses a particular covering role and each form responds to such site characteristics as the slope, views, access and position of the sun. Materials and structure are appropriate to the weather of the region and a podium 'roots' the houses into the slope. Each site produces a different response which determines the character of each villa. Fallet is elaborate, Stolzer is powerful, Jaquemet serene, themes expressed positively in each south facing main gable and then taken up consistently in side gables, doors, windows, balconies and general surface treatment. Axes represent the main lines of growth and all the parts are balanced in a state of dynamic equilibrium. These principles are retained fifty years later in Le Corbusier's Pilgrimage chapel at Ronchamp.

F A C A D E S

A facade hierarchy gives the greatest importance to one major facade, others diminishing in value. There is a distinct front, back and sides.

ATELIERS D'ART 1910

Jeanneret left Vienna for Paris in 1908 where he worked for Auguste Perret, in the process gaining an insight into the design possibilities of reinforced concrete. In late 1909 he returned to La Chaux-de-Fonds where he prepared a notional design for an Ateliers d'Art. The project combined the teaching of art and craft based disciplines within one building and the design suggests several ideas in his mind at this time.

ABSTRACTION

The design may have been influenced by Schuré's arguments and the cubic forms and degree of abstraction suggest the kind of universality Schuré' was advocating.

GEOMETRY

The symmetrical geometry ensures a harmonious balance of elements with a clear hierarchy of forms.

FUNCTION

Although organised within a geometrical straitjacket, there is a suggestion of functional identification in the way the central pyramid acts as a meeting area with the various teaching units distributed around it.

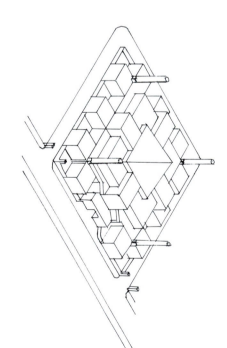

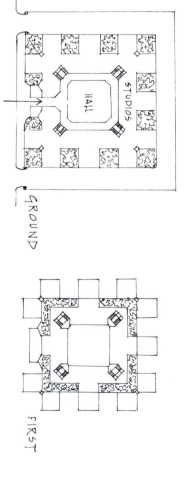

HALL

STUDIOS

GROUND

FIRST

after Jeanneret from drawings reproduced in The Complete Architectural Works 1910-29

CHARTERHOUSE AT GALLUZZO

INDIVIDUAL AND COMMUNAL

While on his study tour of Italy in 1907, Jeanneret had visited a Charterhouse on a hilltop at Galluzzo near Florence. On three sides of the hill the monks live in small houses around cloisters, each having their own garden adjacent, with the church refectory and meeting halls situated in a group at the other side.

Not only does the Ateliers d'Art physically resemble the charterhouse in the arrangement of gardens next to studio units and in the way these relate to a central communal space, but this distinction between communal and individual activities seems to have been retained as a general principle by Jeanneret.

In 1922 as Le Corbusier he organised the Immeuble Villas, apartment blocks in his city for three million people, in the same way. Citrohan houses are placed together in a large block each with a garden alongside. These apartments were connected to communal facilities available to the entire block.

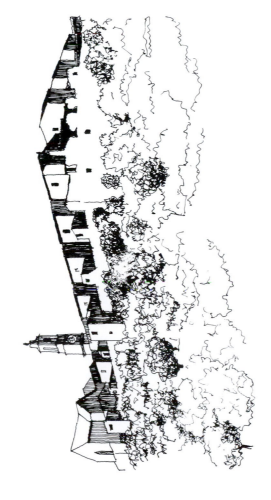

The Carthusian monastery at Galluzzo near Florence

HISTORICAL PRECEDENT

With its centralised hierarchical build-up of elementary forms, the Ateliers d'Art in principle bears a resemblance to Hagia Sophia, with even a suggestion of 'minarets'. The Ateliers illustrate typically diverse influences affecting Jeanneret's design approach.

PROVENSAL AND SCHURÉ

PROVENSAL

Around 1908 Jeanneret read a book by Henry Provensal entitled L'Art de Demain (Paris 1904) in which it was argued that the role of the artist is to connect man with the eternal principles of what Provensal termed an 'absolute'; this absolute is revealed through divine laws, described as those of unity, number and harmony; a new art would appear that no longer imitated past forms; it would be abstract and universal and more likely to appear through architecture than any other art form. Provensal suggested that a new cubic architecture would emerge as a result of new architectural laws about to be discovered and he argued that ideal beauty expresses mind and spirit, instinct alone being insufficient for the artist.

SCHURÉ

About the same time Jeanneret read Edouard Schuré's Les Grands Initiés (Paris 1908) which is devoted to an examination of eight of the greatest prophets in history: Rama, Krishna, Hermes, Moses, Pythagoras, Plato and Jesus. Pythagoras is singled out as of all the great initiates of the past the most relevant to modern man, with Pythagorean numerology described as a system unfolding mathematically from simple divine numbers. This reminds us of Le Corbusier's Modulor, the mathematical relationships system which he used on many buildings.

For this information I am indebted to Paul Turner The Education of Le Corbusier: A Study of the Development of Le Corbusier's Thought 1900-1920, doctoral thesis, Harvard University, 1971.

3

THE YEARS OF TRANSITION
1912-17

If the first villas in La Chaux-de-Fonds were designed within the Swiss vernacular tradition, Jeanneret's next three houses show signs of influence from those twin ancient styles of Classical and Byzantine architecture which he absorbed during the important Voyage d'Orient of 1911.

On the trip he visited Constantinople and the Acropolis at Athens and was impressed by the vernacular architecture of the Balkans. He also spent some time at the monasteries on Mount Athos, an experience which made a deep impression, but it was the Parthenon which left the deepest mark, confirming tendencies towards Classicism which had been developing for several years.

In the next three villas the emphasis shifts from complex massing towards simple combinations of primary solids. Movement into the houses takes place through zones which relate them to their immediate surroundings and spatial articulation assumes the richness formerly present in exterior surface decoration.

In 1912 Jeanneret attempted to translate ideas of form and its arrangement gained on the journey into two house designs, the first of which was a villa for his parents on the Rue de la Montagne near his earlier houses.

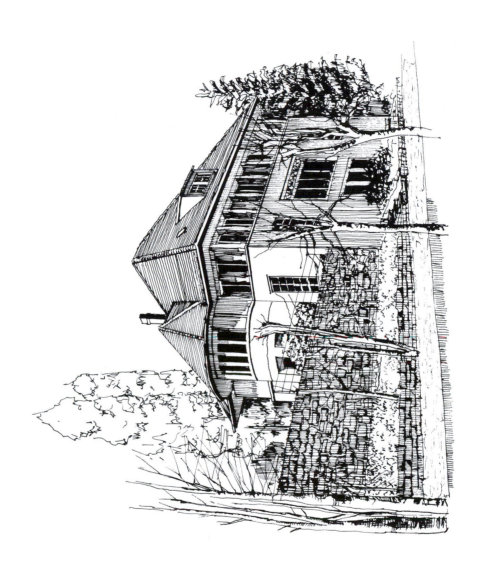

VILLA JEANNERET-PERRET 1912

SITE FORCES

trees on the Pouillerel slope

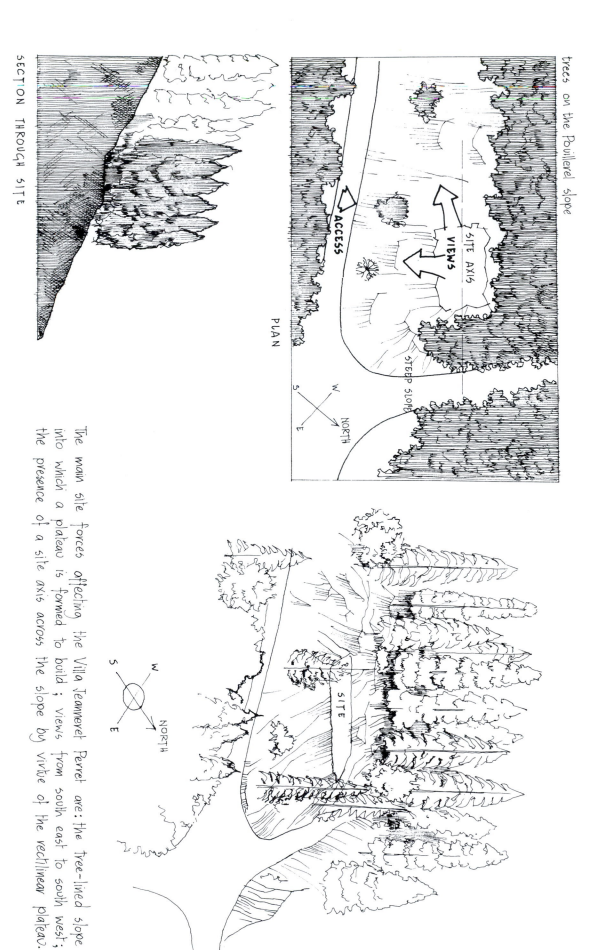

PLAN

SECTION THROUGH SITE

SITE AXIS

VIEWS

ACCESS

STEEP SLOPE

NORTH
W
S
E

SITE

NORTH
W
S
E

The main site forces affecting the Villa Jeanneret Perret are: the tree-lined slope into which a plateau is formed to build; views from south east to south west; the presence of a site axis across the slope by virtue of the rectilinear plateau.

DESIGN CONCEPT

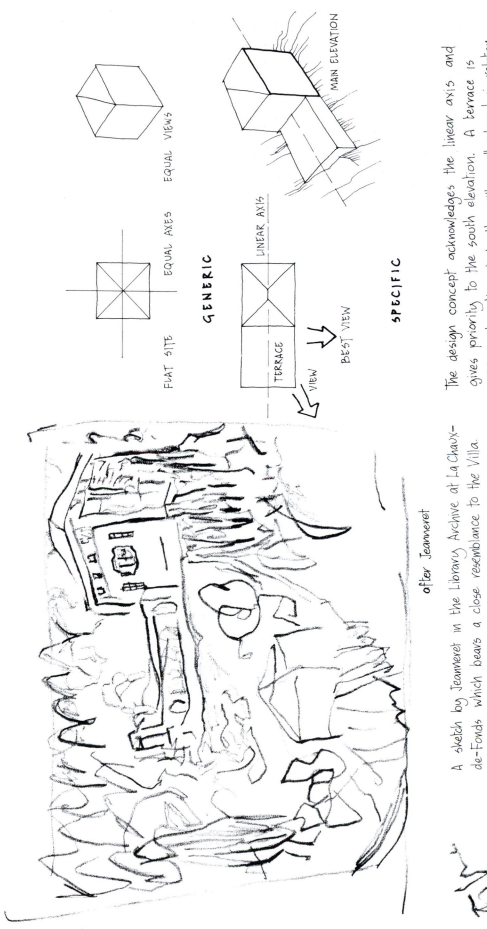

GENERIC

EQUAL AXES   EQUAL VIEWS

FLAT SITE

SPECIFIC

LINEAR AXIS

TERRACE

VIEW

BEST VIEW

MAIN ELEVATION

The design concept acknowledges the linear axis and gives priority to the south elevation. A terrace is established adjacent to the villa, well placed in relation to the sun and views.

after Jeanneret

A sketch by Jeanneret in the Library Archive at La Chaux-de-Fonds which bears a close resemblance to the Villa.

AXIS REINFORCED

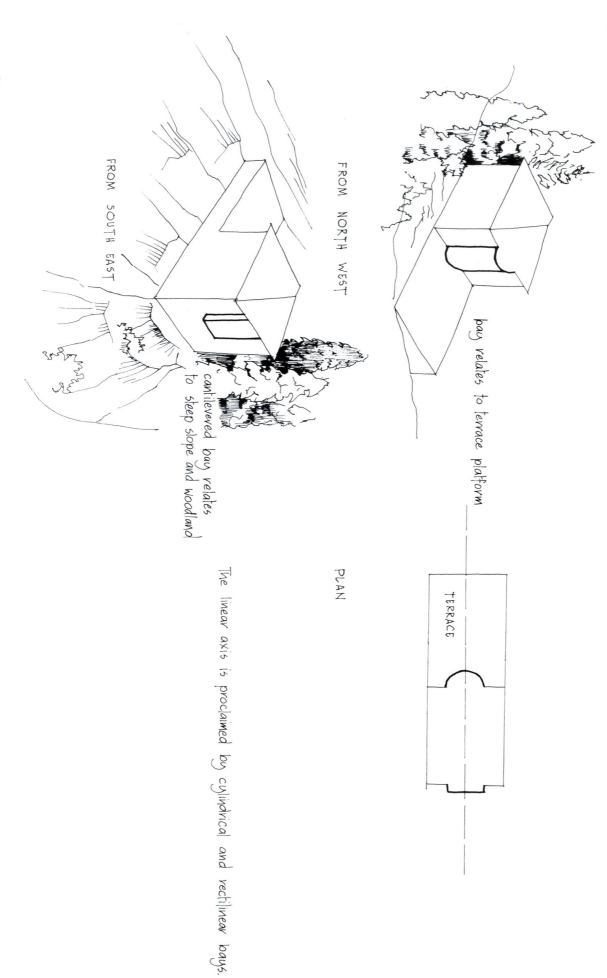

bay relates to terrace platform

FROM NORTH WEST

FROM SOUTH EAST

cantilevered bay relates
to steep slope and woodland

PLAN

TERRACE

The linear axis is proclaimed by cylindrical and rectilinear bays.

SPACE ZONES

Perhaps influenced by the processional route past the Parthenon, Jeanneret creates a movement progression which is the first example of his use of the 'promenade architecturale'.

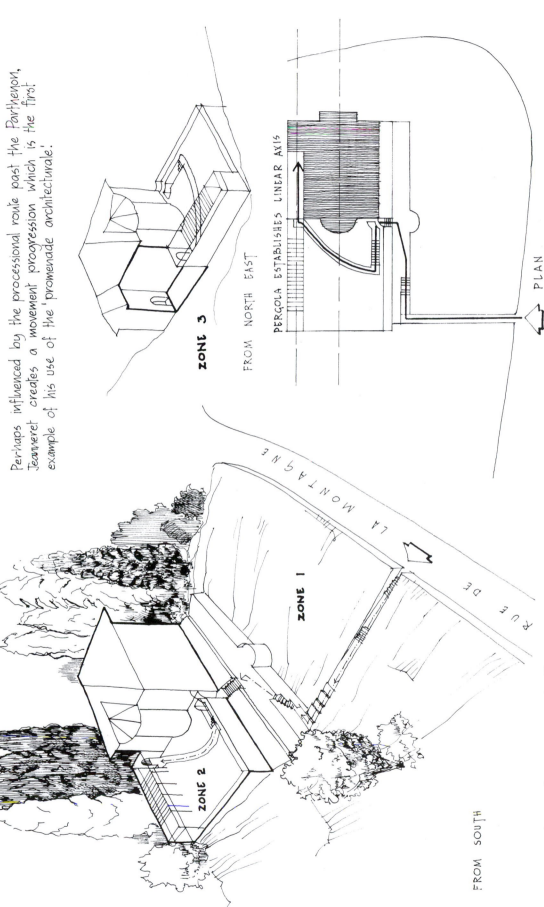

ZONE 3

FROM NORTH EAST

PERGOLA ESTABLISHES LINEAR AXIS

PLAN

The route takes in a zone outside the complex where the south facade provides the main impact; a 'terrace zone' is dominated by the cylindrical bay, with finally the confined space before entry.

LA MONTAGNE

RUE DE

ZONE I

ZONE 2

FROM SOUTH

By progressively confining the route, Jeanneret gradually effects the transition from outer space to that of the building.

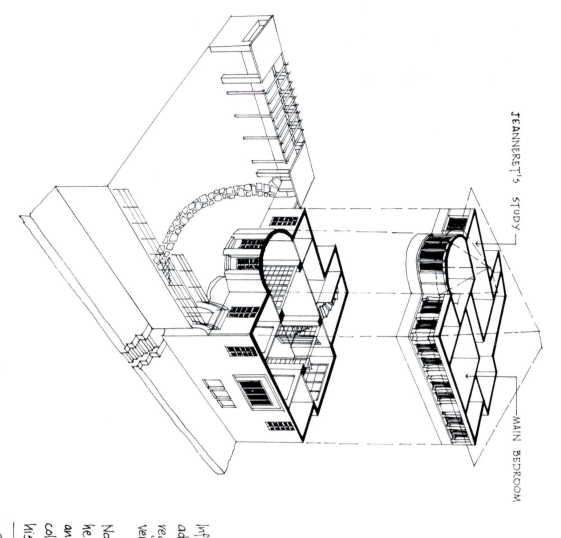

JEANNERET'S STUDY

MAIN BEDROOM

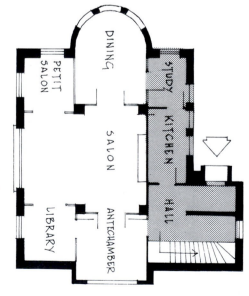

MAIN FLOOR PLAN

DINING

PETIT SALON

SALON

LIBRARY

ANTECHAMBER

STUDY

KITCHEN

HALL

Influenced by his Voyage d'Orient and by a book [1] advocating a 'calm simplified classicism' for the region, Jeanneret abandons his earlier decorative vernacular mode for a more formal composition.

No longer concentrating on the external massing, he achieves a happier fusion between plan and elevations, using four reinforced concrete columns to free the interior and thereby create his first internal space of real quality.

1 Cingria Vaneyre, Entretiens de la Ville du Rouet, Geneva 1908

CLASSICAL FRAME

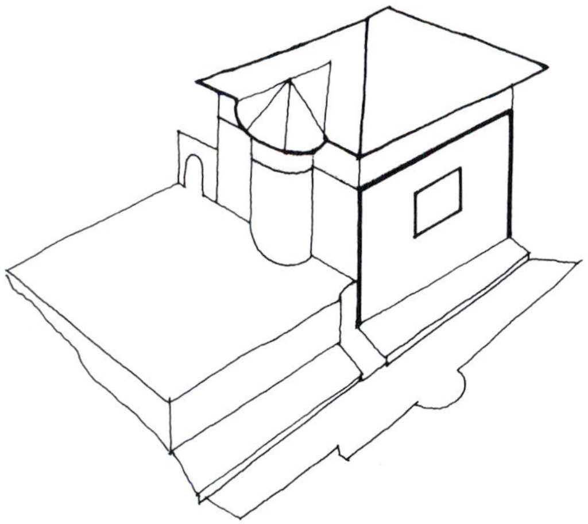

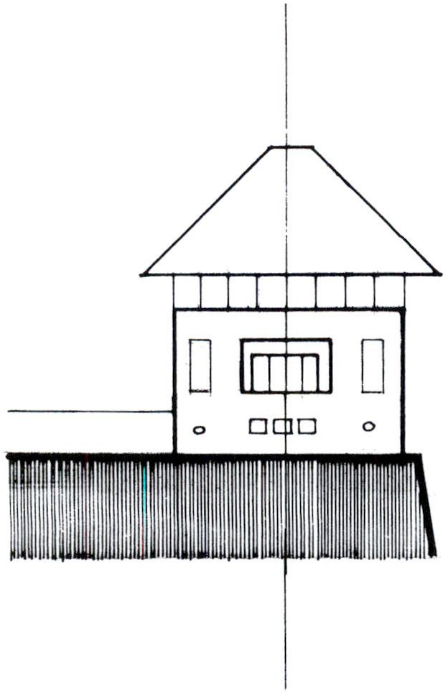

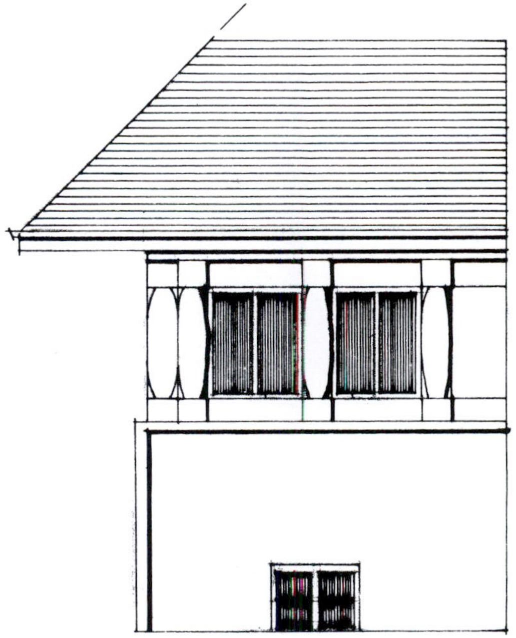

CORNER DETAIL

SOUTH ELEVATION

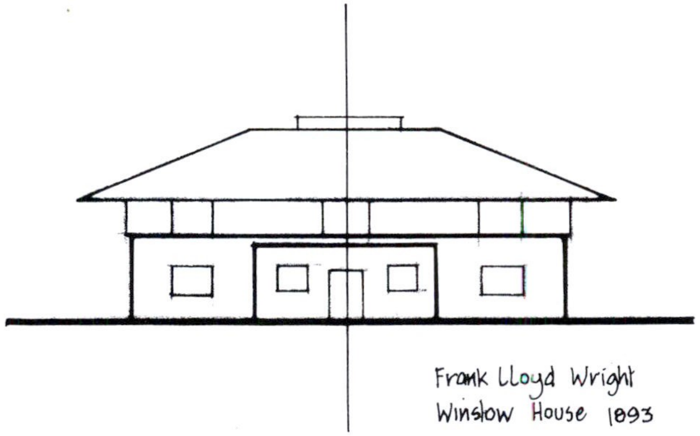

Frank Lloyd Wright
Winslow House 1893

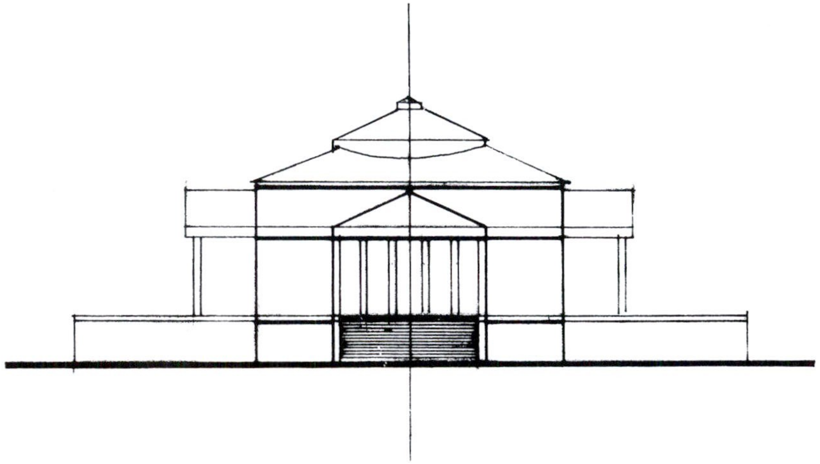

Andrea Palladio Villa Capra ('Rotonda') 1552-70

The facades are framed in the classical manner using the elevated main floor as a piano nobile with a 'frieze' of windows immediately below the roof. There is a resemblance in technique to Frank Lloyd Wright's Winslow House (1893).

In the same year that he designed the villa for his parents, Jeanneret received an important commission, being asked by the founder of the local Zenith watch factory to design a large residence near Le Locle, the next town along the valley from La Chaux-de-Fonds.

The site was a long narrow piece of land on the steep side of a hill overlooking the town, and as with his parents' residence Jeanneret employs a classical architectural expression.

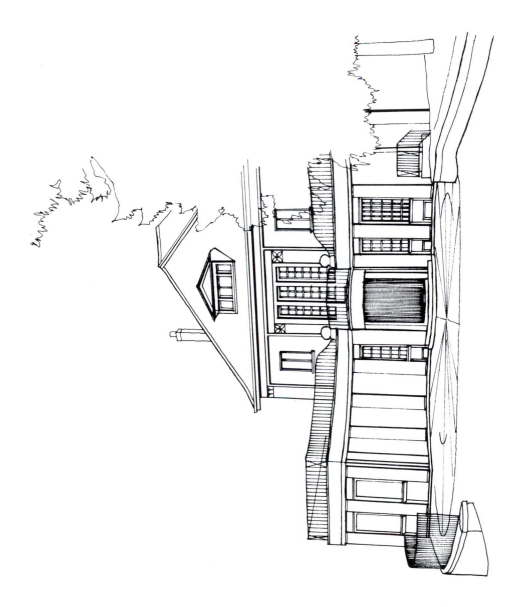

VILLA FAVRE–JACOT 1912

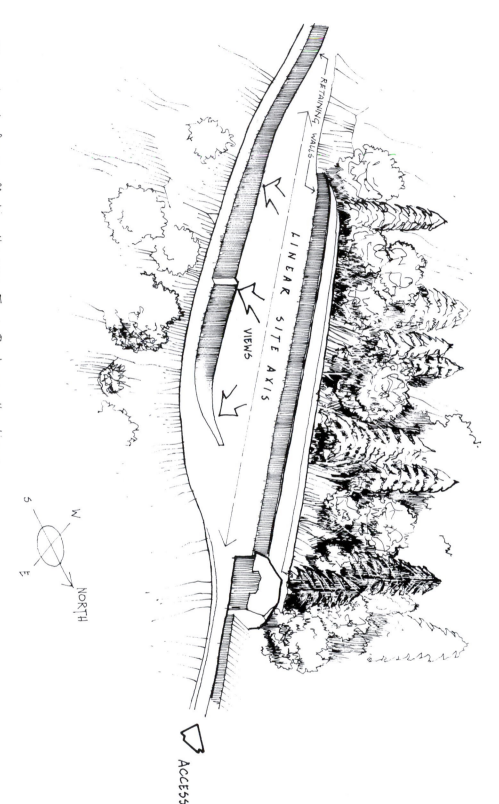

RETAINING WALLS

LINEAR SITE AXIS

VIEWS

ACCESS

S
W
E
NORTH

The main site forces affecting the Villa Favre-Jacot are the linear site axis along the plateau built into the hill; the elevated location on a steep wooded slope with views across the valley; the access route from Le Locle which continues immediately below the site.

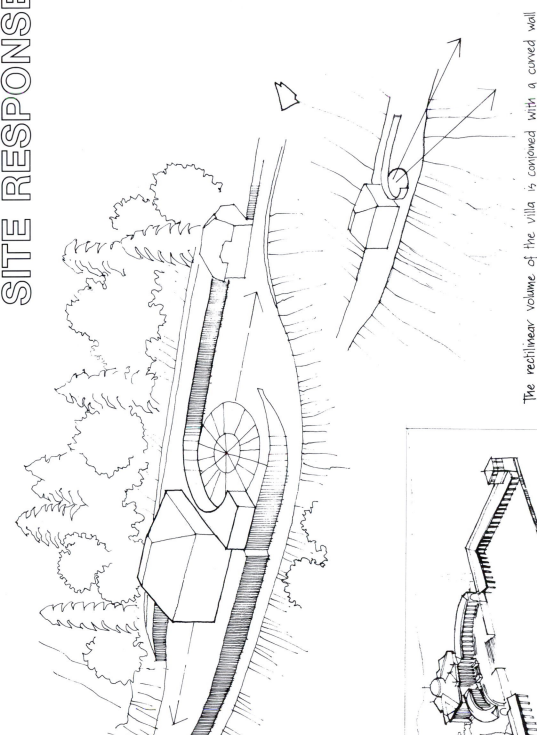

The rectilinear volume of the villa is conjoined with a curved wall which extends around a turning circle to embrace those who move towards it. The wall stops short of complete enclosure to relate to the valley above which the villa is poised. This welcoming gesture remains formal, the prelude to a work of substance, using a technique which forms part of the classical repertoire.

Andrea Palladio   VILLA TRISSINO Meledo   after Francis D. Ching.

GENERAL STRATEGY

THE ENCLOSURE OF SPACE BY
VOLUMETRIC PROJECTION

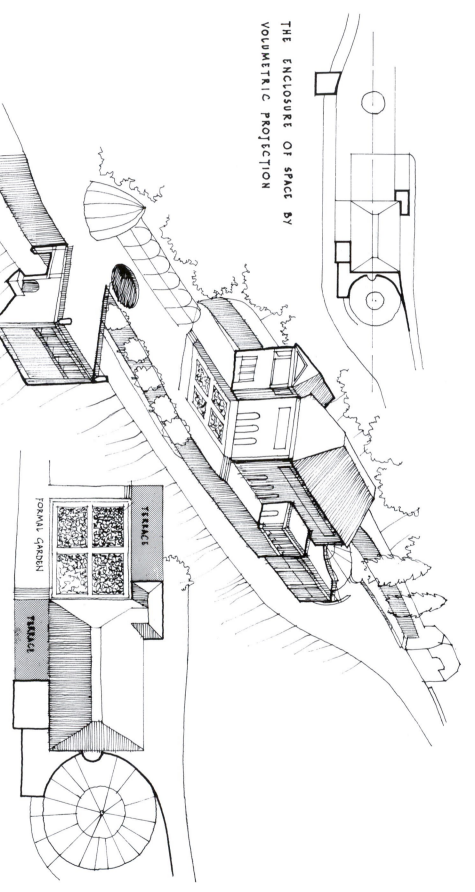

By the addition of volumes to the main mass Jeanneret defines
spaces around the villa. A pergola, pool, and domed pavilion
extend this idea, while a gazebo spans the road to take full
advantage of the view across the valley.

FORMAL GARDEN

TERRACE

TERRACE

CURVILINEAR ENTRY THEME

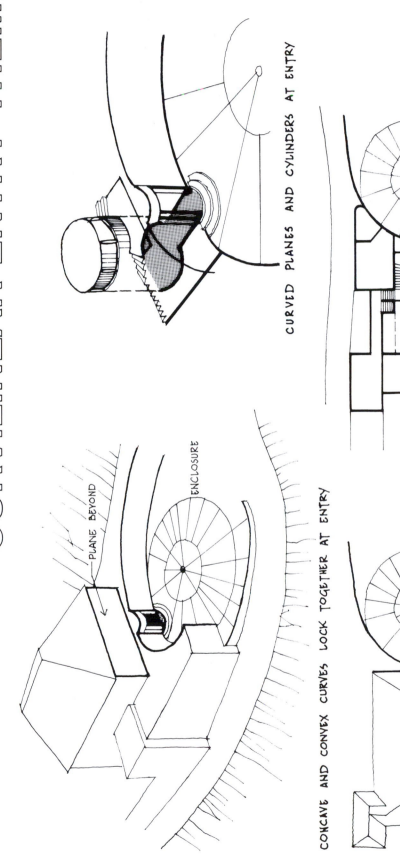

CURVED PLANES AND CYLINDERS AT ENTRY

CONCAVE AND CONVEX CURVES LOCK TOGETHER AT ENTRY

PLANE BEYOND

ENCLOSURE

LINEAR AXIS

LINEAR AXIS DOES NOT PASS THROUGH CENTRE OF TURNING CIRCLE

Stairs wind around this drum, which is the first example in his work of the deliberate imposition of an unexpected spatial device intended to remain as a memorable event. In both villas of 1912 Jeanneret exercises careful control of entry.

CURVES INTERLOCK

ENTRY BECOMES A FOCAL POINT

Taking up the theme established by the turning circle, Jeanneret creates a movement progression in which the cylindrical porch projection is followed by a cylindrical internal space extending through two floors.

AXIAL PLANNING

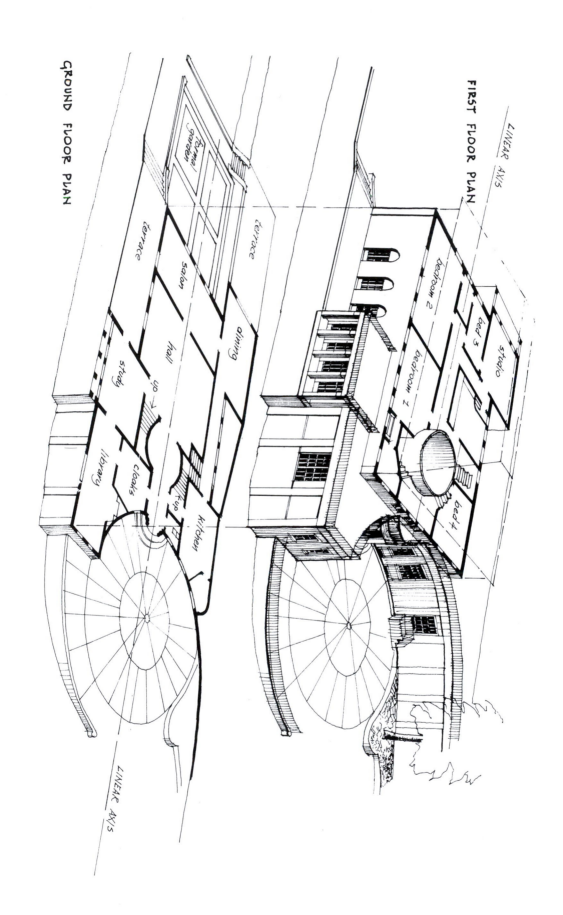

FIRST FLOOR PLAN

LINEAR AXIS

studio

bed 3

bedroom 2

bedroom 1

bed 4

GROUND FLOOR PLAN

formal garden

terrace

terrace

salon

dining

hall

study

up

library

cloaks

kitchen

LINEAR AXIS

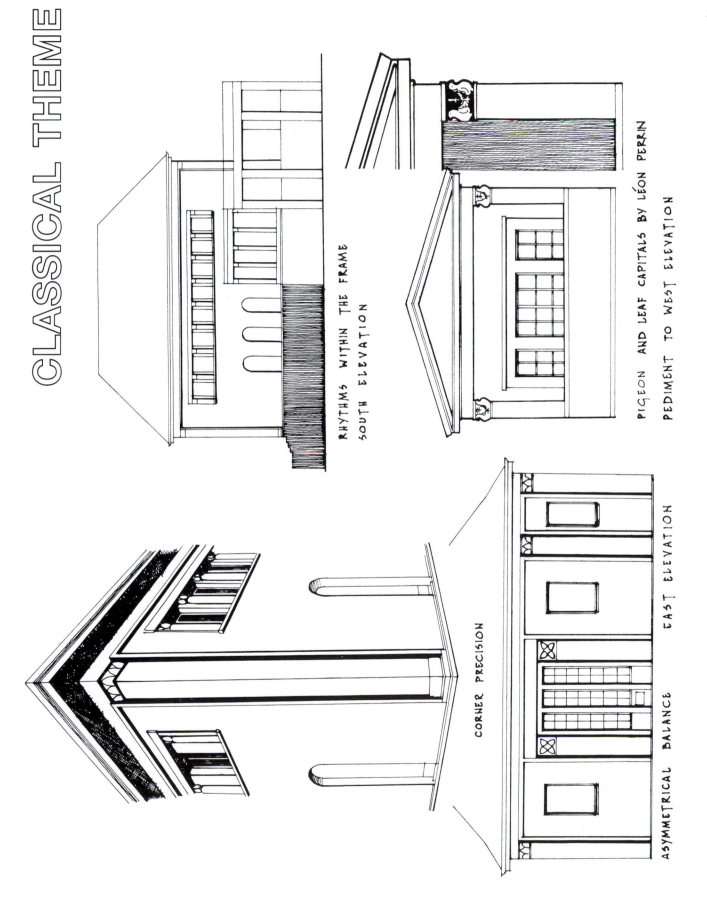

RHYTHMS WITHIN THE FRAME
SOUTH ELEVATION

PIGEON AND LEAF CAPITALS BY LÉON PERRIN

PEDIMENT TO WEST ELEVATION

CORNER PRECISION

EAST ELEVATION

ASYMMETRICAL BALANCE

REINFORCED CONCRETE

Jeanneret's interest in reinforced concrete was partly due to the influence of Auguste Perret for whom he worked during his visit to Paris in 1907. This interest developed further as a result of contact with an engineer friend Max Du Bois. Together Jeanneret and Du Bois worked out a concrete constructional system using principles advocated by Professor E. Mörsche who had taught Du Bois at Zurich Polytechnic.

The system used a concrete slab and columns so that houses constructed in this way could be placed next to each other like dominoes. During 1915 Jeanneret sketched various housing layouts using the system but was only able to build in concrete in the Villa Schwob. One of the great advantages which Jeanneret saw in the system lay in the possibilities for standardised forms of construction and he envisaged a production line for houses resembling that of factories producing motor cars.

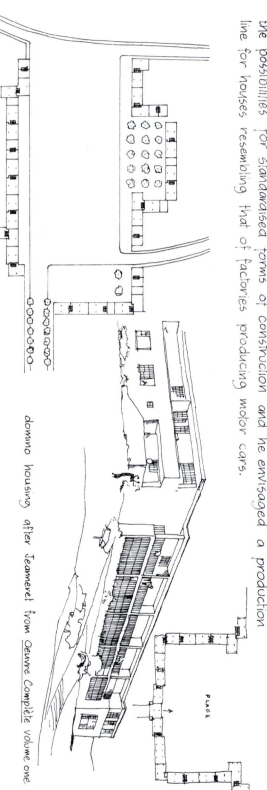

domino housing after Jeanneret from _Oeuvre Complète_ volume one

DOM-INO SYSTEM

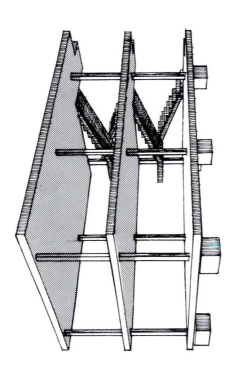

from the diagram in the <u>Oeuvre Complete</u> volume one

the standard Dom-ino model has a concrete floor slab with the columns set back and a cantilevered stair at one end. the slab consists of joist-like beams with steel reinforcement and hollow pots.

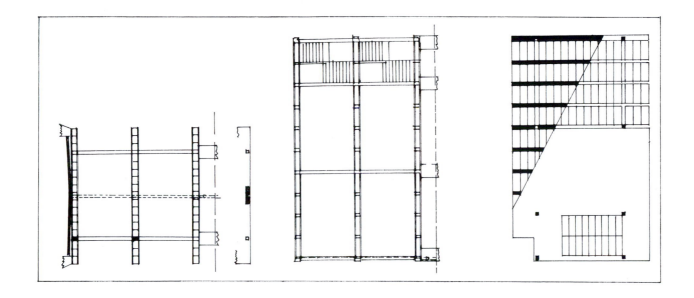

On returning to La Chaux-de-Fonds after his journey to the East Jeanneret became one of the teachers in L'Eplattenier's New Section at the Art School. He taught geometric studies and their application to architecture and the decorative elements in nature and a study of shapes and colours from an ornamental point of view.

Local politicians who believed the staff of the New Section were inexperienced succeeded in closing the section in 1914 and Jeanneret resigned. In 1912 he had become secretary to a group venture called United Art Studios, the other members of the group being Léon Perrin and Georges Aubert.

This was part of an attempt by Jeanneret to establish himself as an architect, interior designer and landscape architect, and for several years a shortage of architectural commissions meant that he was mainly involved in interior design.

It was in his capacity as an Interior Designer that Jeanneret first came into contact with Anatole Schwob, a prominent local industrialist, when in 1913 he was asked to redecorate his smoking room. In the same year Madame Schwob visited the Villa Jeanneret-Perret and was sufficiently impressed to suggest that such a house be designed for her cousin Anatole.

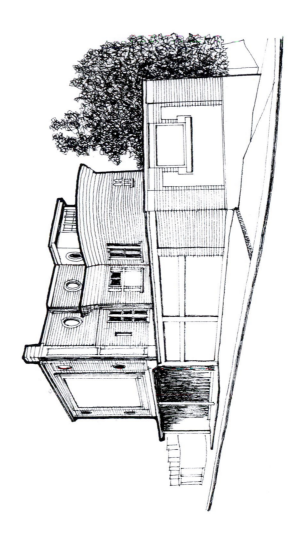

VILLA SCHWOB 1916

SECTION TAKEN THROUGH SITE

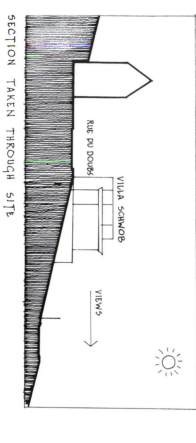

VILLA SCHWOB

RUE DU DOUBS

VIEWS →

PLAN OF THE CENTRE OF LA CHAUX-DE-FONDS

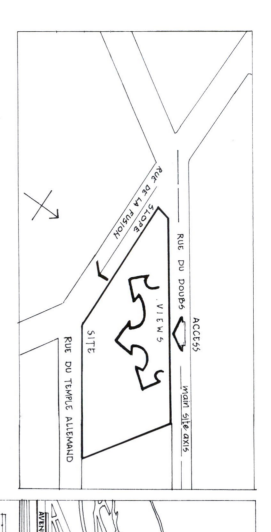

RUE DE LA FUSION

SLOPE

RUE DU DOUBS

ACCESS

· V I E W S ·

SITE

main site axis

RUE DU TEMPLE ALLEMAND

AVENUE LÉOPOLD ROBERT

RUE NUMA-DROZ

VILLA JEANNERET-PERRET
L'EPLATTENIER'S VILLA
VILLA JAQUEMET
VILLA STOTZER
VILLA SCHWOB

VILLA FALLET

PLACE DE LA GARE

CINEMA LA SCALA

RUE DU DOUBS
ART SCHOOL

The Villa Schwob is located at the corner where the Rue de Doubs meets the Rue de la Fusion. The main site forces are the grid plan of La Chaux with the Rue du Doubs acting as the main linear axis of the site. The built-up and therefore restricted site implies a rectilinear approach with views outwards in the direction of the fairly steep slope, a major force characteristic.

INFLUENCES

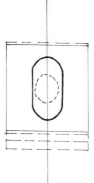

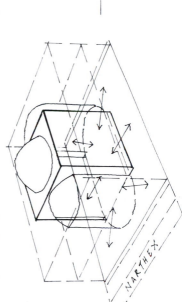

GENERIC CUBE WITHIN HALF CUBE

apsidal projections accentuate the linear axis given direction by entry

NARTHEX

intention to create spatial interaction between central vertical linear space and horizontal layers which surround this.

HAGIA SOPHIA 532-537 AD ANTHEMIUS AND ISODORUS

In the relationship to site with paired entrances, plain facade and double height living volume the Villa Schwob resembles Wright's Thomas P. Hardy house of 1905. In its geometry and sophisticated relationship between the central double height volume and the surrounding space there could be influence from Hagia Sophia, each design being based on a cube within a half cube, and each having apsidal projections and a development along a dominant linear axis.

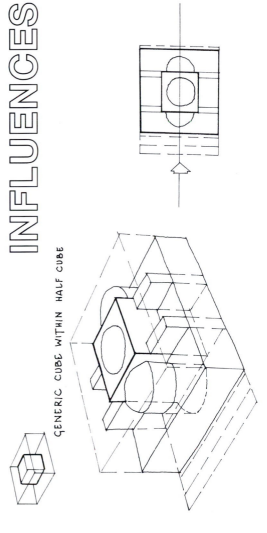

STREET FRONT

BED LIVING BED

GROUND LEVEL

TERRACE KIT DINING BED

LOWER LEVEL

BED UPPER LIVING BED

UPPER LEVEL

THOMAS P. HARDY HOUSE 1905
FRANK LLOYD WRIGHT

DESIGN CONCEPT

THEME OF CURVES AGAINST ORTHOGONALS

A BASIC CONTRAST OF CUBIC AGAINST CYLINDRICAL FORMS

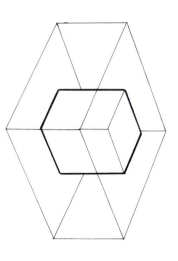

cube within half-cube

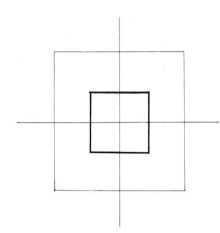

GENERIC

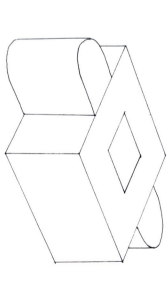

apsidal projections induce linear axis parallel with dominant external axis of Rue du Doubs

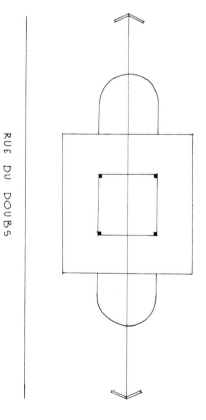

RUE DU DOUBS

four reinforced concrete columns support the centre

SPECIFIC

THEME OF CURVES AGAINST ORTHOGONALS

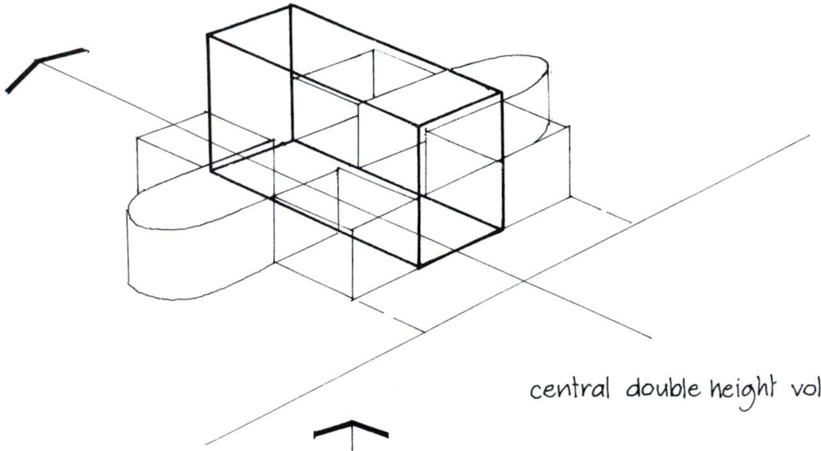

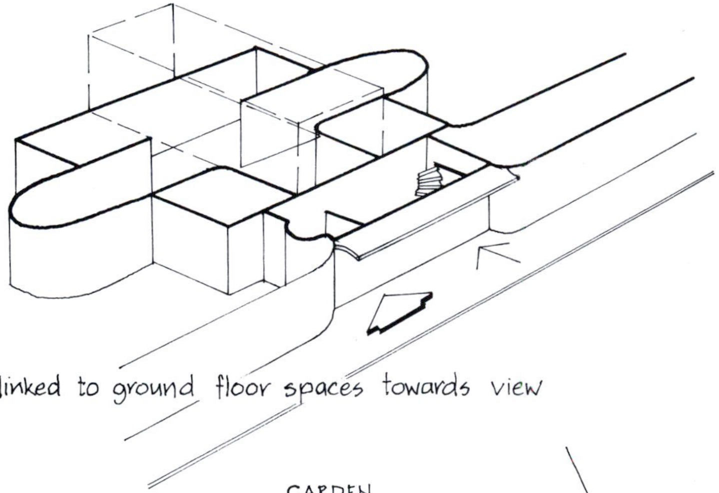

central double height volume is linked to ground floor spaces towards view

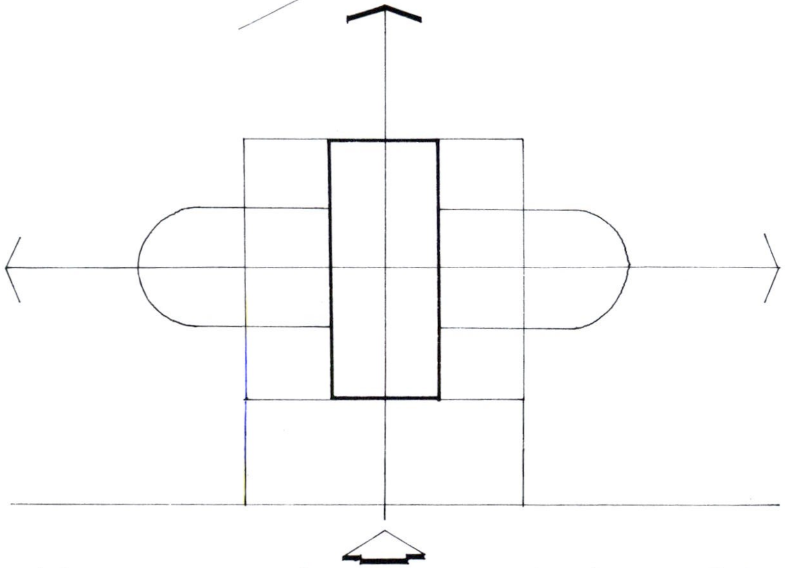

GARDEN

LIBRARY

SALLE

STUDY

LIVING

DINING

TERRACE

CLOAKS

OFFICE

KITCHEN

GROUND FLOOR PLAN

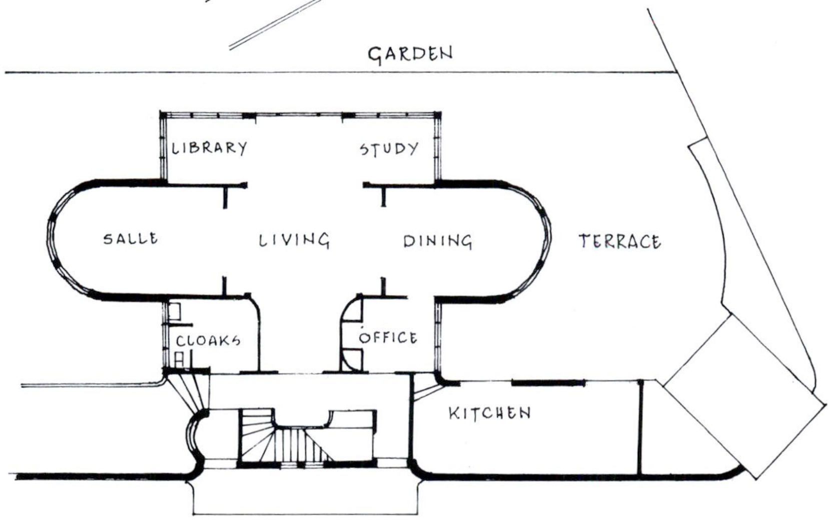

lateral axis developed by double height volume so that movement is towards view

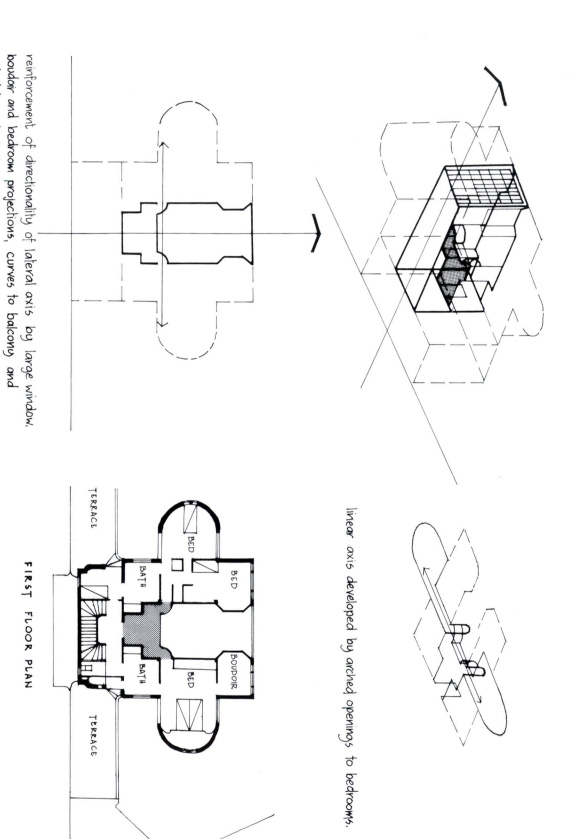

linear axis developed by arched openings to bedrooms.

reinforcement of directionality of lateral axis by large window. boudoir and bedroom projections, curves to balcony and indentations to bathrooms.

FIRST FLOOR PLAN

TERRACE

TERRACE

BED

BATH

BED

BATH

BED

BOUDOIR

GEOMETRICAL ADAPTATION

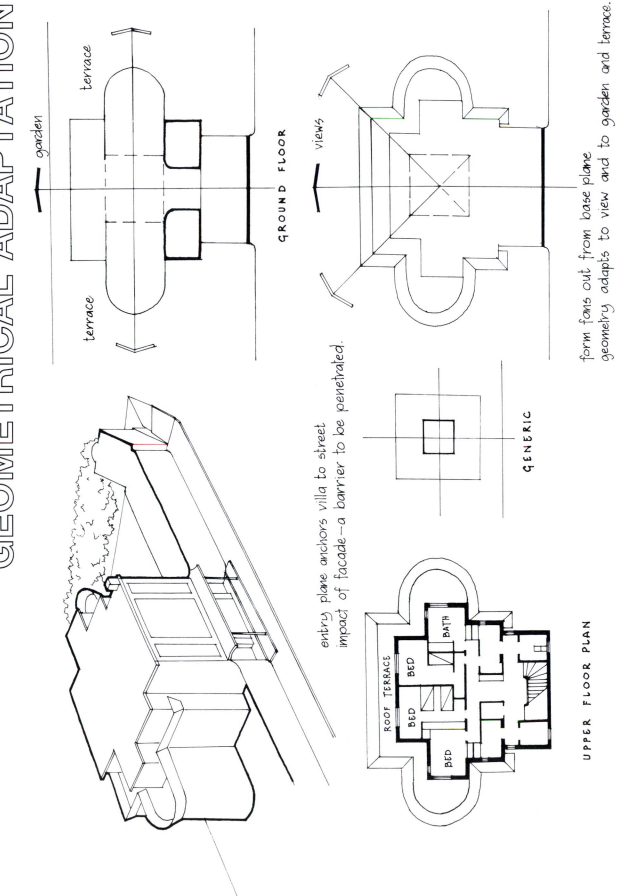

garden

terrace

terrace

GROUND FLOOR

views

entry plane anchors villa to street
impact of facade—a barrier to be penetrated.

GENERIC

ROOF TERRACE

BED BED

BED BATH

BED

UPPER FLOOR PLAN

form fans out from base plane
geometry adapts to view and to garden and terrace.

ZONAL CLARITY

Main zones such as the roof terrace, vertical circulation, sleeping and living zones are clearly delineated in the design. Built in reinforced concrete with a flat roof for the first time in his work and with curves tensioned against orthogonals, the villa anticipates Le Corbusier's later work.

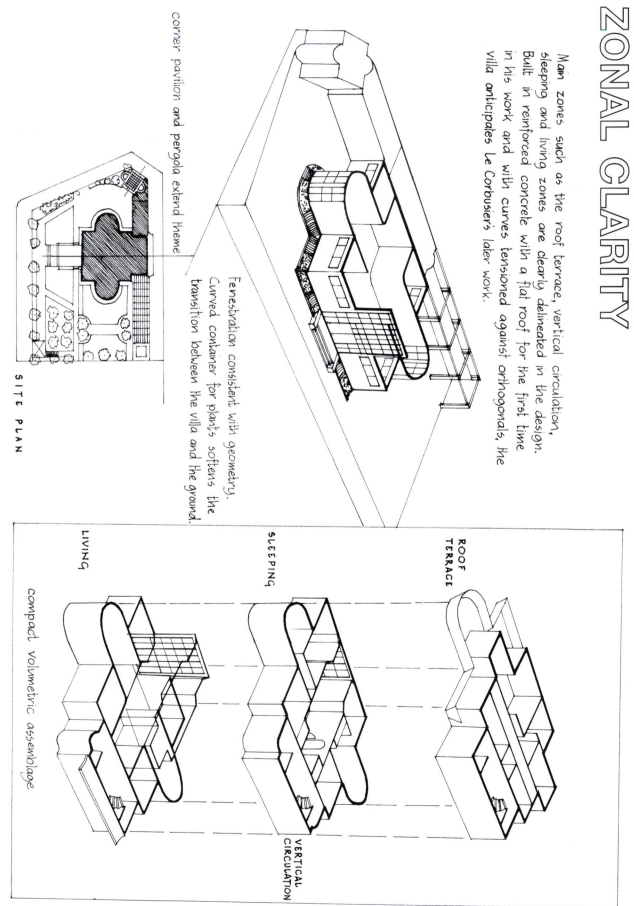

corner pavilion and pergola extend theme

SITE PLAN

Fenestration consistent with geometry. Curved container for plants softens the transition between the villa and the ground.

ROOF TERRACE

SLEEPING

VERTICAL CIRCULATION

LIVING

compact volumetric assemblage

FRAME AND PANEL

As with previous projects, Jeanneret subdivides his surfaces by using a system of framing. The brick veneer to the concrete structure gives a surface having colour, pattern, scale and texture. Brickwork is used as a precise frame for plaster panels and as window mullions, the windows being incised deeply to emphasise the mass.

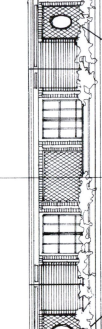

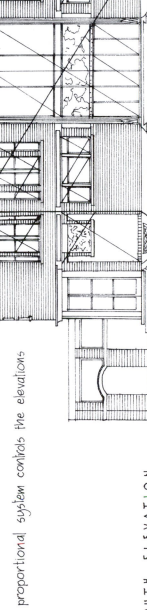

a proportional system controls the elevations

SOUTH ELEVATION
taken from Jeanneret's working drawing

DESIGN PRINCIPLES

MASS
Architecture is the masterly correct and magnificent play of masses brought together in light.

SURFACE
The task of the architect is to vitalise the surfaces which clothe the masses.

PLAN
Mass and surface are determined by the plan. The plan is the generator.

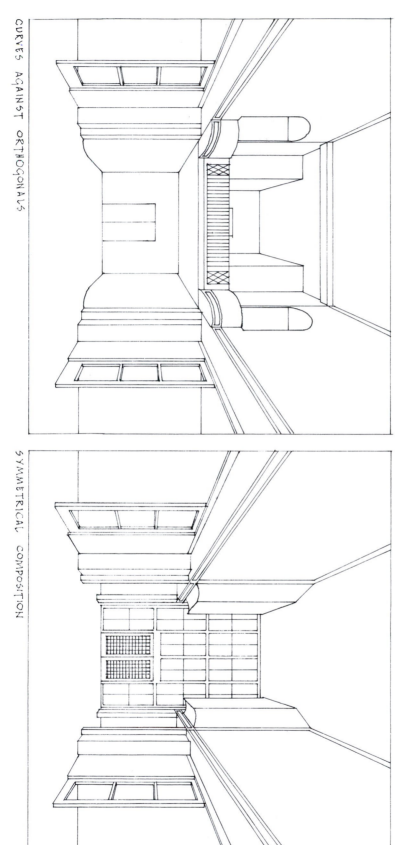

CURVES AGAINST ORTHOGONALS

SYMMETRICAL COMPOSITION

THE VILLA SCHWOB

By the use of inert materials and starting from conditions more or less utilitarian, you have established certain relationships which have aroused my emotions. This is architecture.   Le Corbusier Vers une Architecture

The Villa Schwob brings together some of the design principles that were evolving in Jeanneret's work. These principles formed the basis of his later work and as Le Corbusier he refers to them in Vers Une Architecture.

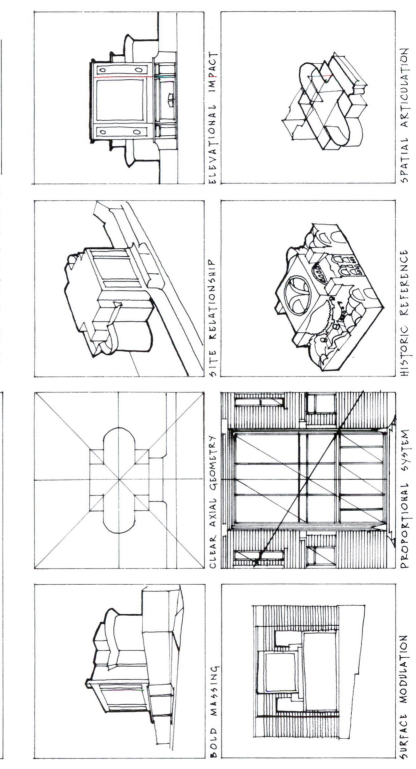

ELEVATIONAL IMPACT

SPATIAL ARTICULATION

SITE RELATIONSHIP

HISTORIC REFERENCE

CLEAR AXIAL GEOMETRY

PROPORTIONAL SYSTEM

BOLD MASSING

SURFACE MODULATION

LIMITED INVENTION

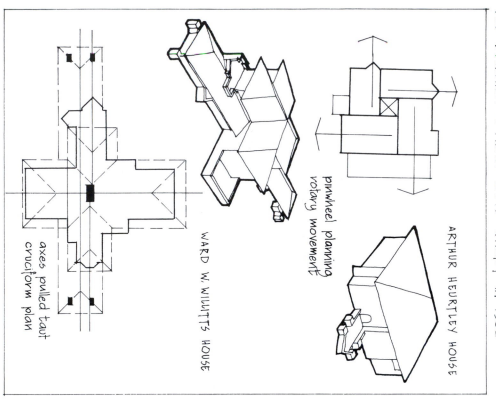

ARTHUR HEURTLEY HOUSE

pinwheel planning
rotary movement

WARD W. WILLITS HOUSE

axes pulled taut
cruciform plan

With the exception of the Villa Favre-Jacot, Jeanneret's first houses are concerned more with the development of existing ideas than with inventing new forms.

The villas Stotzer and Jaquemet follow similar design tenets to the Villa Fallet, and the Villa Schwob, although suggesting Byzantine and Wrightian influence, is derived from the Villa Jeanneret-Perret.

Favre-Jacot is the exception, but in none of these houses do we sense the compositional versatility evident in Wright's work in which pinwheel and cruciform planning appeared as early as 1902.

The most limiting compositional factor in Jeanneret's technique was his reliance on bilateral symmetry, from which he did not progress until the partnership with Ozenfant gave him the skills which were explored through the medium of painting in the movement known as Purism.

The deployment of axes, contrast between curves and rectangles, proclamation of the main elevation and dependence on geometric control, formed the basis of all his later work. He always tended towards deep rooted ideas and preferred to design within a framework of rules.

THE EARLY VILLAS

BILATERAL SYMMETRY   AXIAL CONTROL   DOMINANT MAIN FACADE   RELIANCE ON POWERFUL CONTRASTS.

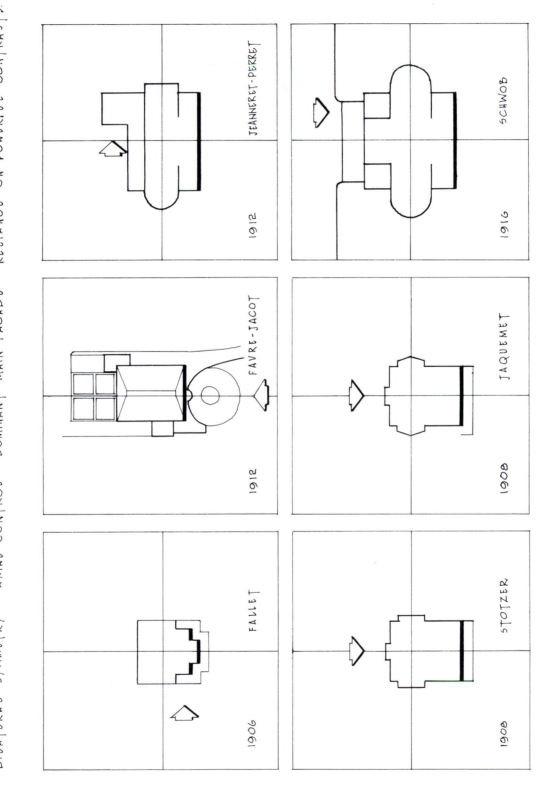

FALLET

1906

FAVRE-JACOT

1912

JEANNERET-PERRET

1912

STOTZER

1908

JAQUEMET

1908

SCHWOB

1916

ABATTOIRS BORDEAUX AND CHALLUY 1917

Two main changes are evident in Jeanneret's work after the Voyage d'Orient; changes of philosophy and technique. Nature as a direct source is overtaken by classicism, so that whereas in the Villa Fallet natural references prevail, in the Villa Favre-Jacot these are largely replaced by classical motifs. In the later villas, references to nature are peripheral, Jeanneret being concerned with clarity and order, expressed through simple combinations of primary forms.

Although the forms and surface treatment are simpler than before, the architecture becomes more complex in the external organisation of zones and the internal organisation of space. The most significant thematic devices are the way movement into the form now affects its arrangement and the positive use of curves as contrast to rectangles. The Villa Schwob takes all these ideas furthest with equilibrium achieved through geometrical control.

Yet this control was based on symmetry, and the villa, with its sculptural panels by Léon Perrin, did not evoke those dynamic aspects now coming to the fore in modern life. Jeanneret realised that the machine and mass production would become major forces in the twentieth century and sought an architectural language capable of reflecting the zeitgeist. In 1917 he designed two abbatoirs, neither of which was built, and freed from the constraints of domestic imagery he was able to concentrate on a purely functional assemblage of elements arranged in accordance with manufacturing processes.

FUNCTIONAL AESTHETIC

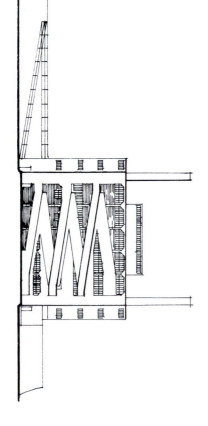

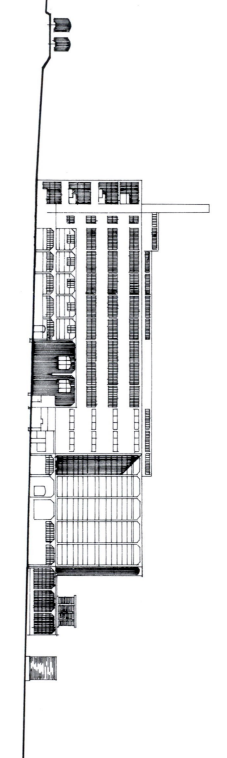

ABATTOIR BORDEAUX 1917

The domino column and slab system is used with the columns expressed elevationally and industrial glazing units stretched out ribbon fashion along the facade. Movement is visually dramatised by the ramp arrangement at the front of the block, the first appearance of this device in Le Corbusier's oeuvre.

A NEW ARCHITECTURAL LANGUAGE

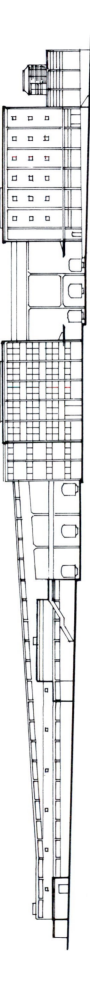

ABATTOIR CHALLUY 1917

ORTHOGONAL FRAME

VISUAL DYNAMISM THROUGH RAMP AND EXTERNAL STAIRS

CLEAR IDENTIFICATION OF FUNCTIONAL UNITS

INTEGRATION WITH CIRCULATION NETWORKS

INDUSTRIAL VOCABULARY

NO DECORATION AS SUCH

BI LATERAL SYMMETRY

AIRCRAFT IMAGERY

The ramp for animals follows the main longitudinal axis with Jeanneret retaining the symmetrical format of earlier designs. Outside stairs give separate access for male and female workers at each side of the building leading to an ablutions block.

The abattoirs are organised so that animals move up a ramp to the top of the building where they are killed in a slaughterhouse, the carcasses then being conveyed downwards to various plants before reaching a delivery bay at ground level.

Carcasses were to be moved manually along ceiling rails following a prescribed route, along which they would be bled skinned and cut into pieces. Conveyor belts and lifts distribute the cuts to the various parts of the building from which the animal emerges in tins, as frozen meat and sausages.

refrigeration

ablutions

access

ramp

access

CANAL

With the abbatoir projects, Le Corbusier's new architectural language of reinforced concrete frame and slab with cubic forms, flat roofs and industrial windows had arrived. The industrial symbolism was appropriate in buildings which manage to express their function directly and the ramps are perhaps the most significant device in demonstrating how functional elements can provide aesthetic drama.

At a stroke, therefore, Le Corbusier acquired a technique by which he could control the organisation of his buildings within a discipline that combined several emerging ideas. The abbatoirs express their function like aeroplanes, ships and cars and now the structure itself becomes an orthogonal grid which provides an ordering framework not just for elevations but for the entire design.

The abbatoirs are also linked to a communications network and as such become much more than merely an answer to a specific problem. The design strategy embodies a grander concept in which nature (animals) is harnessed through farming and made available as a consumer product by an industrial process, to be finally distributed through a national communication network.

Ideas of efficiency inherent in such an integrated design approach remained with Le Corbusier, becoming part of his Utopian city strategy. But if the abbatoirs advanced Le Corbusier's technique and philosophical base they retained his somewhat limited bilaterally symmetrical compositional method. A further stage of development was needed both to free him of this constraint and explore further the whole question of meaning. Both objectives were realised through the association with Amadée Ozenfant which led to the formulation of the movement which became known as Purism.

PURISM

In February 1917 Jeanneret left La Chaux-de-Fonds to take up permanent residence in Paris. The following May he met Amédée Ozenfant, an established painter, who had produced a series of articles and comments under the title *L'Élan* in which he argued against the decorative tendencies of Cubism.

Ozenfant shared several of Jeanneret's views about art and the two men collaborated to develop an artistic theory which became known as Purism. These ideas were first published in 1918 in a book entitled *Après le Cubism* (Beyond Cubism). Addressing themselves to what they regarded as the distinctive features of the twentieth century, Ozenfant and Jeanneret set out to recognise those forces in life made manifest in science and the machine.

They believed that machines and other man-made artefacts respond to the same laws of economy and selection through fitness of purpose that are apparent in nature. They were convinced that this was a universal principle, one of the results of which was a tendency towards harmony, order and balance in all things. They put forward the idea that art could enable man to establish contact with the universal force that governs existence.

In 1920 Ozenfant and Jeanneret launched the magazine *L'Esprit Nouveau*, which became a forum for discussion of the ideas on which Purism was based. They explained the movement as being concerned with the universal properties of the senses and the mind, and articles in *L'Esprit Nouveau* extended the discussion beyond the arts to include the sciences, psychology, biology and sociology. Two issues were uppermost, the one to establish universal principles by means of logic, relating man to nature, and the other to study and if possible clarify the relationship between sensation and aesthetics.

In searching for a means by which an aesthetic language could communicate universally, Ozenfant and Jeanneret advocated the use of primary forms and colours. They also insisted that objects depicted in paintings should have a significance beyond their utilitarian function and should hold meanings that symbolise key principles.

The human form was seen as the most perfect result of natural selection and an example of what they termed the 'Law of Economy,' in which fundamental needs produced an objet type realised through laws of adaptation and economy. From this it followed that certain objects of particular usefulness and economy of means, such as glasses, bottles, plates etc. could be idealised as embodying universal principles.

Although on the surface nature seems to have infinite variety, Ozenfant and Jeanneret argued that this variety was based on certain laws which do not vary and which produce constant unchanging organisms. These organisms are clear in their forms, which are always based on geometrical structures. It followed therefore that geometry should be the underlying discipline for works of art, a means by which order and clarity could be preserved.

Ozenfant and Jeanneret believed that art was lagging behind science and technology in failing to come to terms with the principles which govern nature. Scientific knowledge was able to demonstrate these principles, and the machine in particular was an admirable expression of them. By contrast Cubist art floundered in a chaotic representation of ambiguities and shifting relationships that failed to convey 'the essence' of life. That this essence was a manifestation of order was a cornerstone of the Purist philosophy, as was the fact that order relies on rules, and if it was to be represented by art, any such art must have communication as a high priority.

Accordingly Jeanneret applied himself to the task of using the _objets types_ in his paintings to represent certain constants or universal principles apparent in nature, (and therefore demonstrated in such objects), these being organised in complex ways to represent the variety in nature.

In his paintings, the extension of themes to include different kinds of rhythmic effects and a variety of contrasts and tensions, were intended to be an artistic symbolisation of the forces of nature that govern life. In the early paintings the plates bottles books and guitars which represented the _objet types_ were portrayed explicitly in order to echo the precision and clarity of science and machine products. This was where Purism took issue with the Cubists and other movements such as De Stijl, rejecting any suggestion of confusion or abstraction.

Ozenfant and Jeanneret recognised that unlike the machine, it was the role of art to make contact with the emotions, and art must therefore not only be intelligable but must convey meaning. Art, in representing those forces which govern existence, should demonstrate that order apparent in nature by resolving tensions and contrasts in an ordered way within the pictorial format.

In the autumn of 1918, Jeanneret produced his first painting entitled _La cheminée_. This simple composition contained a cube placed on a table with a book and pile of notepaper alongside and two more books in the lower left hand corner. The painting is an attempt to establish a meaningful relationship between a primary form and the _objets types_

In a subsequent series of paintings Jeanneret introduced many more object types, gaining the opportunity to extend the range of contrast between for example cylindrical forms such as carafes or glasses and flat planar shapes such as guitars. Transparency and opacity, solid portrayal and shadow projection with representation in plan and in the third dimension, gradually take over as the objects become stylised. A hidden geometrical format of regulating lines ensure a proper balance of the various elements within the pictorial surface.

Between 1918 and 1920 Jeanneret's compositional skill increased dramatically, a period which culminates in his first compositional tour de force, Nature morte à la pile d'assiettes. As in other paintings the format is divided roughly into two halves by the table edge, with foreground incidents set against a background which contains two guitars.

A book is thrust forward, its spine on the central axis, the powerful curve of the stylised pages being echoed at a larger scale but in a lower key by the guitars. Below the table edge dividing line objects are rendered as solids, whilst above they are seen as planes and in silhouette. The second guitar is shown ambiguously as if it is a shadow of the first guitar and the scooped-out bowl of the top plate becomes the main focus of the composition. A green cylindrical container to the immediate right of the book echoes the pile of plates, again in a lower key, whilst two pipes are locked in rotation about a bottle neck which becomes a second focus.

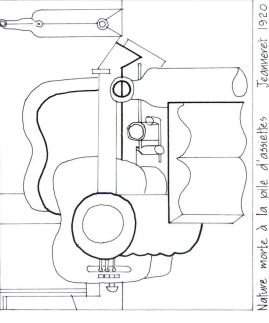

Nature morte à la pile d'assiettes   Jeanneret 1920

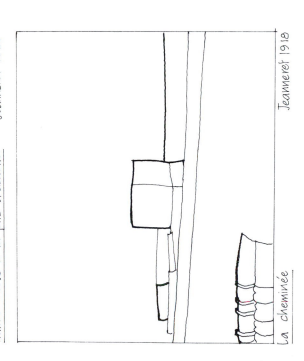

La cheminée   Jeanneret 1918

COMPOSITIONAL TECHNIQUE

By 1920 Jeanneret had arrived in compositional terms, almost entirely through his painterly explorations, of which the final canvas was only the tip of a creative iceberg comprising dozens of sketches for each painting.

Until and including his design for the Villa Schwob, Jeanneret's main compositional armoury consisted of a symmetrical format, enlivened by contrasts between cubic and cylindrical forms in the Parent's house and Villa Schwob. This reliance on primary volumes continued to play an important role in Le Corbusier's architectural repertoire, now embracing the Purist notion that objects themselves can have meaning, something which had become apparent in the ramps to the Abbatoirs, where function became expressed as such.

Now, in the paintings, books, glasses, pipes or guitars became the idealisation of perfect functional expression, whilst affording rich opportunities for arrangement through combinations of their diverse shapes. The technique included overlaps, the merging of objects, rhythms based on curves and echoed in cylinders, greatly extending his compositional range.

Many of these devices could be translated into an architectural idiom, with the _objets types_ being replaced by similarly idealised functional components such as spiral stairs, ribbon windows or roof terraces. Contrasts of planes and solids, rhythmic combinations of various kinds and geometrical control by regulating lines allowed the painterly lyricism to be extended into Le Corbusier's architecture of the twenties.

THE HEROIC DECADE 1920-30

4

Jeanneret adopted the pseudonym Le Corbusier for his architectural work in 1920 although he continued to sign his paintings Jeanneret until 1928. In October 1920 he exhibited his model house at the Salon d'Automne in Paris. He named it the Maison Citrohan as an intended compliment to the Citroën automobile manufacturing company and because he believed it to be as efficient as the new machines which were transforming twentieth century life.

In <u>Vers une Architecture</u> he explained how the concept would replace 'the old world house which made a bad use of space' with its 'incoherent grouping of a number of large rooms' in which 'the space has been both cramped and wasted. Instead' we must look upon the house as a machine for living in or as a tool', 'as serviceable as a typewriter.' This new form of dwelling would have a machine age imagery being 'without a pointed roof, with walls as smooth as sheet iron' and 'windows like those of factories.'

Maison Citrohan was Le Corbusier's answer to prevailing economic conditions in that he intended the side walls to be of masonry so that they could be built by workers anywhere in the country. The floors and roof were to be in reinforced concrete. Compositionally the design exploits techniques developed in Jeanneret's Purist paintings but in its attempt to provide space and good lighting Citrohan was inspired by a restaurant in Paris frequented by Ozenfant and Jeanneret.

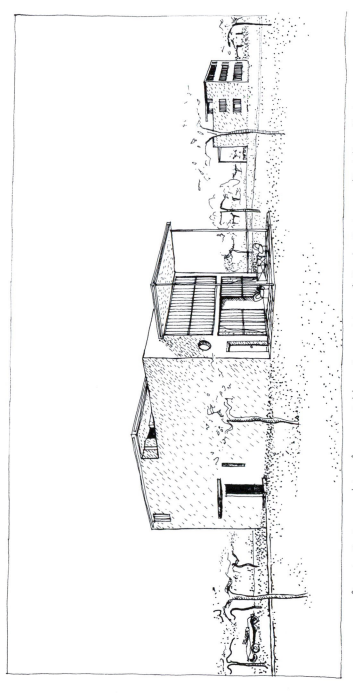

MAISON CITROHAN 1920-27

after Le Corbusier taken from a sketch in the archives of the Le Corbusier Fondation Paris

GENERIC

MAISON CITROHAN 1920

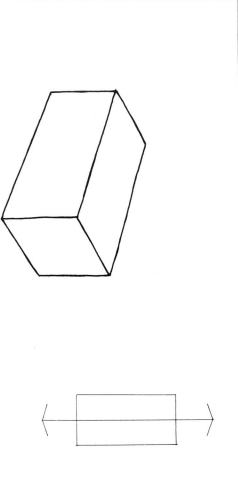

the generic form is a bilaterally symmetrical linear volume

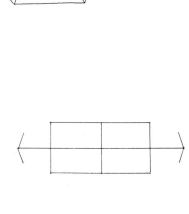

subdivision of accommodation into two cubes

The rectilinear configuration is subdivided into two cubic forms, (each slightly longer than its width), one containing a double height living zone, the other the rest of the accommodation. A gallery overlooks the living area and contains the main bedroom. Below this is the kitchen and dining with further bedrooms at the upper level adjacent to a roof terrace.

Unlike the earlier villas, which were controlled mainly by symmetry and in which modelling and surface treatment were important, the Citrohan house arranges the various elements asymmetrically in an abstract composition.

The various functions of either walking up an external stair or an internal spiral, living in a spacious zone, cooking, dining or sleeping, are placed partly to satisfy each function efficiently and also in such a way that they comprise a satisfying aesthetic composition.

This functional aesthetic with its roof terrace and spacious ambience symbolised that kind of lifestyle which Le Corbusier thought appropriate for the machine age. In its directionality and axial control the design retains techniques used in earlier villas but the imagery is new; with its clean lines and absence of decoration the Maison Citrohan was Le Corbusier's first 'machine a habiter.'

MAISON CITROHAN 1920

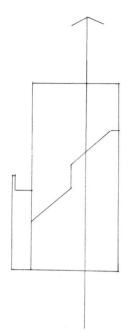

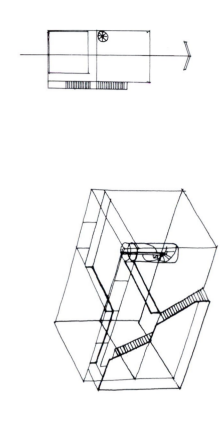

The specific form expresses functional elements with clarity. It is linear, directional and asymmetrical. Major elements such as the external stair, spiral stair, roof accommodation and first floor layer are balanced in a state of dynamic equilibrium.

The directionality of the form is confirmed by the external stair and by the roof.

roof terrace

living

guests

sleeping

cooking

eating

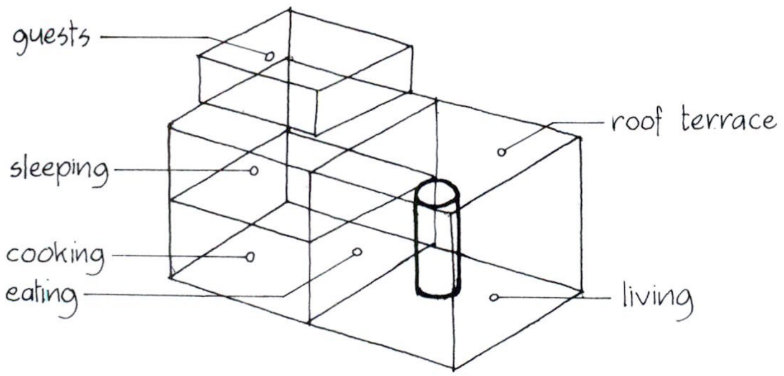

layered accommodation with spiral stair link

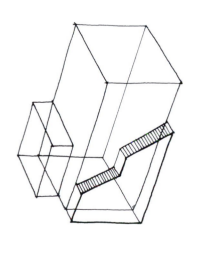

outside stair leads to roof

PLANES

MAISON CITROHAN 1920

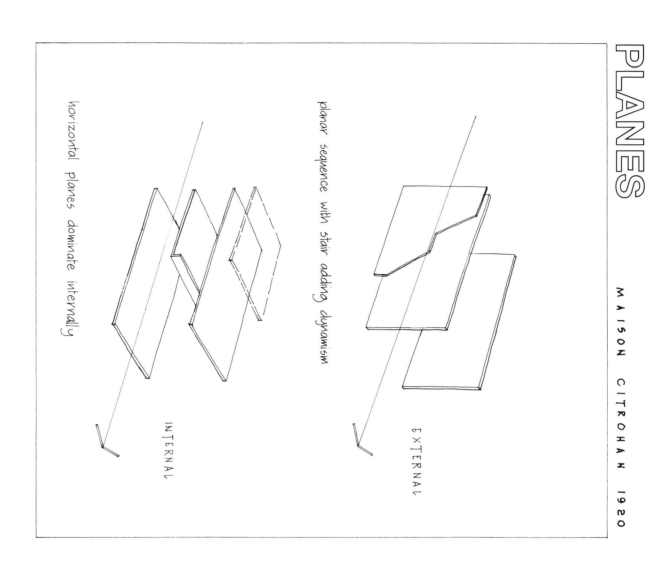

planar sequence with stair adding dynamism

EXTERNAL

INTERNAL

horizontal planes dominate internally

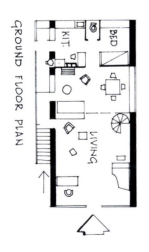

GROUND FLOOR PLAN

BED

KIT.

LIVING

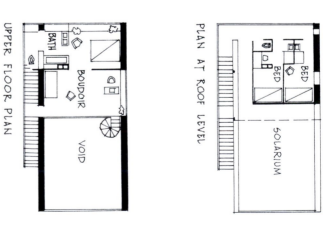

UPPER FLOOR PLAN

BATH

BOUDOIR

VOID

PLAN AT ROOF LEVEL

BED

BED

SOLARIUM

ZONES

MAISON CITROHAN 1920

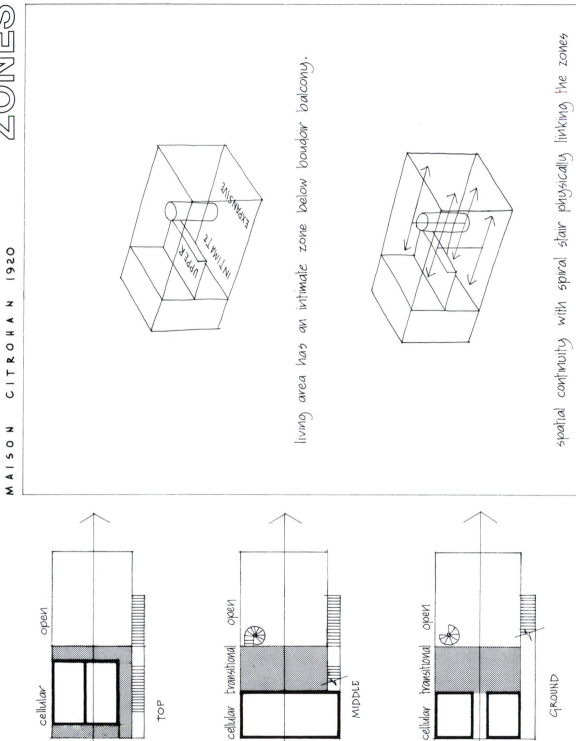

living area has an intimate zone below boudoir balcony.

INTIMATE
UPPER
EXPANSIVE

spatial continuity with spiral stair physically linking the zones

open
cellular
TOP

cellular   transitional   open
MIDDLE

cellular   transitional   open
GROUND

INDUSTRIAL FUNCTIONAL

MAISON CITROHAN 1920

The Citrohan house can be compared with Jeanneret's first three villas in La Chaux-de-Fonds, which had all been rectilinear, with a dominant linear axis and a design emphasis towards a main south-facing facade.

As a form, Citrohan is far simpler than the earlier houses, with industrial windows giving pattern and the triangular plane of the external stair being used to dramatise the composition.

The abstract planar language is based on a functional logic which sees the new materials improving the efficiency of the dwelling by providing more space and light.

The crisp white 'streamlined' image nevertheless obeys those rules of form and geometry discovered by Jeanneret on the study tours.

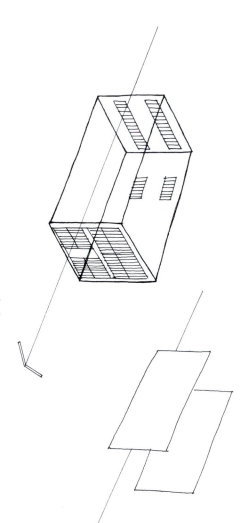

large window expresses importance of living zone fenestration mainly on ends accentuates linear/planar reading

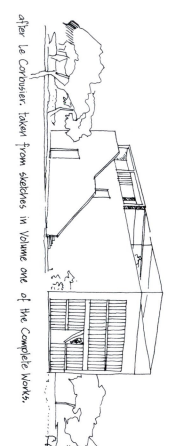

after Le Corbusier, taken from sketches in Volume One of the Complete Works.

the 'shoebox' configuration for a living unit recurs in Le Corbusier's oeuvre

DYNAMIC EQUILIBRIUM

Jeanneret's compositional breakthrough in Purism received architectural expression in Le Corbusier's Maison Citrohan, in which the spiral stair, living units and outer stair have an equivalent role and meaning to the objets types, the pipes books plates and bottles which he used in the paintings.

In the Citrohan house the solids (cellular units), cylinder (spiral stair) and various planes are deployed in a state of dynamic equilibrium resembling in the third dimension the two dimensional technique used in the paintings.

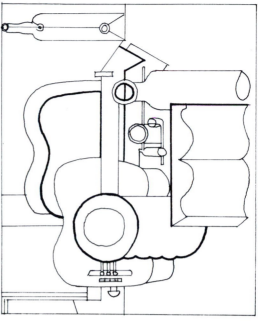

Nature morte à la pile d'assiettes   Jeanneret 1920

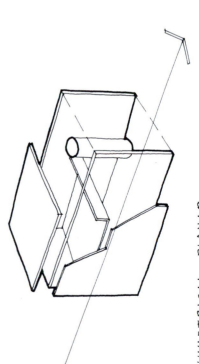

BILATERALLY SYMMETRICAL SOLID

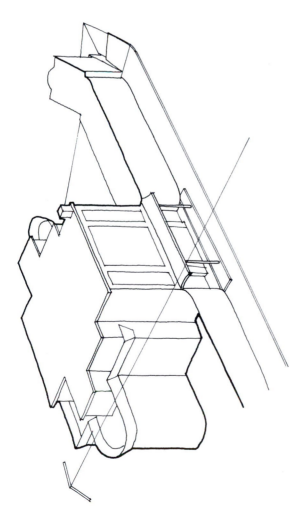

ASYMMETRICAL PLANAR

Like the abbatoir projects, the Citrohan house has broader implications than merely being a solution to the problem of the dwelling. The clear cubic shape obeys those perceptual laws evident in the Parthenon and the mosques, which ensure that form communicates directly with the senses. The houses display a logical approach to both structure and technology in being intended to meet the economic situation and the availability of labour. The kind of space and lighting within the houses suggests the lifestyle of an artist rather than the middle class norm and it was by such means that Le Corbusier intended to elevate the aesthetic consciousness of everyman.

While preparing the design for the Citrohan living units Le Corbusier was working on his Utopian City project, the Ville Contemporaine for three million people. The proposal reacted against the narrow streets and dark confined slums of so many cities by providing spacious well lit apartments and houses in a parkland setting. He put forward the master plan at the Salon d'Automne in Paris in 1922 and the strategy for the city simply extends the ideas demonstrated in the Citrohan house.

The concept is Le Corbusier's most forthright pronouncement of his faith in geometry as an organisational system with major axes forming traffic routes and defining a hierarchical distribution of activity zones. A limited number of building types are proposed, each of which is composed of cubic primary forms.

The layout is bilaterally symmetrical, with the main traffic route running along the linear axis, this being intersected by a major lateral route and by secondary diagonal routes. These diagonals define a diamond shaped central zone containing an air road and rail terminus surrounded by twentyfour cruciform glass skyscrapers. At the edges of this zone are the Immeubles Villas, apartments arranged in a zig-zag manner reminiscent of the Dom-ino system.

VILLE CONTEMPORAINE 1922

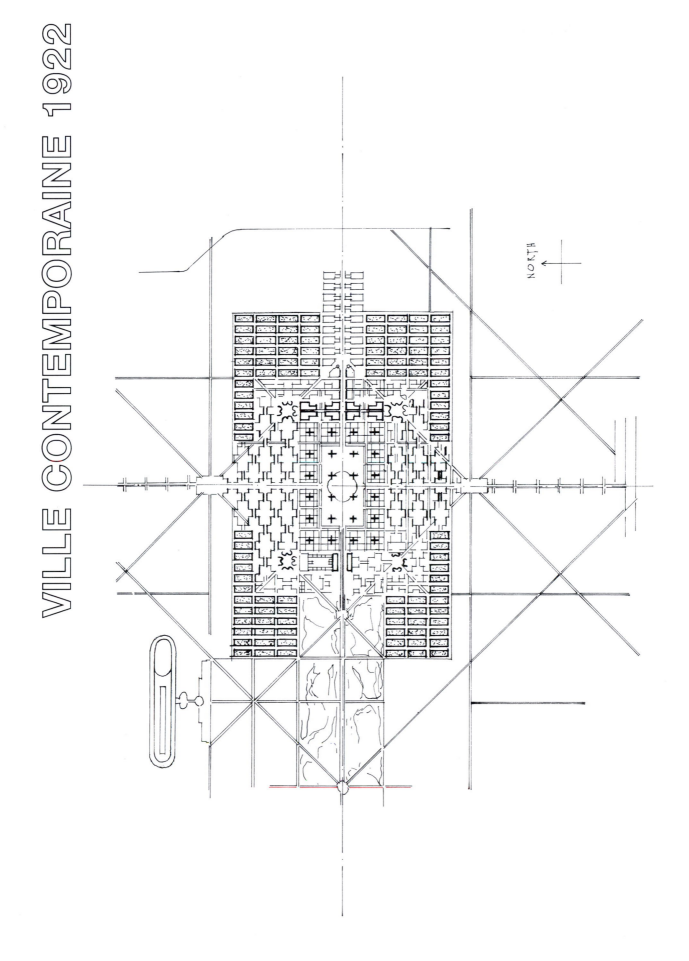

NORTH

The Ville Contemporaine or Contemporary City demonstrates several principles guiding Le Corbusier's strategy at this time.

UTOPIA THROUGH ORDER

In the Ville Contemporaine Le Corbusier irons out the 'chaos' of former cities by imposing an order based on a logical distribution of activities. By this means a framework is provided within which society will prosper, an ideal city similar to those proposed during the Renaissance. As such this is an abstract concept which is essentially a reflection of Le Corbusier's own thought patterns and priorities. This approach is a negation of the pluralistic nature of the city and any 'master plan' imposes a limited system when compared with organic growth. It was because Le Corbusier believed that organic growth had failed that he adopted such an approach.

SYMBOLISM

The city as a whole and each element within it symbolise Le Corbusier's utopian vision. The shimmering glass towers of the business section have an almost mystical significance, elevated high above the sleek axial autoroutes. Elevation in fact becomes a key idea, so that the pilotis which raise buildings above the landscape become powerful symbols, demonstrating that modern technology has liberated man so that he can build at will. An extension of this is the way roof gardens symbolise the idea of health giving relaxation, and in both city and in individual buildings Le Corbusier carries through this philosophy.

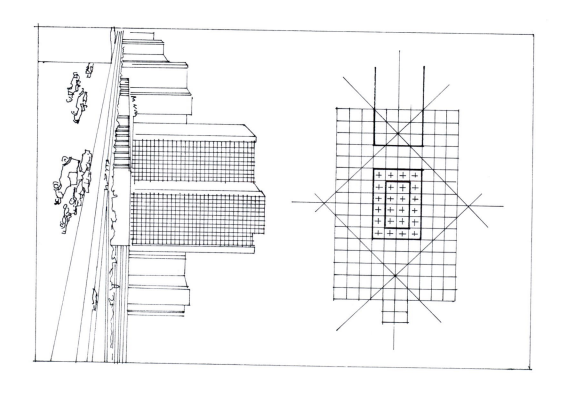

NATURE

Parkland dominates the city along with the geometrical organisation, affirming Le Corbusier's reverence for the twin phenomena, geometry and nature, the one so much part of the other. The city is seen as a biological organism with a heart, (the business centre), lungs, (the parkland), and arteries, (traffic routes). As the blood supply, traffic is given a high priority and Le Corbusier believed that the efficiency of the city depended on a rapid flow of traffic along the major routes. These routes also symbolise the dynamism of modern life, the automobile being a sublime creation within the machine age culture.

HIERARCHIES AND CLASSIFICATION

In the kit of parts comprising the city each element is thought of in accordance with the system of priorities, this being accommodated within the geometrical layout. Activities are defined, classified and fitted into the grand design. Traffic is classified according to the differing needs, with very fast autoroutes, medium speed suburban roads and slow subterranean service roads.

ZONES

Within the classification system zones are designated for business, urban and suburban living, recreation and industry. Space is allowed for expansion within the circulation skeleton.

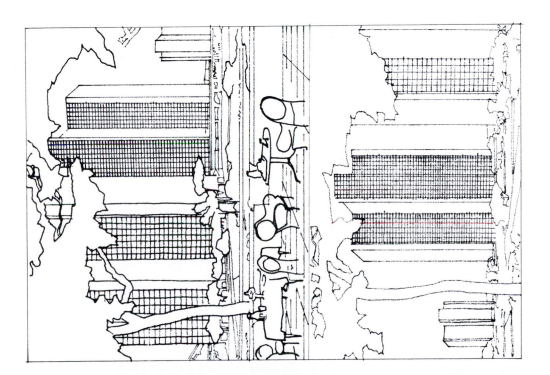

MAISON CITROHAN MARK II 1922

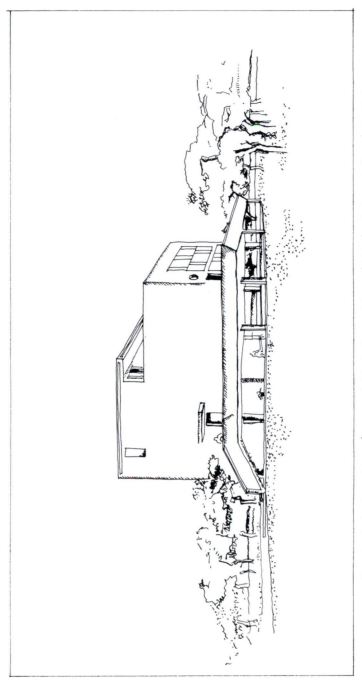

after Le Corbusier taken from a sketch in the archives of the Le Corbusier Fondation Paris

104

MAISON CITROHAN 1922

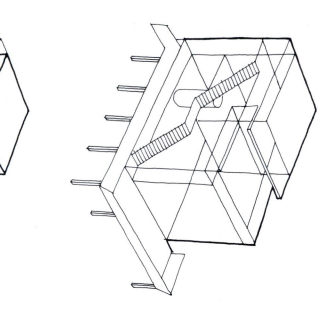

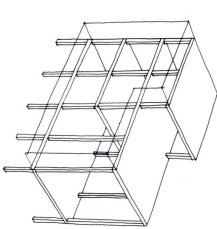

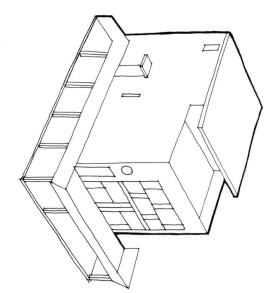

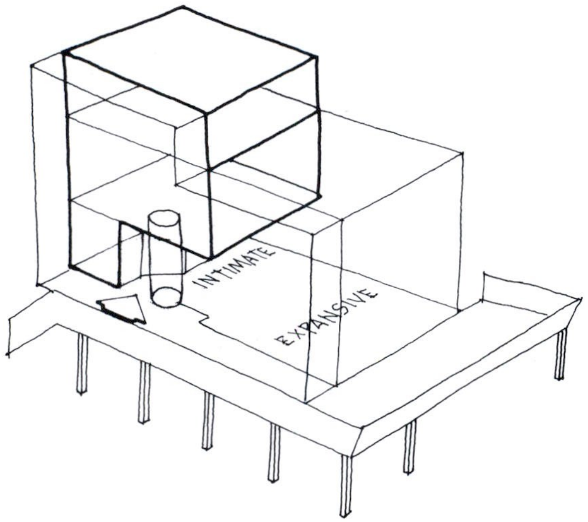

Le Corbusier's modified Citrohan house includes a garage as an integral part of the concept. The garage is placed below the house which is raised by means of a framed structure.

The stair now comes inside the house and instead of the boudoir looking down onto the living space it is closed off although overhanging the dining area as before. The main entrance is to the side with the spiral stair placed alongside so that movement around it leads to the living zone.

INTIMATE

EXPANSIVE

CASCADE THEME

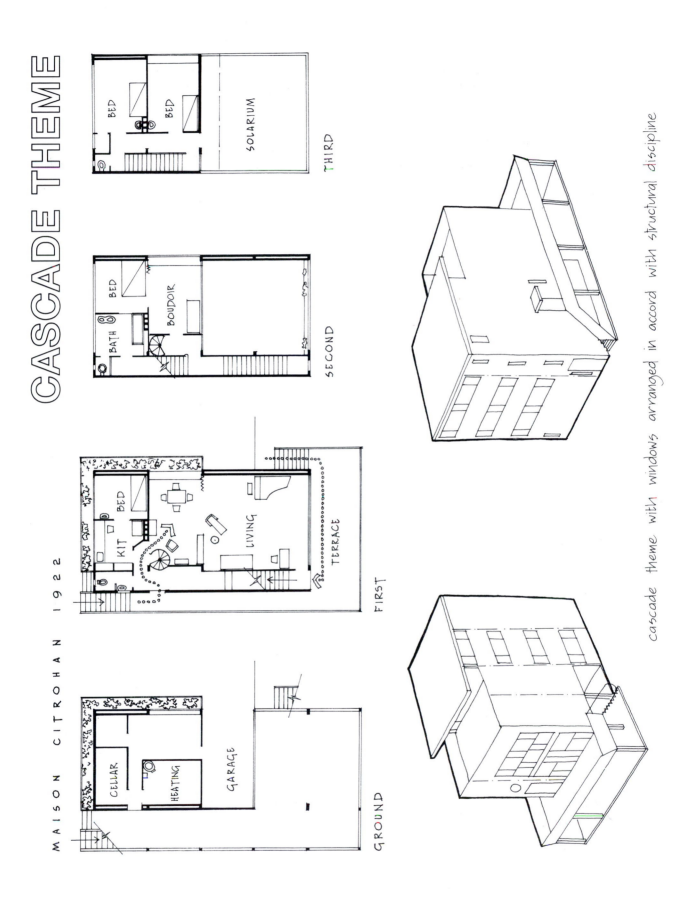

MAISON CITROHAN 1922

BED
BED
SOLARIUM
THIRD

BED
BATH
BOUDOIR
BED
SECOND

KIT
BED
LIVING
TERRACE
FIRST

CELLAR
HEATING
GARAGE
GROUND

cascade theme with windows arranged in accord with structural discipline

105

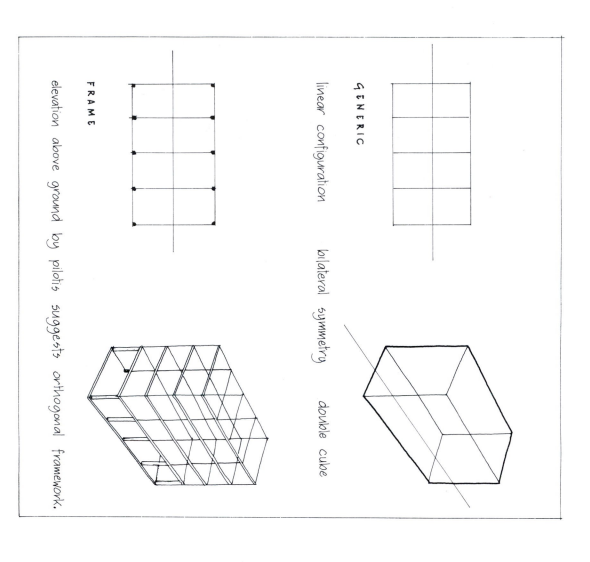

GENERIC

linear configuration   bilateral symmetry   double cube

FRAME

elevation above ground by pilotis suggests orthogonal framework.

The final version of the Citrohan projects was built as one of Le Corbusier's contributions (the other being an apartment block) to the Weissenhof housing exhibition at Stuttgart in 1927.

The solution retains the best features of earlier designs and is a typical example of the way Le Corbusier's ideas evolve. As with the 1922 model the main stair is enclosed, there is a roof terrace, and a framed construction raises the house on pilotis allowing a garage to be placed at ground level.

The spiral stair goes, and the boudoir becomes an open gallery overlooking the living area as in the 1920 design. As then, two cubic forms are placed side by side in an essentially linear configuration. This linearity is intensified by the positioning of the staircase which gains recognition elevationally by a balcony projection thrusting beyond the end plane of the house.

Entry is placed on this secondary linear axis and the edge of the boudoir gallery is set at an angle with a vertical boiler stack plunging through the living space. The oblique form of the stair is revealed in the living area, participating, with the stack and gallery, in a dynamic juxtaposition of functional units.

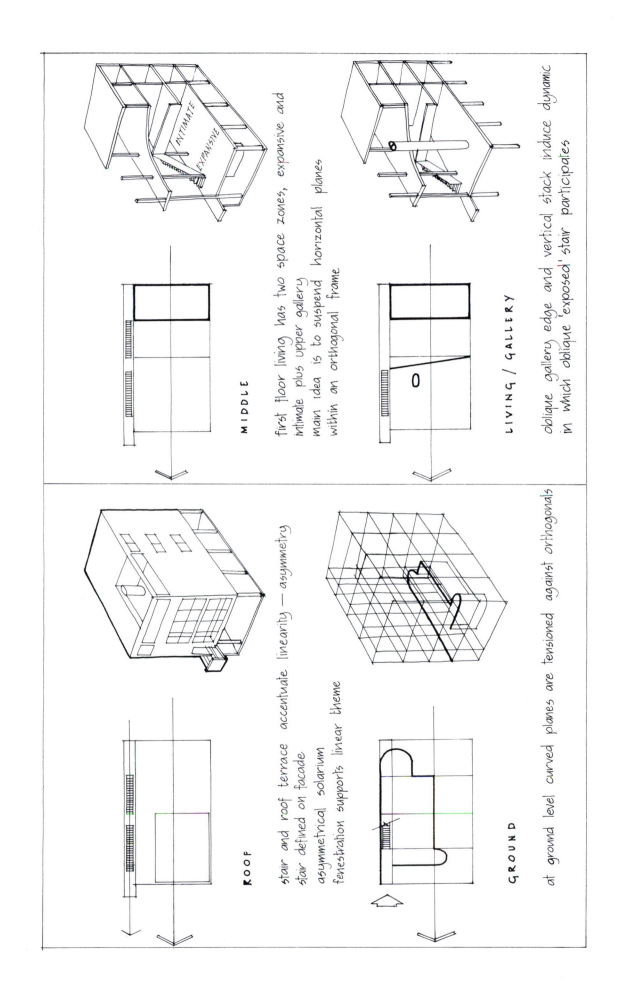

ROOF

stair and roof terrace accentuate linearity — asymmetry
stair defined on facade
asymmetrical solarium
fenestration supports linear theme

GROUND

at ground level curved planes are tensioned against orthogonals

MIDDLE

first floor living has two space zones, expansive and
intimate plus upper gallery
main idea is to suspend horizontal planes
within an orthogonal frame

LIVING / GALLERY

oblique gallery edge and vertical stack induce dynamic
in which oblique 'exposed' stair participates

INTIMATE
EXPANSIVE

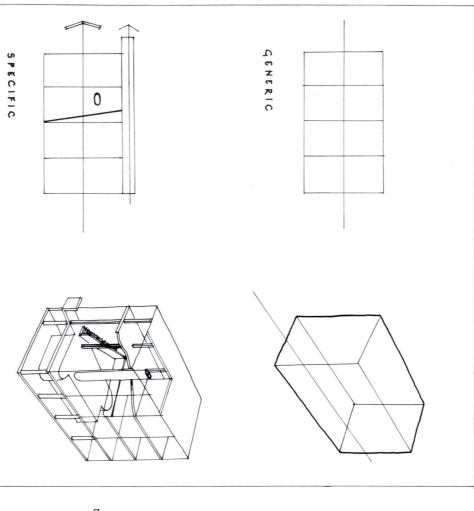

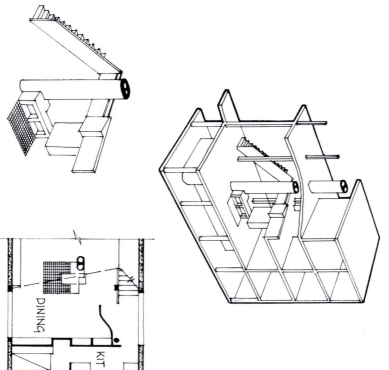

GENERIC

SPECIFIC

Theme is concerned to express a complex three dimensional relationship between functional elements within the discipline of an orthogonal frame.

Le Corbusier develops the theme by locking a series of elements together around the services stack. Using the fireplace and a cubic volume suspended from the gallery as space dividers, he projects a shelf orthogonally from the gallery which emphasises it's contrasting obliqueness.

DINING

KIT

PLANES

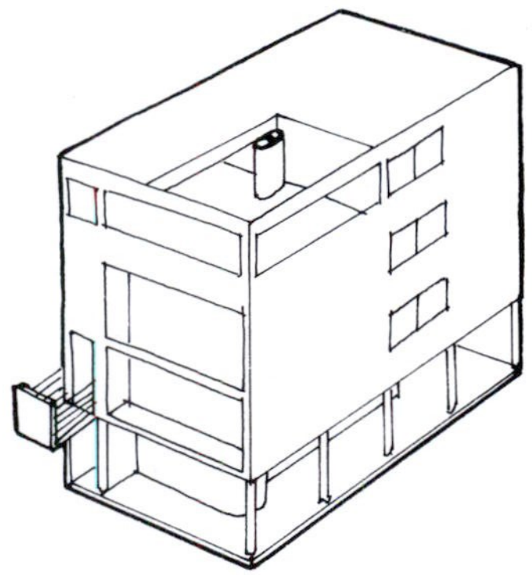

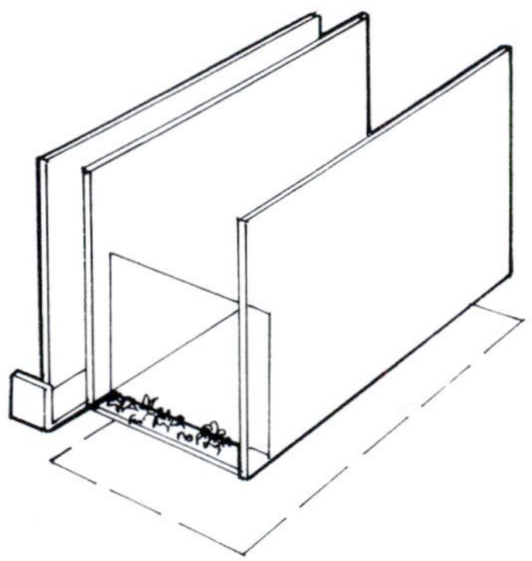

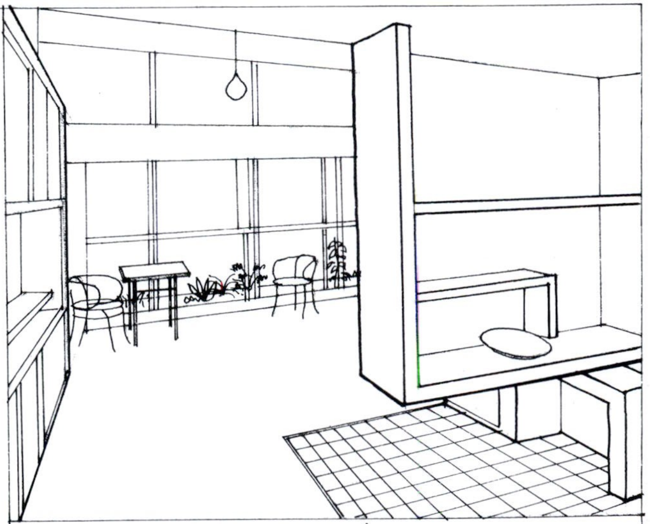

LIVING AREA FROM DINING △
GALLERY SHELF PROJECTION BECOMES WRITING DESK

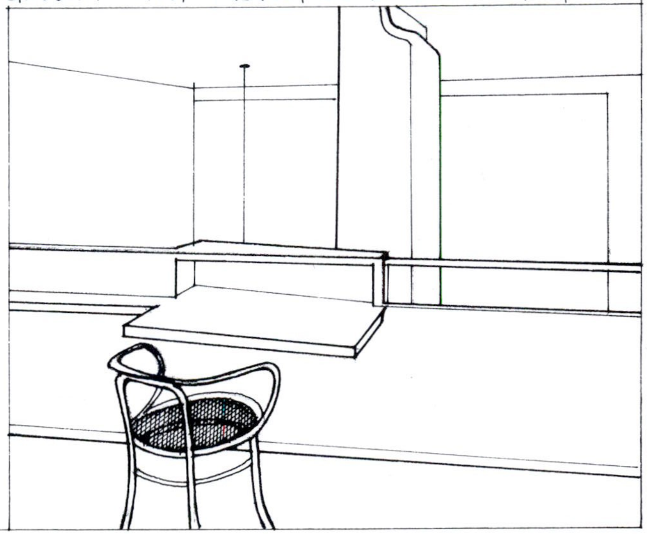

By setting back the living area window
an area of planting is provided and
the vertical planar alignment is emphasised.

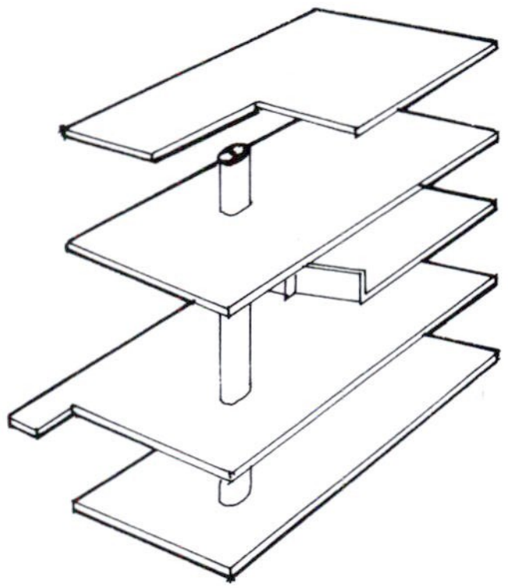

The services stack pins the horizontal
floor planes like a skewer.

110

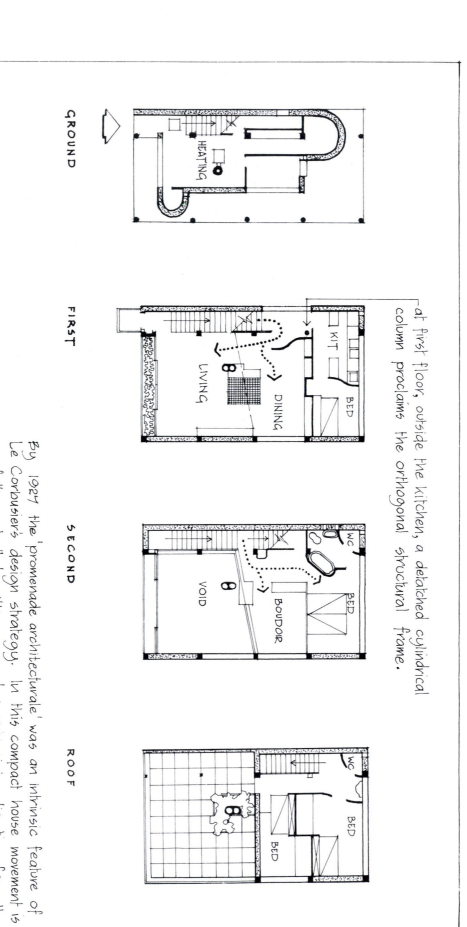

GROUND

FIRST

SECOND

ROOF

HEATING

KIT
LIVING
DINING
BED

VOID
BOUDOIR
BED
WC

BED
BED
WC

at first floor, outside the kitchen, a detached cylindrical column proclaims the orthogonal structural frame.

By 1927 the 'promenade architecturale' was an intrinsic feature of Le Corbusier's design strategy. In this compact house movement is carefully controlled, with a curved screen giving direction from the stair to the living area at first floor, and the inclined bath acting similarly at second floor. Also at second floor the obliquely inclined gallery edge assists movement from the stair landing.

DYNAMISM

With each Citrohan project Le Corbusier deploys functional elements in a state of dynamic equilibrium. By 1927 this technique had become fully developed with a series of important houses which began with the Villa at Vaucresson and studio Apartment for his painter associate Amedeé Ozenfant.

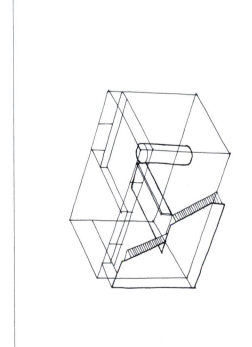

C I T R O H A N   1 9 2 0
stair spiral and gallery in dynamic relationship

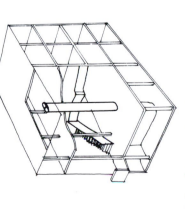

C I T R O H A N   1 9 2 7
stair stack and gallery in dynamic relationship

In 1922 at the Salon d'Automne in Paris Le Corbusier exhibited his Ville Contemporaine and Citrohan II house and it was as a result of visiting the exhibition that M. and M. Georges Besnus (who were regular readers of L'Esprit Nouveau) asked Le Corbusier to design a house for them. The house was built in the Paris suburb of Vaucresson on a corner site that was suggested by Le Corbusier, who persuaded his clients to buy the adjoining site as well.

As with the Citrohan model, garage living and sleeping are on different levels with living again raised as a Piano Nobile. The sloping site is exploited by Le Corbusier and vertical circulation is placed alongside the main form. Along with Ozenfant's studio/apartment these were the first houses to be built using the new architectural language, and Le Corbusier takes the opportunity to demonstrate those design principles already explored in the early Citrohan models.

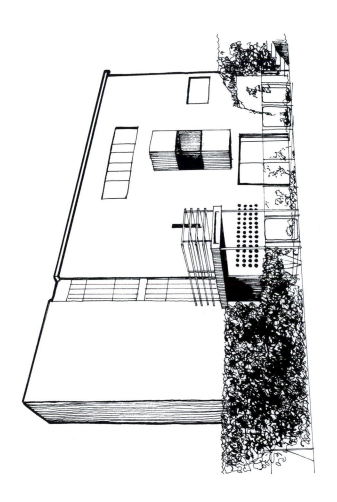

VILLA AT VAUCRESSON 1922

SITE FORCES

The wedge-shaped site faced the Route Départmentale which becomes the dominant external axis. Le Corbusier establishes a plateau, arranging the accommodation on three levels to take advantage of a slope down the Rue Allouard towards the Route Départmentale. The site is without special features in the suburban atmosphere of Vaucresson.

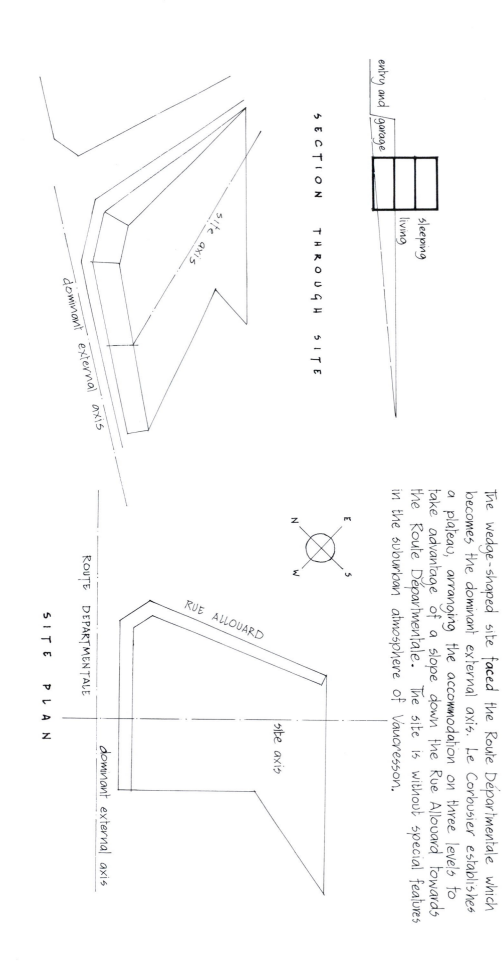

SECTION THROUGH SITE

entry and garage
sleeping
living
site axis
dominant external axis

SITE PLAN

ROUTE DEPARTMENTALE
RUE ALLOUARD
site axis
dominant external axis

GENERIC CONCEPT

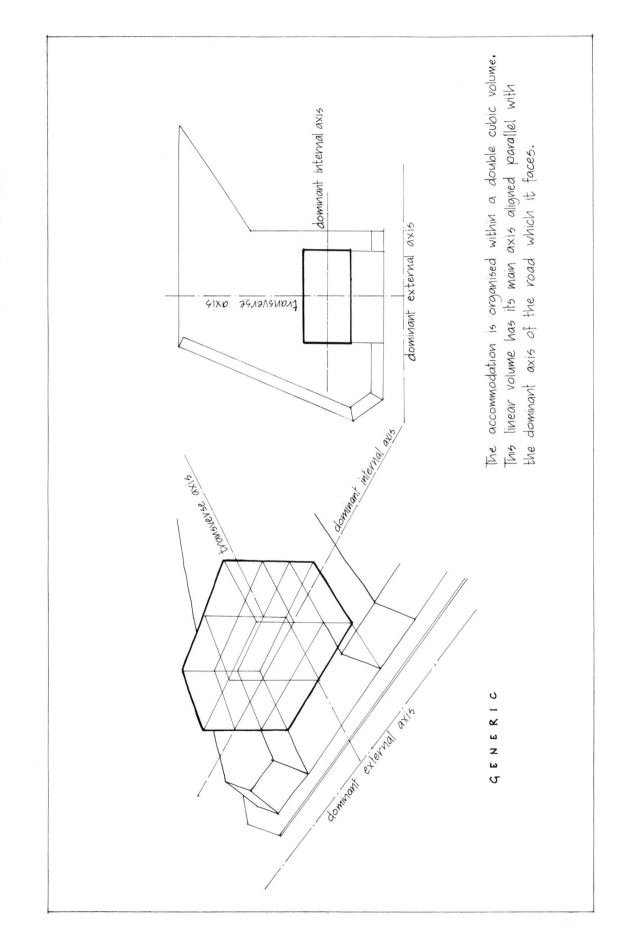

GENERIC

The accommodation is organised within a double cubic volume.
This linear volume has its main axis aligned parallel with
the dominant axis of the road which it faces.

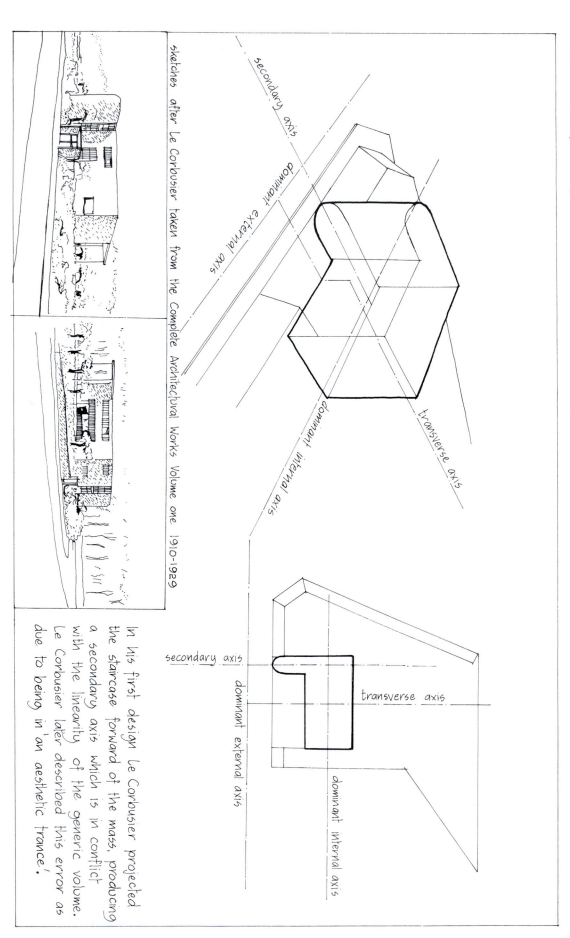

secondary axis

dominant external axis

transverse axis

dominant internal axis

secondary axis

dominant external axis

transverse axis

dominant internal axis

sketches after Le Corbusier taken from the Complete Architectural Works Volume one 1910-1929

In his first design Le Corbusier projected the staircase forward of the mass, producing a secondary axis which is in conflict with the linearity of the generic volume. Le Corbusier later described this error as due to being in an 'aesthetic trance'.

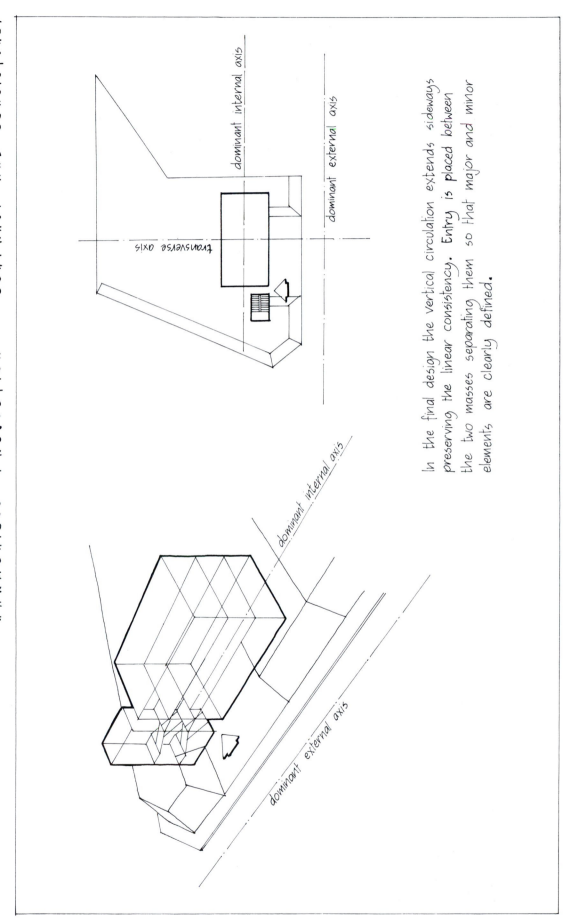

In the final design the vertical circulation extends sideways, preserving the linear consistency. Entry is placed between the two masses separating them so that major and minor elements are clearly defined.

THEME

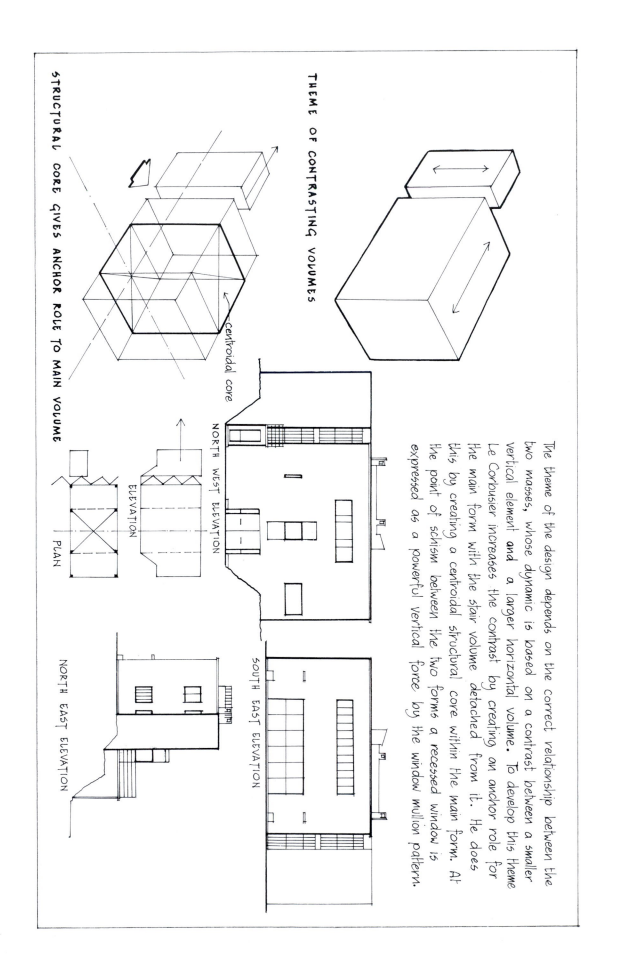

THEME OF CONTRASTING VOLUMES

STRUCTURAL CORE GIVES ANCHOR ROLE TO MAIN VOLUME

centroidal core

NORTH WEST ELEVATION

ELEVATION

PLAN

NORTH EAST ELEVATION

SOUTH EAST ELEVATION

The theme of the design depends on the correct relationship between the two masses, whose dynamic is based on a contrast between a smaller vertical element and a larger horizontal volume. To develop this theme Le Corbusier increases the contrast by creating an anchor role for the main form with the stair volume detached from it. He does this by creating a centroidal structural core within the main form. At the point of schism between the two forms a recessed window is expressed as a powerful vertical force by the window mullion pattern.

CORE

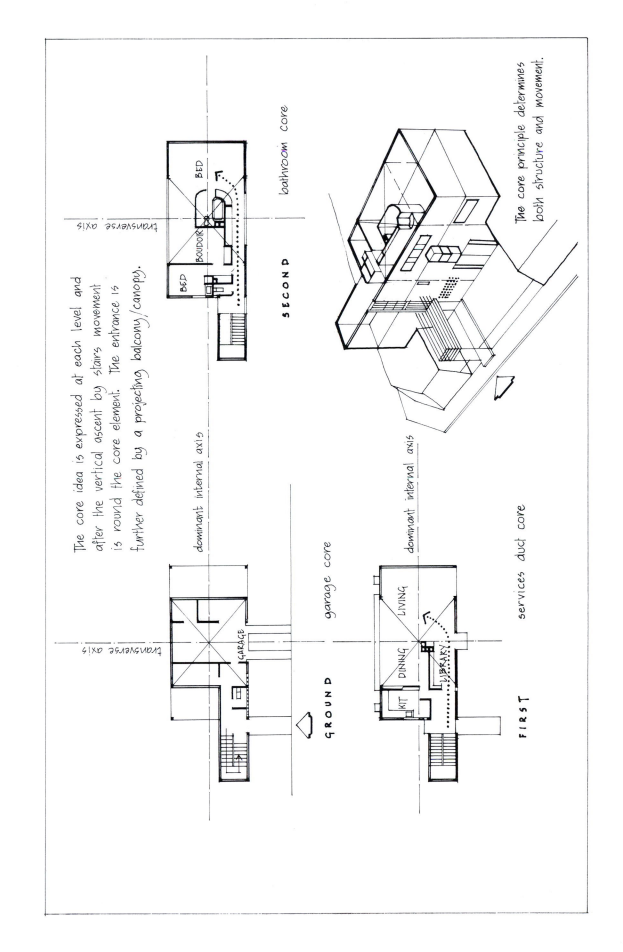

The core idea is expressed at each level and after the vertical ascent by stairs movement is round the core element. The entrance is further defined by a projecting balcony/canopy.

The core principle determines both structure and movement.

SECOND

bathroom core

BED

BOUDOIR

BED

transverse axis

dominant internal axis

GROUND

garage core

GARAGE

transverse axis

FIRST

services duct core

LIVING

DINING

KIT

LIBRARY

dominant internal axis

VERTICALITY   **ANIMATION**   **IMPACT**

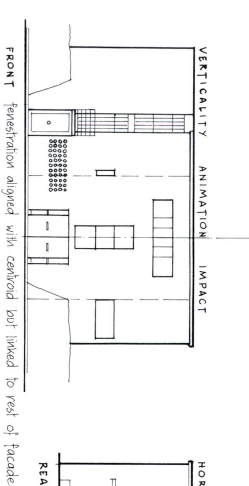

FRONT fenestration aligned with centroid but linked to rest of facade

Le Corbusier treats the front and back differently, acknowledging the different conditions for each, and the properties of the mass. The triple storied front concentrates on verticality with a studied balance between the centroidal section and the rest of the facade.

To the rear the centroid is clearly defined by fenestration, but this time with a horizontal emphasis. A cornice caps the main mass emphasising its primary role, and the bilateral symmetry with twin ledges and bases remind us of those classical design principles of earlier houses in La Chaux-de-Fonds.

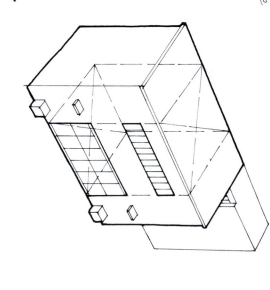

HORIZONTALITY   **SERENITY**

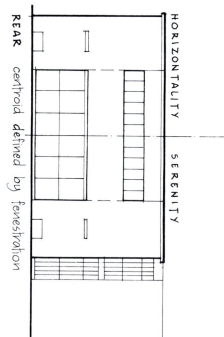

REAR centroid defined by fenestration

PENETRATION OF PLANE

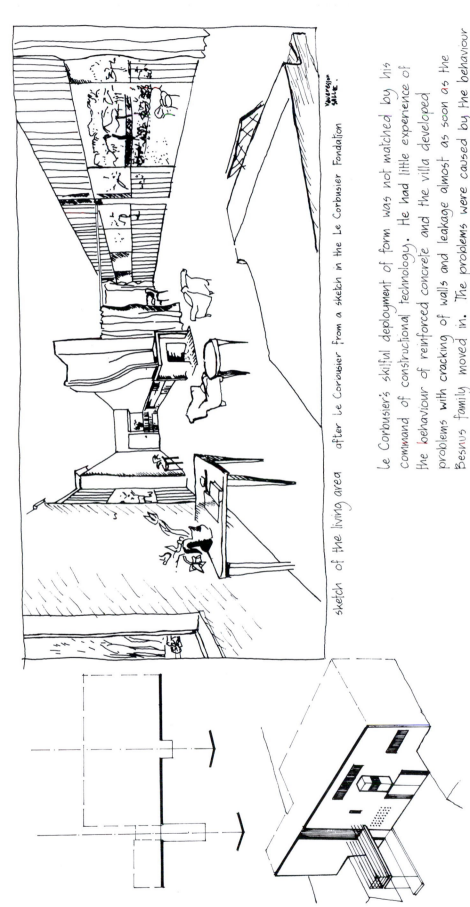

sketch of the living area   after Le Corbusier from a sketch in the Le Corbusier Fondation

Le Corbusier emphasises the planar nature of the front facade by puncturing it with the entry balcony and small bay, defining the transverse axis and division between the forms.

Le Corbusier's skilful deployment of form was not matched by his command of constructional technology. He had little experience of the behaviour of reinforced concrete and the villa developed problems with cracking of walls and leakage almost as soon as the Besnus family moved in. The problems were caused by the behaviour of cement render on concrete blockwork using a reinforced concrete frame in a damp situation. In 1927 large cracks required the reconstruction of a whole wall and other major faults had to be remedied.[1]

1 For this information I am indebted to Joyce Lowman Le Corbusier 1900-1925 The years of Transition unpublished doctoral dissertation submitted to the University of London 1979 pp. 210-211

Amadée Ozenfant commissioned Le Corbusier to design a bachelor studio house on a small corner site in the Avenue Reille Paris. As with the Vaucresson villa Le Corbusier interprets the brief in terms of both the site and the geometrical properties of the form. Circulation and provision of daylight are each handled positively and the solution acknowledges the diagonal condition induced by the corner location.

In many ways this was an ideal vehicle for Le Corbusier, giving him an opportunity to express the Purist ideology uncompromisingly, celebrating the modern machine-made product and the compositional freedom afforded by technology and modern art. Using industrial rooflights for the studio and industrial glazing elsewhere, with ladders reminiscent of a ship, Le Corbusier introduces the functional precision and aesthetic vitality of High Tech.

Ozenfant's main requirement was the provision of a well-lit painting studio; he also needed a gallery in which to display his work to prospective buyers, living accommodation, including a bedroom, bathroom and kitchen, together with a garage and self-contained flat.

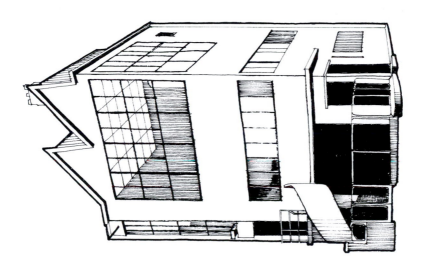

STUDIO APARTMENT FOR OZENFANT 1922

SITE FORCES

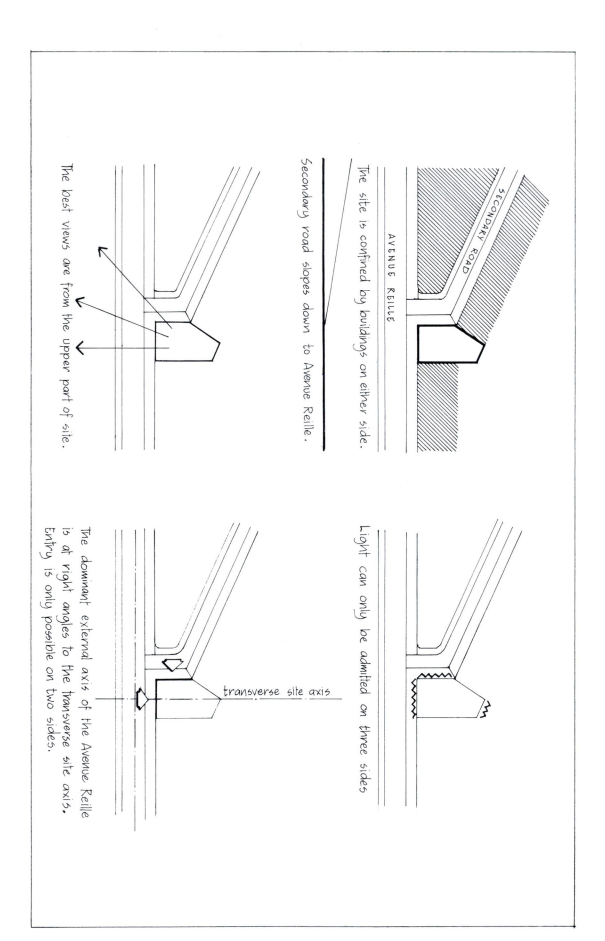

The site is confined by buildings on either side.

Secondary road slopes down to Avenue Reille.

AVENUE REILLE

SECONDARY ROAD

Light can only be admitted on three sides

The best views are from the upper part of site.

The dominant external axis of the Avenue Reille is at right angles to the transverse site axis. Entry is only possible on two sides.

transverse site axis

DIAGONAL CONDITION

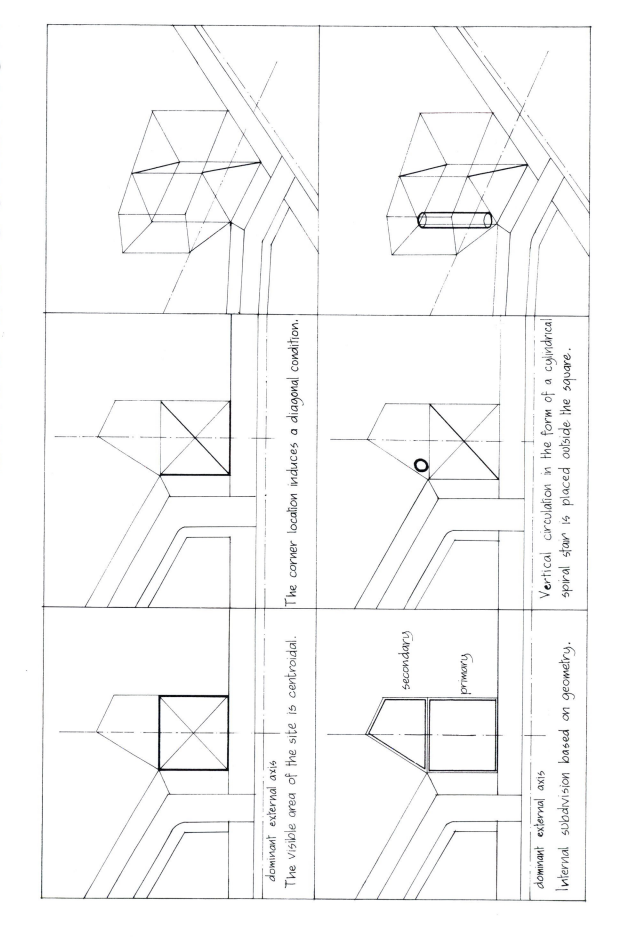

dominant external axis
The visible area of the site is centroidal.

The corner location induces a diagonal condition.

dominant external axis
Internal subdivision based on geometry.

secondary

primary

Vertical circulation in the form of a cylindrical spiral stair is placed outside the square.

PLANAR READING

ACCOMMODATION STACKED ON THREE LEVELS

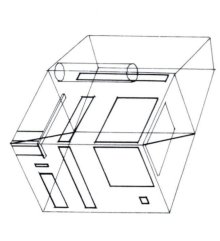

STUDIO

FLAT AND GALLERY

GARAGE AND FLAT

FENESTRATION ORGANISED ABOUT THE CORNER

FENESTRATION CAUSES MASS TO DISSOLVE INTO PLANES

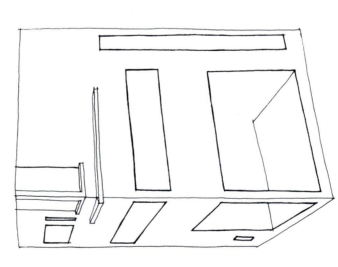
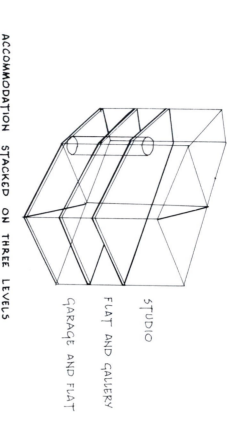

Le Corbusier organises the accommodation on three levels, giving the top floor, with the best lighting and views, to the studio. Large windows are provided for the studio, identifying this element, with a vertical window signifying vertical circulation and illuminating this zone. Fenestration acknowledges the diagonal condition and intensifies the planar reading of the form.

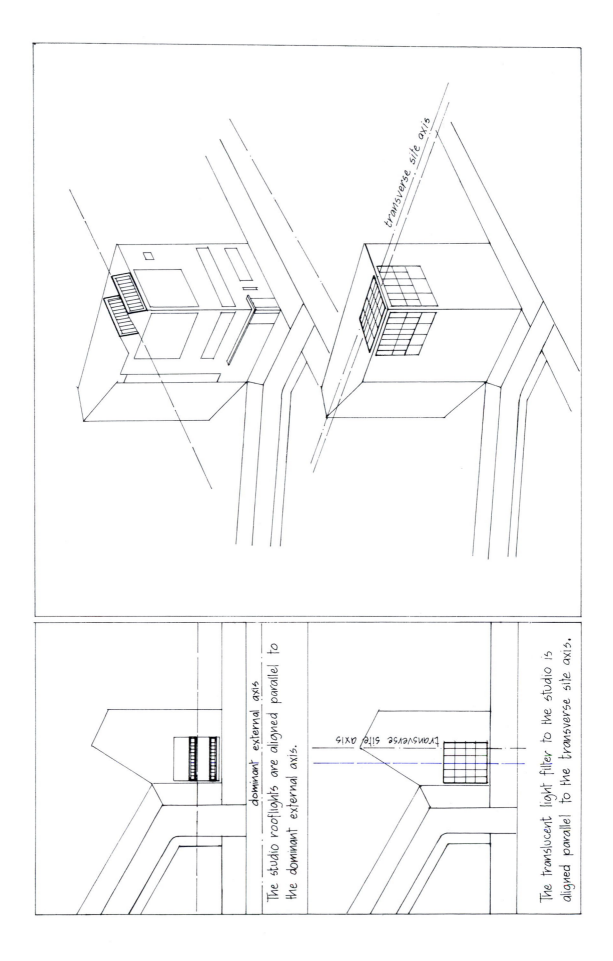

dominant external axis

The studio rooflights are aligned parallel to the dominant external axis.

transverse site axis

The translucent light filter to the studio is aligned parallel to the transverse site axis.

Le Corbusier continues to 'frame' his facades and canopies define entrances. A waterspout expresses contact with the elements and a wiremesh railing contains the entry zone. This transparent membrane extends the planar theme with the three-dimensional spiral stair in dynamic contrast along with the powerful zig-zag of the rooflights.

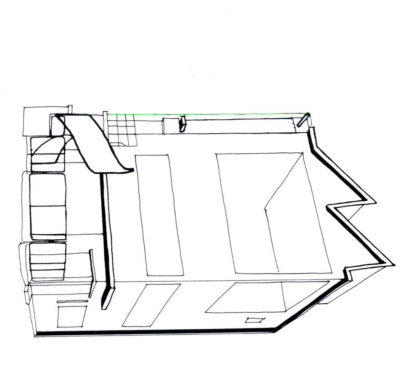

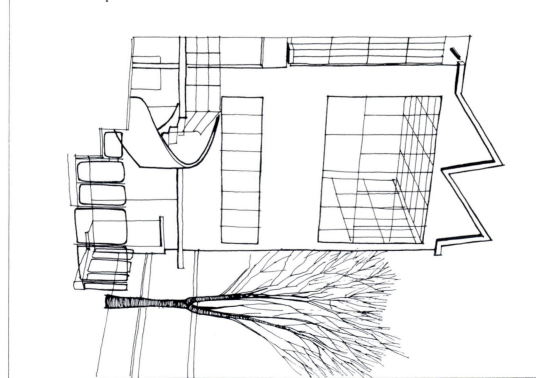

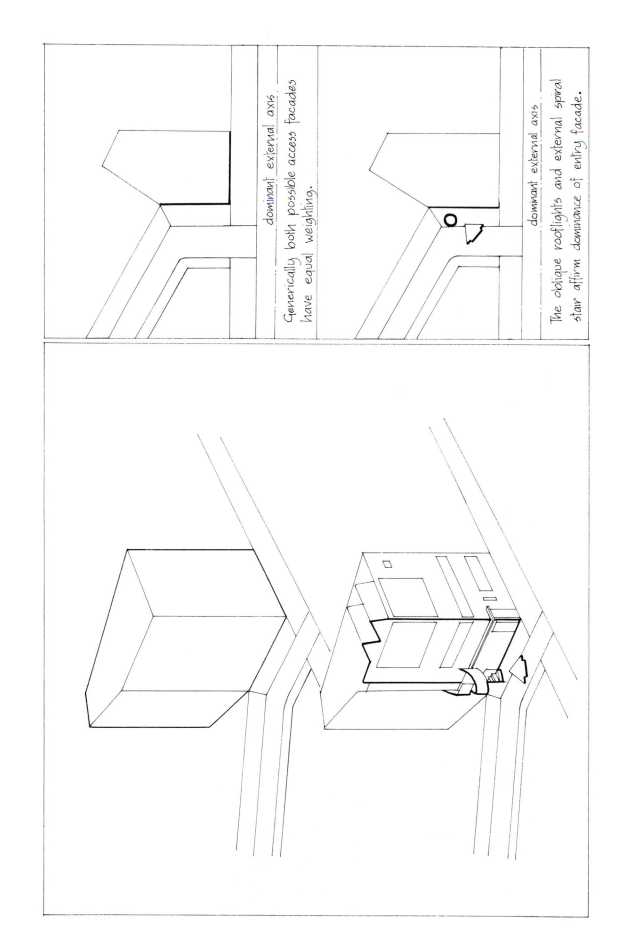

dominant external axis

Generically both possible access facades have equal weighting.

dominant external axis

The oblique rooflights and external spiral stair affirm dominance of entry facade.

FUNCTIONAL TRANSFORMATION

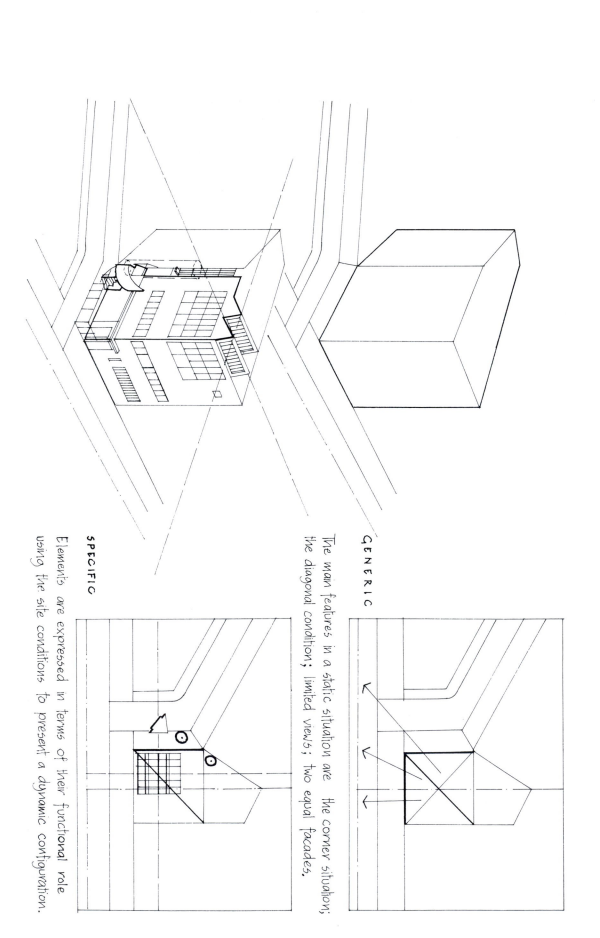

GENERIC

The main features in a static situation are the corner situation;
the diagonal condition; limited views; two equal facades.

SPECIFIC

Elements are expressed in terms of their functional role
using the site conditions to present a dynamic configuration.

MOVEMENT

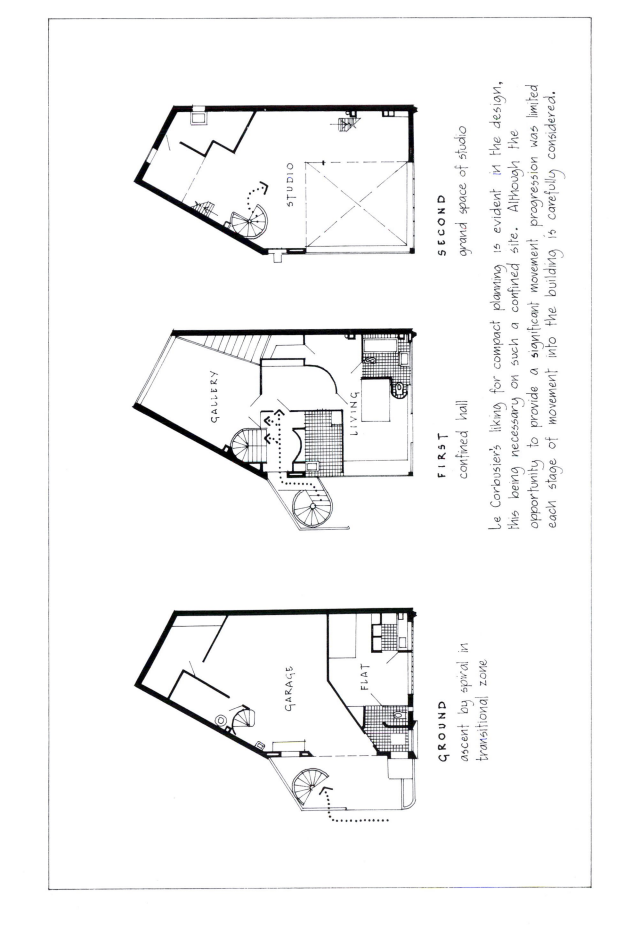

SECOND
grand space of studio

STUDIO

FIRST
confined hall

GALLERY

LIVING

GROUND
ascent by spiral in transitional zone

GARAGE

FLAT

Le Corbusier's liking for compact planning is evident in the design, this being necessary on such a confined site. Although the opportunity to provide a significant movement progression was limited each stage of movement into the building is carefully considered.

UPPER LEVEL OF STUDIO

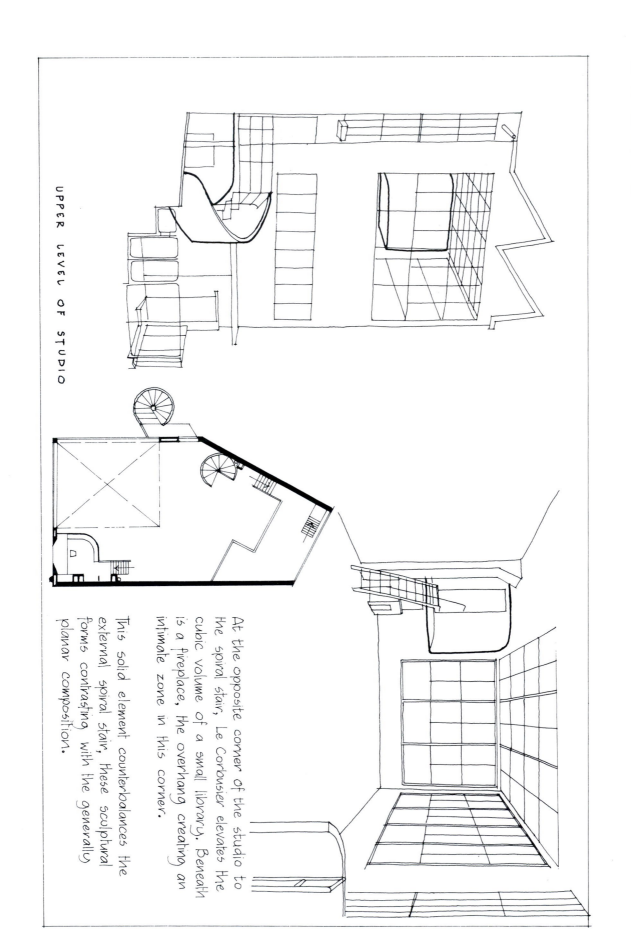

At the opposite corner of the studio to the spiral stair, Le Corbusier elevates the cubic volume of a small library. Beneath is a fireplace, the overhang creating an intimate zone in this corner.

This solid element counterbalances the external spiral stair, these sculptural forms contrasting with the generally planar composition.

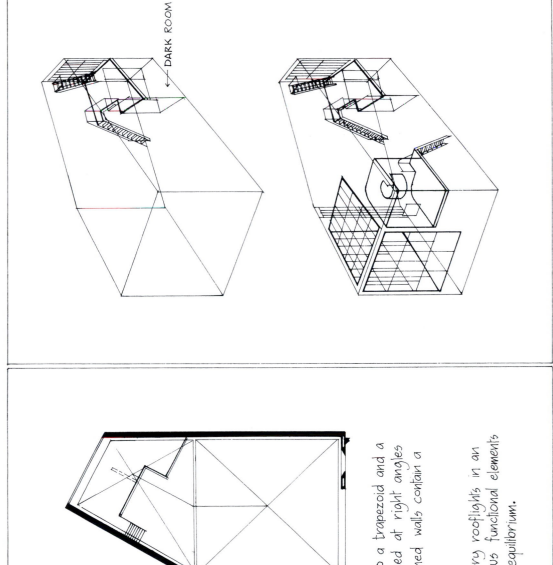

DARK ROOM

The studio space can be subdivided into a trapezoid and a square. A suspended gallery is placed at right angles to the oblique wall. Below this echeloned walls contain a dark room.

Three ladders are used along with factory rooflights in an industrial aesthetic in which the various functional elements are arranged in a state of dynamic equilibrium.

For his distribution of facade elements, Le Corbusier uses a method similar to that used for the elevations of the Villa Schwob. Using a series of parallel diagonals and lines at right angles ensures a relationship between major and secondary elements.

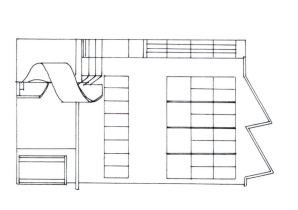

Isolating the vertical section the rectangle is divided in half and the diagonal A₁ is drawn. Diagonal B₁ is drawn and where A₁ and B₁ intersect determines the lowest part of the studio window.

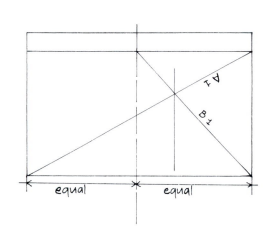

The edge of the window is fixed by the structural column at the corner. Line B₂ is drawn parallel to diagonal B₁ from the top corner of the window. The first vertical window subdivision occurs where B₂ meets the lowest part of the window. A₂ is drawn parallel to A₁.

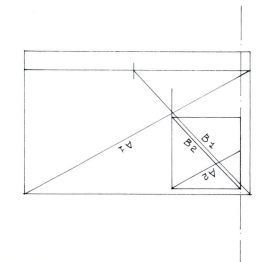

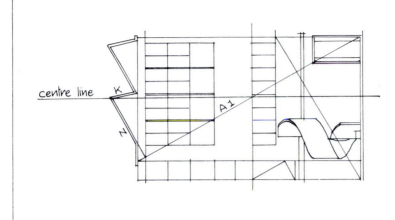

Line z at right angles to A1 forms the rooflight which terminates at the centre line of the rectangle. Return line K links up with the centre of the studio window. The top of the lower window is on the line dividing the rectangle in half and other parallel lines determine door sizes.

centre line

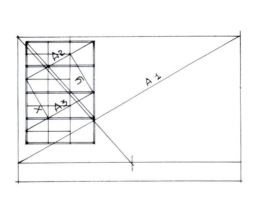

The remaining lines of fenestration can now be located. Where x, y, A2 and A3 meet, the top and bottom of the window determines the verticals. The verticals are located where A3 meets x and where A2 meets y. Each window panel relates to the main rectangle.

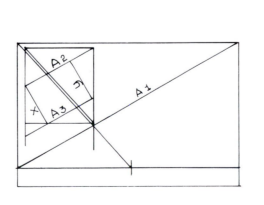

Lines are projected at right angles to A2 (x and y). Where y meets the lowest part of the window, A3 is drawn parallel to A1 and A2.

If _Nature morte à la pile d'assiettes_ [1] may be regarded as Jeanneret's first painterly tour de force, the La Roche-Jeanneret houses became Le Corbusier's first architectural symphony.[2] Purism had been the compositional vehicle through which Le Corbusier had launched his new architectural language and by 1923 this had reached maturity in the two houses.

They were designed for Raoul La Roche, an art collector, and Lotti Raaf who was to marry Le Corbusier's brother Albert Jeanneret. The location was the Square du Docteur Blanche, a small cul-de-sac off the Rue du Docteur Blanche in Auteuil, near the Bois de Boulogne in Paris.

Of the two houses (now the Le Corbusier Fondation) the house for Raoul La Roche gave Le Corbusier his greatest opportunity, the task of displaying a collection of modern paintings. He accordingly arranged the house around the promenade architecturale and movement through the house has been likened to moving through a Purist painting. Using techniques directly inspired by Purism the houses exemplify _L'Esprit Nouveau_ in an ensemble which captures the lyricism of the paintings.

1   see pages 87 and 94.

2   an elaborate orchestral composition of several
    contrasted but related movements.

VILLAS LA ROCHE-JEANNERET 1923-25

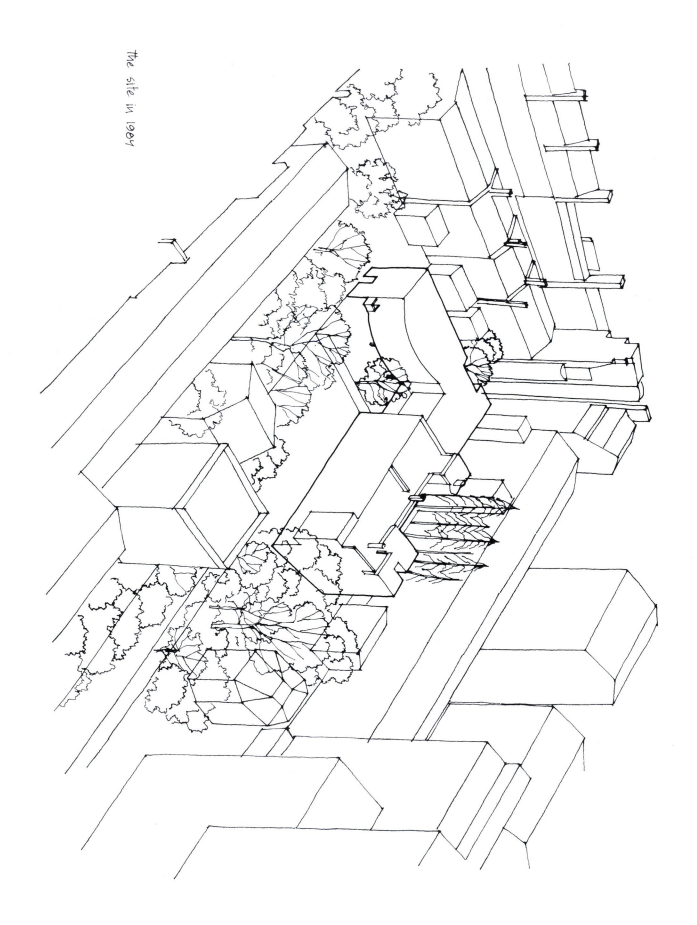

the site in 1984

LOCATION PLAN

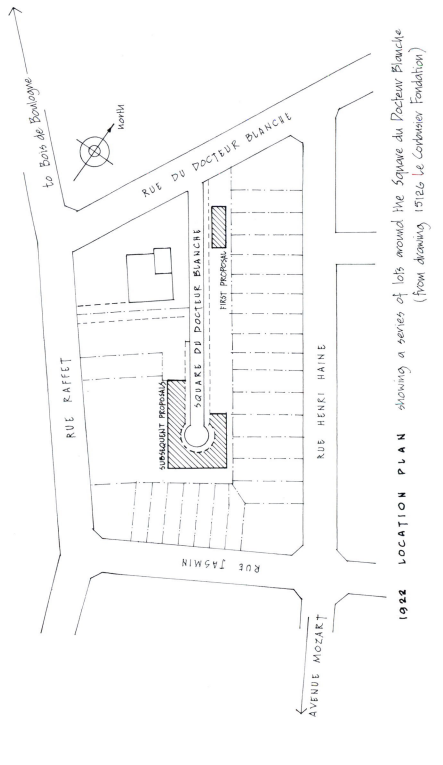

1922 LOCATION PLAN showing a series of lots around the Square du Docteur Blanche
(from drawing 15126 Le Corbusier Fondation)

The final form taken by the La Roche-Jeanneret houses was the result of a series of proposals.
First Le Corbusier suggested three houses on the north side of the square intended for Loti
Raaf, a M. Sarmiento and a Mr Motte. Having failed to gain permission for this he then
proposed three houses around the turning circle at the end of the cul-de-sac. Having
abandoned several schemes on this basis he finally developed a design for two
linked houses for La Roche and Albert Jeanneret and his wife to the south east and
across the end of the Square du Docteur Blanche.[+]

[+] for a full discussion of the various proposals see Tim Benton, The Villas of Le Corbusier 1920-1930
New Haven and London, 1987, pp. 44-45.

SITE FORCES

The Square du Docteur Blanche becomes the dominant external axis to which the site axis runs parallel. The sun path moves around the back of the site from which there are views at high level.

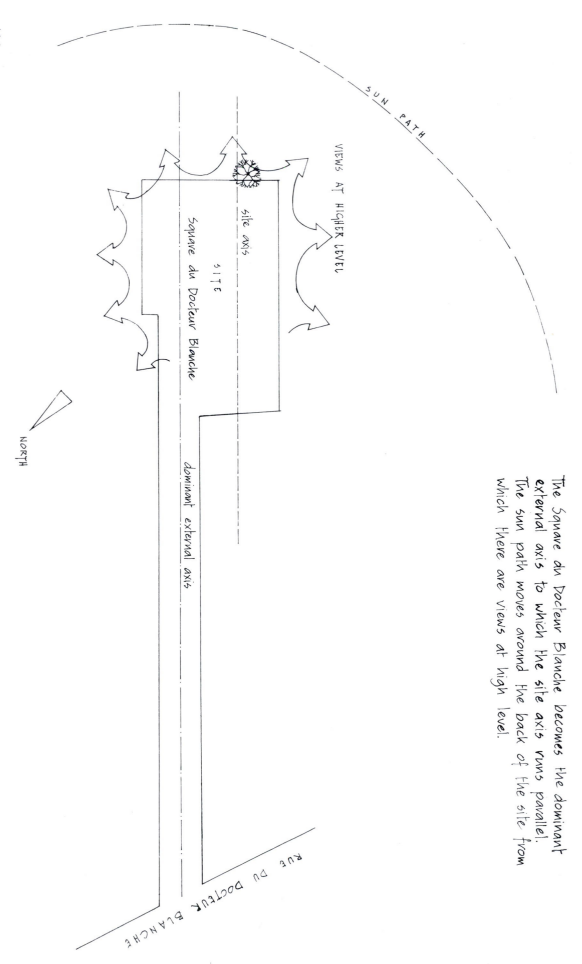

SUN PATH

VIEWS AT HIGHER LEVEL

site axis

SITE

Square du Docteur Blanche

dominant external axis

NORTH

RUE DU DOCTEUR BLANCHE

GENERIC CONFIGURATION

With such a limited and confined site one possible arrangement is to wrap an L shaped configuration around the end of the cul-de-sac. This results in a linear block parallel with the Square du Docteur Blanche and an extension across the private road blunting the linear axis.

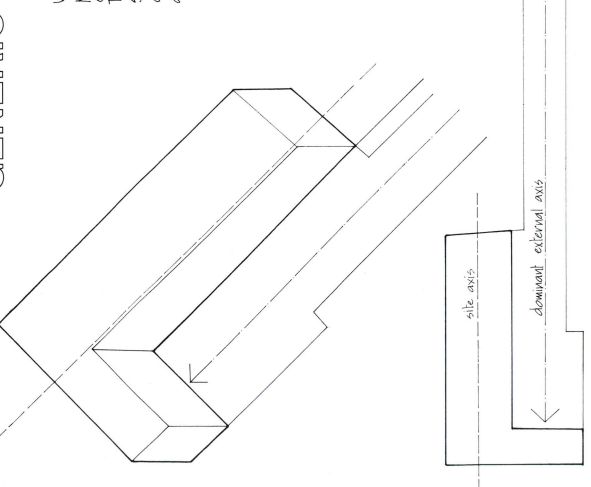

site axis

dominant external axis

SEPARATION

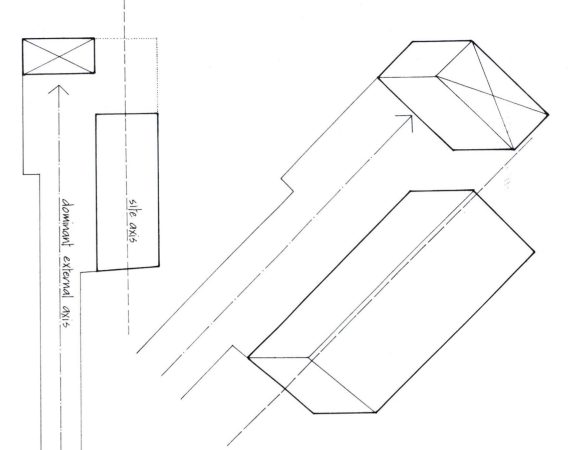

dominant external axis

site axis

The configuration is divided into separate forms, one terminating the linear axis of the Square du Docteur Blanche, the other parallel with it

CONTRAST

The potential contrast between the two forms is exploited by placing the larger block on the ground (assuming the height necessary to contain the required accommodation) and by raising the smaller block so that it forms a pavilion which allows the road axis to continue underneath.

The curved wall of the pavilion responds to the dominant external axis, this being acknowledged by a single cylindrical column placed centrally under the mass. The raised pavilion with its curved wall provides a dynamic contrast to its neighbouring earthbound configuration.

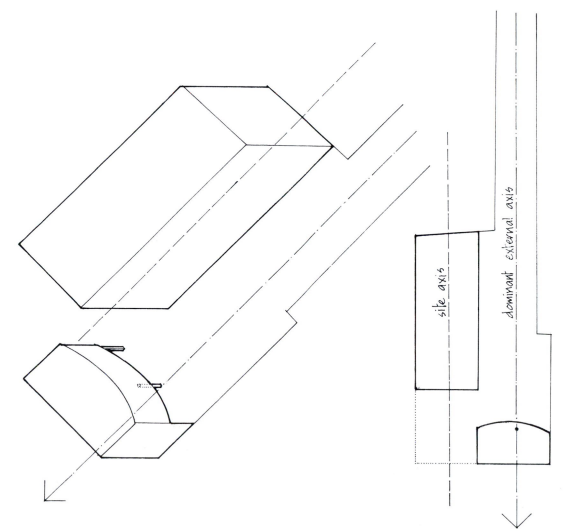

site axis

dominant external axis

NUCLEUS LINK

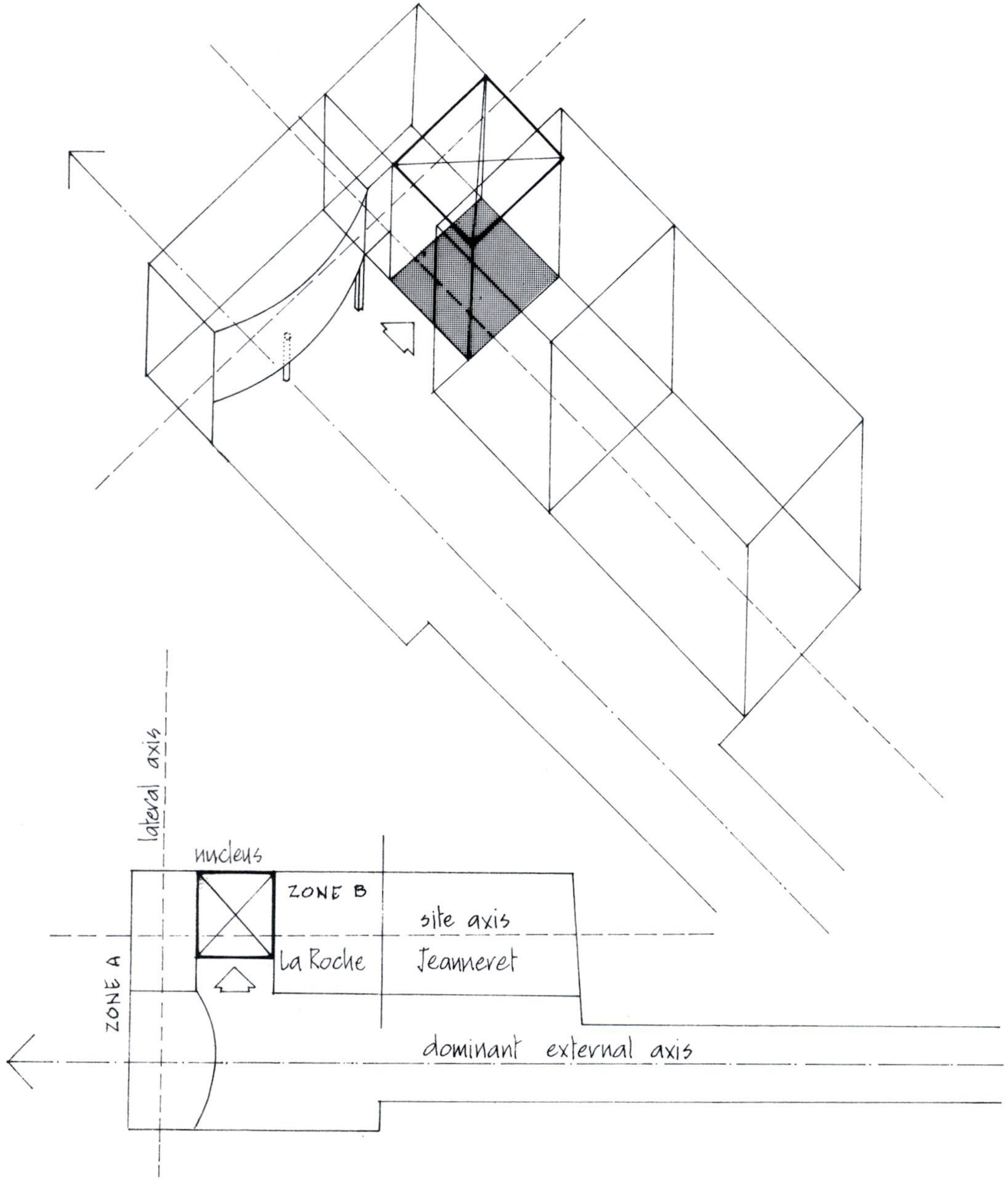

ZONE A

lateral axis

nucleus

ZONE B

La Roche

Jeanneret

site axis

dominant external axis

The two masses are linked by placing a centroidal volume between them, this acting as a fulcrum or nucleus to the configuration. The extension to the pavilion reinforces its lateral axis.

Separation between the two houses is provided within the linear block, and the nucleus becomes the entry to the La Roche house.

The entry nucleus divides the La Roche house into two distinct zones, zone A locating the pavilion and its adjunct, zone B the remainder.

TERMINATION

In each block the composition is terminated by forward projections, the La Roche house by a small balcony, the Jeanneret house by a bay.

The La Roche balcony increases the sense of plane at this end of the pavilion, this being furthered by an opening which reveals the thinness of this plane.

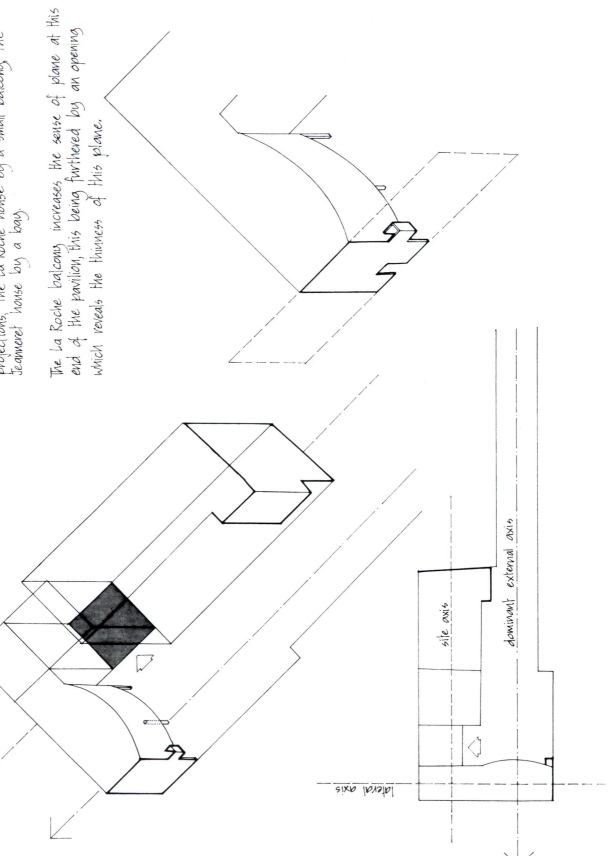

lateral axis

site axis

dominant external axis

INDENTATIONS

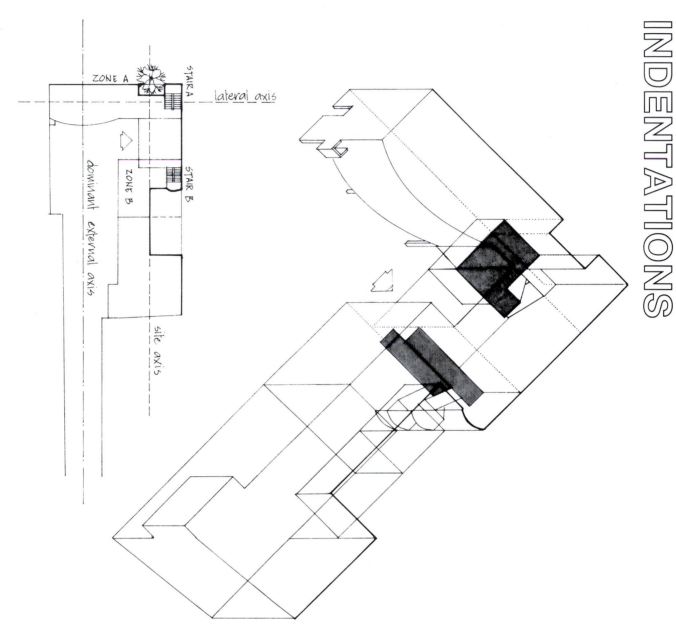

ZONE A

STAIR A

lateral axis

dominant external axis

ZONE B

STAIR B

site axis

Vertical circulation is provided by a staircase in each zone, these being aligned parallel to the site axis.

An indentation into zone A allows for the upper branches of a tree to overhang a small balcony. This set back helps to define the position of staircase A.

An indentation into the linear block forms a roof terrace which faces south west. Staircase B is identified by a curved plane projecting into the terrace indentation.

Each indentation is positioned to receive the sun, fenestration being arranged accordingly, with rooflights on the roof terrace giving toplight below.

MAJOR AND MINOR

A major reading is given to staircase A by the projection of a small balcony into the entry nucleus. The balcony thrusts through plane A signalling the most important direction of movement.

Staircase B is given a secondary reading by its placement with access through a small opening.

The projecting balcony provides an arresting sculptural incident whilst also permitting a view of the entry volume. Below the stair and in line with the balcony is a curved wall. This curve, the adjacent oblique of the stairs, the projecting balcony and plane A, form a complex volumetric ensemble.

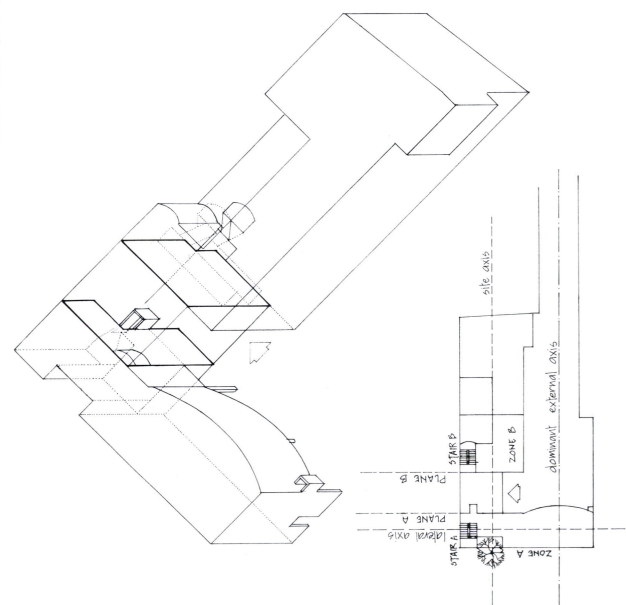

148

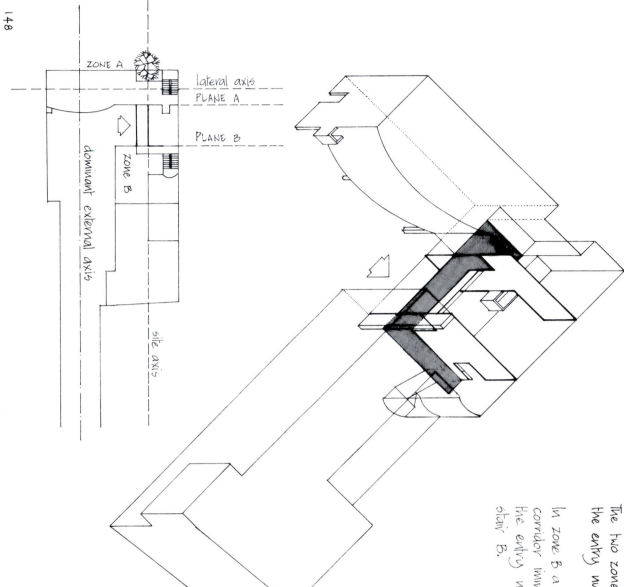

ZONE A

lateral axis
PLANE A

PLANE B

zone B

dominant external axis

site axis

The two zones are linked by a 'bridge' which spans the entry nucleus parallel with the site axis.

In zone B a vertical plane terminates a circulation corridor immediately behind plane B. This overlooks the entry nucleus through an opening opposite stair B.

PRIMARY AND SECONDARY

At the upper level there are views into the entry nucleus from the library in zone A and from the circulation corridor in zone B.

In providing this viewing opportunity each plane is treated differently, a screen of a horizontal and three vertical members ensuring a secondary reading for plane B in contrast with the open balcony edge to plane A.

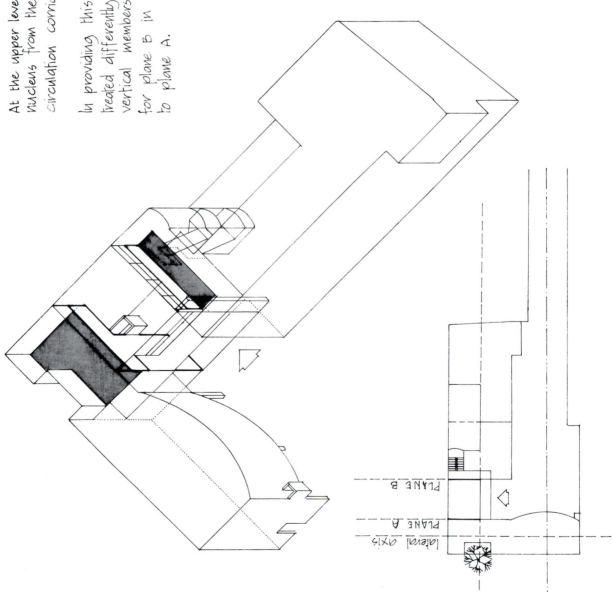

lateral axis
PLANE A
PLANE B

DYNAMIC NUCLEUS

The entry nucleus becomes a dynamic space by the way planes A and B are pierced. This piercing consists of a series of incidents (the bridge, projecting balcony, viewing opportunities and access to stair B) organised so as to state the differing roles of zones A and B.

There is no doubt as to which has priority. Plane B is a 'closed' plane with limited access whereas Plane A has a dramatic event in the form of the projecting balcony at first floor level. The treatment of each plane allows its respective zone to participate appropriately in the entry volume.

The entry nucleus therefore becomes a focus for routes through the house and becomes a receptacle for diverse visual experiences with the observer penetrating the planes, views of the space differing from the various vantage points at different levels.

SLIDING PLANES

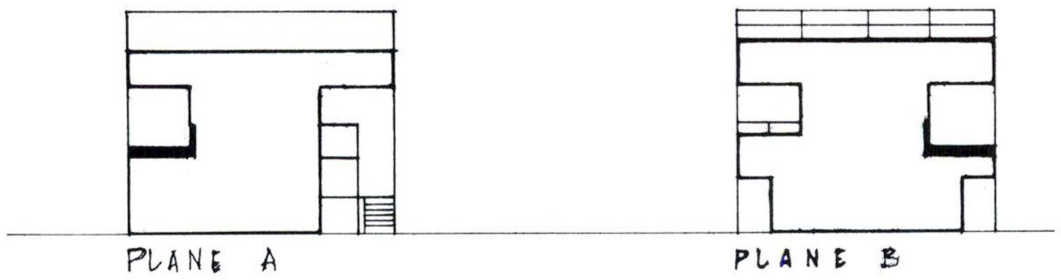

PLANE A

PLANE B

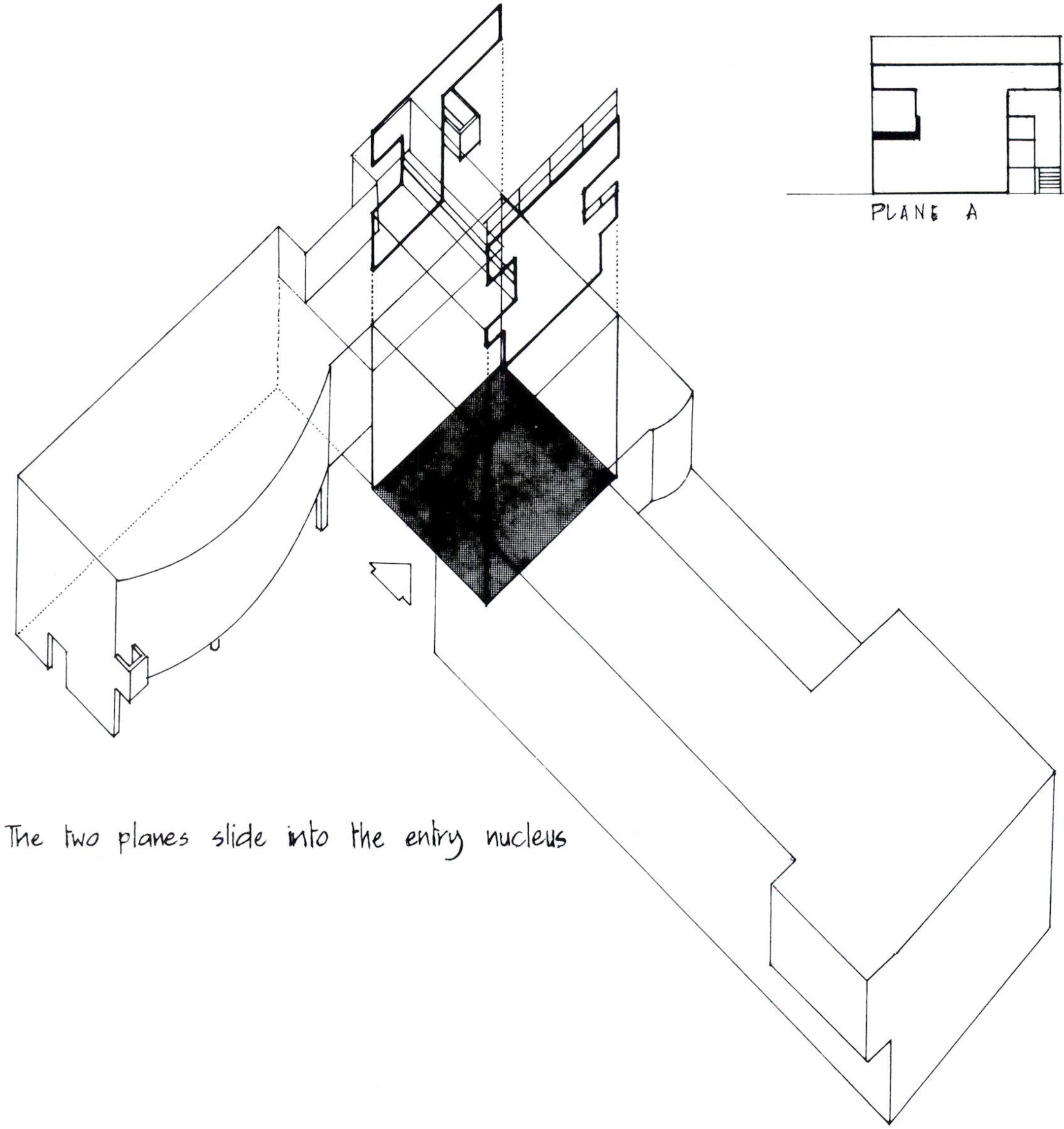

The two planes slide into the entry nucleus

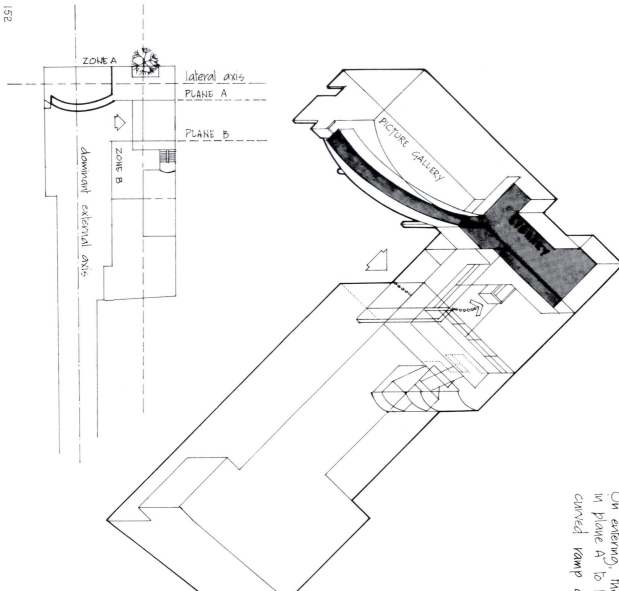

ZONE A

lateral axis

PLANE A

PLANE B

ZONE B

dominant external axis

PICTURE GALLERY

On entering, the main route takes the visitor by the stair in plane A² to the picture gallery, from which a steep curved ramp ascends to the library.

REGULATING LINES

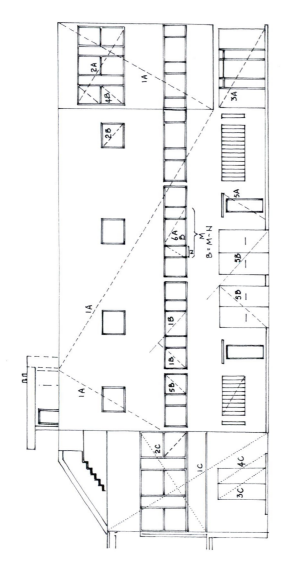

Regulating lines are used to order the facade.

after a drawing from Le Corbusier The Complete Architechtural Works 1910-29,

PAVILIONS

Two roof pavilions conclude the composition, with a roof terrace, so the houses adhere to the principles expressed in Le Corbusier's five points for a new architecture (freedom from the constraint of loadbearing walls, freedom to compose elevations, the use of ribbon windows to maximise views and light, the use of pilotis to raise buildings above the ground and a roof terrace acting as an urban garden).

In the La Roche house, staircase B is expressed at roof level as a small pavilion ensuring that the function of vertical circulation is suitably identified. The curved front of the picture gallery and the fact that it is raised above the ground similarly give functional identification to a major element in the design.

Le Corbusier wrote of the La Roche house : [1]
This second house will be rather like an _architectural promenade._
You enter : the architectural spectacle at once offers itself to the eye. You follow an itinerary and the perspectives develop with great variety, developing a play of light on the walls or making pools of shadow. Large windows open up views of the exterior where the architectural unity is reasserted... Here, reborn for our modern eye, are historic architectural discoveries : the pilotis, the long windows, the roof garden, the glass façade. Once again we must learn at the end of the day to appreciate what is available...

[1] Le Corbusier and Pierre Jeanneret, _Oeuvre Complète, 1, p. 60_ (translation from Tim Benton, _The Villas of Le Corbusier 1920-1930,_ New Haven and London, 1987, p. 43)

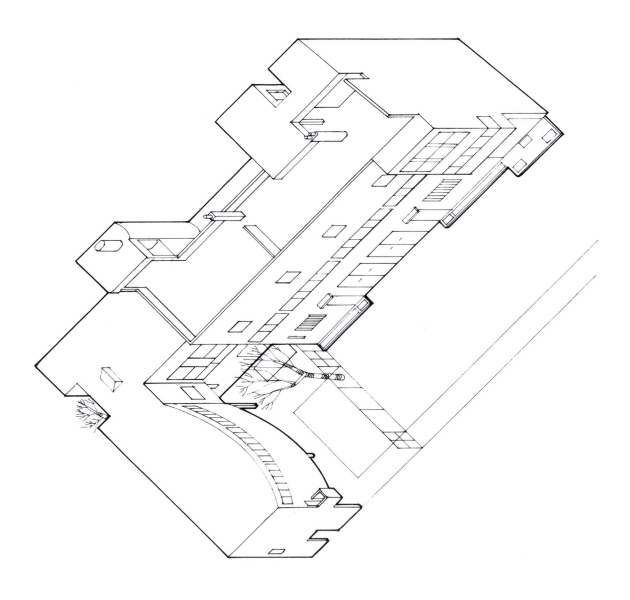

HOUSES FOR WORKERS 1924

Several of Le Corbusier's ideas crystallise in a workers' housing project of 1924. These houses were never built but were intended to provide minimum accommodation using a standardised format.

With its cubic volume, industrial windows, space subdivision with visual emphasis on the staircase, and Purist machine aesthetic, this is a text book solution in terms of Le Corbusier's design principles.

GENERIC CUBE

TRIANGULAR PLATFORM

STAIR ALONG DIAGONAL

SURFACE MODULATION

DIAGONAL CONDITION

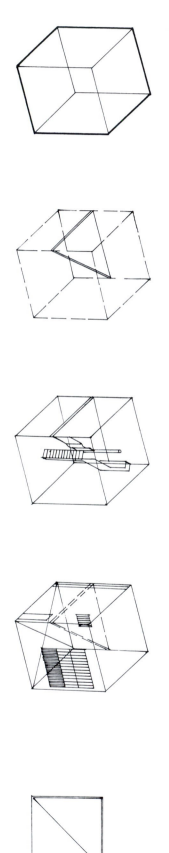

after a drawing by Le Corbusier in _Le Corbusier The Complete Architectural Works Vol 1 1910-1929_

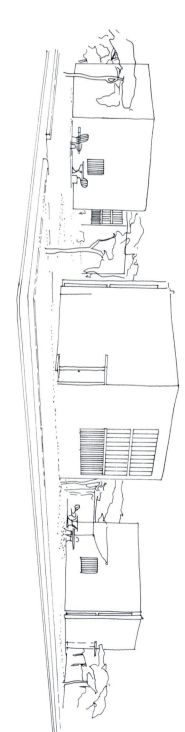

By suspending a triangular platform within a cube, Le Corbusier transforms a primary volume into three activity zones. Placement of the stair intensifies the diagonal, and entry and windows are moved to the corners in acknowledgement of the diagonal condition.

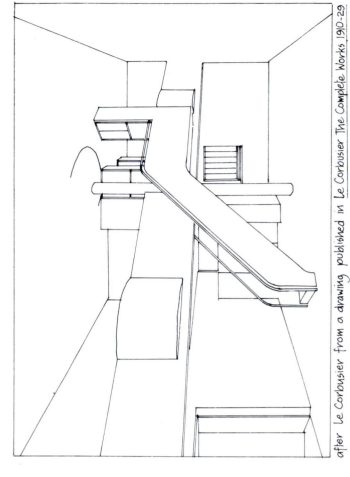

after Le Corbusier from a drawing published in *Le Corbusier The Complete Works 1910-29*

Within a plan only 4 metres square Le Corbusier maximizes the sense of space by using the diagonal. The absolute minimum accommodation is provided and there is no bathroom.

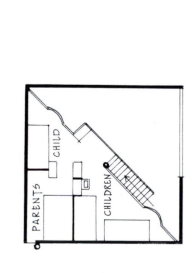

PARENTS

CHILD

CHILDREN

FIRST

KITCHEN

DINING

LIVING

GROUND

The villa known as 'Les Terrasses' was built for Michael (brother of Gertrude) and Sarah Stein on land owned by Gabrielle de Monzie, at Vaucresson, a suburb to the west of Paris. The Steins and Mme de Monzie lived together in the villa, conceived by Le Corbusier as an emblem of his twenties ideology.

This ideology saw the dwelling as temple, work of sculpture and 'machine a habiter,' it's organisation ensuring an interaction with nature that would maximize exposure to sunlight, space and greenery.

Following Purist principles, the mass comprising the villa is sculpted so that it may be read either as mass or as a series of planes in an ambiguous dialogue that sets out to exploit this contradiction. For Le Corbusier, this was the focus of his architectural research at this time as he continually explored design strategies in which internal and external spaces merge, the structural frame allowing an uninhibited deployment of vertical and horizontal planes.

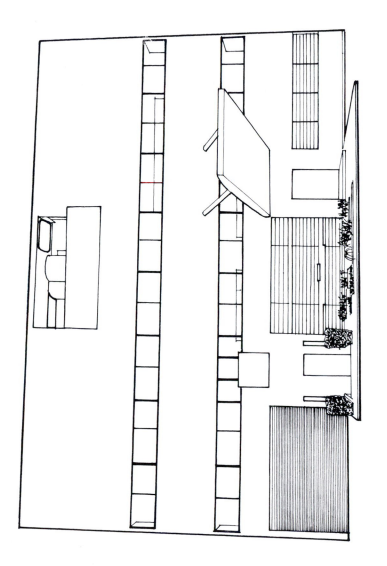

VILLA STEIN-DE-MONZIE 1926-29

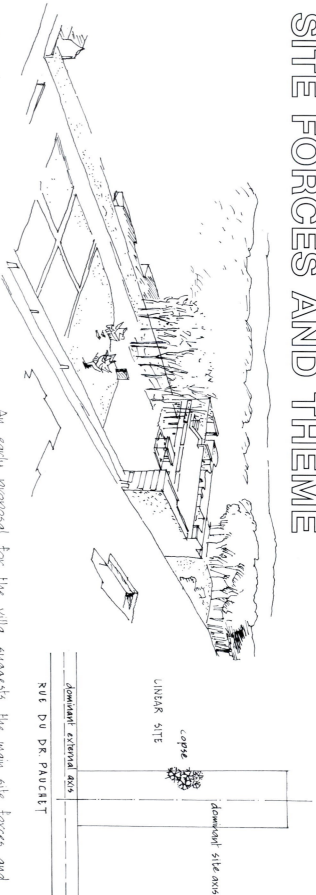

after a drawing by Le Corbusier and Pierre Jeanneret, from Le Corbusier, The Complete Architectural Works 1910-29

RUE DU DR. PAUCHET

dominant external axis

LINEAR SITE

copse

dominant site axis

An early proposal for the villa suggests the main site forces and theme of the emerging design. The site is a long flat strip with a copse of trees midway on the eastern side. The villa takes the form of a slab placed across the site, dividing it into a public zone fronting the block with a private garden to the rear.

Where copse and villa meet, the slab is raised and opened up to establish contact with the garden. The route towards the building leads through the copse, as it turns towards the entrance there is a view under the villa towards the garden. A service wing projects forward on the western side creating a sense of enclosure around the entrance.

The emerging theme is concerned with breaking down the slab to gain maximum contact with the landscape (at this stage linking public and private zones through the 'filter' of the copse). The theme is developed by further subdivision of the slab into a series of terraces which extend the interaction between internal and external space.

EARLY PROJECT

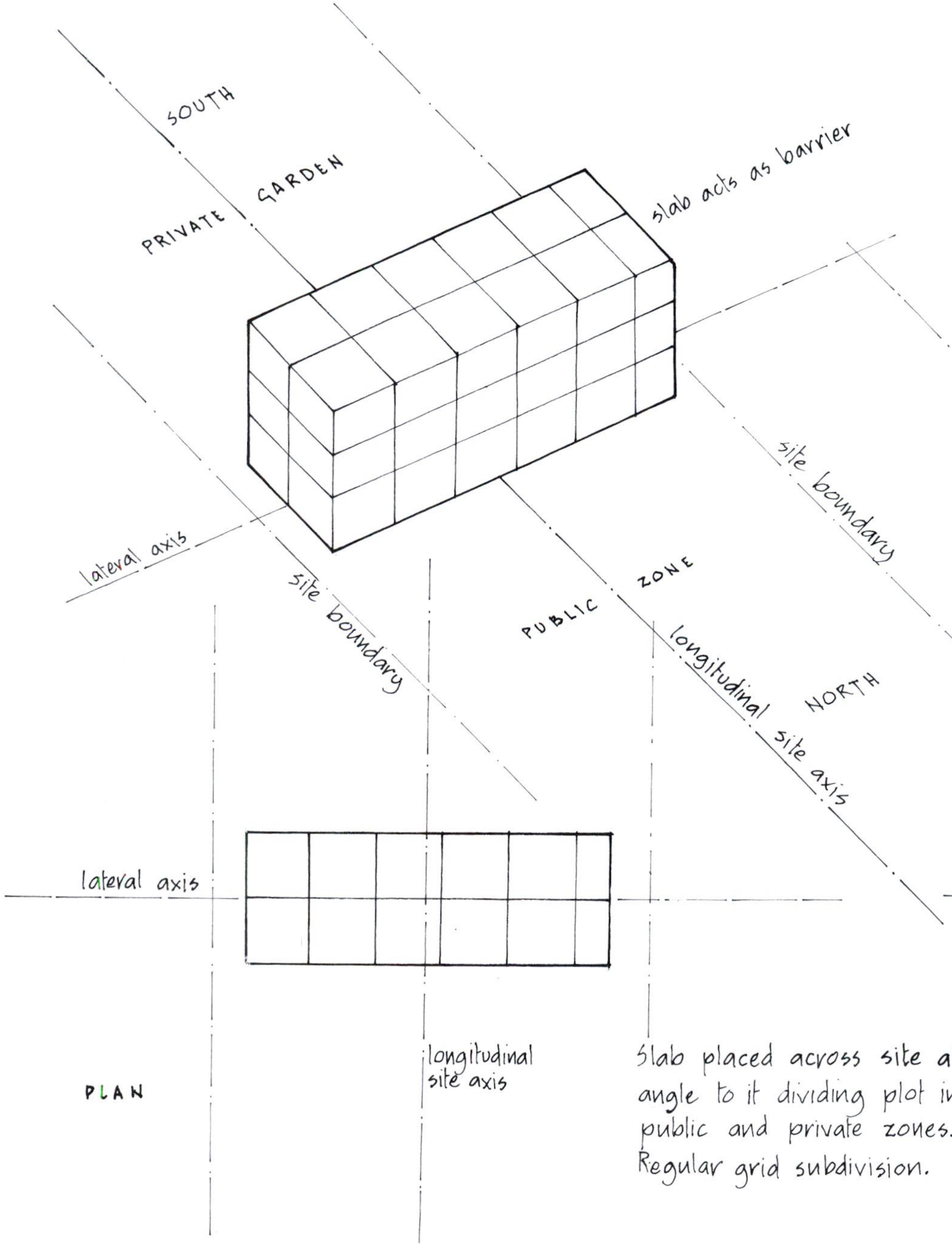

barrier broken

longitudinal site axis

lateral axis

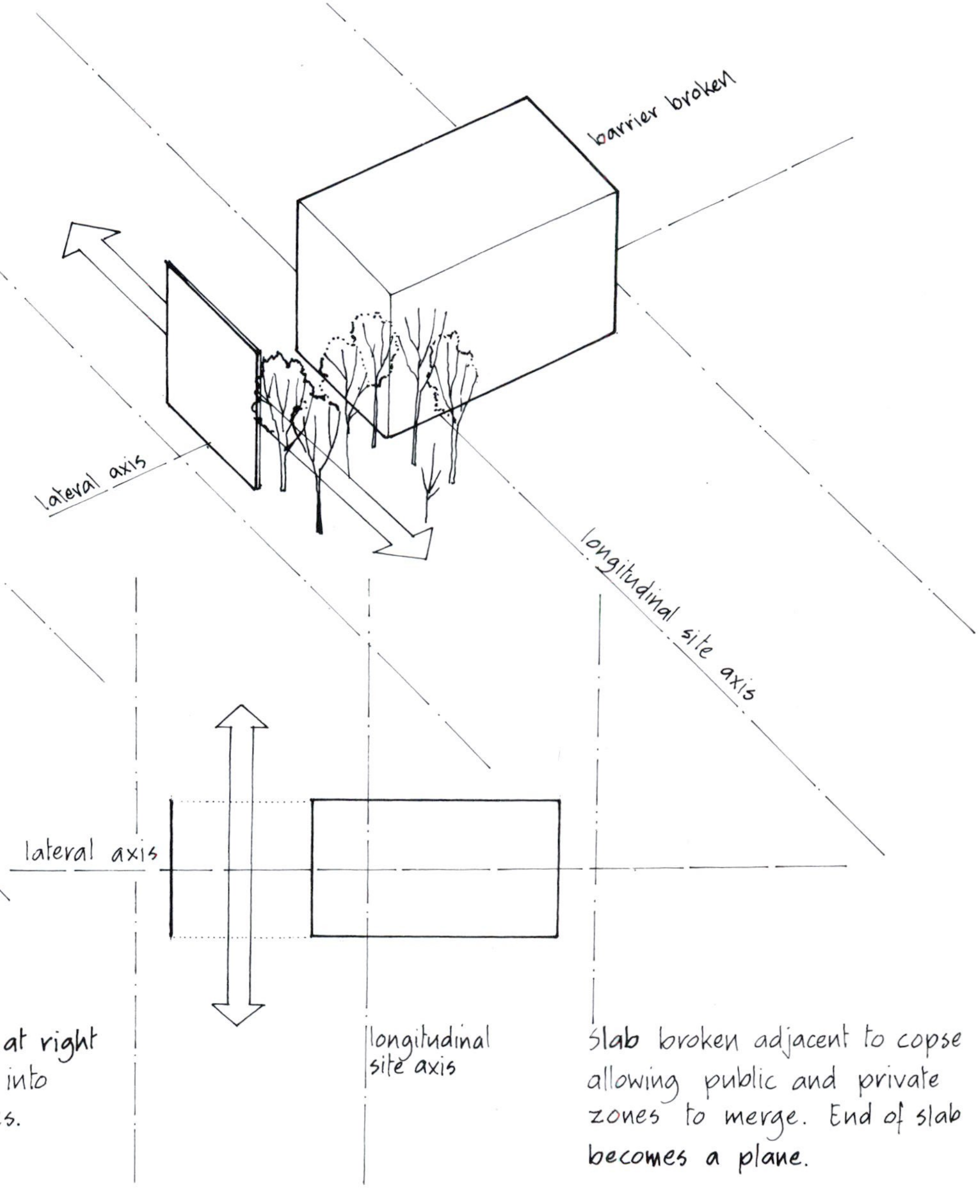

Slab broken adjacent to copse allowing public and private zones to merge. End of slab becomes **a plane.**

longitudinal site axis

lateral axis

slab acts as barrier

NORTH

PUBLIC ZONE

longitudinal site axis

SOUTH

PRIVATE GARDEN

site boundary

site boundary

lateral axis

Slab placed across site at right angle to it dividing plot into public and private zones. Regular grid subdivision.

longitudinal site axis

lateral axis

PLAN

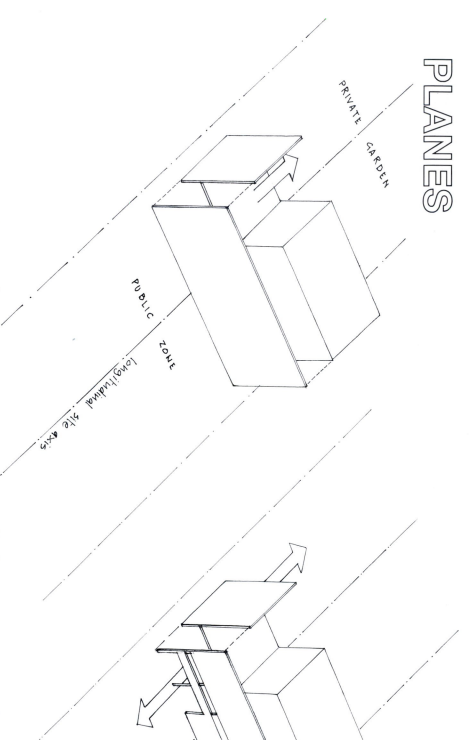

PRIVATE GARDEN

PUBLIC ZONE

longitudinal site axis

longitudinal site axis

A plane is planted onto the configuration reintroducing a barrier across the site. Behind this a horizontal plane acts as a terrace, visually linked to the garden. The forward vertical plane 'completes' the slab reading again, although now the slab has been eroded and from the garden its planar nature is apparent.

The forward plane is pierced, allowing contact from front to back under the terrace. A strip is incised into the plane at piano nobile level. This is left open at the terrace becoming window where it fronts the mass. The strip identifies the piano nobile, increases the planar reading by revealing the thinness of the forward plane and provides an opportunity to express the structural bay rhythm. The strip like the plane itself, helps to 'complete' the slab by partly restoring it.

164

ROOF TERRACE AND ENTRY

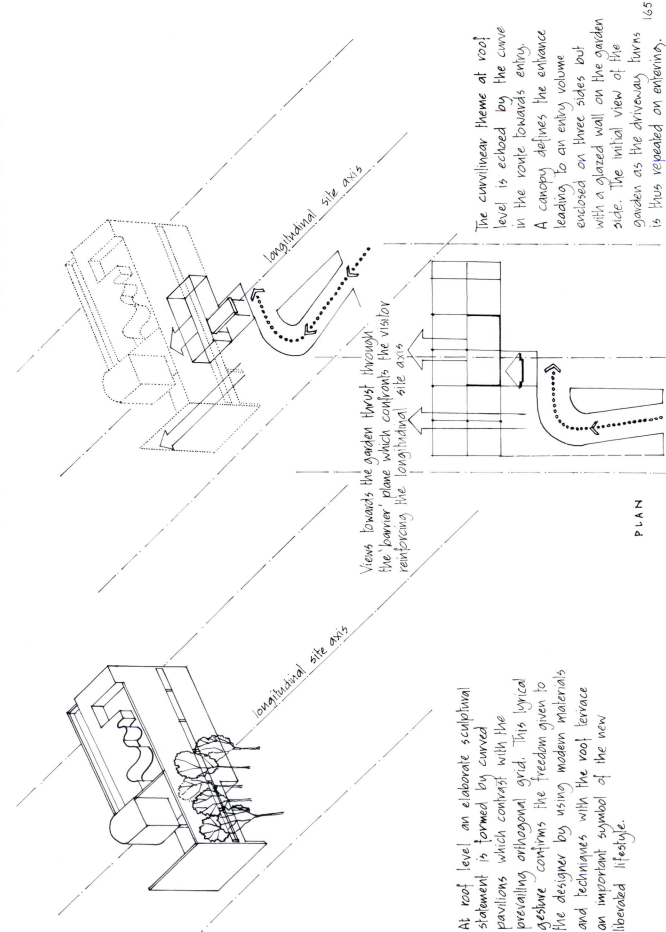

PLAN

longitudinal site axis

longitudinal site axis

Views towards the garden thrust through the 'barrier' plane which confronts the visitor reinforcing the longitudinal site axis

The curvilinear theme at roof level is echoed by the curve in the route towards entry. A canopy defines the entrance leading to an entry volume enclosed on three sides but with a glazed wall on the garden side. The initial view of the garden as the driveway turns is thus repeated on entering.

At roof level an elaborate sculptural statement is formed by curved pavilions which contrast with the prevailing orthogonal grid. This lyrical gesture confirms the freedom given to the designer by using modern materials and techniques with the roof terrace an important symbol of the new liberated lifestyle.

SPATIAL INTERACTION

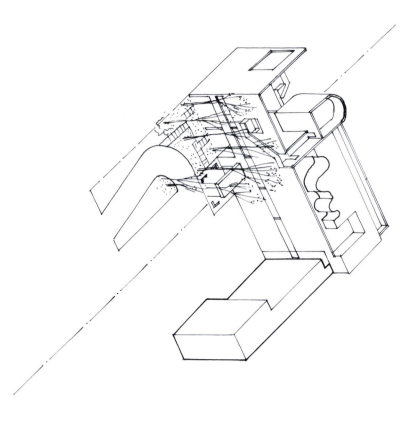

Further recognition of the longitudinal site axis is given by the forward projection of a service wing. Placed opposite the copse this gives further enclosure to the entrance.

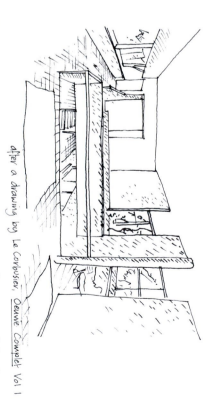

From the entry volume a stair rises, along the lateral axis, through an opening at second floor level. The stair leads to a bridge which leads to the salon.

after a drawing by Le Corbusier, Oeuvre Complet Vol 1

PLAN

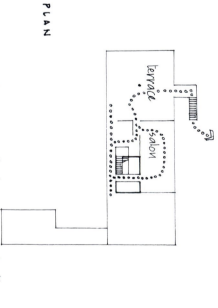

As a result, salon, terrace, first and second floors are all interconnected, movement from one to another being through vertical or horizontal planes.

ELABORATE ROUTE

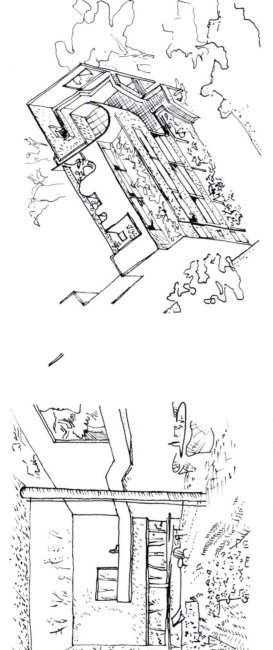

after drawings by Le Corbusier in the *Oeuvre Complet* Vol. 1

The route from roof terrace to garden is an elaborate progression which starts on the top of the half cylindrical enclosed area, then moves out to the front, piercing the 'barrier' plane as it returns inside before descending to the raised terrace by traversing the north and east sides. On each side openings give views at tree top level and finally a stair descends to the private garden.

Le Corbusiers sketches illustrate his main idea, to link the villa to its surroundings by breaking down the slab into a series of terraces and, by means of a movement route, ensuring that all the vertical and horizontal planes can be penetrated so as to form a continuous interaction between internal and external space.

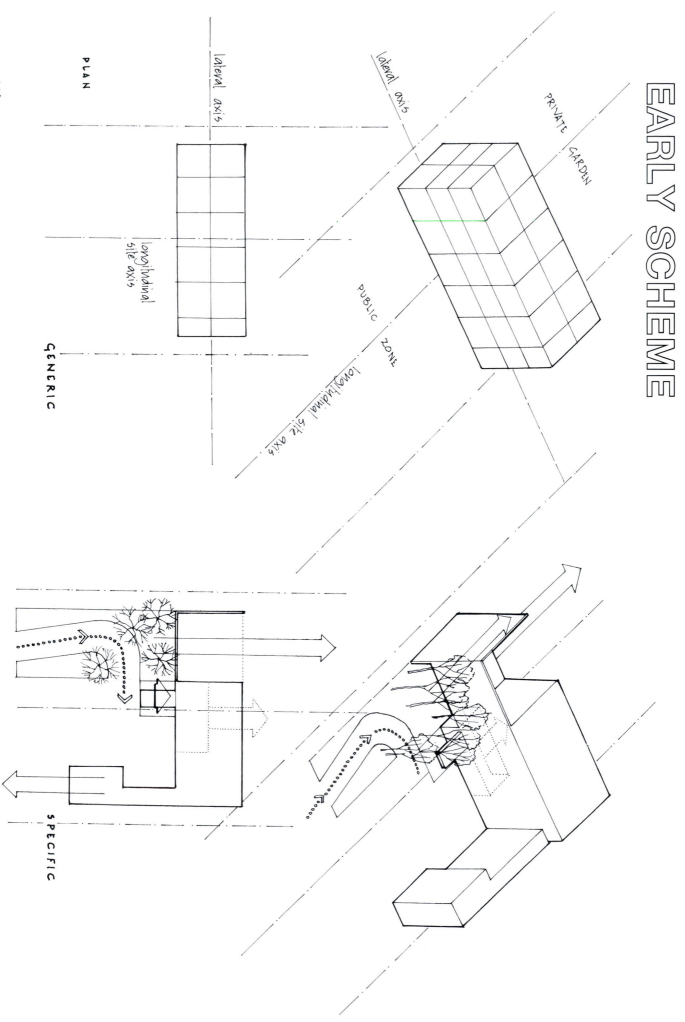

EARLY SCHEME

PLAN

GENERIC

SPECIFIC

lateral axis

lateral axis

longitudinal site axis

longitudinal site axis

PRIVATE GARDEN

PUBLIC ZONE

FINAL DESIGN

The early proposal seems to have been generated by the way an approach to the villa may pass through the copse, giving views of the garden to the rear. The resultant opening up of the slab to further this contact with the garden results in an asymmetrical form with elements pushing and pulling in opposite directions along the longitudinal site axis.

Alongside this proposal and possibly influenced by Palladio's Villa Malcontenta,[1] Le Corbusier worked on an alternative bi-laterally symmetrical design in which the bay rhythm is A B A B A. This compact, regular framework reduces the energy level and degree of fragmentation of the other scheme and successive design investigations[2] show Le Corbusier oscillating between the two ideas. Finally he opts for compaction, with the sense of order and unity of the A B A B A proposal, within which he attempts to retain the spatial and volumetric animation of the alternative proposal.

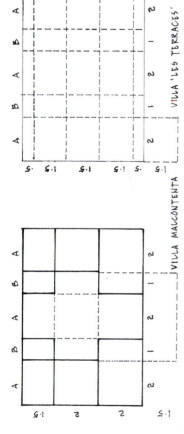

VILLA MALCONTENTA

VILLA 'LES TERRACES'

[1] see Colin Rowe's analysis: Colin Rowe, 'The Mathematics of the Ideal Villa', Architectural Review 1949.

[2] for a full discussion of this see Tim Benton, The Villas of Le Corbusier 1920-1930, New Haven, London, 1987, pp. 164-189

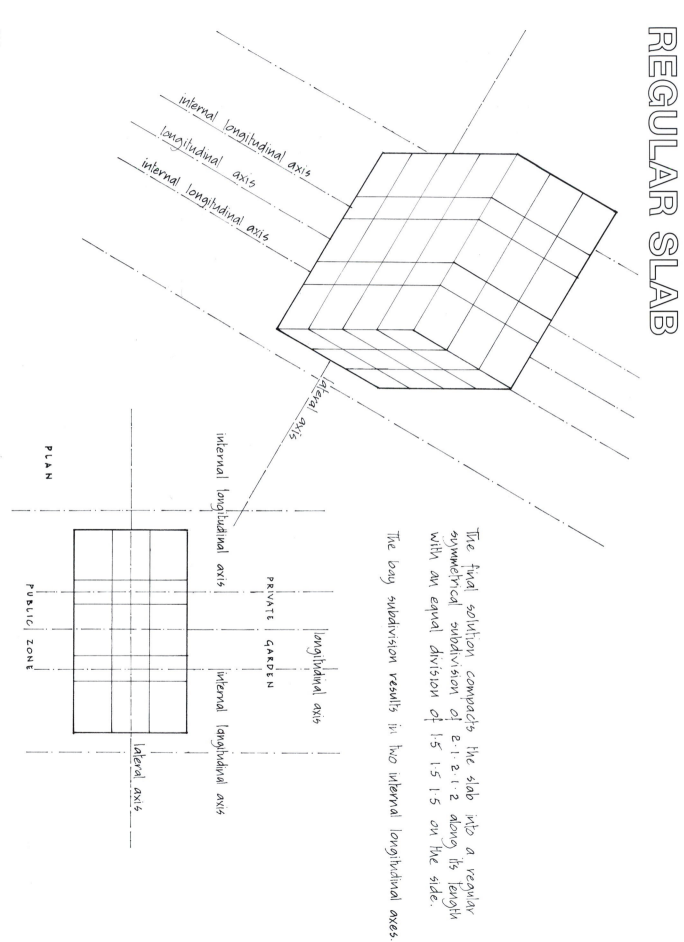

internal longitudinal axis

longitudinal axis

internal longitudinal axis

lateral axis

PLAN

internal longitudinal axis

PRIVATE GARDEN

longitudinal axis

internal longitudinal axis

PUBLIC ZONE

lateral axis

The final solution compacts the slab into a regular symmetrical subdivision of 2·1·2·1·2 along its length with an equal division of 1·5 1·5 1·5 on the side.

The bay subdivision results in two internal longitudinal axes.

DIRECTIONAL SLAB

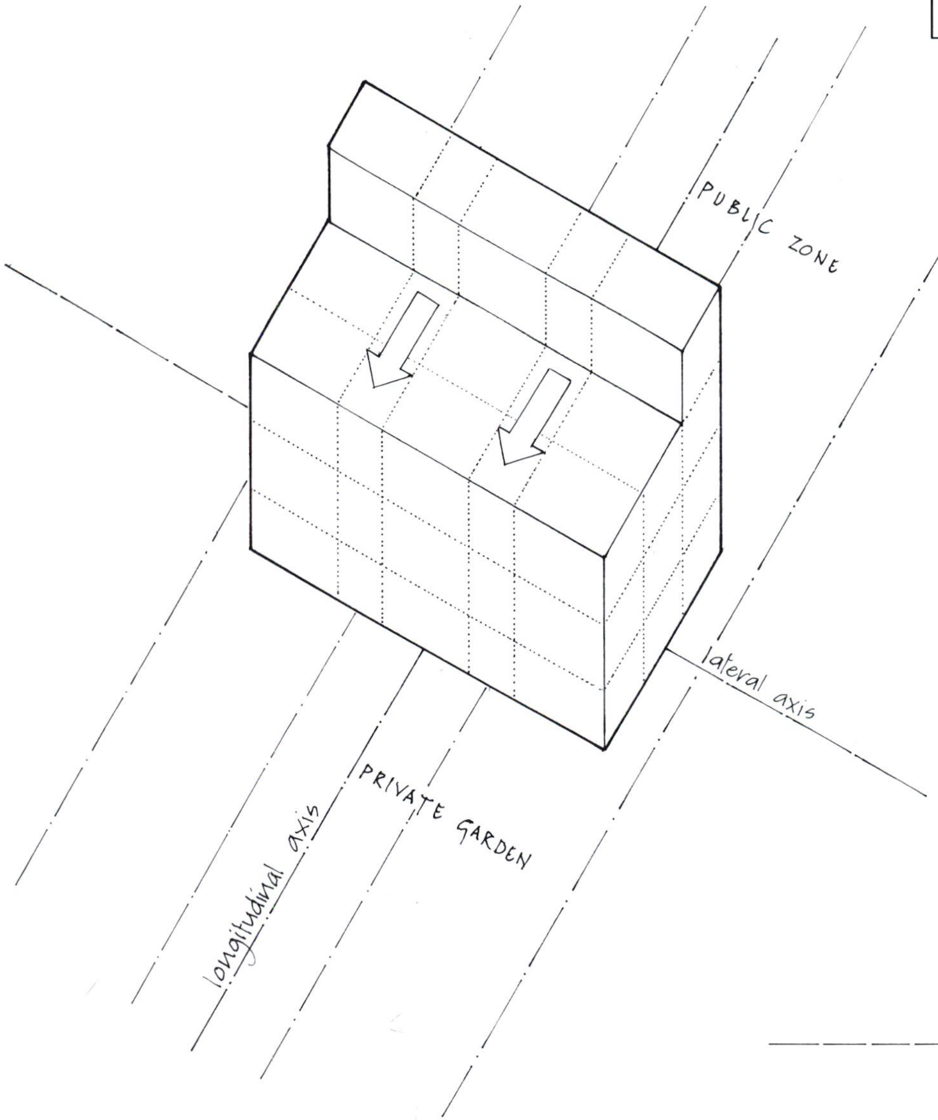

Le Corbusier steps the slab down so that a roof terrace faces onto the private garden. This maintains the regular symmetry of the form and retains the barrier between public and private zones. The form is now directional.

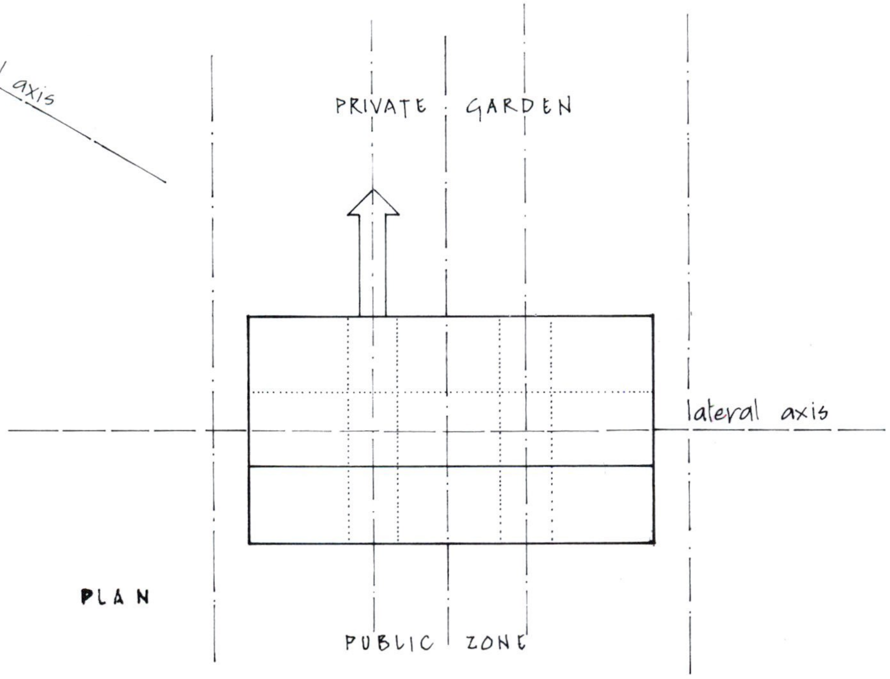

PRIVATE GARDEN

PUBLIC ZONE

lateral axis

PLAN

PUBLIC ZONE

lateral axis

PRIVATE GARDEN

longitudinal axis

172

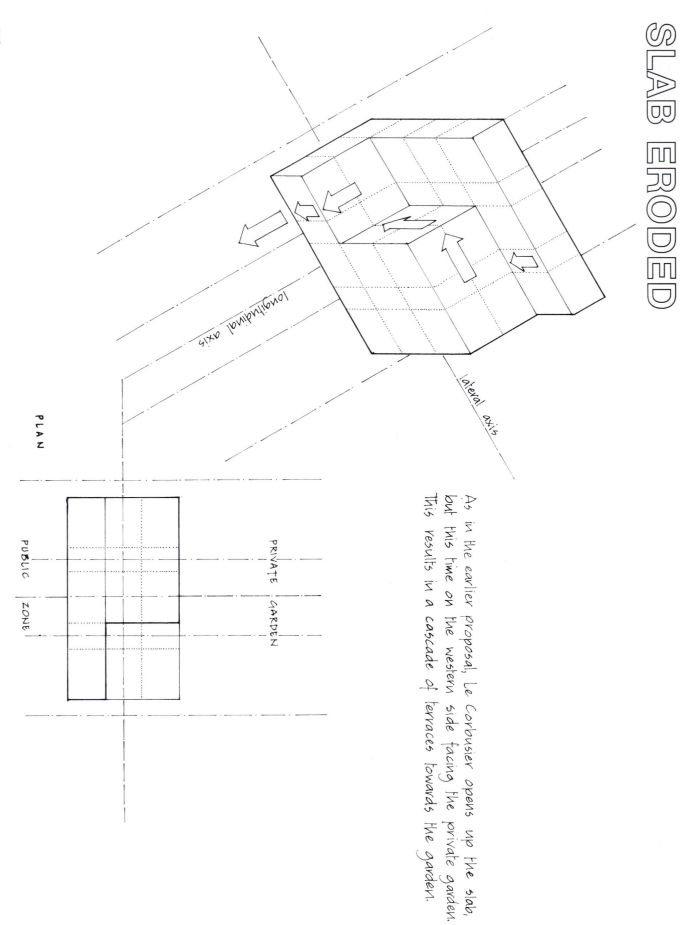

longitudinal axis

lateral axis

PLAN

PUBLIC ZONE

PRIVATE GARDEN

As in the earlier proposal, Le Corbusier opens up the slab, but this time on the western side facing the private garden. This results in a cascade of terraces towards the garden.

SLAB RESTORED

Planes enclose the two sides, restoring the slab reading and unity of the configuration. The erosion of the form remains.

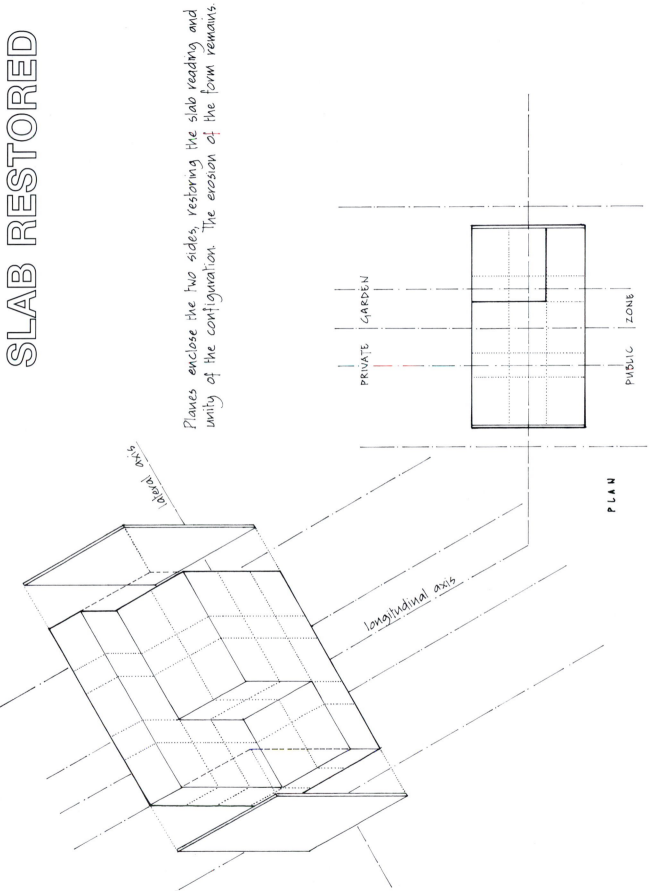

PRIVATE GARDEN

PRIVATE

PUBLIC ZONE

PLAN

lateral axis

longitudinal axis

TERRACE CASCADE

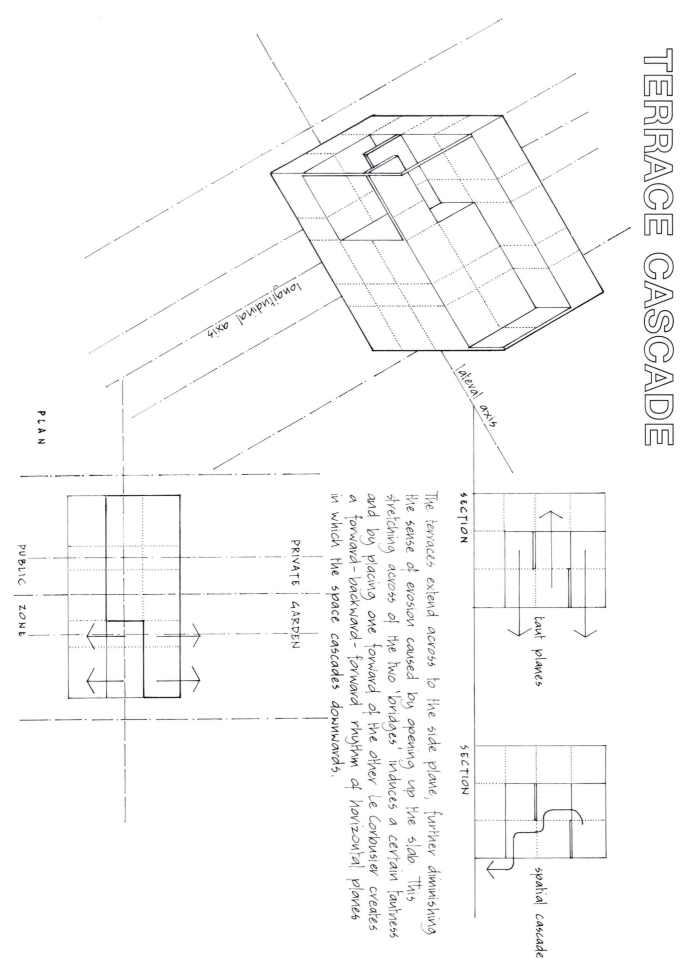

longitudinal axis

lateral axis

PLAN

PUBLIC ZONE

PRIVATE GARDEN

SECTION

taut planes

SECTION

spatial cascade

The terraces extend across to the side plane, further diminishing the sense of erosion caused by opening up the slab. This stretching across of the two 'bridges' induces a certain tautness and by placing one forward of the other Le Corbusier creates a forward-backward-forward rhythm of horizontal planes in which the space cascades downwards.

HORIZONTAL PLANES

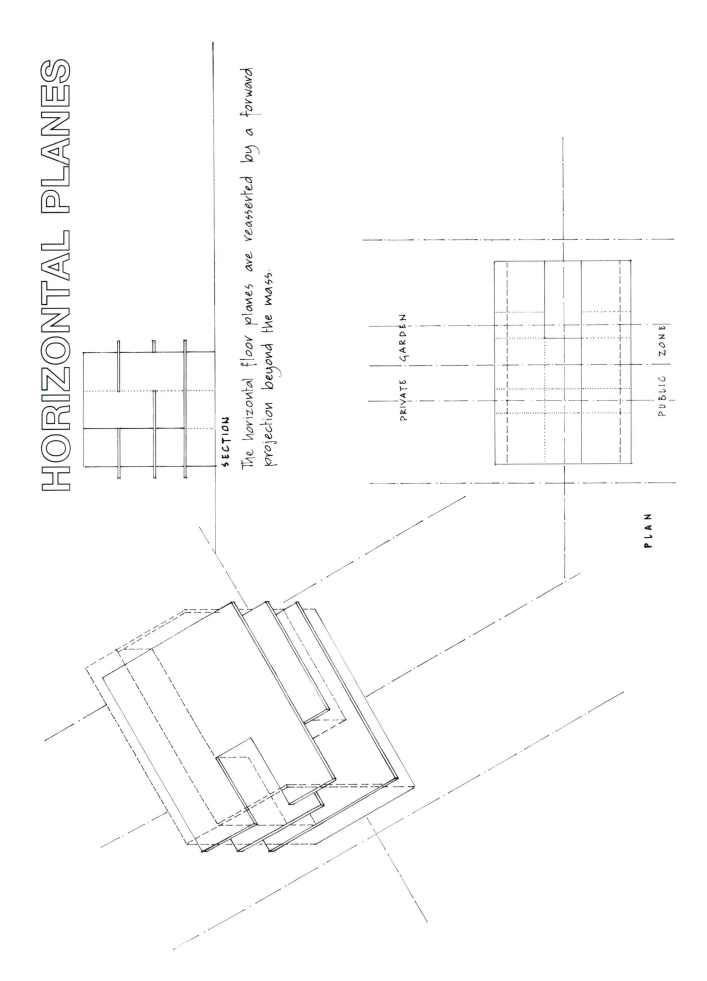

SECTION

The horizontal floor planes are reasserted by a forward projection beyond the mass.

PRIVATE GARDEN

PUBLIC ZONE

PLAN

VERTICAL PLANES

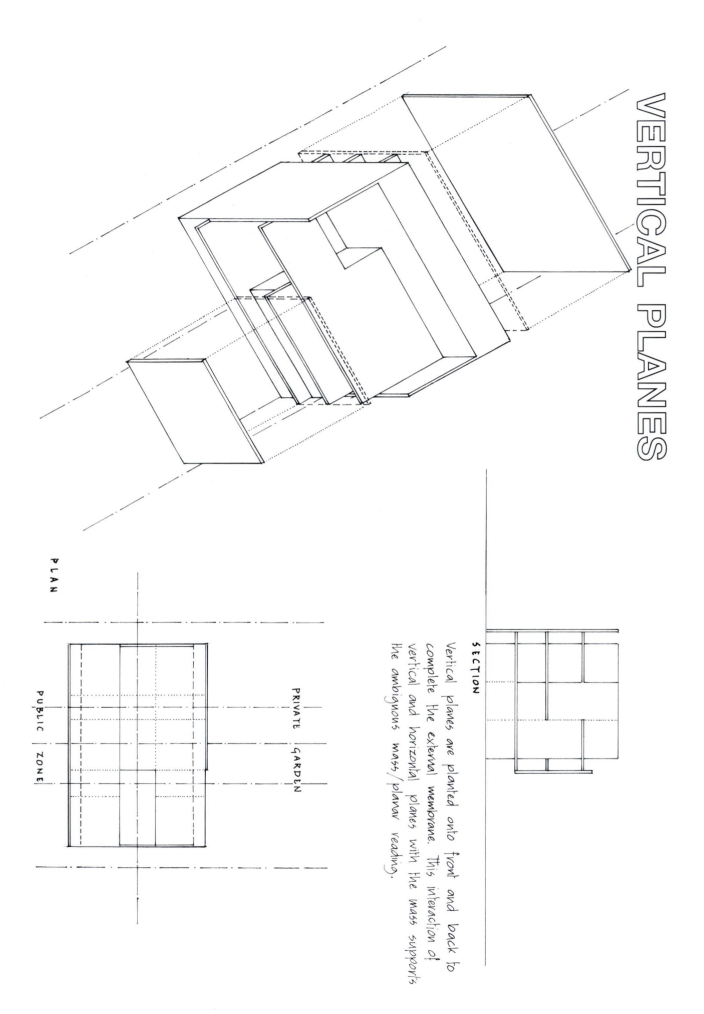

PLAN

PRIVATE | GARDEN

PUBLIC | ZONE

SECTION

Vertical planes are planted onto front and back to complete the external membrane. This interaction of vertical and horizontal planes with the mass supports the ambiguous mass/planar reading.

TERRACES

The lower terrace extends towards the garden, to which it gains access by a stair. The terraces effect the merging of garden and villa.

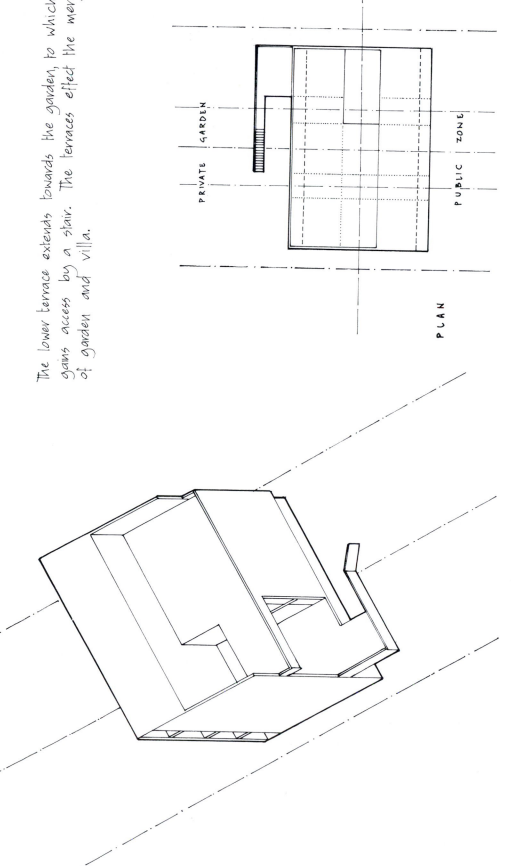

PRIVATE GARDEN

PUBLIC ZONE

PLAN

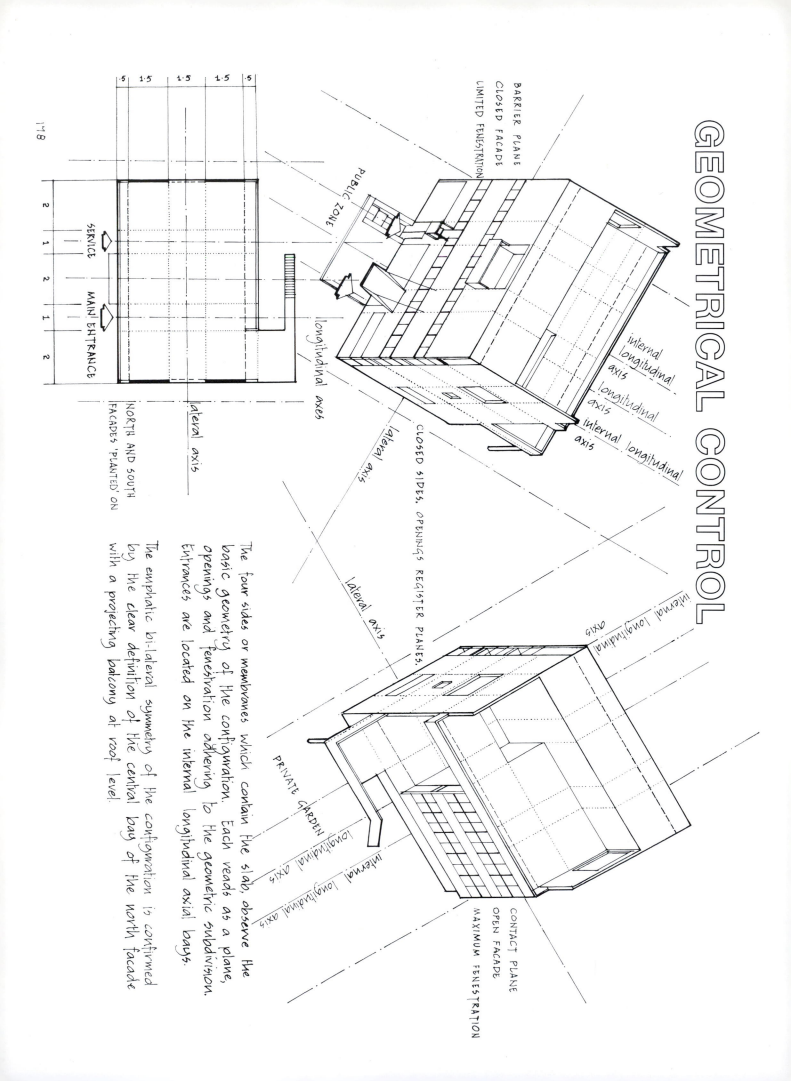

BARRIER PLANE
CLOSED FACADE
LIMITED FENESTRATION

PUBLIC ZONE

internal
longitudinal
axis

longitudinal
axis

internal longitudinal
axis

CLOSED SIDES, OPENINGS REGISTER PLANES.

lateral axis

lateral axis

longitudinal axis

lateral axis

internal longitudinal axis

PRIVATE GARDEN

longitudinal axis

internal longitudinal axis

CONTACT PLANE
OPEN FACADE
MAXIMUM FENESTRATION

SERVICE

MAIN ENTRANCE

NORTH AND SOUTH
FACADES 'PLANTED ON'

lateral axis

The four sides or membranes which contain the slab, observe the
basic geometry of the configuration. Each reads as a plane,
openings and fenestration adhering to the geometric subdivision.
Entrances are located on the internal longitudinal axial bays.

The emphatic bi-lateral symmetry of the configuration is confirmed
by the clear definition of the central bay of the north facade
with a projecting balcony at roof level.

VILLA FALLET

south elevation

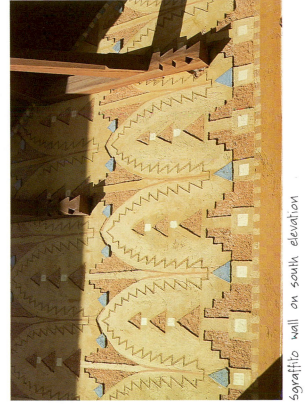

sgraffito wall on south elevation

Pine mullions and cloud shaped railings

VILLA FALLET

View from north-west

Upper landing to hall

Entrance loggia

VILLA STOTZER

View from south-west

View from north-east

View from south-east

VILLA JAQUEMET

North façade

South façade

View from south-east

VILLA JEANNERET-PERRET

West facade

View from salon looking north

View from south-west

Pergola leading to entrance

VILLA FAVRE-JACOT

West facade (roof addition not by Jeanneret)

East facade

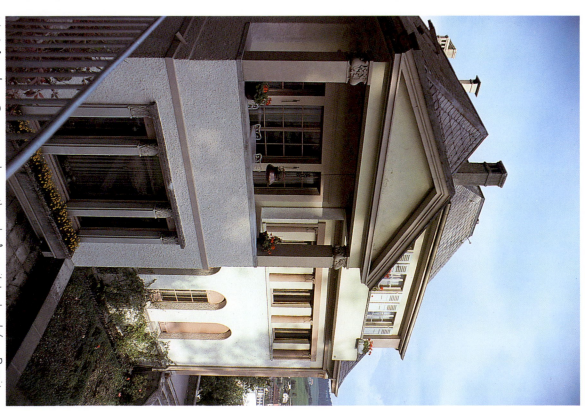

West facade Pigeon and acanthus leaf capitals by Léon Perrin

VILLA SCHWOB

View from north-west

North facade

Balcony to salon

VILLAS LA ROCHE-JEANNERET

Entrance hall looking towards the library

View towards La Roche house from private road

Entrance hall looking towards plane B

VILLA STEIN-DE-MONZIE

Entry facade

Terraces from south-west

Entry facade

VILLA SAVOYE

Entry seen from the south-west

Salon viewed from the terrace

The approach drive and entry volume

Madame's bathroom

PAVILLON SUISSE

View from north-east

View from south-east

View from north-west

View towards entrance hall

Fireplace in house A

JAOUL HOUSES

View towards end wall of living area, house A

Living area house A

NOTRE-DAME-DU-HAUT RONCHAMP

View from east

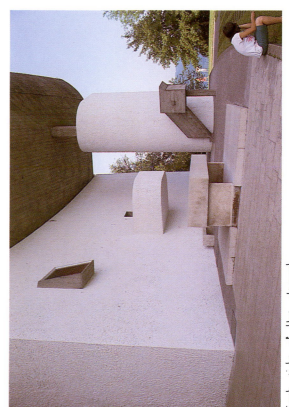

East side of the chapel

South wall and tower

THE MONASTERY OF LA TOURETTE

Interior of the church

Courtyard with atrium roof on circulation spine

Interior of sanctuary

View from the south-west

THE MONASTERY OF LA TOURETTE

Gap between church and rest of complex

North facade of the church

South facade

VILLA SHODHAN

Southwest facade

Exterior detail

Living area

North-west facade

APPROACH ROUTE

On moving towards the villa the visitor is confronted by a vertical plane which virtually blocks the site.

Long windows provide no more than a glimpse of something beyond. That the plane is penetrable is suggested by two balconies which pierce the membrane. Twin supports for the canopy defining the entrance also pierce the facade.

Essentially the facade plane, a typically bold statement, acts as a barrier. It is preparatory, the overture, following which the story of the villa will unfold.

The approach driveway points towards the secondary entrance enabling vehicles to swing round to the main entrance to the right. Located to the left of center, the approach route is a reminder of the earlier project, but the copse has gone.

The entry facade establishes one of the main strategic opportunities which the format provides; this is to develop the internal axes located in the two narrower bays either side of center.

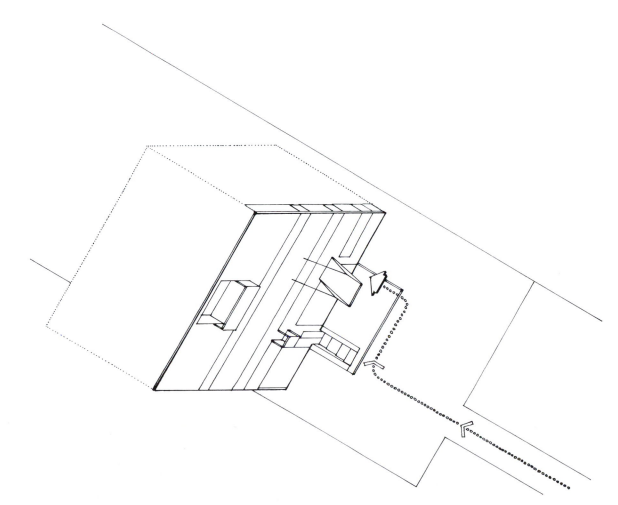

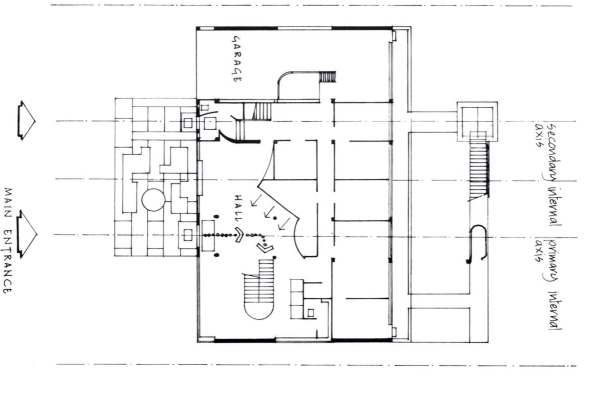

GARAGE

HALL

secondary internal axis

primary internal axis

GROUND LEVEL PLAN

MAIN ENTRANCE

At ground level the main entry is on the right of the twin internal longitudinal axes, with service entry to the left. This duality about a symmetrical format is similar to the location of entry in the Villa Schwob (see pages 69 and 71). As in the Villa Schwob, the entrances are linked, not with floor plane and canopy (Schwob) but with a continuous patterned floor.

To assert the main entry, Le Corbusier suspends a canopy from supports hung from the structure which pierce the front plane. The service entrance is lowered, with access by steps leading down. A small balcony above helps to define this entrance.

On entering the hall, pilotis mark the axis of movement towards the stair at right angles. As with the Villa La Roche this axis leads to a curved plane, a similar device being used in the entry foyer of the Pavillon Suisse. An oblique screen alongside points movement towards the stair.

This elegant spatial movement sequence contrasts with the constrained service entrance, where the vestibule is formed by a curved wall to a w.c. and by an enclosure of space determined by the curve of the secondary stair above. This double twist on entering ensures a secondary reading for the service entrance. The door to the service entrance is placed off axis to complete the series of shifting relationships about the secondary internal axis.

At this level, despite a subtle balancing of the two entry points, the main entrance gives primacy to the internal axis on which it is located.

VERTICAL PLANES

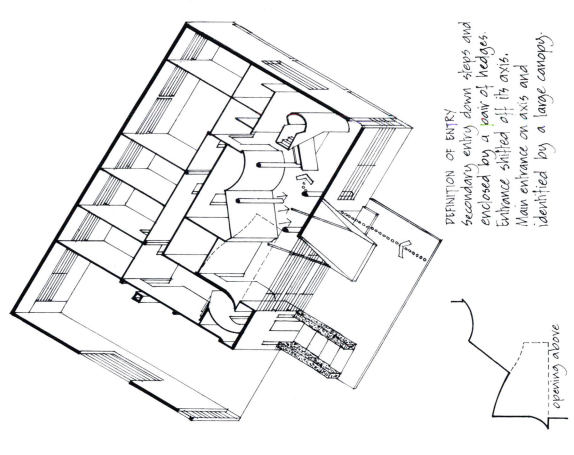

DEFINITION OF ENTRY

Secondary entry down steps and enclosed by a pair of hedges. Entrance shifted off its axis. Main entrance on axis and identified by a large canopy.

PLAN PROFILE OF VERTICAL PLANES

opening above

As a sequence of visual experiences on moving towards and into the villa, 'Les Terrasses' typifies Le Corbusier's visual method in offering a series of contrasting and memorable visual effects.

Following the external view of the entry facade, a compelling and boldly composed vertical plane, the entrance hall presents an entirely different scenario. The juxtaposition of elements has an energy reminiscent of Jeanneret's paintings. This animation establishes a mood to be further developed as the architectural promenade continues.

Initially the four columns defining the entry route enframe the curved screen opposite in a manner both calm and dignified. This restful sequence is enlivened by the oblique screen immediately to the left. As in so much of Le Corbusier's work, the oblique provides a dynamic directional thrust within the orthogonal setting.

To the left and forward of this screen is the curve of an opening in the ceiling giving a sense of the floor above, a hint of the next stage of the experience sequence. The opening terminates at its eastern extremity with the service stair, itself curving into the rectilinear side of the secondary entry vestibule. The plan profile of this series of vertical planes captures the spirit of the villa.

STAIRCASE SCULPTURE

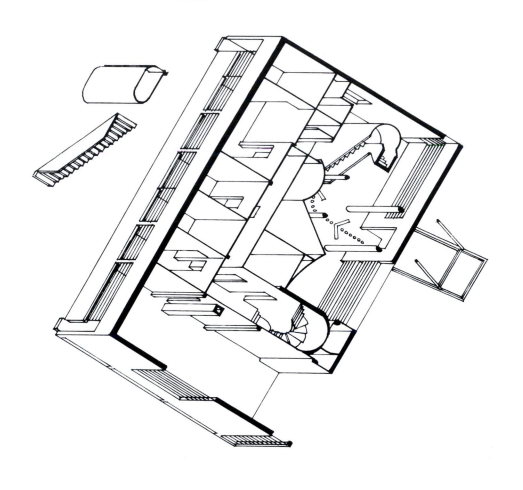

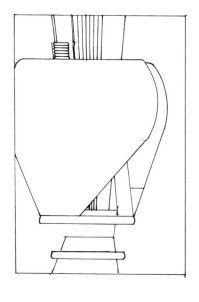

In the entrance hall the staircase becomes a sculptural object, being encased on one of its sides. The independence of this shape is furthered by the gap between stair and opening above.

This level acts as a base to the overall composition of the villa and is given a horizontal reading by long windows to the rear and close spaced horizontal glazing bars throughout.

FORM DISTORTED

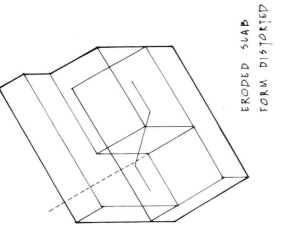

ERODED SLAB
FORM DISTORTED

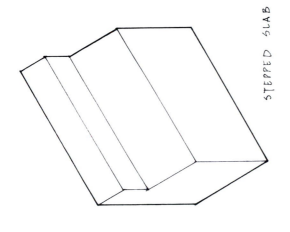

STEPPED SLAB

Despite corrections which help to restore the gestalt slab reading
the configuration remains distorted by the erosion of the corner.
Distortion of a regular grid affords Le Corbusier a typical design
scenario, enabling a dynamic balance of asymmetrical elements
within a symmetrical format.

possibility of fracturing; weak linkage of exposed edge.

FORM DISTORTED WITHIN SYMMETRICAL FORMAT

GENERIC SLAB

'CORRECTED' SLAB

184

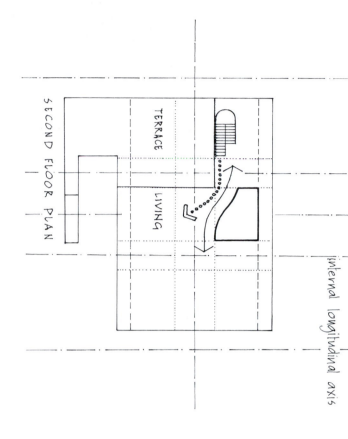

SECOND FLOOR PLAN

TERRACE

LIVING

internal longitudinal axis

Acknowledging the distortion in the form Le Corbusier creates a piano shaped opening which allows movement from the exposed edge into the main space at second floor.

This further weakens the exposed edge and movement from the space below participates fully in the elemental ordering.

The opening mediates between two spaces, the smaller exposed edge next to the terrace and the larger central space of the living room. There is also a visual link with the first floor

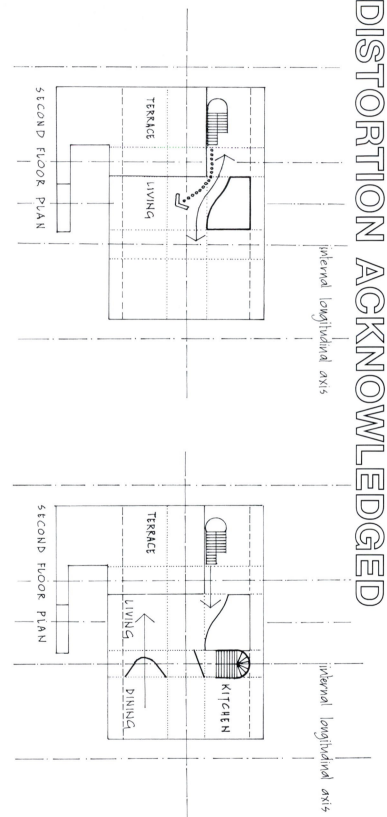

SECOND FLOOR PLAN

TERRACE

LIVING

DINING

KITCHEN

internal longitudinal axis

At second floor level, the stair above the secondary entrance becomes the main vertical circulation.

If the exposed edge is excluded, the remaining configuration is almost a square, having it's own bi-lateral symmetry about the internal longitudinal axis.

At this level, and on upper floors, this internal axis is further developed and strengthened, counterbalancing the erosion of the form where the terraces cascade.

SCULPTURAL ENSEMBLE

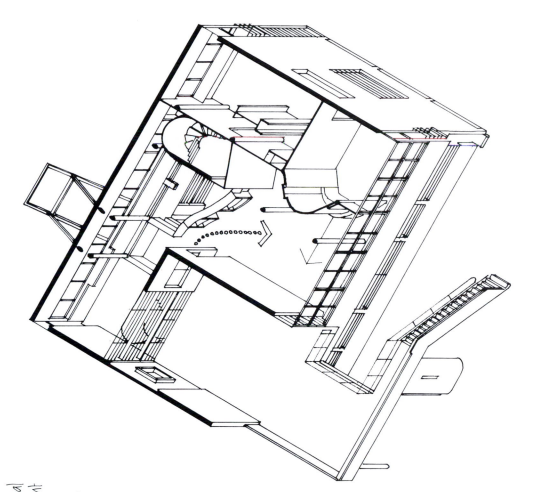

The piano shaped opening is placed within the compositional and structural grid and becomes a three dimensional statement by the way it's sides are built up as shelving. To the north, defining the space between facade and opening, shelving continues beyond the opening, reinforcing the linearity of the long window alongside. Three columns (on grid) pierce the horizontal upper plane of this shelving. The vertical linearity of the long window is furthered by the horizontal plane of a shelf which runs continuously below the window.

A taut bow-like screen encloses the dining area which is next to the kitchen. The screen projects itself into the living area, providing a lateral directional force which echoes the similarly aligned sculptural stair leading from the lower floor.

An oblique screen closes the main staircase area allowing direct contact between the kitchen and living area. The screens and piano shaped opening may be linked with the sculptural stair in the entrance hall in the way these elements form a lyrical sculptural ensemble which acts in concert with the promenade architecturale. The curved shelving to the opening, together with the oblique and bow shaped screens, enclose the living area, which is centrally located with a view towards the garden. Twin columns in the living area enframe the curved screen, itself held by two columns. A door leads from the living area to the adjacent terrace.

FREE PLAN

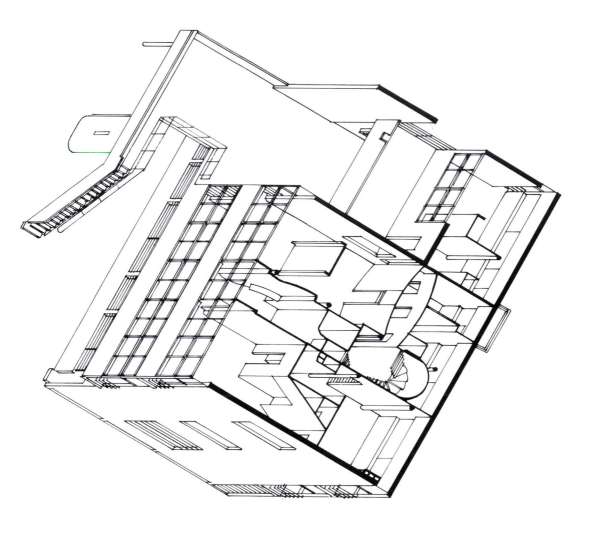

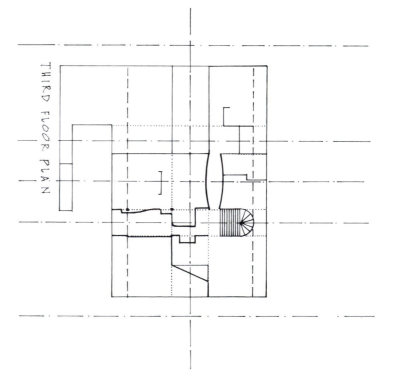

THIRD FLOOR PLAN

At third floor level the internal axis of the staircase bay is developed by the elaborate treatment of a bathroom and dressing space. The undulating wall dividing the bathroom from bedroom 1 exemplifies Le Corbusier's 'free plan.' The wall extends to contain the dressing area before meandering behind two columns. A sensuous curve contains a bathroom fitment terminated at the point where bedroom and boudoir divide.

The third floor plan exemplifies Le Corbusier's desire to accommodate functional needs within an arrangement that aspires towards aesthetic profundity.

Rooms and circulation spaces are enriched by a deployment of vertical planes which do not merely contain or screen but which instead highlight each activity in a manner appropriate to its role in the design.

If the second floor is concerned with spatial interaction, the bedrooms on the third floor are planned for cellular privacy and extravagant convenience. In particular, bathrooms provide opportunities to celebrate the functional beauty of sanitary ware, as lavatory basins, baths, bidets and water closets are displayed like sculpture in an art gallery.

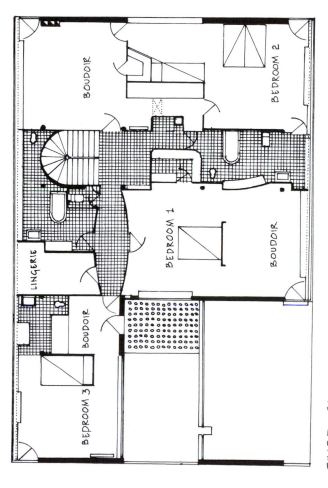

THIRD FLOOR PLAN

The corridor leading from the stair to bedroom 3 has its centrality emphasised by curves which give it the role of a 'bridge' linking the two sides of the configuration. Within a complex and slightly turbulent plan this acts as a stabilising element reiterating the A,B,A,B,A symmetry which underlies the organisation.

An oblique plane containing a dressing area suggests linkage of a different kind between bedroom 2 and its boudoir.

188

The primacy of the stair axis is confirmed at roof terrace level by a curved studio which projects out from the stair. The sculptural weight of this element balances the erosion of the form created by the cascading terraces.

The axis receives further reinforcement in the garden where a paved path leads from the foot of the stair. The driveway towards the villa is also located on this axis.

primary axis

APPROACH AND DRIVE

ROOF LEVEL PLAN

GARDEN PLAN

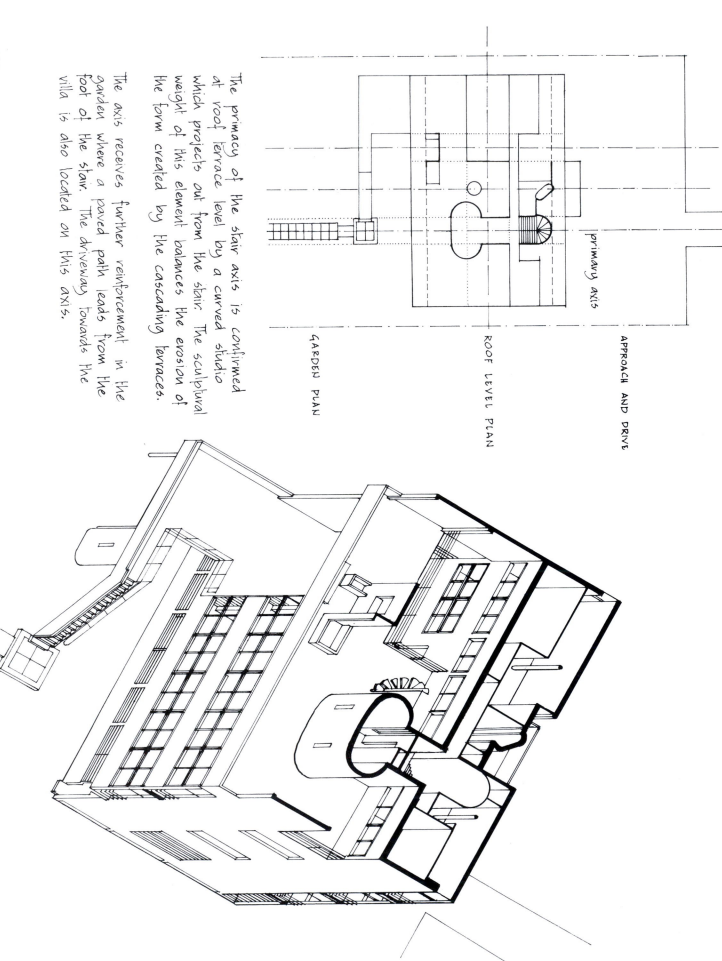

ROOF TERRACE

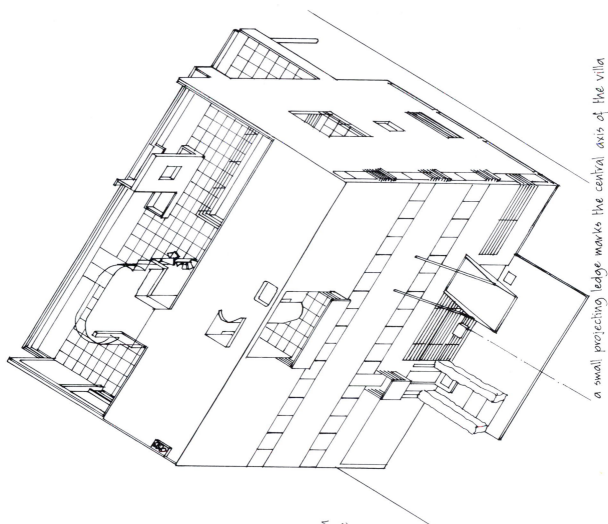

a small projecting ledge marks the central axis of the villa

The distortion of the gestalt acknowledged by the piano shaped opening at second floor level, is further recognised by an oblique indentation where the central balcony punctures the entry facade.

The oblique is curved at either end to enclose a bath, the resultant form echoing both the shape of the rooftop studio and the curved w.c. below the stair leading to the garden.

This device demonstrates a design technique used frequently by Le Corbusier in which a functional element is exploited to serve the manipulation of form. In this case the bath is twisted round so that it is set in a dynamic relationship with the orthogonal grid. Also the shape uses curves which contrast with the grid and the wall containing the bath has a dual role, being functional on one side and sculptural on the other. (The same technique is used on the third floor with the wall dividing a bathroom from bedroom 1.)

A spiral stair leads to the roof of the studio, bounded by a single railing. Spiral stair and studio coexist in a dual role, symbolizing the nautical flavour evident in Le Corbusier's roof terraces and presenting a striking contrast of form.

SLAB TRANSFORMED

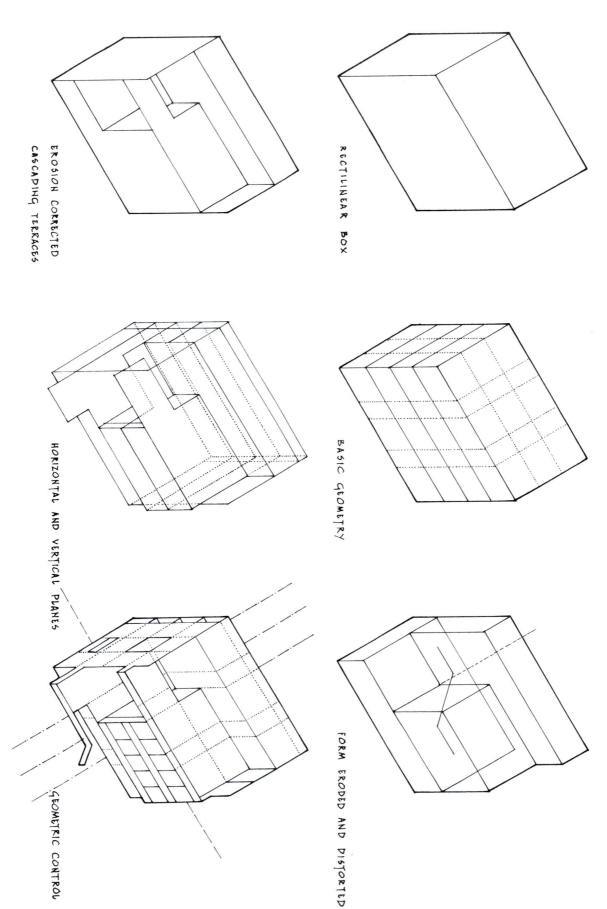

RECTILINEAR BOX

EROSION CORRECTED
CASCADING TERRACES

BASIC GEOMETRY

HORIZONTAL AND VERTICAL PLANES

FORM ERODED AND DISTORTED

GEOMETRIC CONTROL

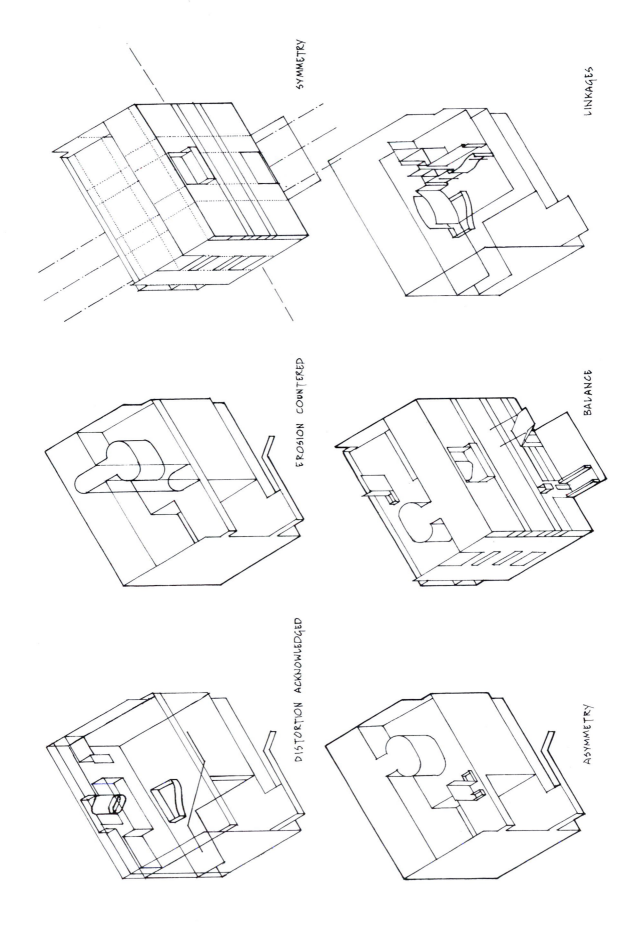

SYMMETRY

EROSION COUNTERED

BALANCE

DISTORTION ACKNOWLEDGED

ASYMMETRY

COMPACTION

The Villa Stein-de-Monzie may be regarded as an icon of the Modern Movement and has been seen by successive generations of architects as having a canonical role in the history of the movement. This is justified by Le Corbusier's capacity to exploit a situation in which he had a site with more opportunities than constraints, clients who could afford an expensive villa, and by the fact that the substantial body of design experience gained during the decade enabled him to effectively bring together several strands of his ideology.

In the Villa he displays consummate technique in the deployment of spaces and volumes, demonstrating the inherent potential of his 'domino' diagram (p 63). Purist maxims are much in evidence in the way the design exemplifies universality, perceptual clarity, a functional basis in the use of _objets types_ (the spiral stair on the roof terrace, long windows, sculpted stairs) and in the use of regulating lines to control proportions.

The elements are brought together within the confines of a rectilinear box, so often the starting point for Le Corbusier's villas. Within the slab, exercising control with a geometric discipline, he distorts the form and compacts the planes to allow a subtle balance between the different kinds of energy within the composition. If the erosion of the slab and opening in the entrance hall ceiling have negative connotations, these are countered by positive sculptural gestures such as the rooftop studio and bow-like screen dividing the living and dining areas. The resultant state of dynamic equilibrium, evident in the work as a whole, is attained by a particularly rich deployment of elements within the bi-laterally symmetrical format.

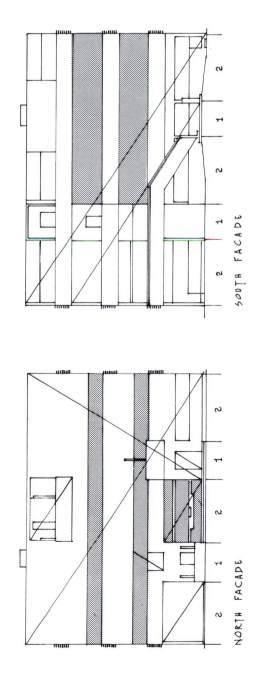

NORTH FACADE

SOUTH FACADE

REGULATING LINES   (from drawings in Le Corbusier The Complete Architectural Works 1910-29 Vol. 1, London, 1964, p 44)

The formal distortion is only apparent from the second floor upwards, and is explored differently at each level as programmatic requirements demand. Symmetry and asymmetry are manipulated in ways appropriate to the geometry of the configuration in a system which uses contrasts and tensions to achieve dynamic equilibrium.

The villa is no longer as originally designed by Le Corbusier, having been subdivided internally and extended to the rear in a manner which destroys the conceptual intention.

The Villa Savoye represents the apotheosis of Le Corbusier's attempt to create the ideal dwelling during the twenties. The design brings to fulfillment ideas first explored in the Citrohan model and developed in a series of major houses during the decade.

The dwelling is seen as a receptacle for sunlight 'elevated above the landscape. This is expressed with Le Corbusier's 'heroic' imagery of sun decks, ramps, spiral stairs and ribbon windows; it uses a language of solids and planes compacted as in a Purist painting.

At the same time the villa crystallises Le Corbusier's classical ideals which can be traced back to his reverence for the Parthenon, although the interpretation more closely resembles a Renaissance villa. The centralised form is set temple-like in the landscape, elevated on pilotis, which can be regarded as a contemporary equivalent of classical columns.

In having both contemporary and historical overtones the villa typifies Le Corbusier's approach. He saw it as one of the components of his utopian city, a symbol of how architecture would enrich life both physically and culturally. The medium as always is form, controlled through geometry and placed in a special relationship with nature.

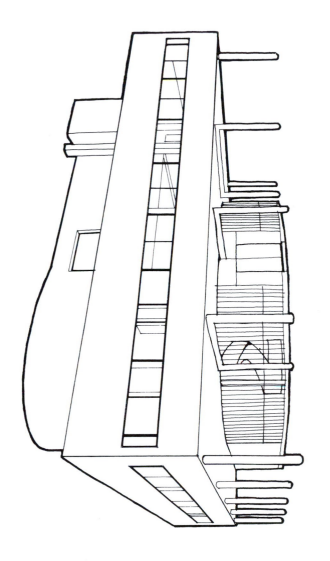

VILLA SAVOYE 1929-31

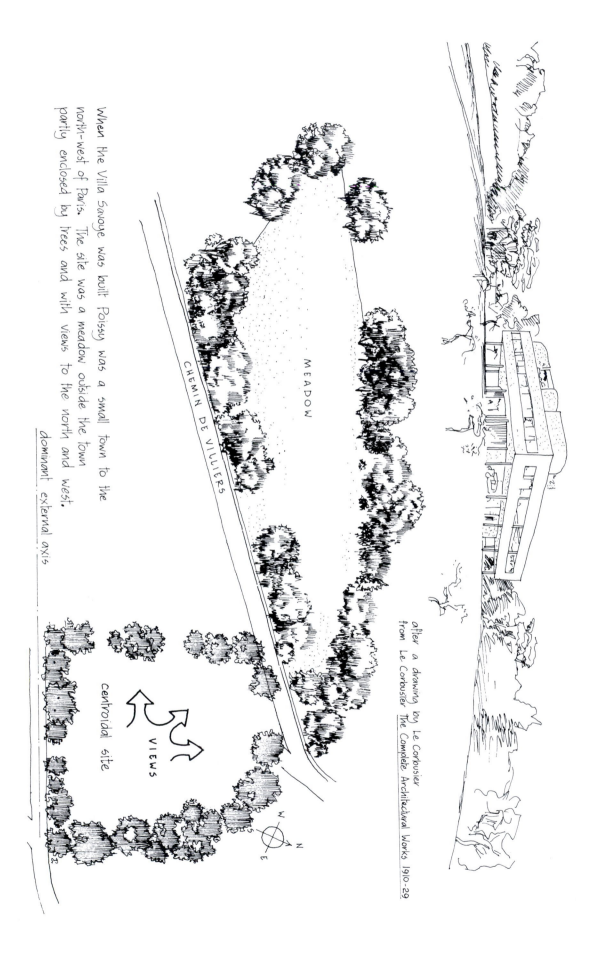

When the Villa Savoye was built Poissy was a small town to the north-west of Paris. The site was a meadow outside the town partly enclosed by trees and with views to the north and west.

dominant external axis

CHEMIN DE VILLIERS

MEADOW

centroidal site

VIEWS

after a drawing by Le Corbusier from Le Corbusier The Complete Architectural Works 1910-29

PROBLEM

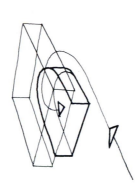

The problem is one of entry into a raised volume.

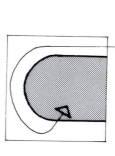

The entry block shape is determined by the turning capability of a vehicle, with the fundamental dynamic of a curvilinear volume tensioned against a rectangle.

GENERIC
equal axes

centroidal

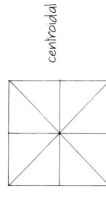

Le Corbusier intended to elevate a cubic volume above the meadow, the geometry of man poised above the geometry of nature.

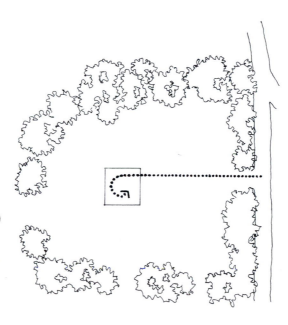

The centroidal form is placed centrally within the centroidal site, a horizontal form in a horizontal situation. Le Corbusier intended a prolonged contemplation of this primary form.

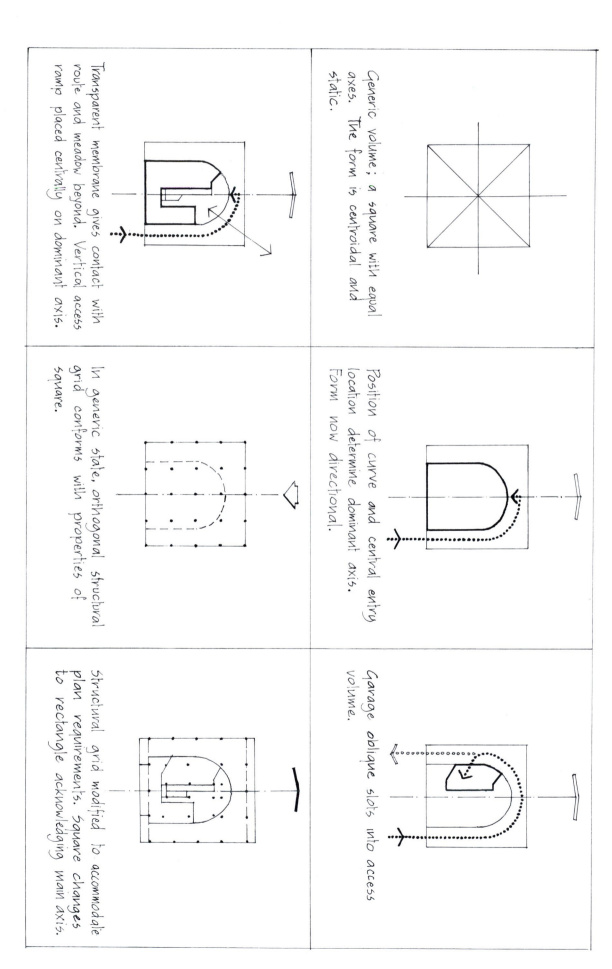

Generic volume; a square with equal axes. The form is centroidal and static.

Position of curve and central entry location determine dominant axis. Form now directional.

Garage oblique slots into access volume.

Transparent membrane gives contact with route and meadow beyond. Vertical access ramp placed centrally on dominant axis.

In generic state, orthogonal structural grid conforms with properties of square.

Structural grid modified to accommodate plan requirements. Square changes to rectangle acknowledging main axis.

BASIC THEME

The theme is concerned to explore the relationship between the 'floating' slab and its surroundings. The slab becomes both a viewing container and a receptacle for sunlight.

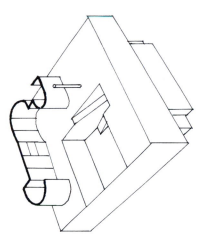

GENERIC CONDITION

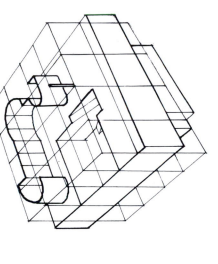

THEME DEVELOPED

This is developed by opening up the slab and by extending the curved imagery at roof level. The idea is controlled within an implicit orthogonal system against which the various elements are tensioned.

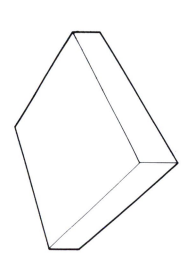

BASIC CONFIGURATION

ORTHOGONAL GRID

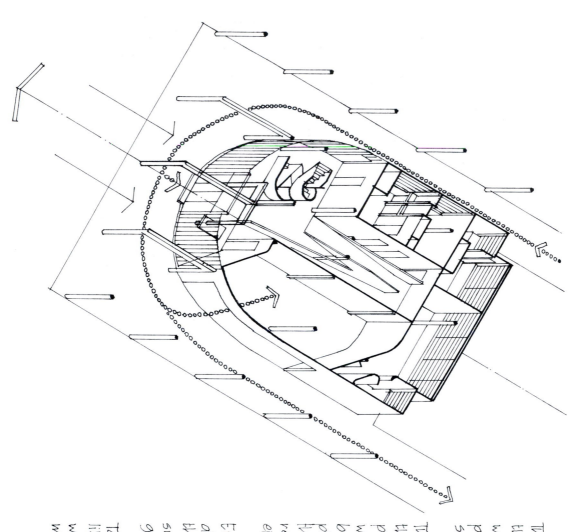

The transparent curved membrane which defines the access zone contrasts in shape and density with the rectilinear slab above. This slab is protective, the zone is preparatory and the soft curved glazing invites penetration.

The enclosing membrane threads it's way through the orthogonal framework of columns and is pierced by a beam linking an outer column with an 'arch' formed by twin columns and a beam within. This T shaped structure is placed on the dominant axis where it marks the point of entry. The entry direction is reaffirmed by beams which link pilotis on either side of centre.

Entry, therefore becomes ceremonial, and, directly ahead, on the axis, a ramp extends this theme by providing a gradual ascent, which suggests that the promenade architecturale will gently unfold.

To the left is the spiral stair which, baldechino-like, provides swirling vertical punctuation within the space, extending the curvilinear movement of the perimeter membrane.

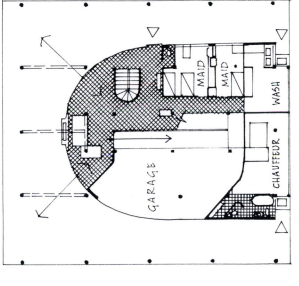

GARAGE

MAID

MAID

WASH

CHAUFFEUR

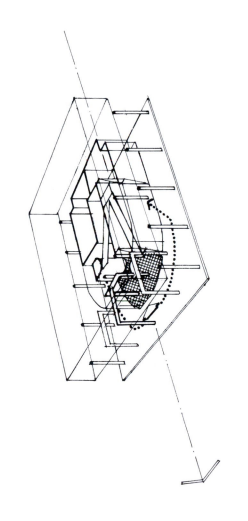

Ramp and spiral, 'perfect' functional objects, are the major
sculptural events in the space, contrasting in shape, each
being placed at a centre of gravity within the zone. Two
vertical planes add further contrast, the one orthogonal,
near the spiral stair, the other oblique, the garage wall.
These elements combine with the curved membrane to give
the space dynamic animation.

Diagonal floor tiles suggest a radial sense of contact
between inside and out. To the right of entry a
'floating' horizontal slab is pierced by a column, a restatement
in a minor key of the main idea of the villa.

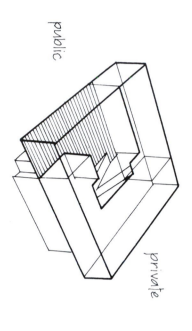

public

private

In general terms a diagonal divides the accommodation into spatial and cellular zones.

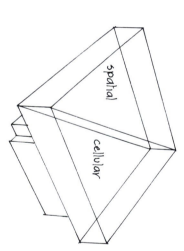

spatial

cellular

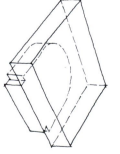

A rectilinear slab placed on top of a curved form

salon

terrace

covered
terrace

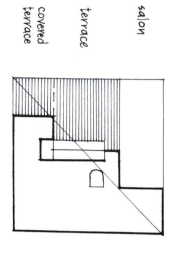

There is continuous spatial contact between the salon, terrace and covered terrace, and the oblique lines of the ramp dramatise an otherwise orthogonal organisation. The plant boxes pick up the slab theme with the terrace table echoing the prevailing horizontality. Rooflights in the plant containers light the garage below.

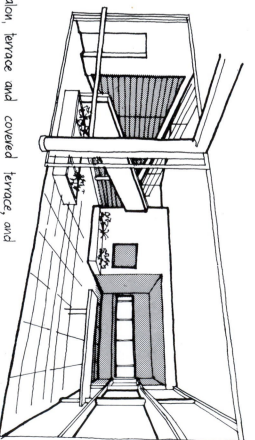

PIANO NOBILE

The living zone, expressed as a piano nobile, has an orthogonal deployment within the rectilinear slab, while being divided on a diagonal into public and private areas separated by the ramp. In the public area the part-glazed box of the salon merges into the open and yet part-closed terrace.

Le Corbusier controls this spatial interpenetration by his handling of solids and opaque and transparent planes, permitting views through in different ways. The ribbon windows are left out of the long side of the terrace giving a narrow frame for the vista and horizontal glazing to the ramp gives views within and without.

The assemblage of solids and planes in grades of open and closed gains an extra dimension with the inclined plane of the ramp, its progression from inside to out exemplifying the versatility of this architectural language.

As the vehicle for the promenade architecturale, the central location of the ramp provides contrasting experiences as one moves from confined enclosure to the sense of spatial expansion of the terrace. The continuity of the ramp is a reminder of the interrelationship between the three levels of the villa.

SON'S BED

GUEST BED

TERRACE

KITCHEN

MADAME'S BEDROOM

BOUDOIR

SALON

SLABS AND PLANES

Slablike wardrobes subdivide the space in the bedrooms. Shelves under windows and in wardrobes act as planes.

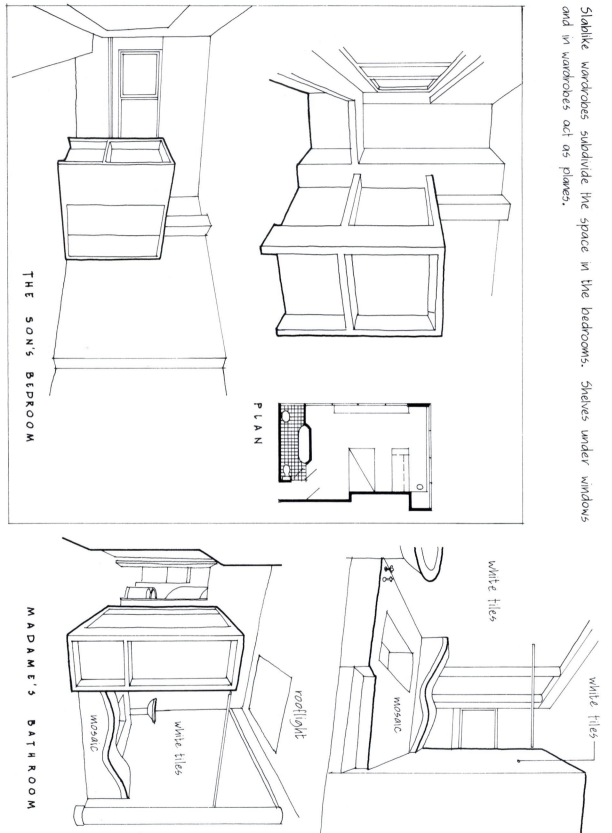

THE SON'S BEDROOM

PLAN

MADAME'S BATHROOM

white tiles

white tiles

mosaic

mosaic

white tiles

rooflight

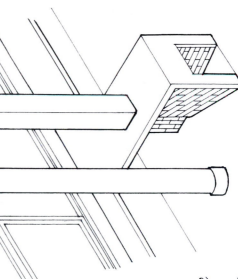

At the heart of the cellular private zone Madame's bedroom merges into the bathroom in a volumetric arrangement similar in its richness to the spatial organisation where salon, terrace and ramp conjoin. The bathroom is animated by contrasts of shape, surface and colour with a mosaic cladding to the bath and reclining slab. Toplights illuminate the bath and w.c.

Bathroom and terrace suggest the fitness ethic symbolising the health-giving virtues of sun, air and cleanliness.

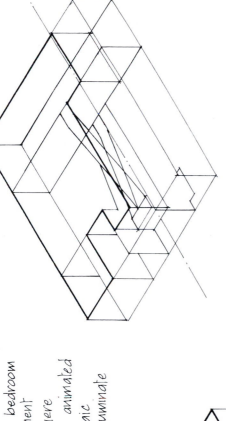

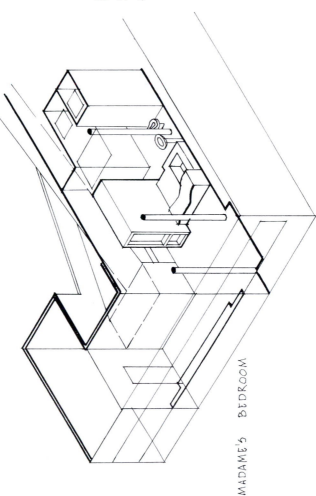

MADAME'S BEDROOM

SALON FIREPLACE

The horizontal plane of the window ledge is used to considerable effect around the perimeter. In the salon this plane projects outwards to contain the fireplace, being pierced by the chimney flue. The hearth is built simply of brick, a statement of function expressed within the planar discipline.

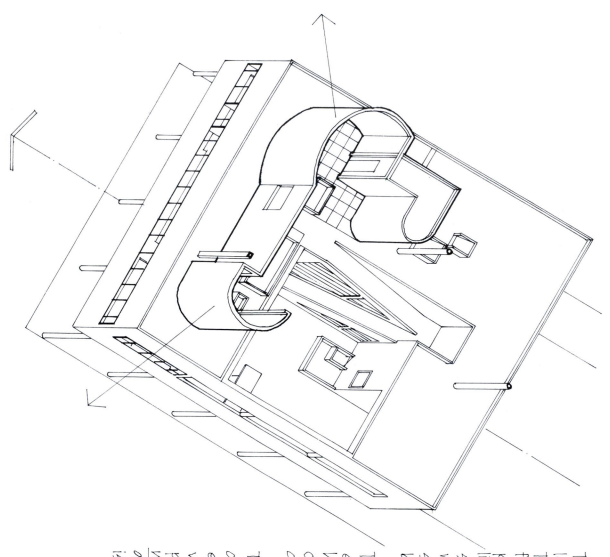

The promenade architecturale concludes at roof level where Le Corbusier creates a further terrace. This is enclosed by a screen which acts as the final flourish of the design, a flamboyant gesture proclaiming the sense of freedom and idea of liberation made manifest in the villa. As a statement about the nature of the villa, this screen resembles the Greek temple pediment in which a sculptural composition conveys the message of the building.

The concave/convex planes of the screen both enclose and also proclaim the villa to distant horizons. This is a variation on the theme of contact with the surroundings established on each of the lower levels.

The screen is controlled by the orthogonal discipline of the design and has a solid component which encloses the spiral stair. Depending on the viewpoint the entire screen may be read as solid or planar, an ambiguity similar to that of the piano nobile box, read as a solid container except where a glimpse of the terrace is provided. The screen is stabilised by the solid stair container.

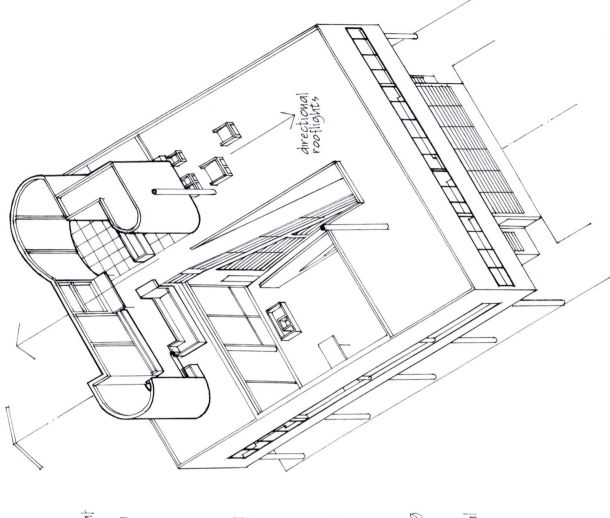

directional
rooflights

Each end of the roof terrace screen has a
definite termination and edges to this level are
protected by plant containers. Structural ribs
supporting the screen are expressed suggesting that
the screen is a thin wrap-around membrane. This
rib and panel statement resembles ship construction
and railings to the ramp add to the nautical
metaphor.

The membrane is pierced by an opening which
reveals the thickness of the screen and terminates
the promenade architecturale. This event is marked
by a concrete table which projects out from the
base of this opening, a similar device being
used at the perimeter of the living zone terrace.
The opening enframes a distant view, and close
by, the edge of the largest of the plant containers
projects out and is raised, helping to define the
route.

At piano nobile level the continuous strip of glazing
is echoed by the horizontal plane of the window
ledge. The opening in the roof screen with its
adjacent table confirms this idea. From a practical
viewpoint the screen gives shelter from the
north and east while admitting the afternoon
sun.

FORM

The basic configuration provides a perceptual image that is both clear and simple, contrasting a curved form with a rectilinear slab.

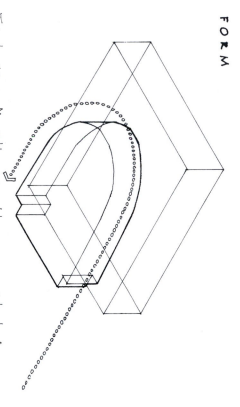

deep incision for ramp

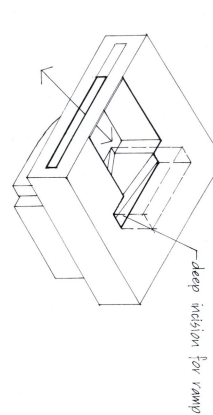

Biting out part of the form allows sunlight to penetrate deep into the building as in all courtyard planning. The slab has an ambiguous reading being only part solid.

The theme of contact with the surroundings is explored through the media of form and space to provide several kinds of enclosure, exposure and spatial interaction.

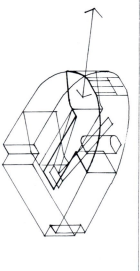

The entry volume preserves contact with the meadow and is a space of some complexity.

SPACE

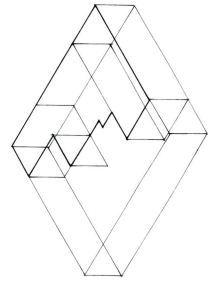

Spatial continuity affords grades of enclosure and exposure.

PLANES

At access level the surface treatment recognises certain characteristics of the mass. The closely spaced glazing mullions give a rhythmic ripple effect at one with movement around the curve. To the rear, the strength suggested by the corners helps to stabilise the form, reminding us of its directional nature.

The taut membrane of the roof screen both proclaims and contains.

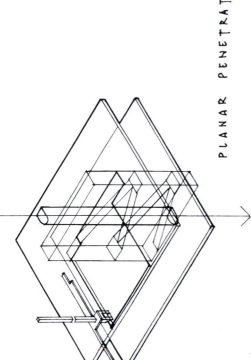

PLANAR PENETRATION

The horizontal planes of the slab are pierced by the ramp and spiral stair, which corkscrews through the layers down to basement level. This vertical piercing is expressed in a minor key by the chimney flue in the salon which penetrates the ceiling plane and the horizontal perimeter shelf plane. At roof level this vertical flue punctuates the roof screen.

The static generic form is transformed into a dynamic configuration by Le Corbusier's handling of the planes. The perimeter ribbon windows increase both the planar reading and sense of horizontality. Adjacent to the ramp the glazing bar pattern creates a stretching effect which echoes the linear thrust of the ramp itself. The rear of the access volume becomes a particularly taut surface, being read in conjunction with the edge of the slab above because it is in the same vertical plane. At the opposite end the roof screen is an overt statement of the freedom and lyricism of the design.

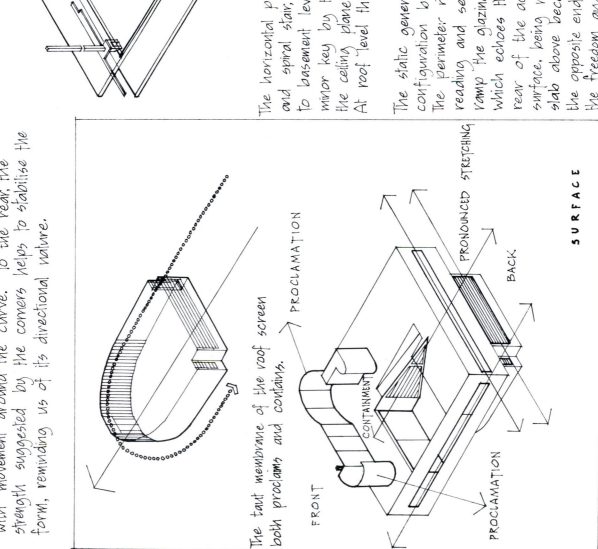

FRONT

PROCLAMATION

PROCLAMATION

CONTAINMENT

PRONOUNCED STRETCHING

BACK

PROCLAMATION

SURFACE

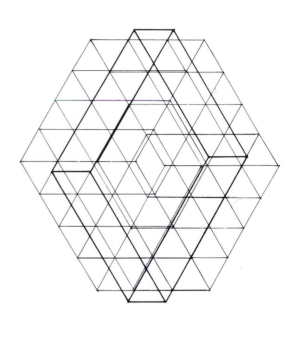

NON-DIRECTIONAL ORTHOGONAL GRID

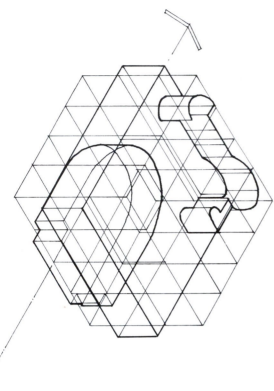

CURVES TENSIONED AGAINST GRID

The basic geometrical system is a non-directional orthogonal grid within which Le Corbusier establishes the major volumetric unit, the rectilinear living zone. This regular cubic form provides an ordering baseline which states the major theme of the design, that of the relationship between an elevated cubic volume and its surroundings.

The roof screen and access volume explore the fundamental tension between curves and the orthogonal system, each having directional components which respond to functional and symbolic requirements within the design.

Further tension is apparent in the diagonal spatial/cellular subdivision of the <u>piano nobile</u> and in the vigorous animation of the form by surface modulation and planar penetration. The dynamism induced is controlled within the orthogonal system and particularly by the two major forces implanted into the system by the disposition of forms : the first of these is the dominant longitudinal axis, reinforced by the ramp, and the second is the living zone volume. Of these the living zone exerts the greater effect, and the degree of animation within the design becomes possible because this is always subservient to the overriding power, serenity and unity provided by the <u>piano nobile</u> volume.

Within the orthogonal grid the structural system brings to fruition the Domino principle of columns and slab, with a columnar organisation sufficiently flexible to respond to particular requirements of the plan.

MOVEMENT

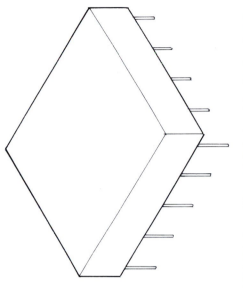

STATIC SYMMETRY OF THE BOX

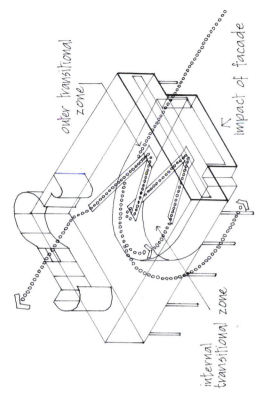

outer transitional zone

impact of facade

internal transitional zone

DYNAMIC CONTINUITY OF THE ROUTE

As in all Le Corbusier's work during the twenties, the movement route has special significance, being the means of linking the successive experiences provided by the villa. The sequential nature of these events becomes the thread which holds the design together, and Le Corbusier cross-references the various relationships of elements with the way these are perceived along the movement route.

In threading experiences together, the route is a linear element with a dynamism and sense of continuity which contrasts with the static symmetry of the raised box which is the dominant perceptual image of the villa. Unlike the arrangement of the villa, the route has a time dimension and a potency which is increased by the form taken by the movement sequence.

The sense of dynamism is encouraged by the way the route curves around the access volume and by the dramatic exploitation of the ramp. This important symbolic element does move rather than reinforce the main axis, scything through the layers and becoming like an escalator on which the observer is conveyed through the very heart of the design.

Following the initial impact of the form, successive experiences take in the external transitional zone where the route first moves under the box; ceremonial entry is followed by the internal transitional zone of the entry-volume, in which contact is preserved with the exterior, in which there is no sense of rest, and in which the ramp exerts a strong directional pull. Stable rectilinear spaces create a holding zone at the piano mobile and movement concludes with the enclosed spaces of the roof deck. Continuity is maintained by the opening enframing the distant view.

MACHINE AESTHETIC

The hard surfaces and geometrical purity of the villa reinforce the rational and intellectual implications of Le Corbusier's symbolism. Order and clarity were central to his architecture at this time, reflecting an idealistic attitude towards form which was seen as analogous to the precision and efficiency of machines.

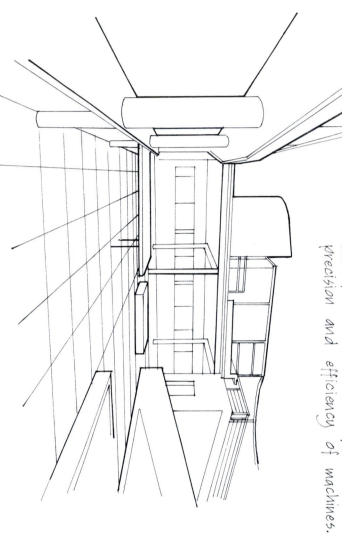

Each level of the villa has symbolic connotations, with forms and materials reflecting Le Corbusier's attitude towards the machine age. The motor car directly affects the shape of the access volume, the roof deck evokes images of ocean liners and the living zone demonstrates that dematerialisation of form and space associated with a new kind of freedom for man. In fact the living zone consists largely of a sun terrace, one of Le Corbusier's most pervasive symbols throughout the decade. Reinforced concrete and glass are the means by which liberation is attained and the idea of standardisation is seen as intrinsic to modern technology.

UNIVERSAL LANGUAGE

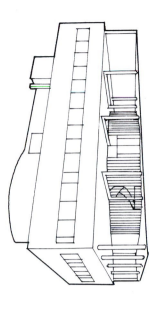

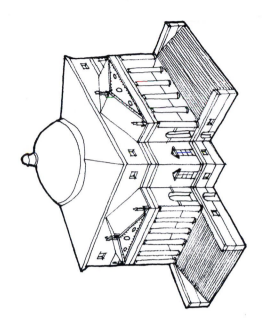

ANDREA PALLADIO   VILLA CAPRA VICENZA

In symbolic terms, the villa embodies a series of philosophical principles expressed in the architectural idiom which Le Corbusier had established at the beginning of the decade. This doctrinaire approach ranges over such factors as the perceptual potency of primary volumes and the use of such 'perfect' evolutionary functional elements as spiral stairs or ribbon windows, standard items of a universal architectural language.

The idea of an elevated villa, poised serenely above the landscape, was basic to Le Corbusier's idealistic vision at this time, a modern equivalent, in its sense of unity and equilibrium, of the Renaissance villa. Here the comparison is telling in that each form is essentially cubic and centralised, each employs a piano nobile and each uses a standard architectural language with a rich and appropriate vocabulary.

As the means by which the Villa Savoye attains both its elevation and sense of compositional freedom, the pilotis have special symbolic significance. They liberate the ground and signify a special kind of structure reflecting twentieth century technological advance. No less important than classical columns, pilotis represent a particular kind of structural discipline, recognising architecture's fundamental concern with the resolution of structural forces.

Although in simple terms the villa may be seen as an access volume, piano nobile and roof deck arranged so as to maximise opportunities for contact with nature, the elaborate development of this concept may properly be termed symphonic. The sophisticated articulation and lyricism of the design underscore Le Corbusier's prime symbolic intention that this modern temple should offer a profound emotional and intellectual experience, giving man contact with those cosmic forces which govern the Universe.

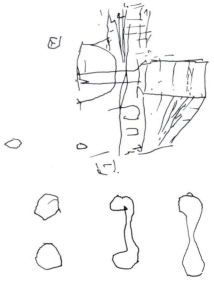

The Pavillon Suisse ranks with the villas Stein-de-Monzie and Savoye as a sublime icon of the Modern Movement, and its architectural language resembles that of these villas so that they all belong to the family of forms that would constitute the modern city.

The Pavillon exemplifies Le Corbusier's design method by the manner in which a generic orthogonal concept is modified in acknowledgement of site and programmatic forces. This transformation takes movement towards and into the form as a prime generator, this promenade architecturale being integral with the deployment of axes.

The route and axial discipline are organised within a Purist ensemble of planar layers. Functional components are clearly identified to confirm Le Corbusier's allegiance to the Modernist canon, but their fluent, poetic arrangement and the introduction of a natural material, stone, with pilotis shaped like bones, mark a crucial turning point in his work. Henceforth, the machine ceases to dominate his World view, so that increasingly, he returns to a concern for climate, nature and ecology as being fundamental to the human condition.

Santiago Calatrava has described the Pavillon Suisse as 'the absolute fruit of the most advanced and rigorous interpretation of the science of building of that period.'[1] Calatrava points out the dual structural image of the building in that the main slab and stair tower comprise a steel frame, this resting on a base of béton brut pilotis. These, in turn, rest on cylindrical concrete piles sunk deep into the ground. This subterranean penetration of the earth gives the building 'roots', evoking recollections of tree roots sketched when Jeanneret was a student in La Chaux-de-Fonds. This synthesis of nature and technology, first apparent in the craft-oriented Villa Fallet, reaches maturity in the Pavillon Suisse.

1 Santiago Calatrava, 'The Open Hand Architecture - Engineering,' In the footsteps of Le Corbusier, edited by Carlo Palazzolo and Riccardo Vio, Rizzoli, New York, 1989, p 192

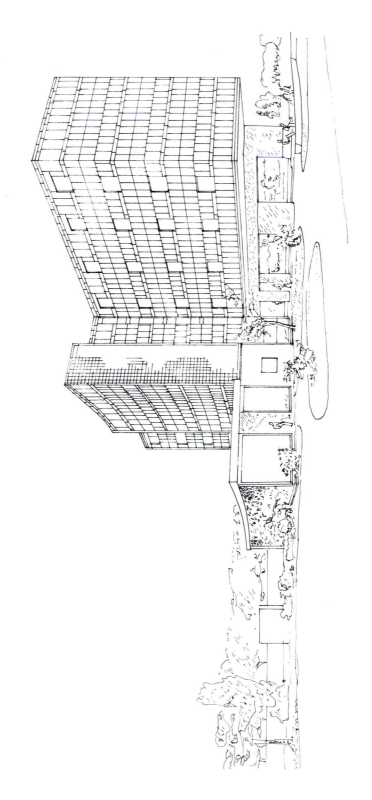

PAVILLON SUISSE PARIS 1930-32

SITE FORCES

Although the site has a dominant longitudinal axis at its southern boundary, several angled streets and a turning circle create a complex condition. The main approach is from the Boulevard Jourdan.

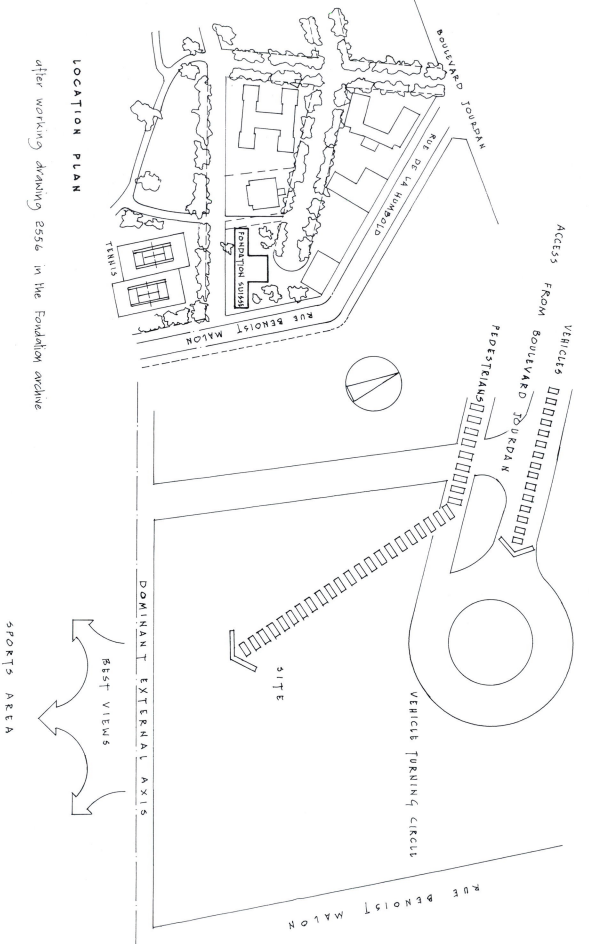

ACCESS FROM BOULEVARD JOURDAN

VEHICLES FROM BOULEVARD JOURDAN

PEDESTRIANS

SITE

VEHICLE TURNING CIRCLE

RUE BENOIST MALON

DOMINANT EXTERNAL AXIS

BEST VIEWS

SPORTS AREA

BOULEVARD JOURDAN

RUE DE LA HUMBOLD

RUE BENOIST MALON

FONDATION SUISSE

TENNIS

LOCATION PLAN

after working drawing 2556 in the Fondation archive

FIRST PROJECT

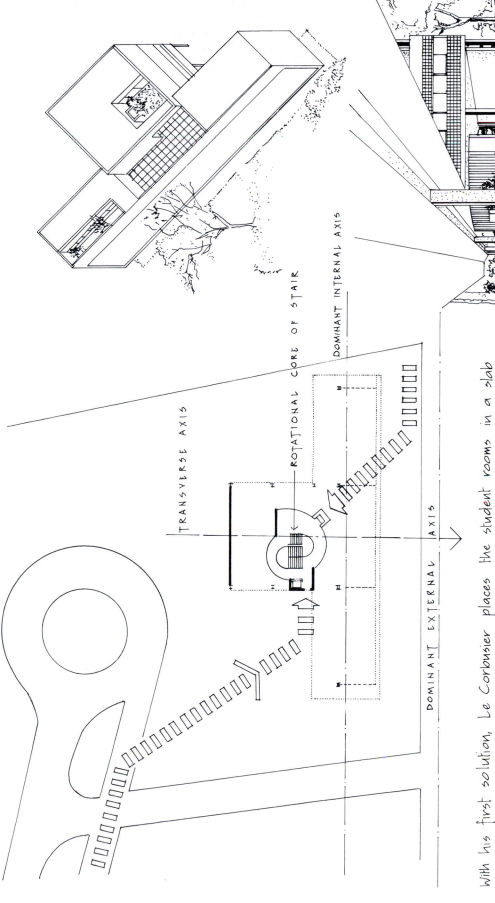

PROGRAMME : To provide a student hostel with rooms for 42 students; a Director's apartment; a library/refectory with small kitchen; an office for the concierge; two bedrooms for staff; a solarium.

TRANSVERSE AXIS

ROTATIONAL CORE OF STAIR

DOMINANT INTERNAL AXIS

DOMINANT EXTERNAL AXIS

With his first solution, Le Corbusier places the student rooms in a slab block overlooking the sports area, elevated by steel pilotis. To the north, he places a rectilinear block containing vertical circulation, bathrooms and communal services. This also being raised on steel pilotis. Entry is on two sides of a glazed module, the stair and curved edges having a rotational implication that echoes the turning circle nearby. To the rear, a wall closes the planar sequence at ground level

'Ribbon' windows, pilotis and entry glazing resemble the Villa Savoye.

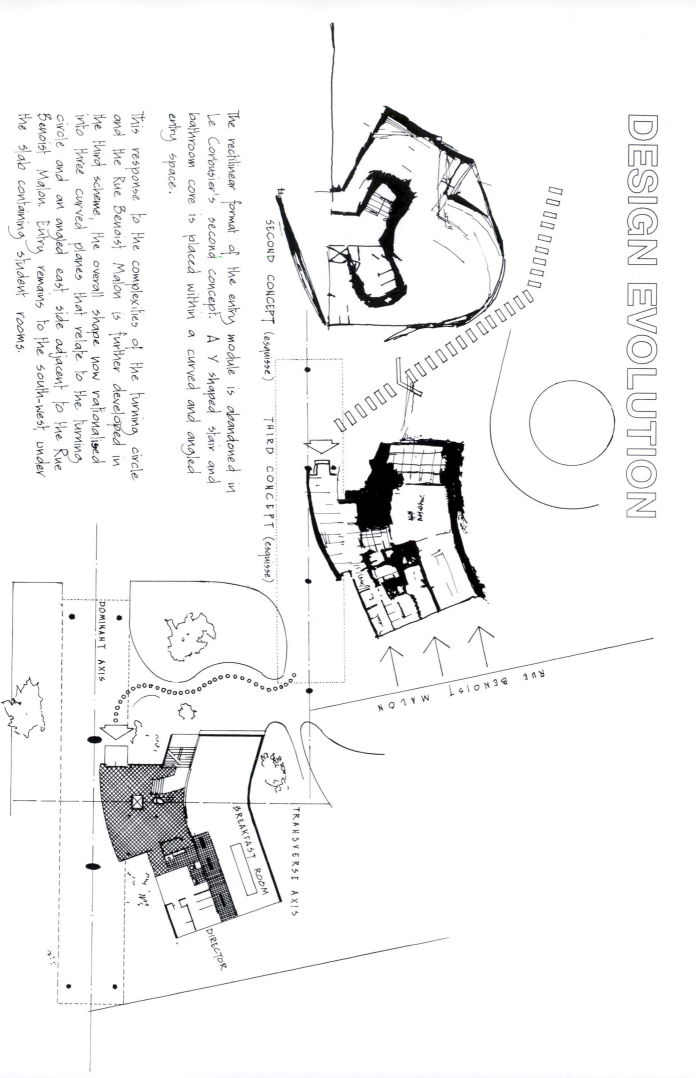

SECOND CONCEPT (esquisse)

THIRD CONCEPT (esquisse)

RUE BENOIST MALON

DOMINANT AXIS

BREAKFAST ROOM

TRANSVERSE AXIS

DIRECTOR

THIRD CONCEPT

The rectilinear format of the entry module is abandoned in Le Corbusier's second concept. A Y shaped stair and bathroom core is placed within a curved and angled entry space.

This response to the complexities of the turning circle and the Rue Benoist Malon is further developed in the third scheme, the overall shape now rationalised into three curved planes that relate to the turning circle and an angled east side adjacent to the Rue Benoist Malon. Entry remains to the south-west, under the slab containing student rooms.

esquisse sketches after drawings by Le Corbusier
218

SLAB TOWER AND PAVILION

As in the first concept, the planar sequence within the entry pavilion is closed with a solid wall. The central curved plane, attached to the stair, is part solid, part transparent. The third plane (under the slab) is transparent, confirming the layering from south to north as being from transparent to solid.

Three functional elements (stairs, a duct and an elevator) are displayed in the tiled entrance hall, the duct and elevator being located on the transverse axis, this marking the point of maximum curvature of the north wall. These elements ascend vertically within the stair/bathroom tower that is attached to the slab block. This tower locks the entry pavilion into the accommodation slab, acting as an intermediary between the two.

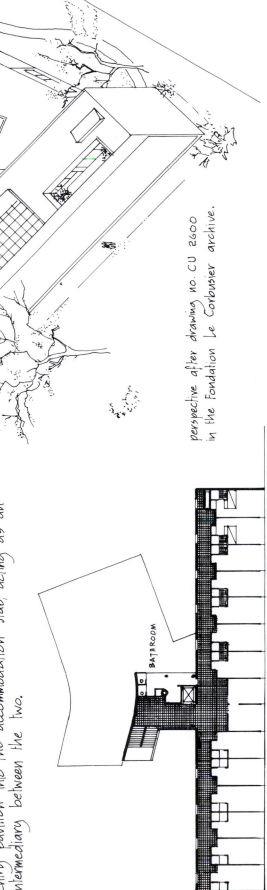

perspective after drawing no. CU 2600 in the Fondation Le Corbusier archive.

BATHROOM

PLAN OF TYPICAL FLOOR IN ACCOMMODATION BLOCK

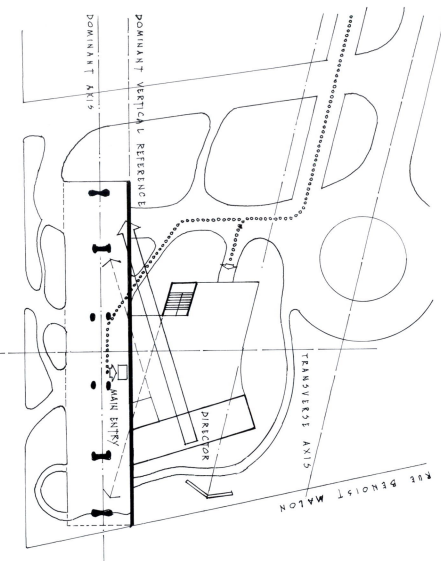

DOMINANT VERTICAL REFERENCE

DOMINANT AXIS

TRANSVERSE AXIS

RUE BENOIST MALON

MAIN ENTRY

DIRECTOR

EARLY PLAN OF THE FINAL SOLUTION SHOWING LE CORBUSIER'S 'PURIST' LAYOUT OF ROUTES AROUND THE BUILDING after working drawing CU 3007 in the Le Corbusier Foundation

A significant change in the final solution is the shifting of directional emphasis in the curved stone wall to the pavilion. In the third concept the longest straight section of this wall supported the thrust from the Rue Benoist Malon. In the final solution this wall is aligned with the access route.

In the third, and in his final solution, Le Corbusier aligns the north wall of the lower pavilion in two directions. The one, from north-west to south-east, follows the direction of the road leading towards the turning circle. The wall then curves in an alignment almost at right angles to the Rue Benoist Malon.

These two opposing directional thrusts are represented by incisions into the pavilion where it meets the vertical slab. To the west, this break in the form identifies the stair, and to the east, the break defines the Director's apartment.

The western edge of the pavilion is parallel with the transverse axis, a reminder of the orthogonal field generated by the rectilinear slab.

The juxtaposition of raised slab and adjacent pavilion gives added emphasis to the point where they meet and the north plane of the slab may be read as a dominant reference in the configuration.[1]

1   I am indebted to Peter Eisenman for this observation (in his doctoral dissertation 'The formal basis of modern architecture' p 204).

PROMENADE ARCHITECTURALE

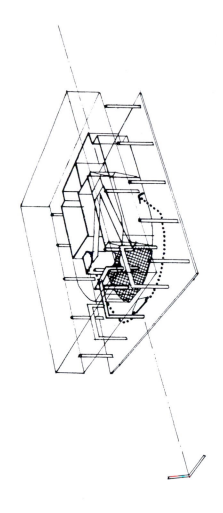

In his final solution, instead of allowing the lower pavilion to 'slide' under the vertical slab, Le Corbusier aligns its southern edge along the northern plane of the slab. This allows the entry route to be drawn onto the dominant longitudinal axis (formed by the pilotis) and then turned at a right angle to effect entry. The visitor is thus pulled towards the dominant axis established by the pilotis and is directed along this spine towards entry. [1]

THE VILLA SAVOYE (1929-31)

This progression towards entry is similar to that in the Villa Savoye in the way the route takes the visitor from one side of the building to the other, in the process moving under a slab in each case in a way that fully engages with the ensemble.

There are other strategic similarities. In each concept the promenade architecturale is directed onto the dominant longitudinal axis (the pilotis in the Pavillon Suisse and the ramp in the Villa Savoye). And in each project the slab generates an orthogonal field, its regular mass having a stabilising and unifying effect on those forms adjacent to it.

after a sketch by
Le Corbusier

[1] see Eisenman, ibid, pp. 201, 202.

COMPRESSION AND TENSION

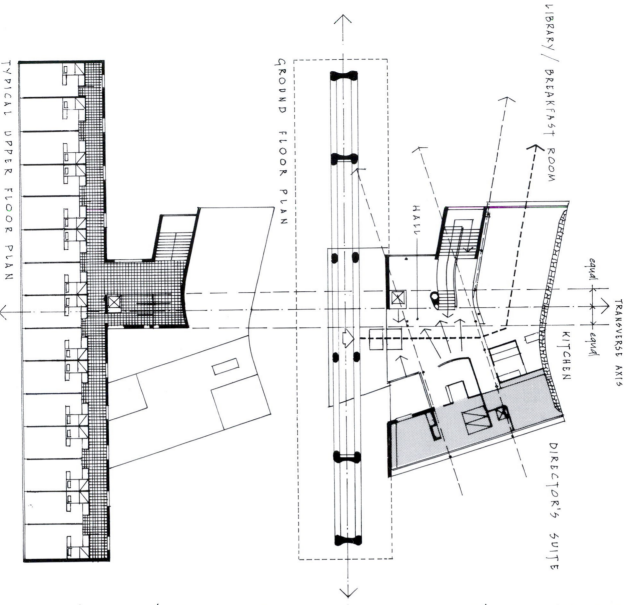

TYPICAL UPPER FLOOR PLAN

GROUND FLOOR PLAN

LIBRARY / BREAKFAST ROOM

TRANSVERSE AXIS

equal | equal

HALL

KITCHEN

DIRECTOR'S SUITE

Entry is through a vestibule that acts as a draught lobby. This 'box' is compressed between the elevator and an oblique glazed wall to the east. Moving forward, the space expands prior to further compression between the stair and curved screen opposite.

The stair emerges onto a low platform that twists round the service duct, the final descent being directed towards the curved screen opposite. This movement is then directed radially back into the entrance hall.

Finally, movement through a curved glazed screen into the library/breakfast room is pushed by the oblique kitchen wall along the north-west direction of the stone wall, towards the start of the movement sequence.

Columns on either side of the glazed wall act as directional markers in the space. The 'chest expander' outward pull of the pilotis intensifies the longitudinal axis, establishing a dynamic tension against the curved and oblique pavilion.

The curved walls are pulled inwards towards the longitudinal axis, their points of maximum curvature being equidistant from the lateral axis.

The western edge of the pavilion and the western edge of the entry platform are securely fixed onto the orthogonal grid exerted by the slab. The pavilion is thus 'held' by this field to the west and south.

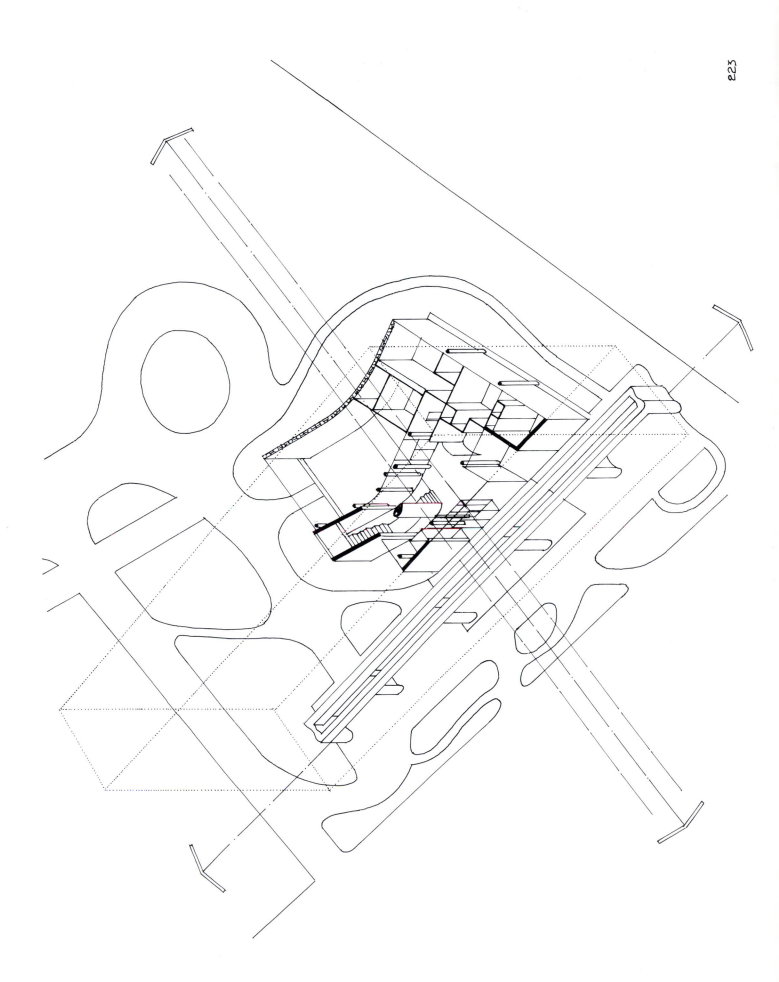

By introducing rubble walling and pilotis that 'evolve' into eroded 'bones', and then bone shapes, Le Corbusier recognises that the abstract imagery of machine-age functionalism is an inadequate representation of the human condition. Although the stone is presented in an abstracted surface format (as opposed to its traditional load-bearing role) this is a natural material, and references to bones send a message about the relationship between man and nature.

224

PILOTIS EVOLVE TO EXTEND OUTWARDS

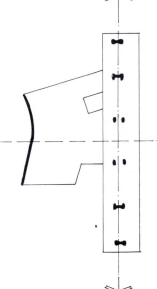

STATIC GENERIC PILOTIS

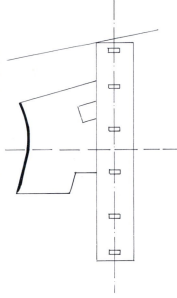

GROUPING OF WINDOWS ON NORTH ELEVATION ALSO SUGGESTS OUTWARD EXTENSION

POSSIBLE EVOLUTION OF PILOTIS INTO OVAL SHAPES

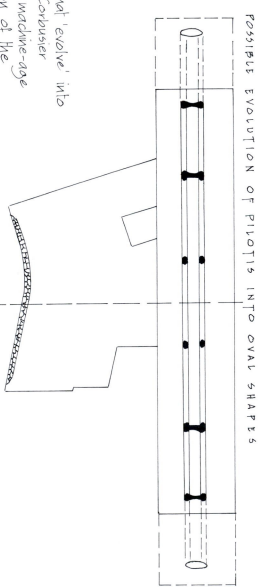

Pilotis grow in successive stages from the centre. This outward pull furthers the stretching of the longitudinal axis against which the curved and oblique forms of the pavilion are tensioned.

I was first alerted to this implication of extension at the Pavillon Suisse by Peter Eisenman: see p. 218 of 'The formal basis of modern architecture' (doctoral dissertation, University of Cambridge, 1963).

PLANAR LAYERING

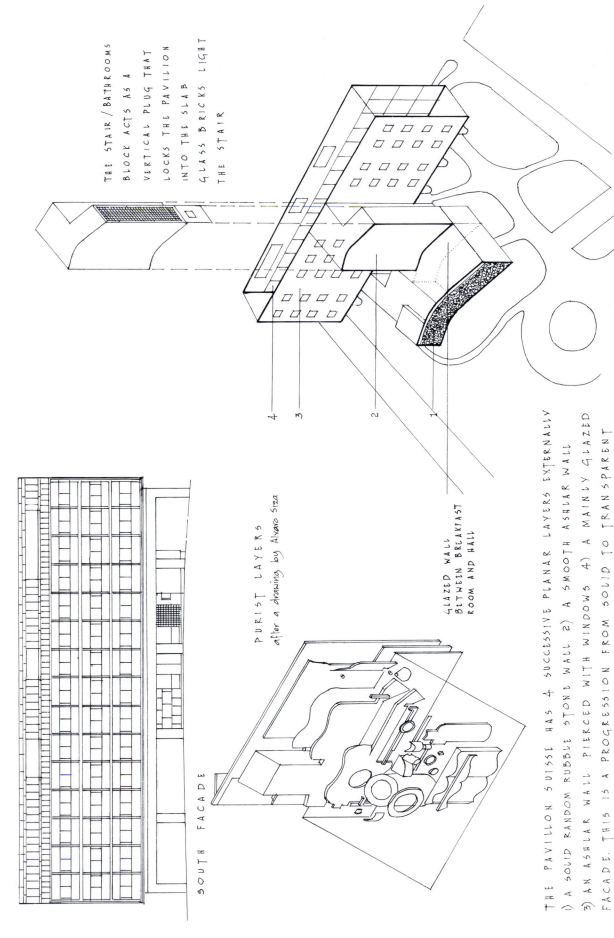

THE STAIR/BATHROOMS
BLOCK ACTS AS A
VERTICAL PLUG THAT
LOCKS THE PAVILION
INTO THE SLAB
GLASS BRICKS LIGHT
THE STAIR

4
3
2
1

SOUTH FACADE

PURIST LAYERS
after a drawing by Alvaro Siza

GLAZED WALL
BETWEEN BREAKFAST
ROOM AND HALL

THE PAVILLON SUISSE HAS 4 SUCCESSIVE PLANAR LAYERS EXTERNALLY
1) A SOLID RANDOM RUBBLE STONE WALL 2) A SMOOTH ASHLAR WALL
3) AN ASHLAR WALL PIERCED WITH WINDOWS 4) A MAINLY GLAZED
FACADE. THIS IS A PROGRESSION FROM SOLID TO TRANSPARENT

THE WALL RE-DEFINED

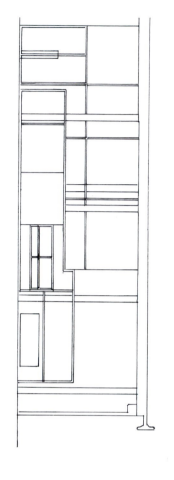

ELEVATION OF CURVED WALL

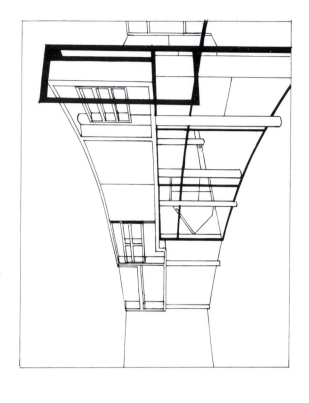

VIEW FROM BREAKFAST ROOM / LIBRARY

The curved glazed screen between the hall and breakfast room/library is one of Le Corbusier's most sophisticated compositions. A cupboard and shelves form a sculptural ensemble that rises at the point where the main stair occurs, with columns piercing the shelving and cupboard.

At the heart of the pavilion, the wall connects and separates the hall from the breakfast room. It participates in the planar layering as a three-dimensional construct that epitomises the functional lyricism and compositional freedom of Le Corbusier's Purist mode.

The wall participates in and visualises the complex directional energy inherent throughout the concept. Its curves and columns identify the twin thrusts of the pavilion, its taut formation being connected to and held by the obliquely placed stair.

The stair extends out into the hall as a twisting platform, in its final descent being wrapped around the services duct. The duct, like the columns that pierce the shelving in the breakfast room/library, stabilises a curving form. On either side of the curved wall, the columns continue towards the exterior, concluding beyond the Director's suite by being placed outside the pavilion. This positioning externalises the edge of the pavilion. This positioning externalises the directional thrust from the Director's suite towards the south-west. With this complex wall, Le Corbusier re-defined the role of the wall in twentieth century architecture, in the process proclaiming his liberation of architecture with the <u>plan libre</u>, structural flexibility, functional sculpture and planar layering.

FUNCTIONAL CLARITY

In the pavilion, the distinction between public and private space is marked by raising the ceiling in the breakfast room/library with clerestory lighting from the east. Rooflights are used over the kitchen and bedroom and the Director's office also has a raised ceiling. Externally, this identifies an important room and strengthens the corner with yet another directional thrust, this time to the north.

The window walls to the east and west are encased in timber frames, a panel reading that gives a substantial weighting to these extremities (as opposed to being merely glass walls). The stone wall is abstracted from its traditional load-bearing role by its surface treatment as pattern within pronounced mortar joints.

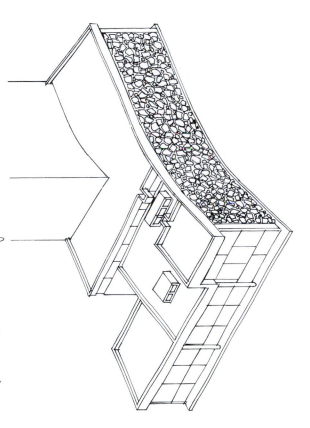

Le Corbusier encased the glazed end walls of the Jaoul Houses (1954-56) in a similar manner to his treatment of this condition at the Pavillon Suisse (see page 244).

PUBLIC | PRIVATE

5 THE POST-WAR PHASE

Towards the end of the twenties, Le Corbusier's infatuation with the machine began to recede in favour of a return towards fresh interpretations of nature. Natural forms including bones, shells and the human figure were introduced into his paintings; stone was used on the Swiss Pavilion at the University of Paris; and during the thirties a series of 'primitive' buildings emerged using stone and timber construction.

These ideas crystallized in the Weekend House in a Paris suburb (1935)[2], built in stone, using glass bricks, with a grass-covered roof of reinforced concrete. This low, ground-hugging image, with such a natural material as stone, was diametrically opposed to the elevated cubic architecture of the twenties. This new approach drew on Le Corbusier's constant fascination with vernacular architecture, and reflects an attempt to evolve an appropriate contemporary language using natural materials.

This attitude was the result of many factors, one of which was the failure in a practical sense of many of Le Corbusier's twenties' buildings. The rooflights on Ozenfant's studio had to be removed and the metal windows on several buildings became rusty and twisted. The concrete blocks which comprised the walls of many buildings were poor insulators with the stucco surface also causing problems. Many buildings (including the Salvation Army Building in Paris and Le Corbusier's own apartment) were overglazed and suffered from solar overheating, causing him to invent the brise soleil.

By the 1950's Le Corbusier had reassessed his position and his post-war work shows a redeployment of both form and materials in response to fresh priorities. In the domestic sphere, the Maisons Jaoul demonstrate this shift in strategy, offering a model intended as a universal solution, which in most respects reverses the techniques and ideology of the twenties decade.

1 see diagrams on pages 225 and 227
2 see diagram on page 337

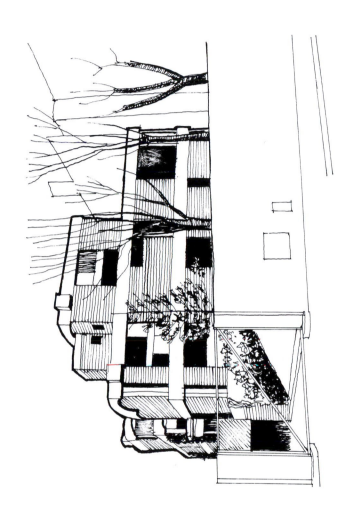

THE JAOUL HOUSES 1954-56

SITE FORCES

The Jaoul houses are located in the fashionable Neuilly area of Paris, fairly near the Bois de Boulogne. Two houses were required, providing typical family accommodation for the parents and for their son, his wife and children. This relationship between the parents and their son and his family became a central concern in Le Corbusier's concept.

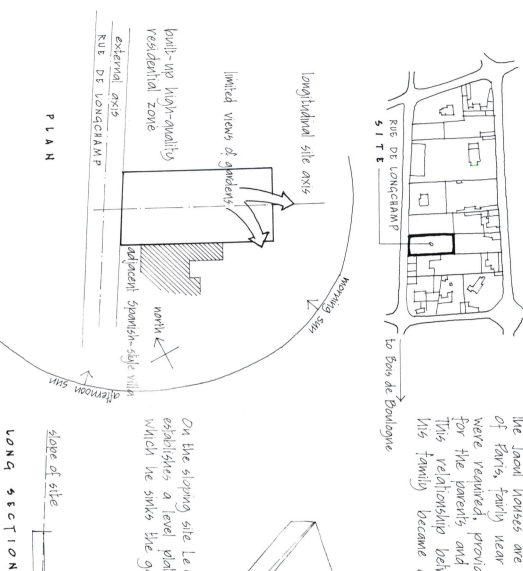

RUE DE LONGCHAMP

SITE

to Bois de Boulogne

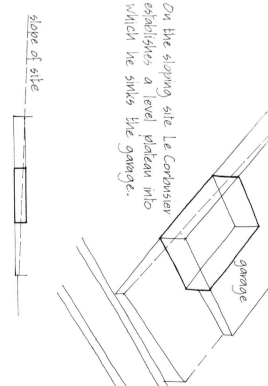

longitudinal site axis

limited views of gardens

built-up high-quality residential zone

external axis
RUE DE LONGCHAMP

adjacent Spanish-style villa

north

morning sun

afternoon sun

PLAN

slope of site

garage

On the sloping site Le Corbusier establishes a level plateau into which he sinks the garage.

LONG SECTION

INTERLOCK

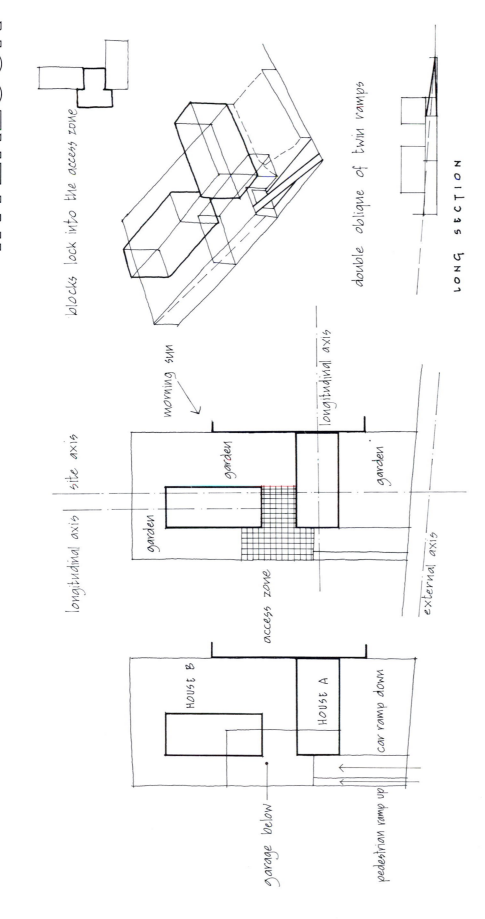

blocks lock into the access zone

double oblique of twin ramps

LONG SECTION

morning sun

site axis

longitudinal axis

longitudinal axis

garden

garden

garden

access zone

external axis

HOUSE B

HOUSE A

car ramp down

garage below

pedestrian ramp up

The houses are arranged at right angles giving a secluded garden to the rear. Ramps lead up to the access zone and down to the garage.

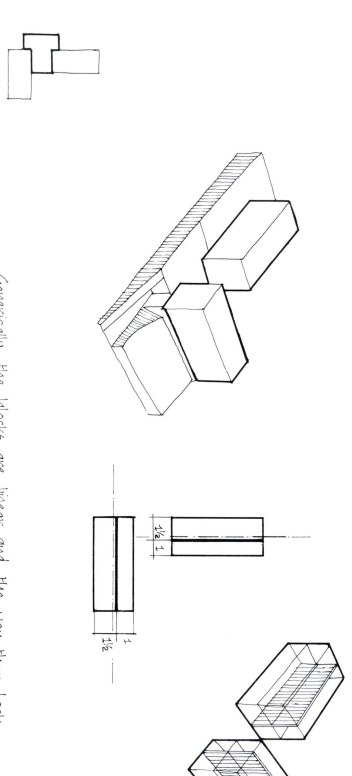

Generically the blocks are linear and the way they lock into the access zone suggests a possible relationship between them. The space between the houses therefore has special significance.

Spine walls increase the linearity, reduce the span and divide the blocks into major and minor cells.

VAULTED SYSTEM

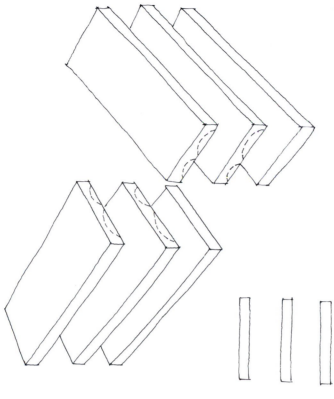

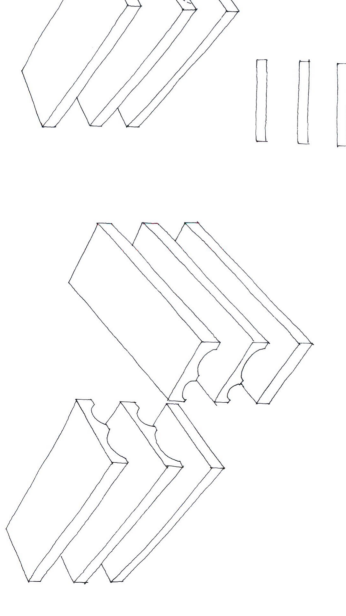

Vaults are contained within the slab in a 'sandwich' statement of horizontal stratification.

The floor slabs are vaulted in accord with the plan subdivision.

VAULTS EXPRESSED

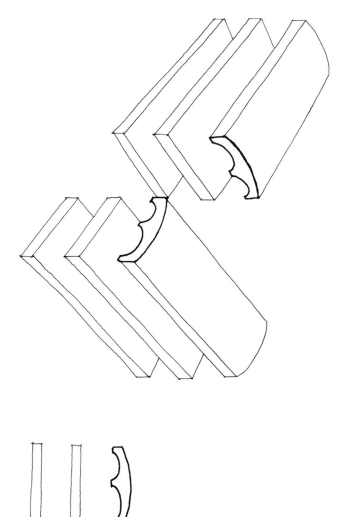

Each configuration is transformed by the curvature of the roof and by the expression of the vaults at roof level only. Horizontality remains the dominant idea with the main contrast between the rectilinear slab floors and the curvilinear roof.

TRANSFORMATION

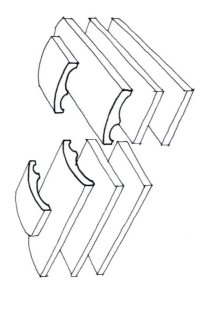

ADDITIONAL CURVED ROOFS

The generic cubic mass is divided into horizontal layers which are transformed by the curved roof and vaulted expression at roof level. Additional curved roofs and the alignment of the blocks add vitality to the configuration.

HORIZONTAL LAYERS

VAULTS AND CURVED ROOF

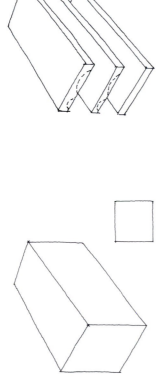

GENERIC STATIC CUBIC

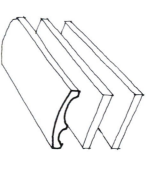

CURVED ROOF

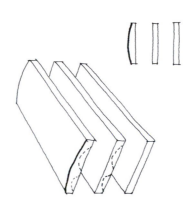

TRANSFORMATION OF THE CUBIC MASS

PRIMARY CONCEPT

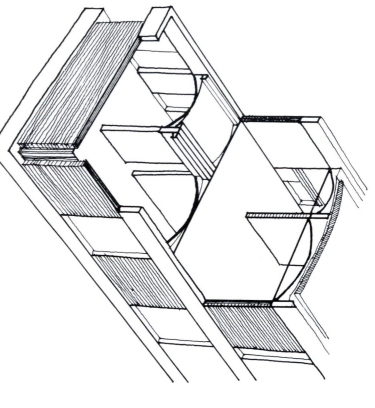

The primary concept of the Jaoul houses is that of vaults supported continuously by beams resting on loadbearing brick panels. The contrast between brick panel and concrete beam is essential to this theme and tie bars express the tension between vault and support. To preserve the clarity of the statement slabs project beyond the ends of the panels, which do not meet at the corners.

BASIC STATEMENT

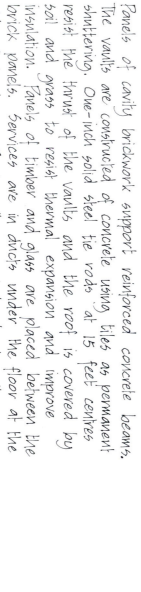

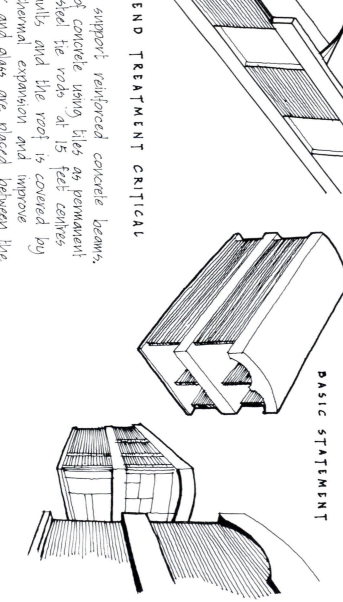

END TREATMENT CRITICAL

Panels of cavity brickwork support reinforced concrete beams. The vaults are constructed of concrete using tiles as permanent shuttering. One-inch solid steel tie rods at 15 feet centres resist the thrust of the vaults and the roof is covered by soil and grass to resist thermal expansion and improve insulation. Panels of timber and glass are placed between the brick panels. Services are in ducts under the floor at the side of the beams. Brick walls are plastered internally.

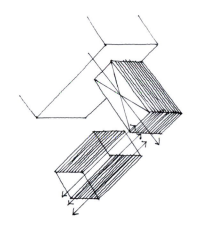

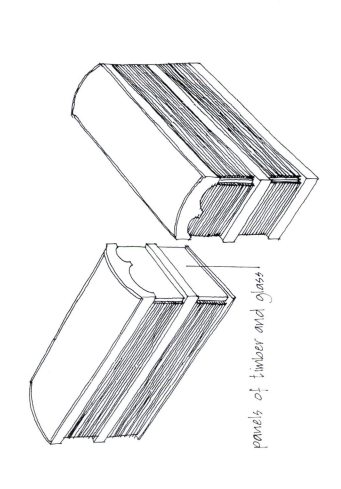

panels of timber and glass

The end treatment intensifies the linearity in House B and reduces the linearity in House A thereby establishing an anchorage role for House A and a link role for House B.

The corner treatment of House A ensures a panel reading, preserving consistency between the membranes in both houses.

GEOMETRY

The stairs in House B are aligned with the extremity of the garage below. Similarly the stairs in House A lead to the garage and are placed in line with the spine wall of House B.

The upper blocks on houses A and B are placed in the same relationship to the spine walls. By these means the two houses are geometrically related to each other.

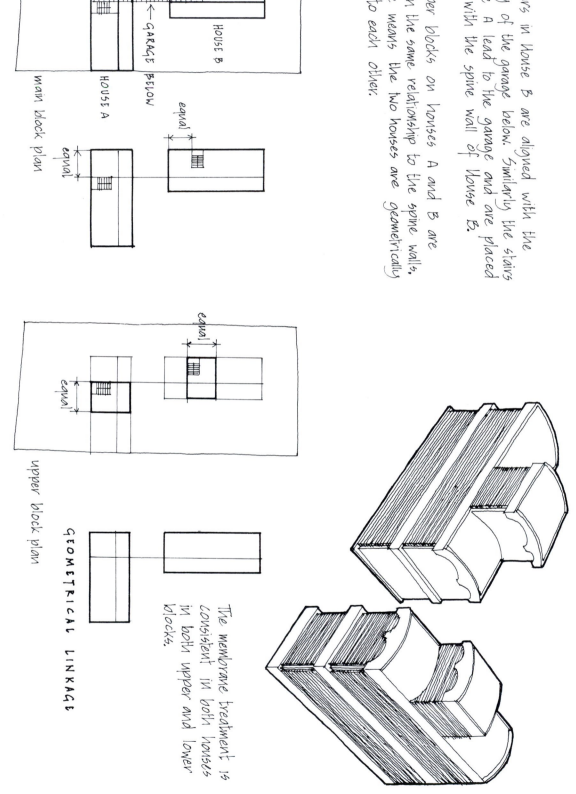

HOUSE B

← GARAGE BELOW

HOUSE A

equal

equal

main block plan

equal

equal

upper block plan

GEOMETRICAL LINKAGE

The membrane treatment is consistent in both houses in both upper and lower blocks.

PRIMACY OF HOUSE A

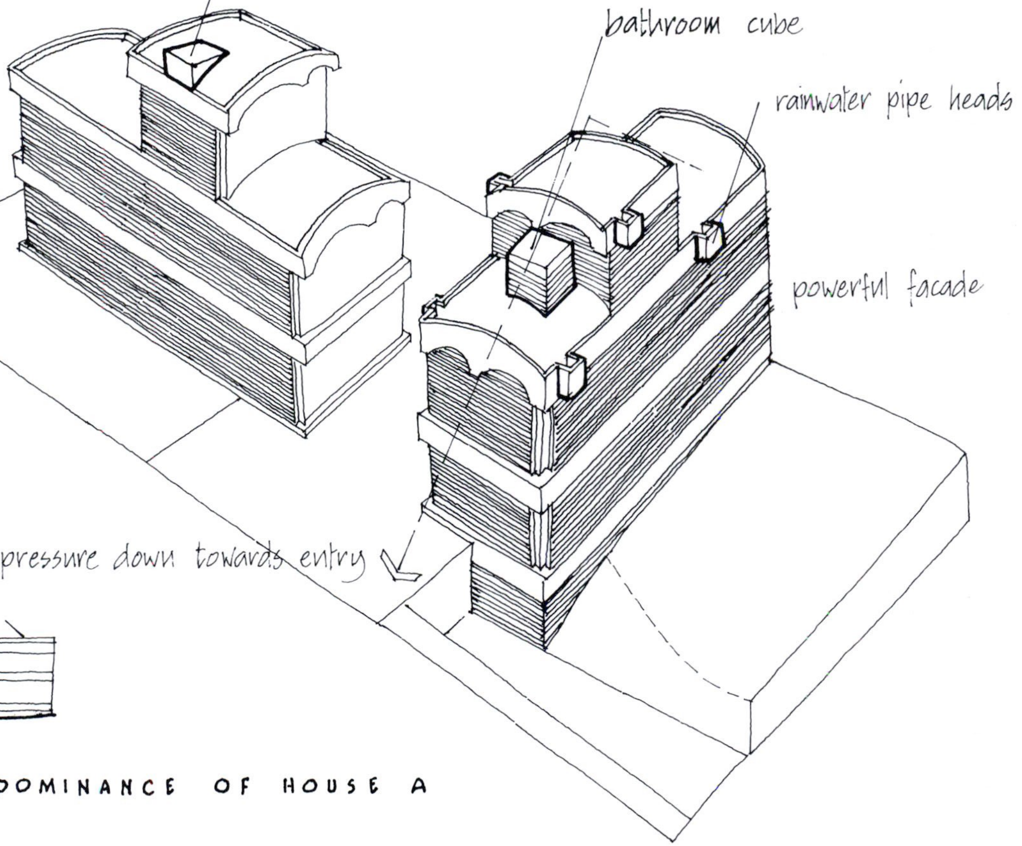

rooflight to studio on House B

bathroom cube

rainwater pipe heads

powerful facade

pressure down towards entry

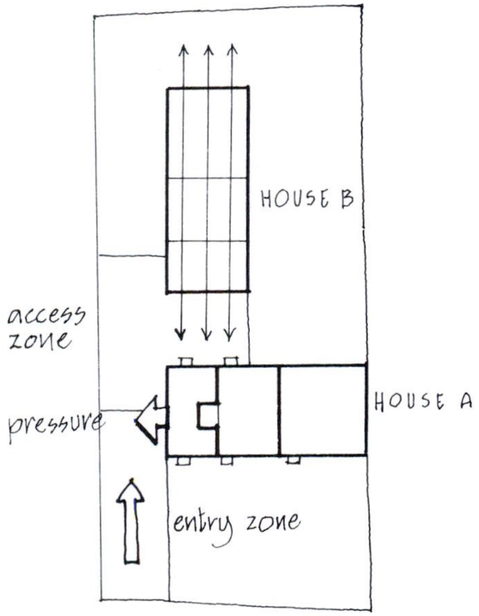

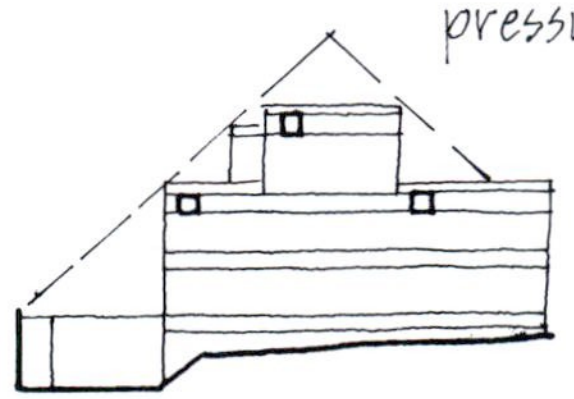

PYRAMIDAL DOMINANCE OF HOUSE A

HOUSE B

HOUSE A

access zone

pressure

entry zone

pressure

PRESSURE TOWARDS ENTRY

The heads of rainwater pipes are expressed as projecting cubes on House A. A small bathroom cube is added to the upper block of House A so that it forms part of a pyramidal formation which exerts pressure as the visitor moves past the end of the house. House A assumes primacy with a protective anchorage role.

241

THEME AND TACTICS

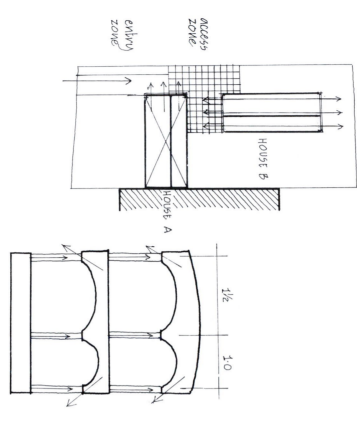

access
zone

entry
zone

HOUSE A

HOUSE B

1½

1:0

The interdependent relationship between the two families forms the basis of the Jaoul houses theme. This receives expression through the arrangement, in which House A (the parents house) assumes primacy with a sheltering protective role of stable anchorage. House B is relegated to a secondary, though more dynamic role, being linked to House A by its end treatment and by the way both houses lock into the access zone.

The theme is developed in a number of specific ways which demonstrate ie Corbusier's changed view of the dwelling and include the following tactical measures:

1) a vaulted structure of thrust and counter thrust

2) the support role of loadbearing walls.

3) the importance of end and corner treatment in each house

4) the horizontality, oblique thrust **and** 1½-1 rhythm of the vaults themselves

5) the exertion of a directional pressure from House A towards the entry zone

6) intensification of the linearity of House B with its implication of linkage to House A

7) the location of entry and access zones to further the general intention

8) a particular strategy towards the external membrane treatment including fenestration

9) the up-down oblique contrast of the entry ramps

242

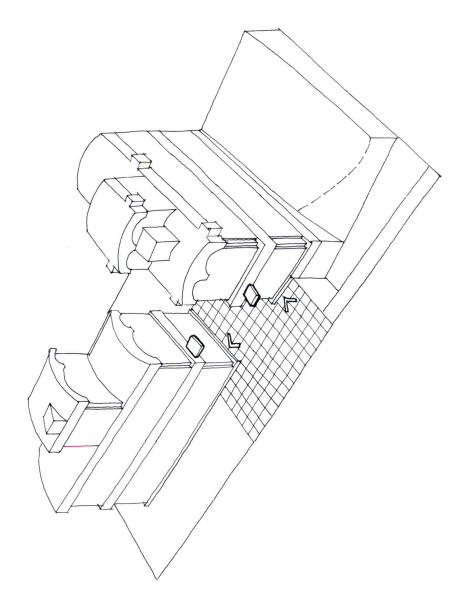

Entry to each house is located in the access zone and
defined in each case by a simple cantilevered concrete canopy.
Points of entry conform to the linearity of each block.

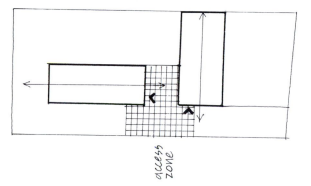

access
zone

ENTRY ELEVATION

LIVING

STUDY

DINING

KIT.

VESTIBULE

WC

main entry

secondary entry

GROUND PLAN HOUSE B

Panels are faced with plywood.
They have glazed inserts and
have shelves and shutters inside.

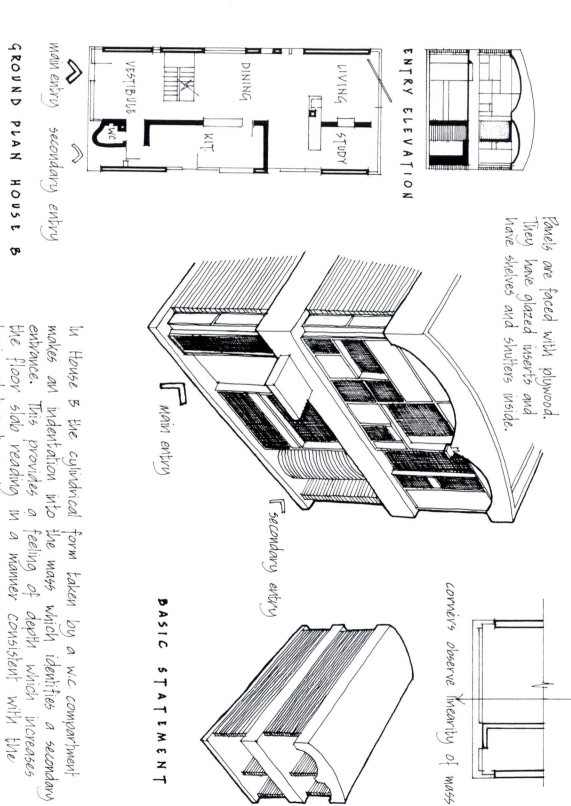

main entry

secondary entry

BASIC STATEMENT

corners observe linearity of mass

In House B the cylindrical form taken by a w.c. compartment
makes an indentation into the mass which identifies a secondary
entrance. This provides a feeling of depth which increases
the floor slab reading in a manner consistent with the
basic statement.

FENESTRATION

The Jaoul window design is similar to the treatment of the south wall of the Chapel at Ronchamp in providing varied shapes, sizes and three-dimensionality of the glazing. The changing quality of light throughout the day adds to the sense of animation which this system affords.

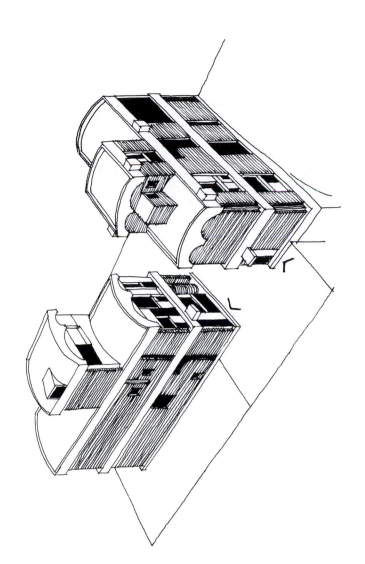

The fenestration membrane at each end of House B consists of non-loadbearing timber and glass screens framed in accord with the Modulor [1] to form a complex three-dimensional construction containing solid, opaque and transparent panels.

The use of a structural frame for this fenestration provides a pattern which gives human scale to the building while indicating that these are panels fixed on to the ends of the loadbearing walls. Being to some extent solid (by having depth) makes these panels of a similar order through different function to the brick panels on the end of House A. By this means the individual character of each house is retained within a uniform design system of panel and beam.

The edge beams distribute the vault thrust evenly along the supporting walls and allowed Le Corbusier freedom to distribute windows as he wished, giving far more flexibility than had been possible with the ribbon windows of the twenties. During the Purist period, windows had formed part of a skin apparently stretched tightly over a frame. With the Jaoul Houses the structural nature of the wall changes the role of the fenestration so that windows are recessed and arranged to intensify the load bearing structural reading of the brick panels.

1 Le Corbusier's mathematical proportional system based on the human figure

BALCONIES

Balconies project out from each house to receive sun and obtain a view. In House B where the balcony is an extension to the vault a cantilever is used; in House A, where this is not the case, a support column is used. Balcony edges are detached so as not to interfere with the main slab reading of each mass.

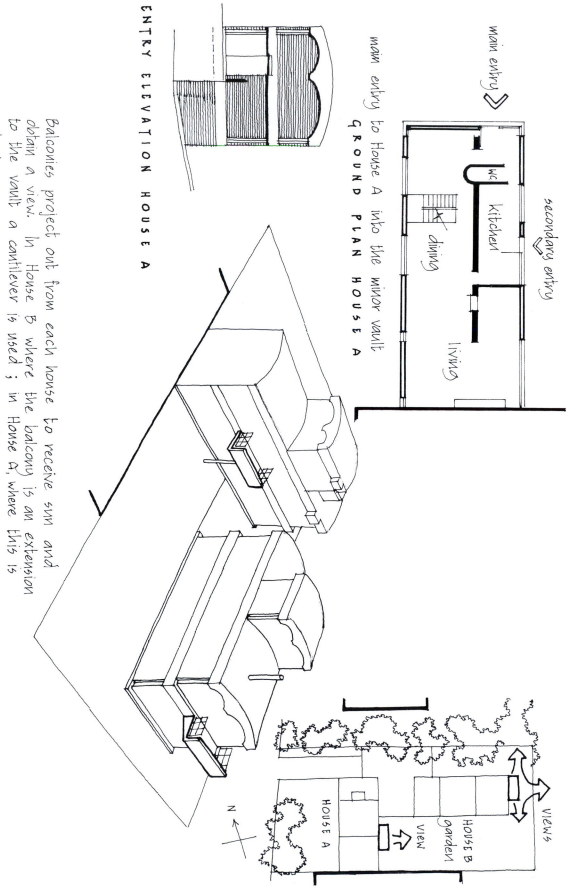

ENTRY ELEVATION HOUSE A

main entry to House A into the minor vault

GROUND PLAN HOUSE A

main entry

secondary entry

wc

kitchen

dining

living

HOUSE A

HOUSE B

garden

VIEW

VIEWS

N

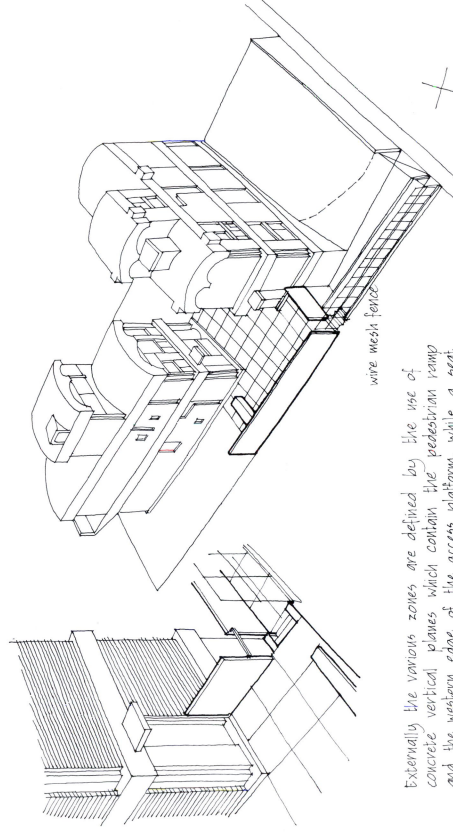

wire mesh fence

Externally the various zones are defined by the use of
concrete vertical planes which contain the pedestrian ramp
and the western edge of the access platform, while a seat
containing a window to light the garage below defines the
access platform where it meets the lawn to the north
of House B. Square concrete paving slabs are used in
the access zone and a concrete wall and seat contain the
zone at the northern boundary of the site.

MOVEMENT SEQUENCE

As usual, Le Corbusier controls the movement sequence in relation to his massing arrangement. From the road the first impression is one of compact power, the houses having considerable visual impact by virtue of their unusual form and complexity.

The pedestrian ramp is like a bridge effecting the transition from public to private domain. The ramp gives a sense of confinement furthered by the close proximity of the end of House A.

The access zone is separated from the ramp by steps, with a concrete wall above the garage helping to define this special area. In contrast to the confined ramp, the access platform is expansive, a resting place prior to entry which allows full contemplation of the complex. In this it is similar to a square in providing a formal setting which links the houses.

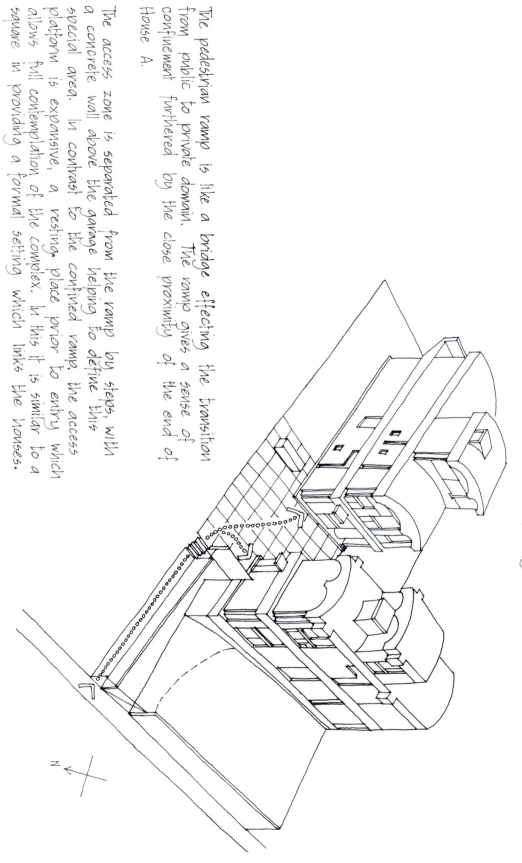

N

HOUSE A

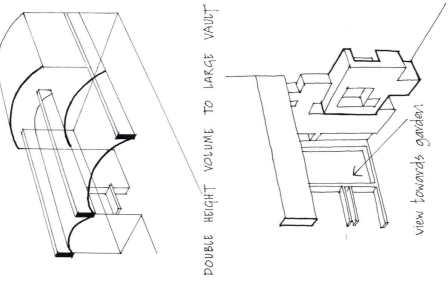

DOUBLE HEIGHT VOLUME TO LARGE VAULT

view towards garden

COMPLEX MODELLING REDUCES SCALE

vertical space

horizontal space

PROBLEM OF LINKING TWO KINDS OF SPACE

top light

FIREPLACE ACTS AS DIRECTIONAL LINK

HORIZONTALS AND OBLIQUES ASSIST SPATIAL LINKAGE

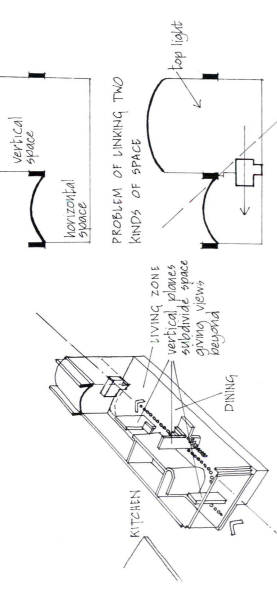

KITCHEN

LIVING ZONE vertical planes subdivide space giving views beyond

DINING

On entry the tiny vestibule gives a glimpse of the space beyond. Movement is then directed around the curve of the w.c. along an axis defined by the vertical plane supporting the stair.

Le Corbusier allows light to fall on the end wall from a large window in the upper part of the double height volume which identifies the living zone. This well-lit wall draws the observer towards it where attention is then focussed on the fireplace. This is carefully modelled to link the major and minor spaces and bring down the scale.

HOUSE B

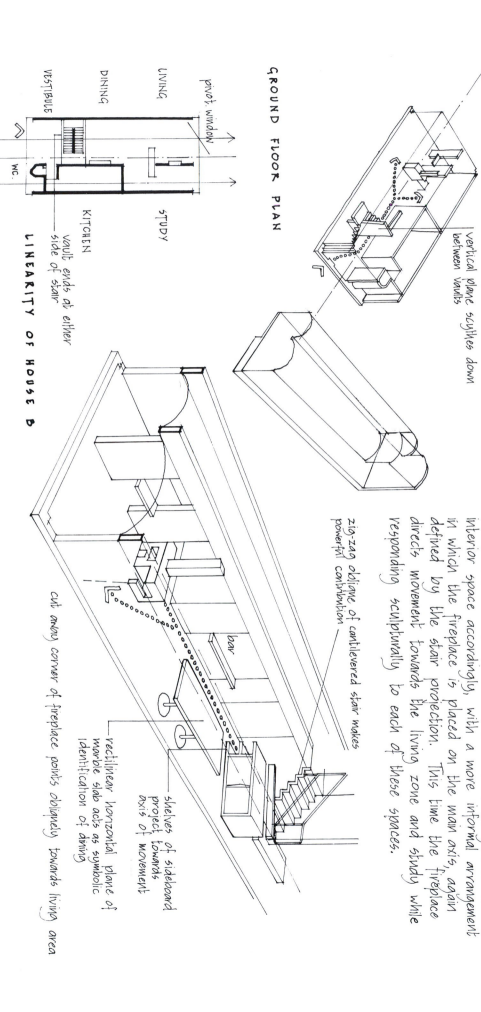

vertical plane scythes down between vaults

GROUND FLOOR PLAN

pivot window

VESTIBULE
DINING
LIVING

STUDY

KITCHEN

vault ends at either side of stair

LINEARITY OF HOUSE B

cut away corner of fireplace points obliquely towards living area

rectilinear horizontal plane of marble slab acts as symbolic identification of dining

shelves of sideboard project towards axis of movement

bar

zig-zag oblique of cantilevered stair makes powerful combination

Unlike House A with its termination at an end wall and primary anchorage role, House B has a pronounced 'open ended' linear characteristic. Le Corbusier organises the interior space accordingly, with a more informal arrangement in which the fireplace is placed on the main axis, again defined by the stair projection. This time the fireplace directs movement towards the living zone and study while responding sculpturally to each of these spaces.

FIREPLACE SCULPTURE

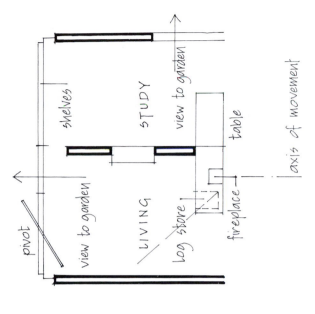

shelves

view to garden

pivot

STUDY

LIVING

Log store

view to garden

fireplace

table

axis of movement

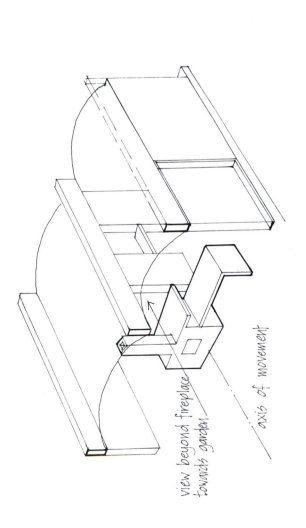

view beyond fireplace
towards garden

axis of movement

The fireplace becomes a composite relating to both living zone and study by the attachment of a concrete table. The axial location is recognised by the chimney which becomes a focus on the movement route and significantly unlike the fireplace in House A which is a visual stop, the 'open ended' linearity of House B is recognised by the view over and beyond the fireplace towards the garden. The fireplace becomes a work of sculpture which symbolises the activities of two adjacent spaces.

MEANING

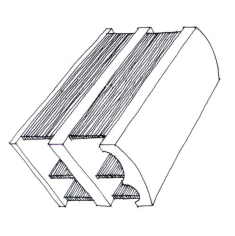 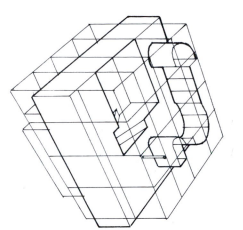

The Jaoul Houses bear no resemblance to the white cubic architecture of the twenties. The Utopian vision of houses elevated above the landscape to maximise contact with sun and nature is replaced by an introverted almost defensive approach in which privacy, strength and security seem paramount.

Instead of a framed structure, a 'stretched skin' membrane with large glazed areas and interpenetrating planes, the Jaoul Houses project an image of heavy vaults supported by loadbearing brickwork.

The machine is no longer the leitmotif, and analogous reference to aircraft, liners or factories is displaced by a shift of emphasis away from abstract idealism towards fundamental questions relating to the family unit. If the most pervasive symbol of the twenties language is the roof terrace, its replacement by vaults suggests profound symbolic implications which allude to man's evolutionary past.

Man once lived in caves, the Romans used concrete vaults extensively, and the soft feminine curves and tunnel-like shelter afforded by the Jaoul Houses show Le Corbusier now preoccupied with ideas of the dwelling as a maternal refuge, womb-like and rooted in mother earth.

The doctrinaire certainty of the twenties, demonstrated in an architecture of clear prisms and precise primary forms is replaced by an acknowledgement of the mystery of the life-force with forms that are not immediately comprehensible, containing ambiguities and contradictions.

TECHNIQUE

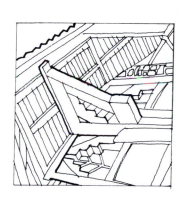

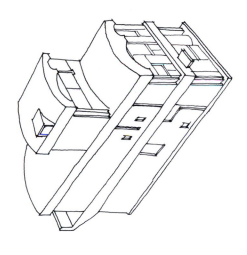

In technique, Le Corbusier returns to the interest during his formative years in surface texture, pattern and the properties of materials. In his powerful handling of concrete we are reminded of the way stone was used in his early villas in La Chaux-de-Fonds, and the kind of elaborate pattern displayed on the ends of House B is reminiscent of the gables of the Villas Fallet and Stotzer. Similar too is the use of a firm base and expressive roof, and the Jaoul Houses are compact 'closed' linear forms with powerful massing controlled by geometry.

The corners of the Villas Jeanneret-Perret and Favre-Jacot had been clearly defined and they receive special attention in the Jaoul Houses. Within the vaulted framework, interior spaces are intimate with the loadbearing support theme using vertical planes to give glimpses of spaces beyond. Colour is used in a very positive way, with cream floor tiles throughout and terra cotta quarry tiles to the underside of vaults. Walls are in white plaster, with panels of blue, yellow, vermilion and dull green giving warmth or coldness where appropriate, using a colour coding developed by Le Corbusier during the Purist phase.

Perhaps the most striking difference between Le Corbusier's pre and post-war work, and particularly evident in the Jaoul Houses, is the quality of light in interior spaces. With more flexible fenestration, light is deployed with drama and subtlety so that the houses express varied moods, having a serenity and emotional content impossible to achieve to the same degree with the earlier architectural language.

The site of the chapel at Ronchamp has had religious significance for centuries, being mentioned for the first time in 1269 as a place of pilgrimage. In the autumn of 1944, French artillery attacked German troops occupying the area, and in the ensuing battle the existing chapel was destroyed.

At first Le Corbusier was not interested in the project, remembering the difficulties he had encountered on the St. Baume scheme. According to Joseph Savina,[1] it was to give pleasure to his mother that he accepted the commission.

Le Corbusier visited the site for the first time in June 1950, and according to a story, having insisted on walking up the hill, he exclaimed 'It will be good that the chapel will give a welcome for the people coming up because they will be out of breath.'[2]

Intended as a chapel to be visited on twice yearly pilgrimages. The brief required space for an outdoor mass for the assembled multitude. In addition, three small chapels were required, permitting celebration of the office independent of the collective mass. A choir stall, altar and pulpit were needed outside as well as inside for ceremonies in the open air on pilgrimage days. A sacristy was also needed and a small office. It was also a requirement of the brief to collect rainwater which falls on the hill.

_____

1   Joseph Savina 'Sculptures de Le Corbusier temoinages,' Art and Architecture no 51 Nov 1955 pp. 96-101.

2   quoted from a doctoral dissertation by Danièle Pauly, La Chapelle de Ronchamp de Le Corbusier, Universite des Sciences Humaines de Strasbourg, p. 31.

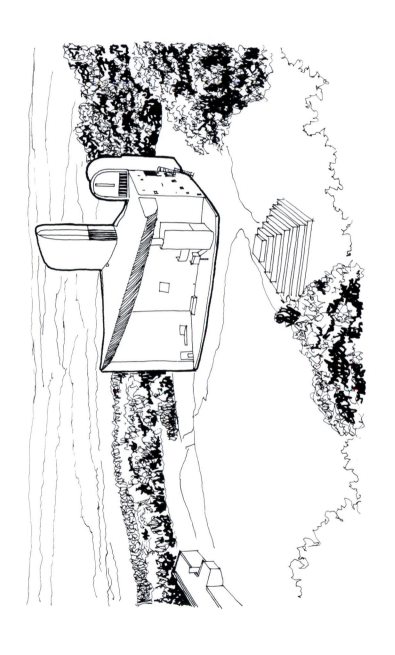

NOTRE-DAME-DU-HAUT RONCHAMP 1950-55

SITE FORCES

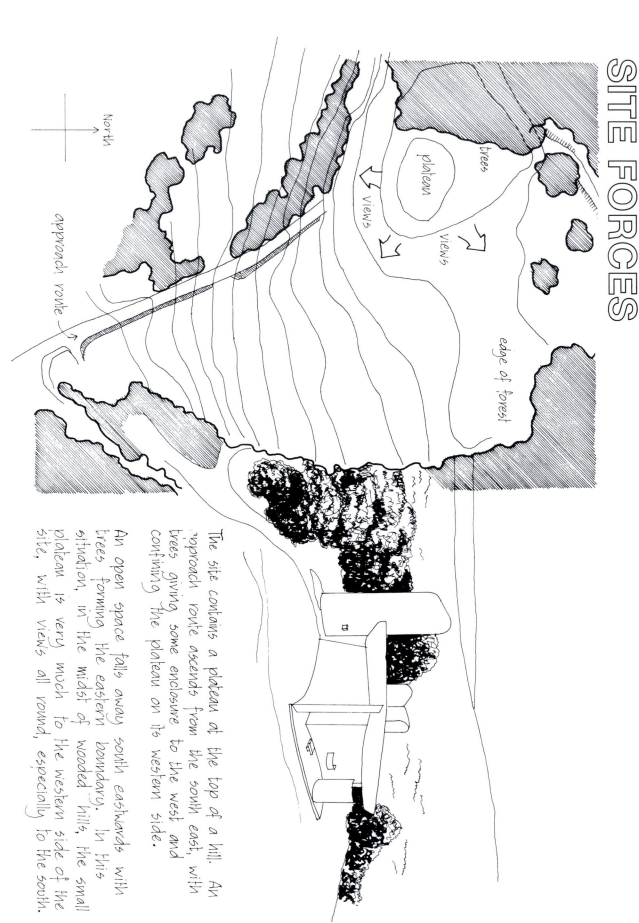

North

approach route

plateau

trees

Views

Views

edge of forest

The site contains a plateau at the top of a hill. An approach route ascends from the south east, with trees giving some enclosure to the west and confining the plateau on its western side.

An open space falls away south eastwards with trees forming the eastern boundary. In this situation, in the midst of wooded hills, the small plateau is very much to the western side of the site, with views all round, especially to the south.

Geoffrey H. Baker 1988

SITE IMPLICATIONS

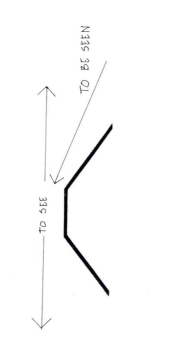

The plateau and its hilltop location suggest a monument of some visual consequence.

GENERIC CIRCLE

The plateau has centroidal implications and the liturgical requirements of a chapel may be interpreted in centroidal terms.

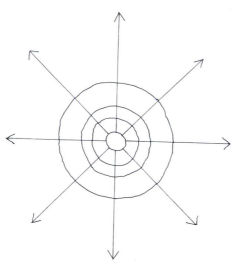

Any vertical structure placed on the site must act as a beacon visible for miles.

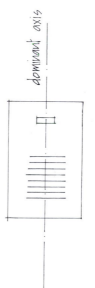

dominant axis

However Le Corbusier opts for a rectilinear configuration with a dominant linear axis.

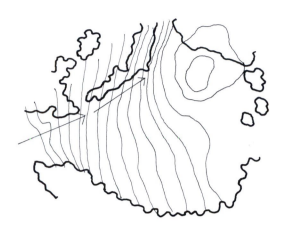

The approach route is from the south east flanking the open area, with the contours also giving a south eastern slope.

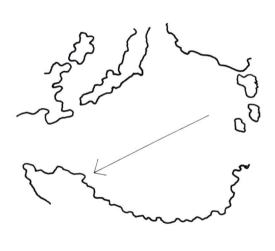

The site has an oblique characteristic.

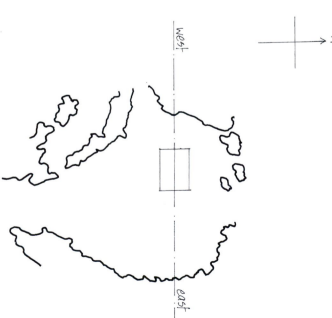

The chapel is placed at the high point on an east-west axis.

N

west

east

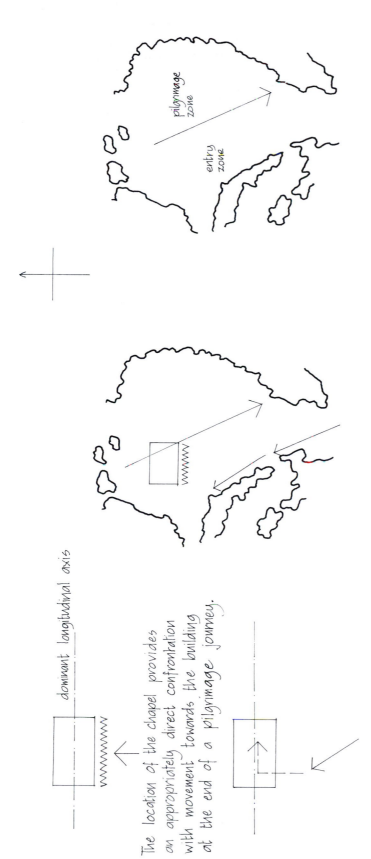

dominant longitudinal axis

The location of the chapel provides
an appropriately direct confrontation
with movement towards the building
at the end of a pilgrimage journey.

The initial problem is how to turn
the oblique approach on to the
longitudinal axis.

pilgrimage zone

entry zone

Le Corbusier establishes separate zones
for entry and pilgrimage assembly,
separated by the site oblique.

The situation is therefore one of confrontation
between movement and the building within
the circumstances of an oblique site condition.

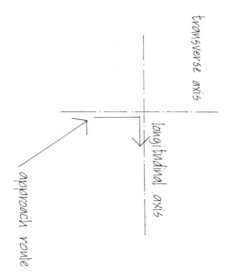

transverse axis

longitudinal axis

approach route

The movement route towards the chapel is turned on to the longitudinal axis by forming a transverse axis.

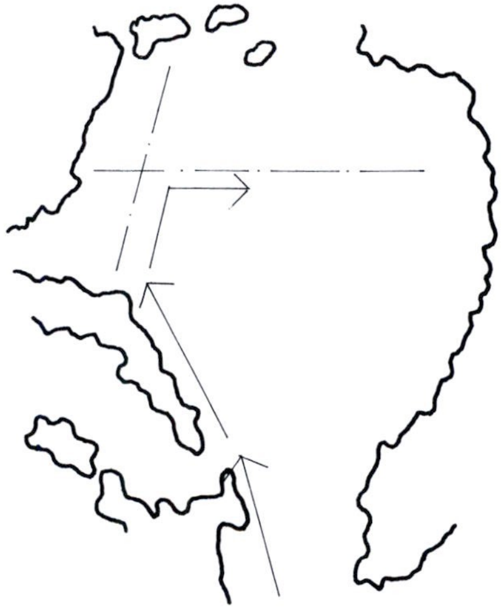

Tilting of the transverse axis responds to the enclosing trees to the west and helps to draw movement onto the longitudinal axis.

A concave form contains the movement sequence at the latter part of the approach route.

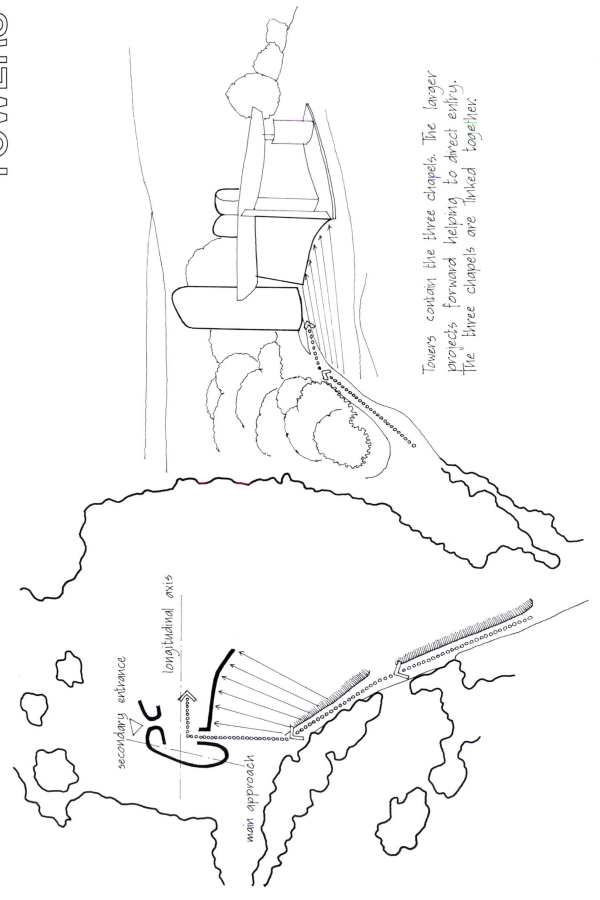

Towers contain the three chapels. The larger projects forward helping to direct entry. The three chapels are linked together.

secondary entrance

longitudinal axis

main approach

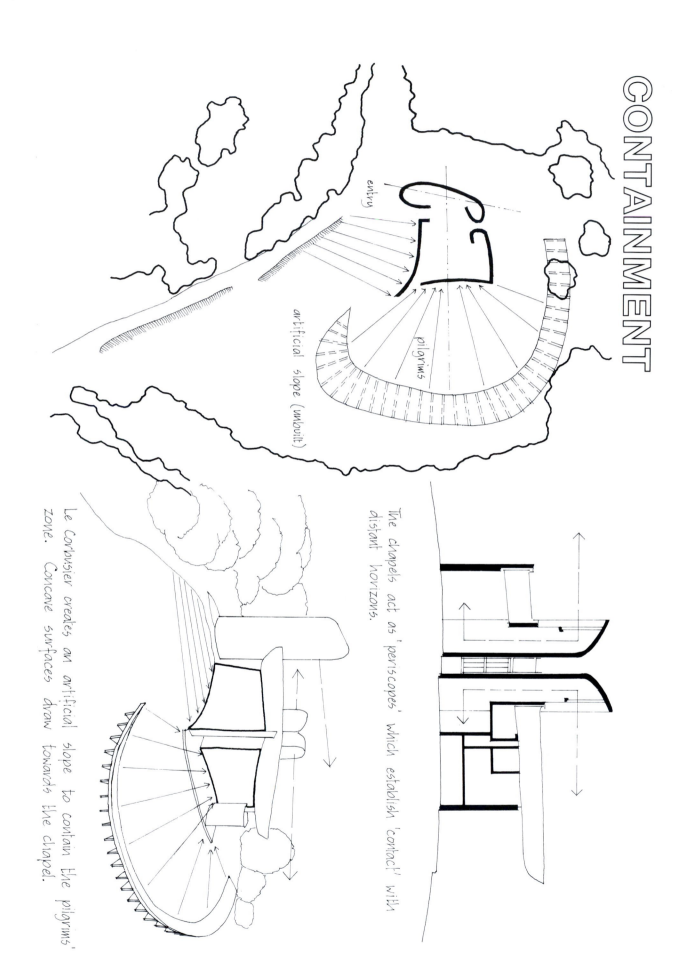

entry

pilgrims

artificial slope (unbuilt)

The chapels act as 'periscopes' which establish 'contact' with distant horizons.

Le Corbusier creates an artificial slope to contain the pilgrims' zone. Concave surfaces draw towards the chapel.

CONTRAST

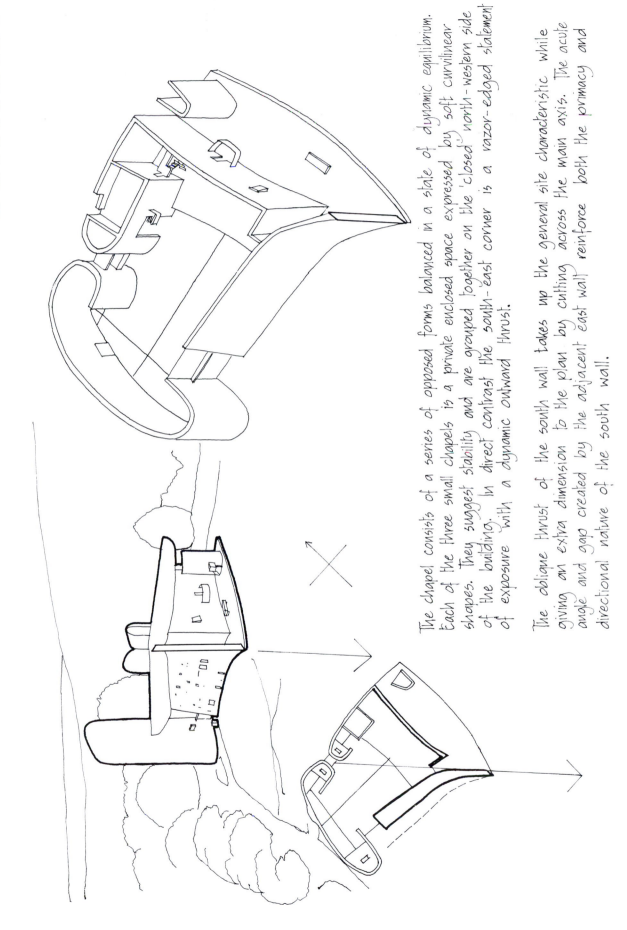

The chapel consists of a series of opposed forms balanced in a state of dynamic equilibrium. Each of the three small chapels is a private enclosed space expressed by soft curvilinear shapes. They suggest stability and are grouped together on the 'closed' north-western side of the building. In direct contrast the south-east corner is a razor-edged statement of exposure with a dynamic outward thrust.

The oblique thrust of the south wall takes up the general site characteristic while giving an extra dimension to the plan by cutting across the main axis. The acute angle and gap created by the adjacent east wall reinforce both the primacy and directional nature of the south wall.

DIRECTIONAL FORM

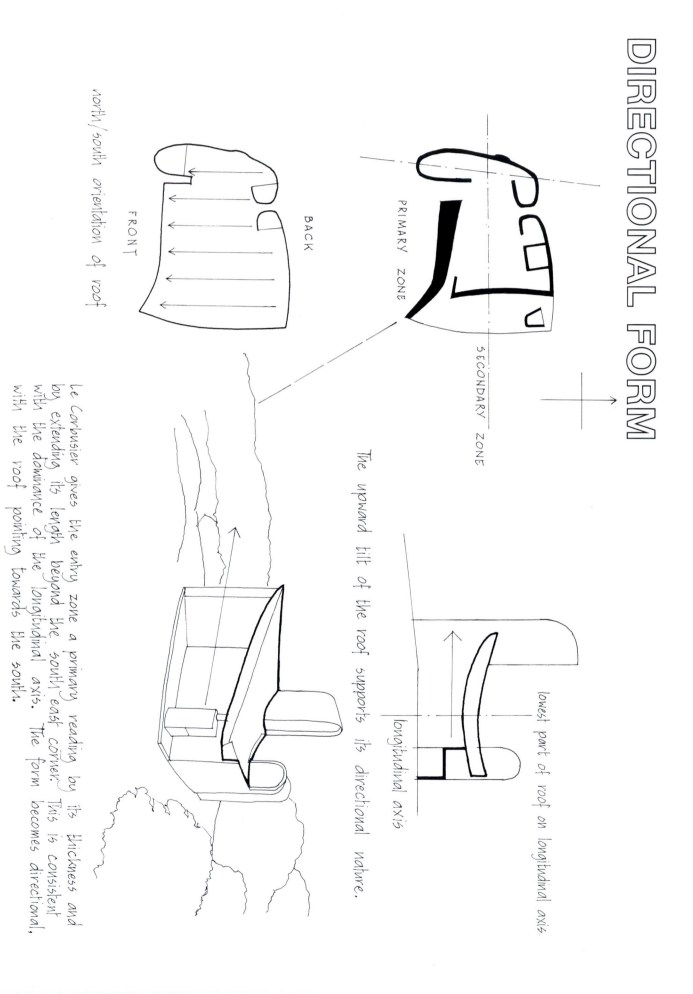

PRIMARY ZONE

SECONDARY ZONE

The upward tilt of the roof supports its directional nature.

lowest part of roof on longitudinal axis

longitudinal axis

BACK

FRONT

north/south orientation of roof

Le Corbusier gives the entry zone a primary reading by its thickness and by extending its length beyond the south east corner. This is consistent with the dominance of the longitudinal axis. The form becomes directional, with the roof pointing towards the south.

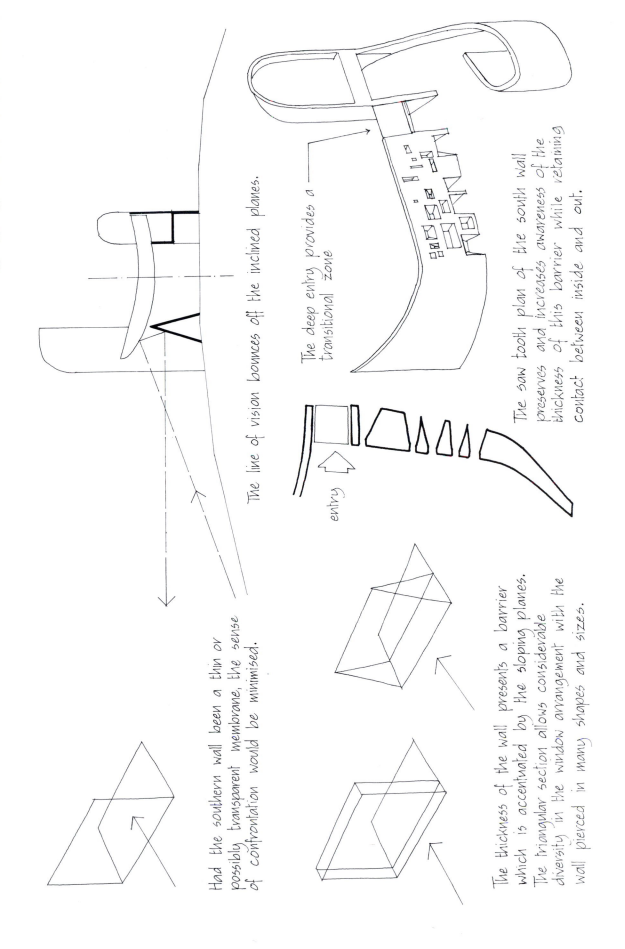

Had the southern wall been a thin or possibly transparent membrane, the sense of confrontation would be minimised.

The line of vision bounces off the inclined planes.

The deep entry provides a transitional zone

entry

The saw tooth plan of the south wall preserves and increases awareness of the thickness of this barrier while retaining contact between inside and out.

The thickness of the wall presents a barrier which is accentuated by the sloping planes. The triangular section allows considerable diversity in the window arrangement with the wall pierced in many shapes and sizes.

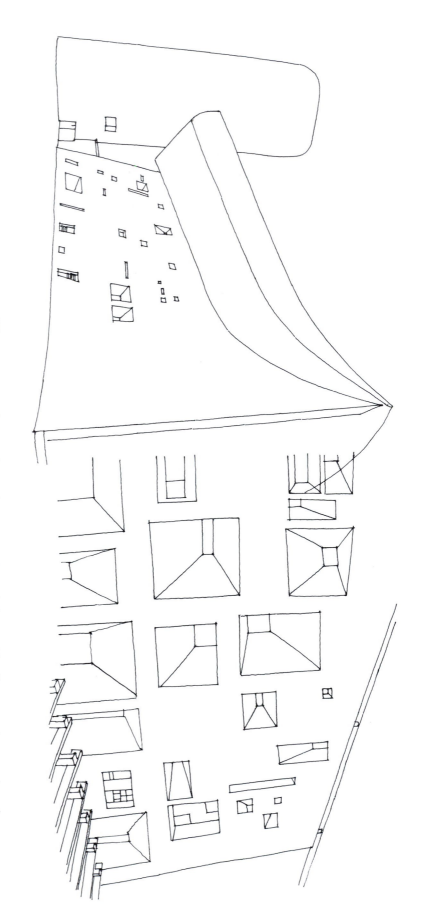

The south wall therefore draws in the visitor with its curvature, yet acts as a barrier to be penetrated as a result of the sloping wall. On the outside the small window openings increase both the apparent scale and sense of solidity, the inclined surface increasing the effect of thickness. Facing south, it acts as the major surface receptacle for light in the chapel, and it is through the medium of light that the interior space is understood.

STRUCTURE

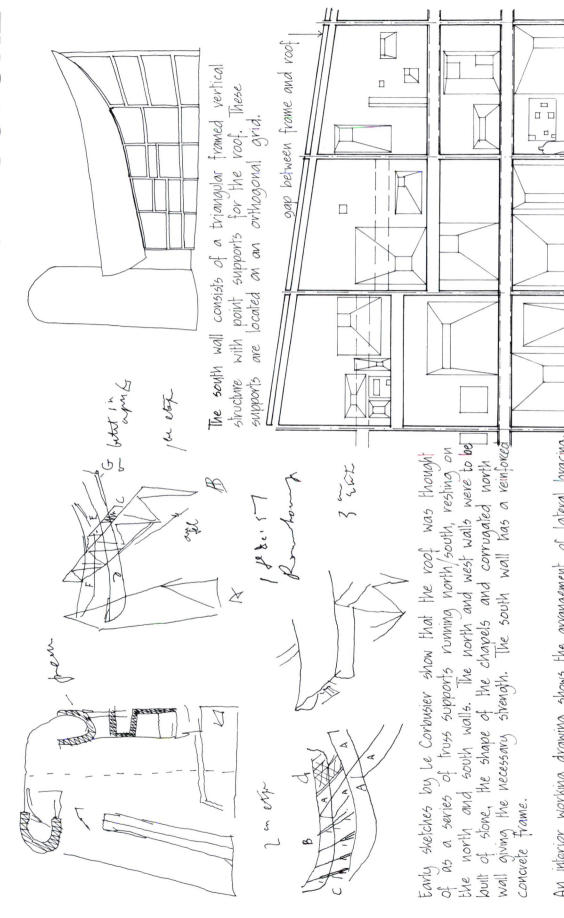

The south wall consists of a triangular framed vertical structure with point supports for the roof. These supports are located on an orthogonal grid.

Early sketches by Le Corbusier show that the roof was thought of as a series of truss supports running north/south, resting on the north and south walls. The north and west walls were to be built of stone, the shape of the chapels and corrugated north wall giving the necessary strength. The south wall has a reinforced concrete frame.

An interior working drawing shows the arrangement of lateral bracing. Internal members are shown by a continuous line, external members having a broken line.

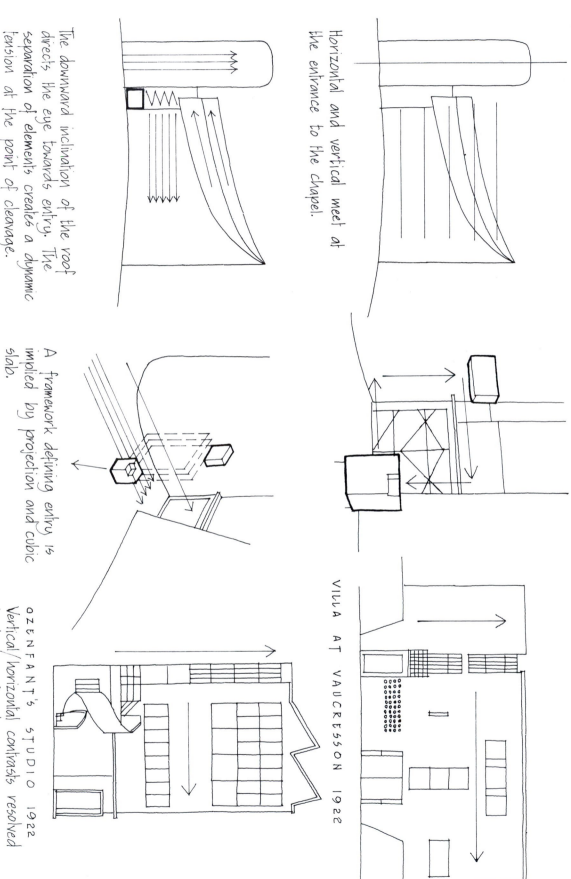

The downward inclination of the roof directs the eye towards entry. The separation of elements creates a dynamic tension at the point of cleavage.

Horizontal and vertical meet at the entrance to the chapel.

A framework defining entry is implied by projection and cubic slab.

VILLA AT VAUCRESSON 1922

OZENFANT'S STUDIO 1922
Vertical/Horizontal contrasts resolved in terms of entry.

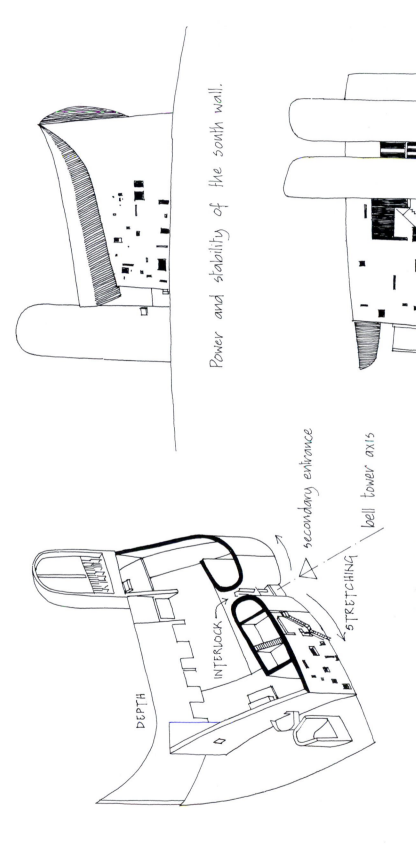

Power and stability of the south wall.

Stretched skin of the north wall.

secondary entrance

STRETCHING ..... bell tower axis

DEPTH

INTERLOCK

In contrast to the reassuring stability of the south wall the north wall is taut, with the twin chapels locked together about the secondary entrance. From this entrance an axis was to lead to a bell tower which has not been built.

The need for dual facilities inside and out is recognised by the interlocking choir stalls and by the framed madonna placed in the east wall.

The internal altar is located on the longitudinal axis and raised on a shallow podium. The concave edge to this zone indicates that this is an area of containment.

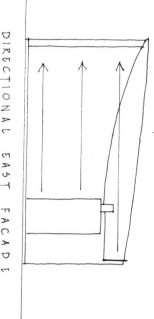

- altar
- choir stalls
- framed madonna

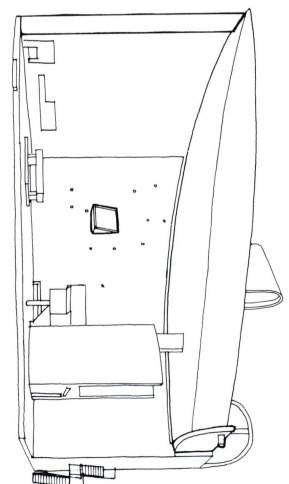

Contrary to its curvilinear appearance, the chapel is designed using the discipline of an orthogonal grid. This receives expression with two vertical planes, the edge of the south wall at its eastern extremity, and the north eastern edge of the roof.

These planes are at right angles to each other, and the back of the roof is separated from the adjacent wall plane by a slight set-back, and from the roof by being raised just above its edge.

DIRECTIONAL EAST FACADE

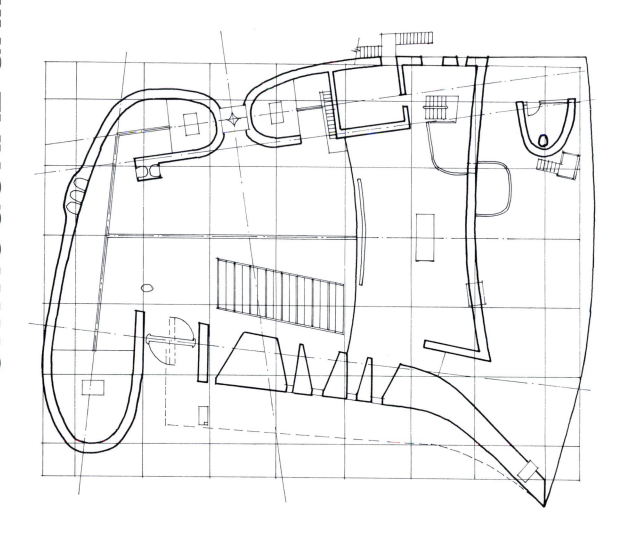

P L A N   O F   T H E   C H A P E L

after a working drawing

LIGHT

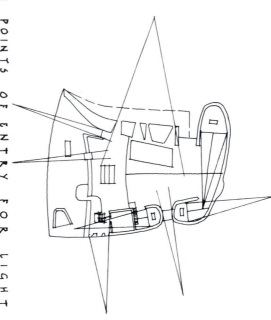

MAIN POINTS OF ENTRY FOR LIGHT

The different ways light is admitted to the chapel create a sense of mystery. The variety and contrasts of light echo and modulate the forms and spaces.

The south wall provides a flood of multicoloured light whereas in the chapel's light is gently reflected down through concrete baffles on to the altars below. In the east and west facing chapels this indirect light changes in intensity with the movement of the sun, but in the north facing south chapel the illumination is constant.

ELEVATION

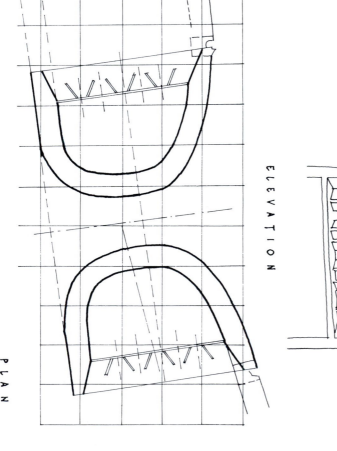

PLAN

setting out plan (from a working drawing) of the twin interlocking chapels showing the arrangement of the concrete diffuser baffles

WEST FACADE

directional thrust of gargoyle gives external identification of internal longitudinal axis

The pews in the chapel are placed on a platform and are aligned close to the south wall, being pulled towards it by its strength. This placing reinforces the angle of the south wall and gives space in the centre for a standing congregation.

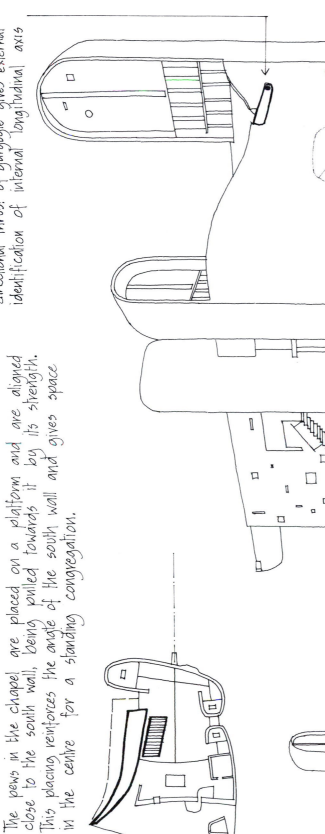

A gargoyle celebrates the shedding of rainwater on the western side, water being received in a concrete trough. The gargoyle is placed on the longitudinal axis at the point where the roof dips to its lowest and the trough acts as a sculptural foreground incident set against the plain curved wall.

Inside the chapel the roof dips to the longitudinal axis, the direction being towards the middle of the chapel. By contrast the floor follows the contours, sloping down towards the east. The pressure of the roof bearing down within the chapel, is relieved by the light admitted through the south wall.

FACADE THEMES

Each of the four facades explores a different theme through massing surface treatment and foreground incident.

The north wall, with twin chapels at one end is the most animated facade. A sense of dynamism is imbued by the taut interlocked chapels and by the stretched skin of the facade pulled outwards by the back of the roof. Different shaped windows puncture the surface, and the spiky stair with its upper flight against the wall and its lower flight detached, adds to the sense of animation.

The west facade, held at each end by a tower, is a mass statement. The wall curves down to the longitudinal axis and bulges outwards with the confessionals.

Concrete water receptacle, bulge and gargoyle act together as a triple foil to the plain white wall in an expression of grandeur and serenity.

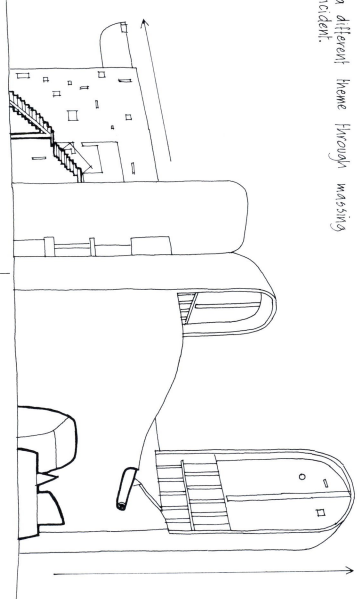

The south wall is also a mass statement, a barrier to be penetrated, in contrast to the carving into the form in the adjacent east facade. Here the roof acts as a shelter for the activities taking place below.

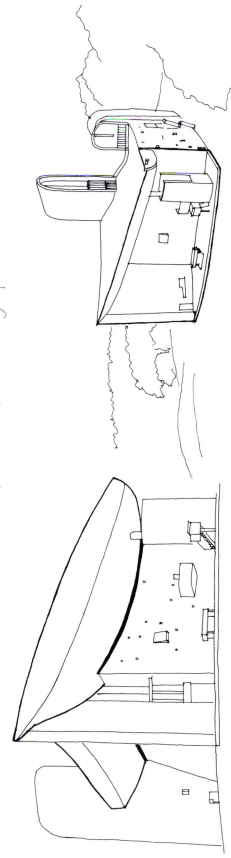

The east side is like the proscenium arch in a theatre, with an implicit spatial curtain bounded by the edges of the floor and roof.

Within this space a series of symbolic functional objects are displayed: the altar, pulpit and choir stall needed for services in the open.

The two receptive sides of the chapel are signified by the overhang of the roof. This is raised slightly above the walls below to permit a narrow strip of light to enter the chapel on the south and east sides only.

Small openings in the east wall admit pinpoints of light behind the altar.

MEANING

With the exception of functional items such as the altars, the cross and the framed Madonna on the east wall, meaning is not specific and aspects of existence are suggested through the combined media of form and light.

The chapel is placed in the landscape so that it reacts to its surroundings in a way which affirms Le Corbusier's belief in the relationship between 'man, nature and the cosmos.' It was a requirement of the brief that water had to be gathered on the hill, and it is received on the roof from which it cascades into a concrete trough, exemplifying the fact that not only the landscape but also the elements participate in the architecture.

The summit location becomes a major factor as the chapel projects itself while acting as a receptacle through the three towers. Concave and convex surfaces contain and proclaim the building while the roof acts as a shelter outside, exerting pressure internally as it bears down on the central axis.

The whiteness of the chapel helps to clarify the form which is reassuringly solid, a sacred private world which has to be penetrated. At the point of penetration the large door pivots round to allow entry and the internal illumination suggests both mystery and abundant joy with the south wall radiant with coloured light.

The chapel is a statement of contrasts; contrasts of form which suggest a multitude of cross-references with the life situation. The shapes are at once powerful and serene; walls both enclose parts of the internal space while allowing other parts to expand; there is stability and tension, drama and repose; lighting is direct and indirect, mysterious and radiant, sometimes changing, sometimes not.

Forms are part continuous and yet there are precise breaks; the chapel is intravert and extravert, answering a brief with internal and external needs. Nothing is explicit in a complex statement exemplified by the diversity of light and shape induced by the varied profiles of the openings in the south wall. On the interior this 'penetrable' wall is a myriad of shapes sparkling with light in contrast to the pressure exerted by the roof, which being raised and separated from the wall seems to be unsupported. The internal sloping wall is almost the opposite of its external face with its fortress-like slope and suggestion of mass.

In many ways the chapel typifies Le Corbusier's mature work. The certainty of the twenties has gone, to be replaced by apparently deliberate contradictions and ambiguities. It seems to be a looser, more open-ended approach posing questions instead of providing answers, factors certainly evident in the Jaoul Houses and the Monastery of La Tourette. In all these buildings meaning no longer demonstrates the explicit and literal transcription of the machine age, but instead becomes manifest in allegorical interpretations of nature, which by inference are an interpretation of life itself.

STAIR TO CHOIR

STAIRS WORKING DRAWING

after the original in the archive at the Le Corbusier Fondation Paris

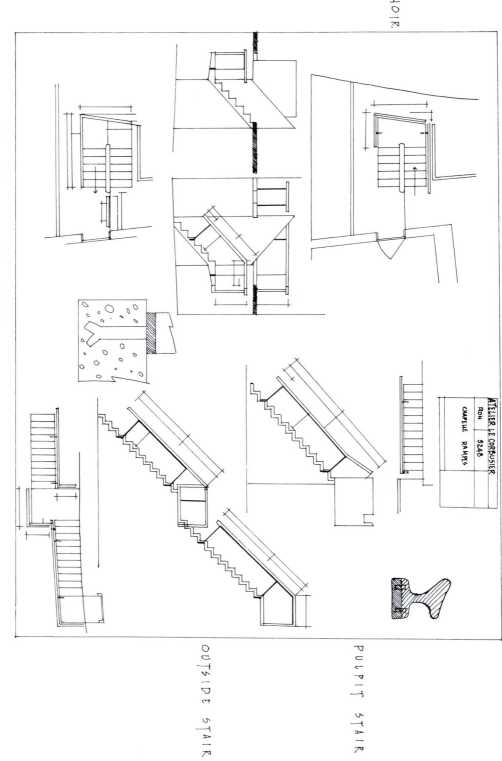

ATELIER LE CORBUSIER

RON   5268

CHAPELLE   RAMPES

OUTSIDE STAIR

PULPIT STAIR

Le Corbusier wrote of the chapel:

In the brain the idea is born, indefinite it wanders and develops. On the hill I had meticulously drawn the four horizons. There are only four: to the east, the Ballons d'Alsace; to the south, the last spurs leave a vale; to the west the plain of the Saône; to the north, a small valley and a village. These drawings are missing or lost, it is they which unlocked, architecturally, the echo, the visual echo in the realm of shape. On the 4th June 1950 ... Give me charcoal and some paper...

The shell of a crab picked up on Long Island near New York in 1946 is lying on my drawing board. It will become the roof of the chapel: two membranes of concrete six centimetres thick and 2m. 26cm. apart. The shell will lie on walls of the salvaged stones...'

The key is light and light illuminates shapes and shapes have emotional power. By the play of proportions by the play of relationships unexpected, amazing...

But also by the intellectual play of purpose: their authentic origin, their capacity to endure, structure, astuteness, boldness, even temerity, the play of those vital abstractions which are the essential qualities the components of architecture.

quoted from Le Corbusier, The Chapel at Ronchamp, trans. by Jacqueline Cullen, Architectural Press, London, 1957, pp. 89, 90 and 27.

In 1952 The Reverend Father Couturier on behalf of the Provincial Chapter of the Dominicans of Lyon asked Le Corbusier to construct a church and dwelling place for the members of his order. Accommodation would include a cloister, chapter, classrooms, library, refectory, kitchens and a hundred cells.

Le Corbusier began work on the project in 1953 and the friars took possession of the monastery on July 1st 1959. Founded by Saint Dominic in the thirteenth century, the order broke with established religious custom by situating their monasteries in the hearts of towns and cities so that they could mix with the people. Essentially a teaching order, the monks were pledged to a life of study and service to the community, a tradition which continues today. They are also a democratic order, electing senior members, and their simple lifestyle is not concerned with material possessions.

In a letter to Le Corbusier Father Couturier outlined some important requirements; the bareness of the building must be very severe, without any superfluous luxury and yet all the vital common necessities must be respected : silence, a temperature warm enough to permit continuous intellectual work, a distance for the goings to and from reduced to the minimum ... Remember ours is a completely community life and as a result requires no personal differentiations within the groups.[1]

Giving some reasons why Le Corbusier was chosen as the architect, another member of the community, Father Belaud, has explained : Why ? For the beauty of the monastery to be born of course. But above all for the significance of this beauty. It was necessary to show that prayer and religious life are not bound to conventional forms, and that harmony can be struck between them and the most modern architecture, providing that the latter should be capable of transcending itself.[2]

---

1 and 2 are taken from Jean Petit, Un Couvent de Le Corbusier Les Cahiers Forces Vives, Paris, 1961. pp. 26 and 17.
translated by Andrew Fairbairn

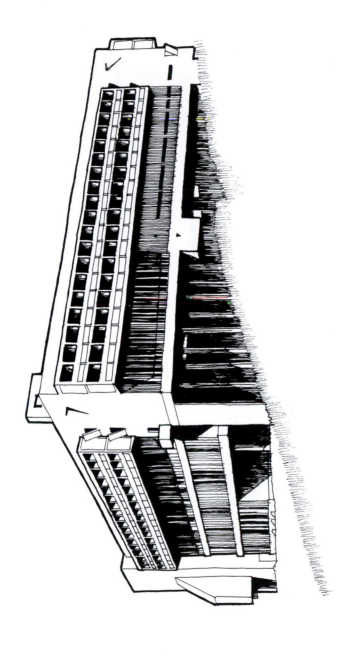

**THE MONASTERY OF LA TOURETTE
1957 – 60**

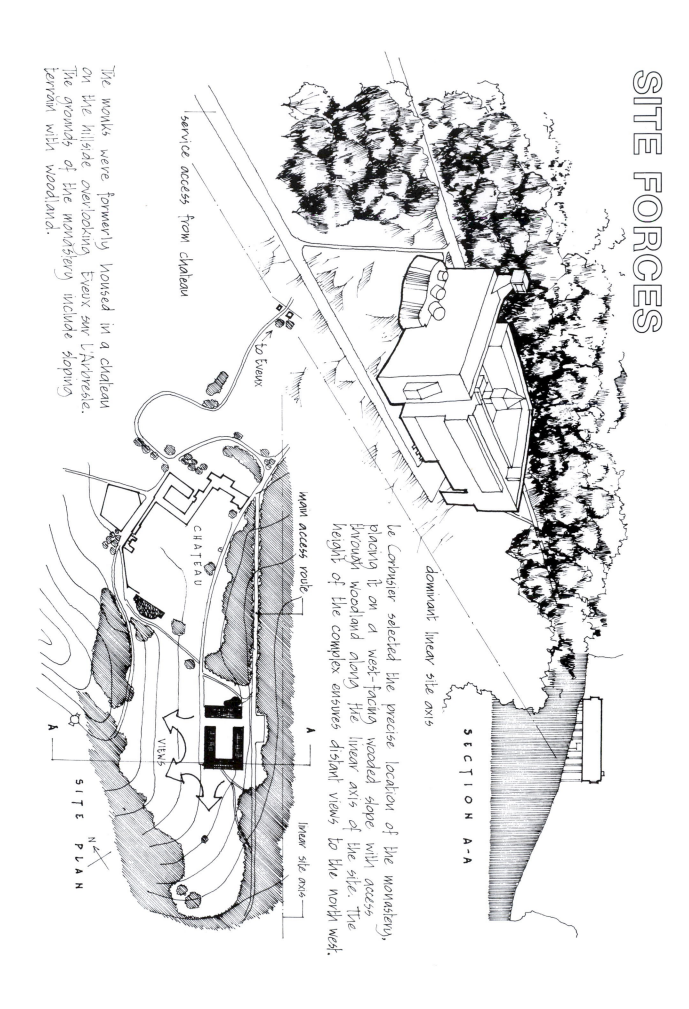

SECTION A-A

dominant linear site axis

le Corbusier selected the precise location of the monastery, placing it on a west-facing wooded slope with access through woodland along the linear axis of the site. The height of the complex ensures distant views to the north west.

linear site axis

service access from chateau

to Evreux

main access route

CHATEAU

A

A

VIEWS

SITE PLAN

N

The monks were formerly housed in a chateau on the hillside overlooking Evreux sur L'Arbresle. The grounds of the monastery include sloping terrain with woodland.

LE THORONET

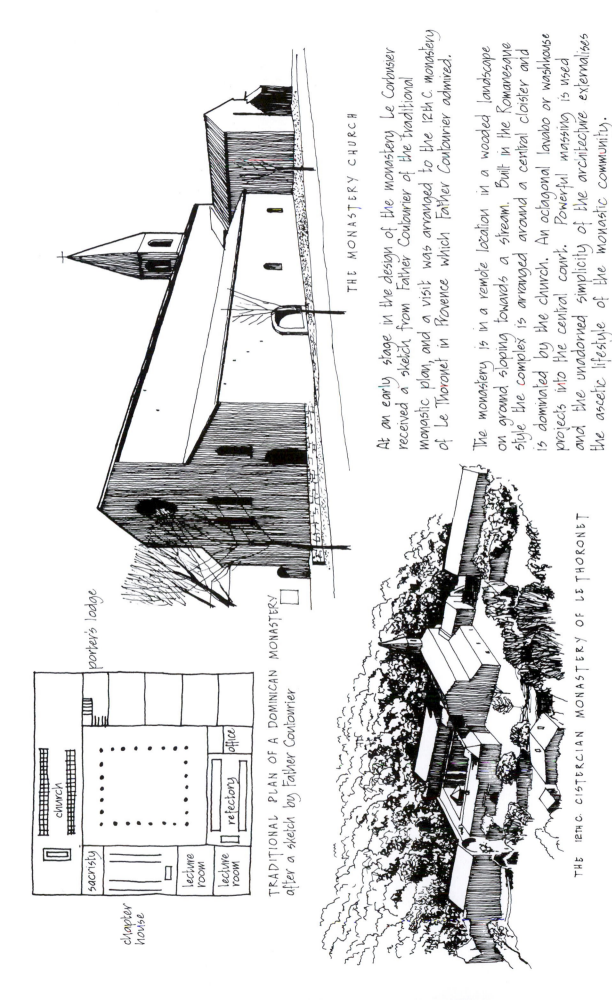

THE MONASTERY CHURCH

At an early stage in the design of the monastery Le Corbusier received a sketch from Father Coutourier of the traditional monastic plan, and a visit was arranged to the 12th C. monastery of Le Thoronet in Provence which Father Coutourier admired.

The monastery is in a remote location in a wooded landscape on ground sloping towards a stream. Built in the Romanesque style the complex is arranged around a central cloister and is dominated by the church. An octagonal lavabo or washhouse projects into the central court. Powerful massing is used and the unadorned simplicity of the architecture externalises the ascetic lifestyle of the monastic community.

THE 12th C. CISTERCIAN MONASTERY OF LE THORONET

porter's lodge

chapter house

church

sacristy

lecture room

lecture room

refectory

office

TRADITIONAL PLAN OF A DOMINICAN MONASTERY after a sketch by Father Coutourier

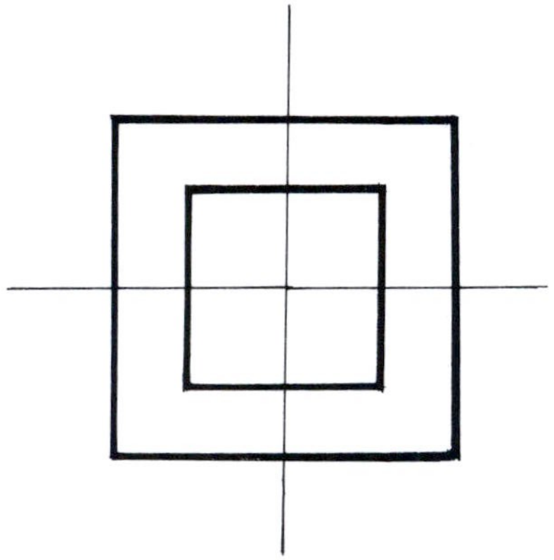

The generic antecedent of the specific form is the traditional monastic court, a square form with equal axes.

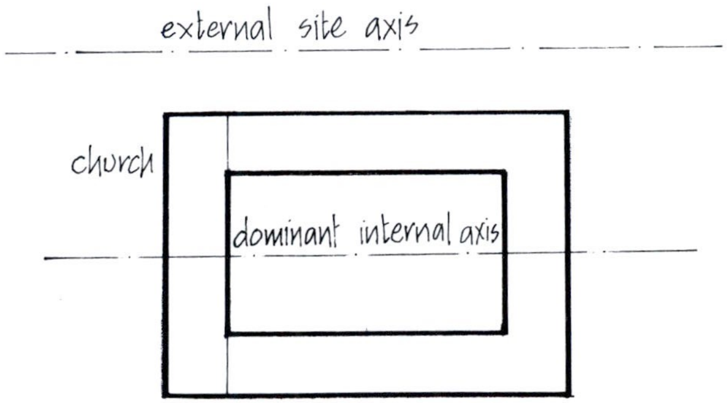

external site axis

church

dominant internal axis

The initial distortion takes account of the external site axis, changing the square to a rectangle.

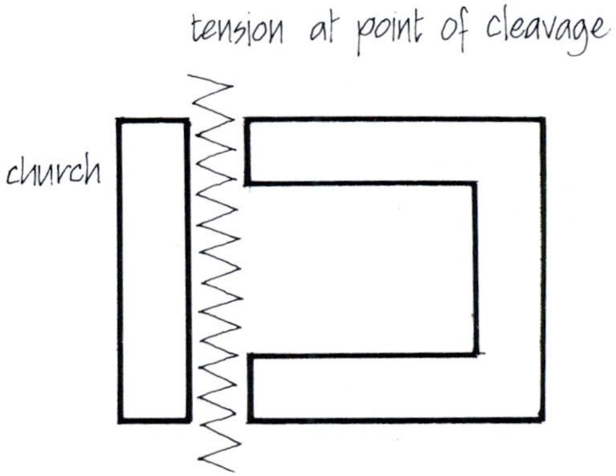

church

tension at point of cleavage

The second distortion is caused by separating the church from the rest.

Le Corbusier retains the traditional courtyard grouping for the monastic complex, placing the church along the northern side. The form becomes rectilinear in acknowledgement of the linear site axis and by detaching the church a potential tension is created at the point of cleavage between the forms.

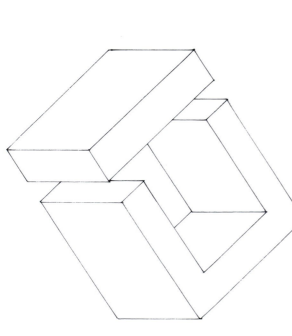

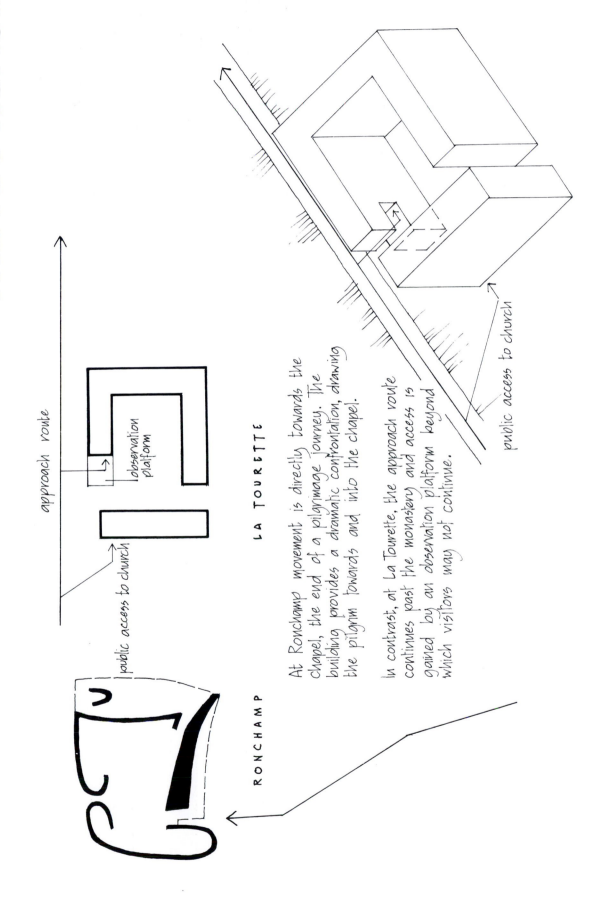

approach route

observation platform

public access to church

LA TOURETTE

public access to church

RONCHAMP

At Ronchamp movement is directly towards the chapel, the end of a pilgrimage journey. The building provides a dramatic confrontation, drawing the pilgrim towards and into the chapel.

In contrast, at La Tourette, the approach route continues past the monastery and access is gained by an observation platform beyond which visitors may not continue.

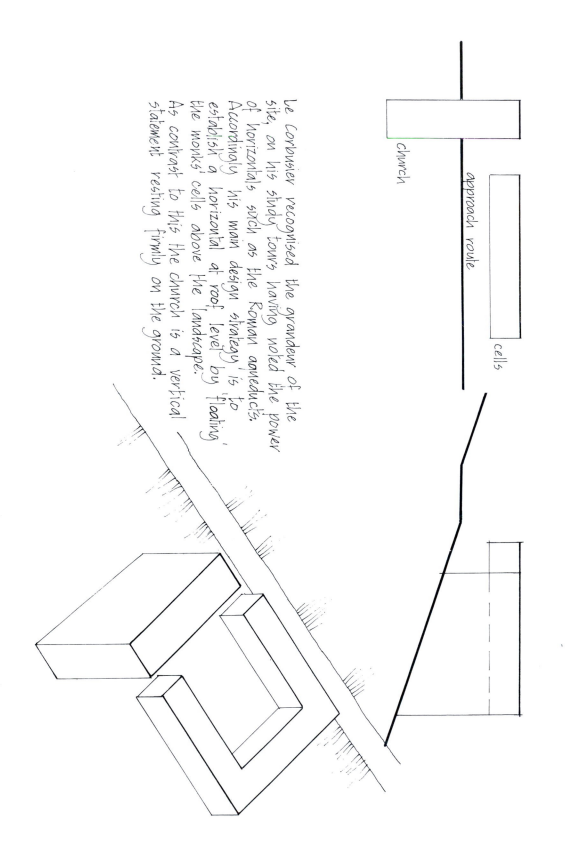

church

approach route

cells

Le Corbusier recognised the grandeur of the site, on his study tours having noted the power of horizontals such as the Roman aqueducts. Accordingly his main design strategy is to establish a horizontal at roof level by 'floating' the monks' cells above the landscape. As contrast to this the church is a vertical statement resting firmly on the ground.

When the monastery was finished, Le Corbusier on a visit had a friendly conversation with the whole religious community, during which he explained his approach to the site:

I came here, I took my notebook as usual, I drew the road, I drew the horizons, I put in the orientation of the sun. I smelled out the topography. I decided the place where it would be, for the place wasn't fixed at all. In choosing the place I was committing the criminal or valid act. The first gesture to make is the choice, the nature of the site and then the nature of the composition one will make in these conditions. Here in the landscape which was so flowing I said to myself I am not going to set the building down on the ground since it would hide itself or else it would cost as much as an Assyrian fortress. The money is not there and this is not the moment to do this.

Let us take the setting of the foundations aloft to the horizontal line of the building at the top, which line will harmonise with the horizon. And starting from that horizontal line at the top we will measure everything, from there we shall reach the ground at the moment when we touch it. It is an obvious remark but it's like that. It is thus that you have a building very precise in its upper part and which little by little determines its organisation in descending and touches the ground as and how it can. It is a thing which is not in the mental conception of everyone, it is an original aspect of the monastery, very original. [3]

3 Jean Petit Un Couvent de Le Corbusier, Les Cahiers Forces Vives, Paris, 1961. p. 28
  translated by Andrew Fairbairn

THE CLOISTER

The monks are accommodated according to seniority, with novices in the east block and senior brethren in the west block. Instead of the traditional cloister, Le Corbusier suspends a circulation spine along the contours, giving a processional route from the atrium to the church.

A link to the spine is provided from the novices block and they also have their own route to the church. Senior members of the community descend to the atrium by spiral stair within a cylindrical tower.

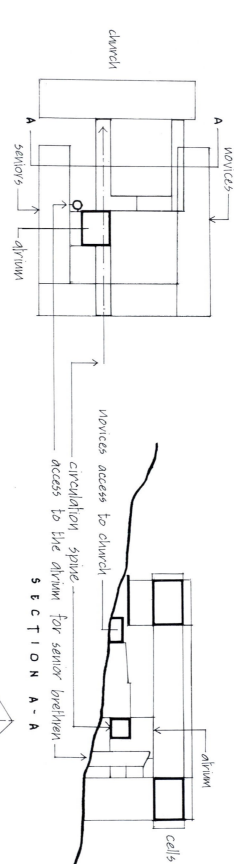

church

A — A

seniors

atrium

novices

novices access to church

circulation spine

access to the atrium for senior brethren

S E C T I O N   A - A

atrium

cells

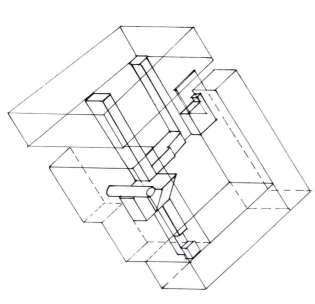

CELLS ROTATE

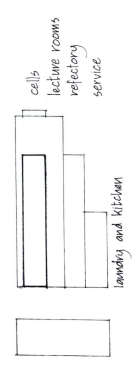

cells
lecture rooms
refectory
service

laundry and kitchen

The layered arrangement has a teaching floor comprising lecture and seminar rooms with library below the cells. Lower down the slope on the west side only are the refectory and service facilities.

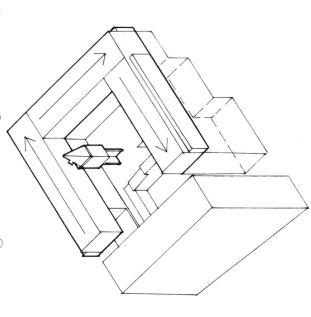

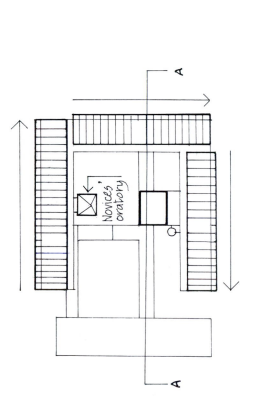

The cells rotate around the atrium in a pinwheel formation. A small chapel or oratory is provided for the novices by a cubic projection with pyramidal roof on cruciform supports.

Novices' oratory

A

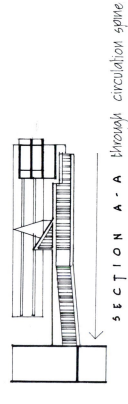

S E C T I O N   A - A   through circulation spine

The roof of the circulation spine maintains the horizontality established by 'floating' the cells initially. The pitched roof of the atrium identifies this important gathering point (prior to movement towards either church or refectory).

EFFECT OF SLOPE

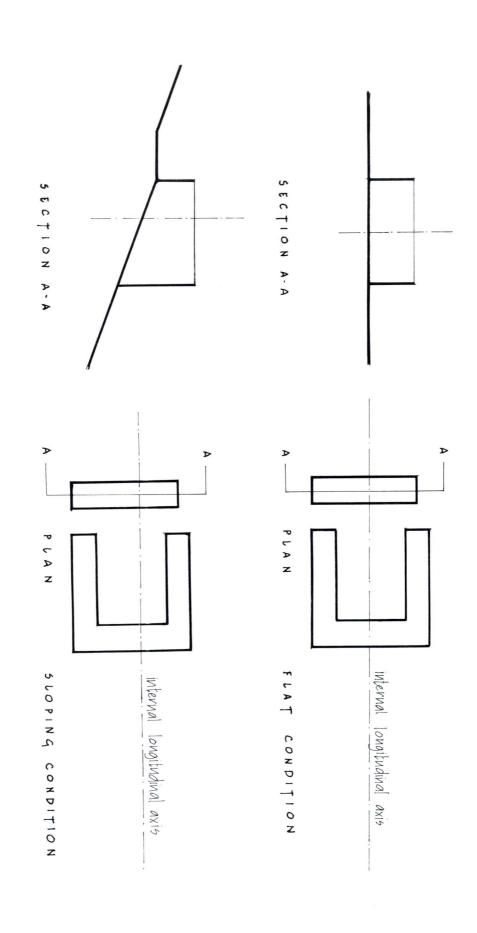

SECTION A-A

SECTION A-A

A   A

A   A

PLAN

PLAN

FLAT CONDITION

SLOPING CONDITION

internal longitudinal axis

internal longitudinal axis

If the monastery had been placed on flat terrain, such a configuration would have its longitudinal axis centrally located. In sloping conditions this axis is pulled in to shift the centre of gravity.

CHURCH STABILISES

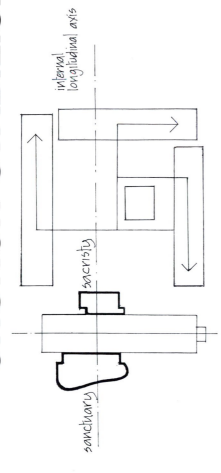

internal longitudinal axis

sacristy

sanctuary

Le Corbusier gives further stability to the church by placing the sanctuary and sacristy on either side. These elements are located on the internal longitudinal axis.

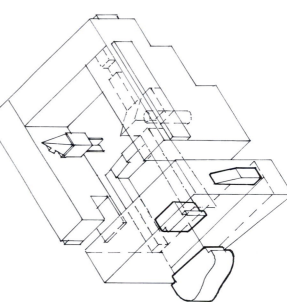

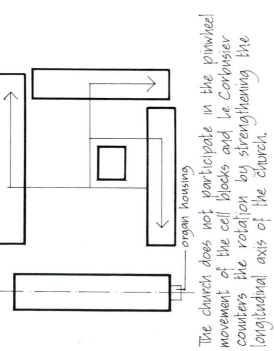

organ housing

The church does not participate in the pinwheel movement of the cell blocks and Le Corbusier counters the rotation by strengthening the longitudinal axis of the church.

This is done by inscribing the axis in the floor of the church and by expressing the organ housing on the axis externally.

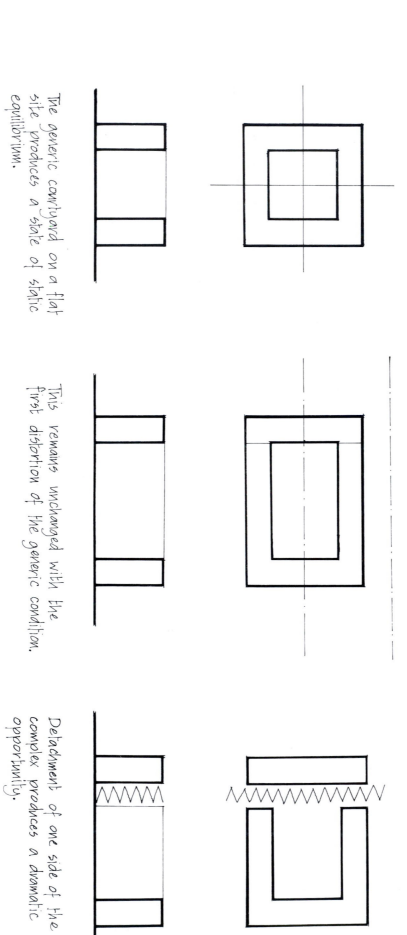

The generic courtyard on a flat site produces a state of static equilibrium.

This remains unchanged with the first distortion of the generic condition.

Detachment of one side of the complex produces a dramatic opportunity.

DRAMA WITH SLOPE

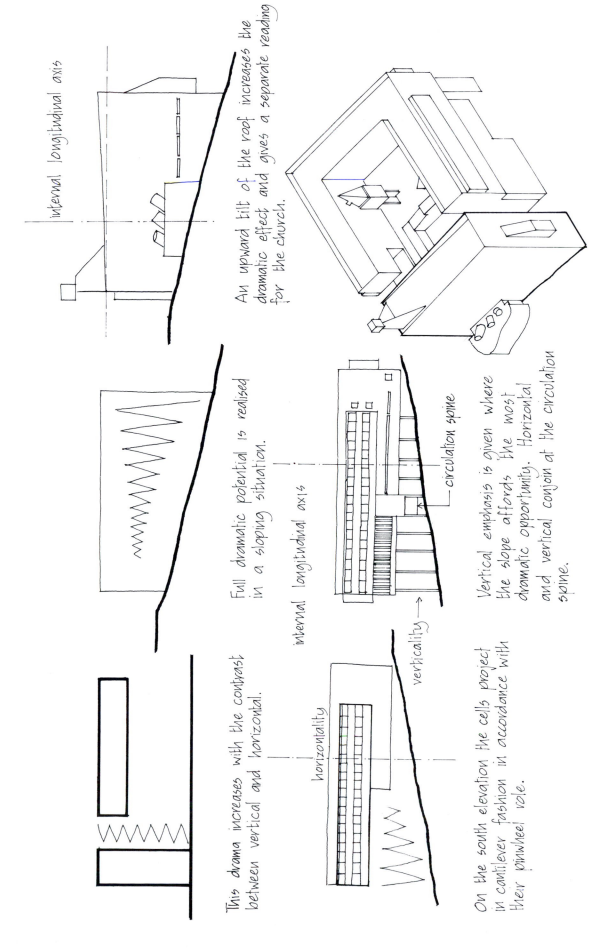

internal longitudinal axis

An upward tilt of the roof increases the dramatic effect and gives a separate reading for the church.

Full dramatic potential is realised in a sloping situation.

internal longitudinal axis

circulation spine

Vertical emphasis is given where the slope affords the most dramatic opportunity. Horizontal and vertical conjoin at the circulation spine.

This drama increases with the contrast between vertical and horizontal.

horizontality

verticality →

On the south elevation the cells project in cantilever fashion in accordance with their pinwheel role.

The public are separated from the monks by the zone of worship. The sanctuary, approached only from the sacristy under the church, is the devotional heart of the monastery, where the monks pray at a series of private altars.

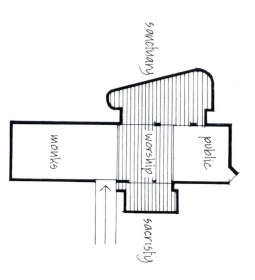

sanctuary

worship

public

monks

sacristy

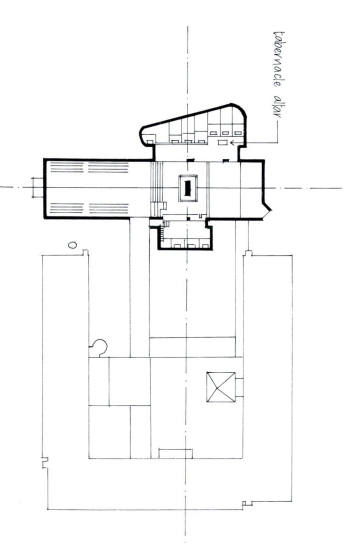

tabernacle altar

The altar is placed where the main axes of the complex meet.

Discussing the church Le Corbusier explained:

It is with the altar's that the centre of gravity will be marked, also the value, the hierarchy of all things. There is in music a key, a diapason, a chord. It is the altar, which lending sacredness by its magnificence gives this tone thus setting the radiance of the work in motion.[4]

4. taken from Jean Petit _Un Couvent de Le Corbusier_ Les Cahiers Forces Vives, Paris, 1961. p. 29. translated by Andrew Fairbairn

SPATIAL FLOW

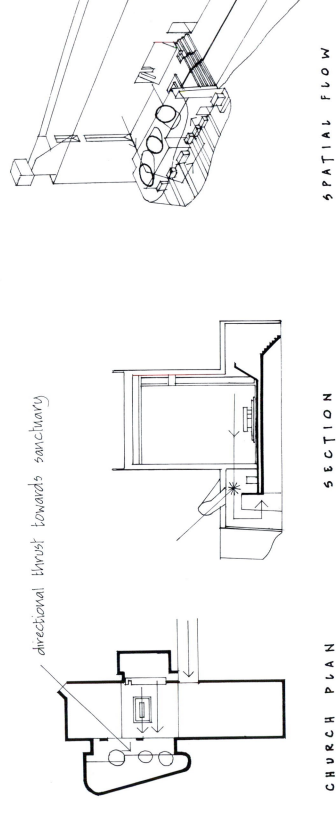

directional thrust towards sanctuary

CHURCH PLAN

SECTION

THE ALTAR

SPATIAL FLOW

Le Corbusier directs spatial movement within the church towards the sanctuary. The altar points in this direction and is supported by the angled vertical window on the east wall and by the sloping screen wall dividing the church from the sacristy. The most powerful pull is provided by three light sources distributing light over the sanctuary and tabernacle altar. Spatial flow descends to the sanctuary, then down the slope, finally turning back towards the church where the altars are placed.

SACRISTY AND SANCTUARY

SANCTUARY

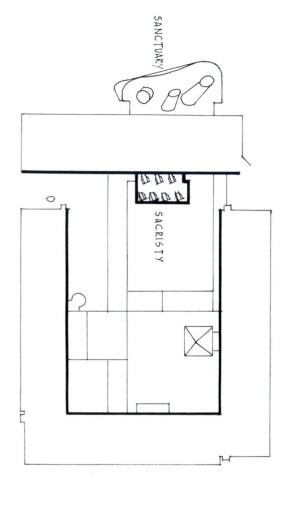

SACRISTY

The rectilinear form of the sacristy responds to the rectilinear format of the courtyard. The regular pattern shape and disposition of the light sources contrasts with the dramatic effect contrived in the sanctuary.

The fluid shape of the sanctuary reflects its role as a place for private prayer and its position in the open landscape outside the complex.

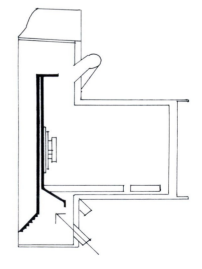

Each source allows light to enter the sacristy along the same diagonal.

LIGHT SOURCES

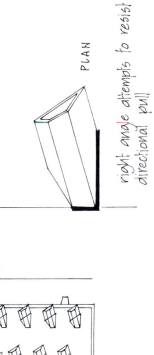

PLAN

right angle attempts to resist
directional pull

The light sources participate in the pinwheel.

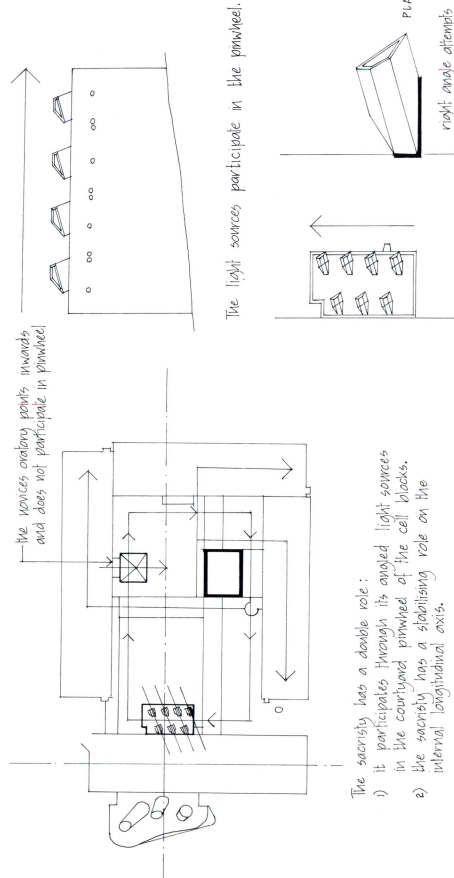

the novices oratory points inwards
and does not participate in pinwheel

The sacristy has a double role :
1) it participates through its angled light sources
in the courtyard pinwheel of the cell blocks.
2) the sacristy has a stabilising role on the
internal longitudinal axis.

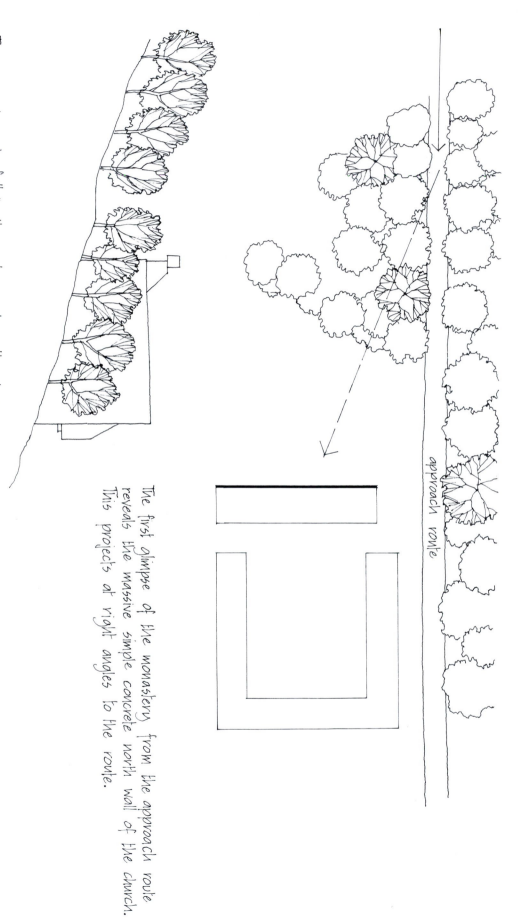

The approach route follows the contours along the slope through a corridor formed between the trees.

The first glimpse of the monastery from the approach route reveals the massive simple concrete north wall of the church. This projects at right angles to the route.

approach route

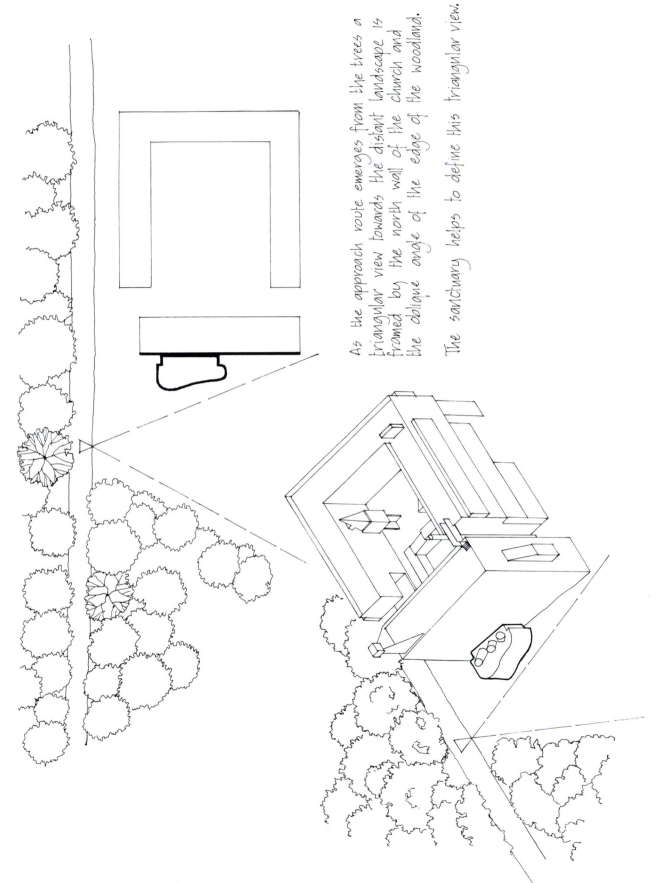

As the approach route emerges from the trees a triangular view towards the distant landscape is framed by the north wall of the church and the oblique angle of the edge of the woodland.

The sanctuary helps to define this triangular view.

SANCTUARY

Three possible readings of the sanctuary:

as a form growing out of and responding
directly to the sloping terrain

as dramatic foreground incident framing the distant view

as a sculptural form in a figure/ground
relationship with the vertical plane of
the north wall of the church

RIDGE TURRET

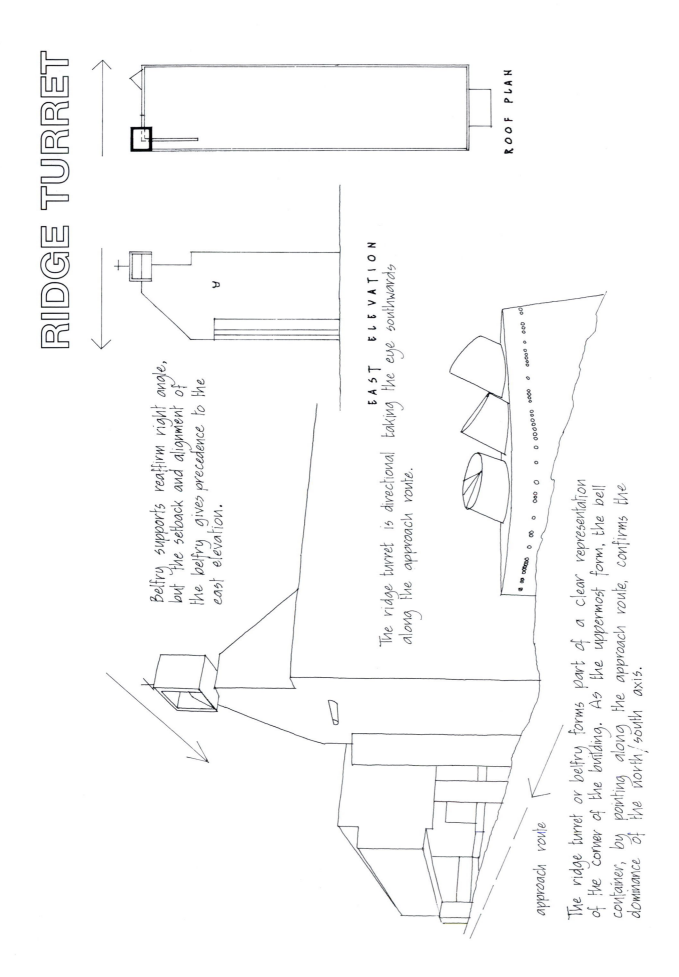

ROOF PLAN

A

EAST ELEVATION

Belfry supports reaffirm right angle, but the setback and alignment of the belfry gives precedence to the east elevation.

The ridge turret is directional taking the eye southwards along the approach route.

approach route

The ridge turret or belfry forms part of a clear representation of the corner of the building. As the uppermost form, the bell container, by pointing along the approach route, confirms the dominance of the north/south axis.

The insistent right angle of the bell tower proclaims the orthogonal characteristic of the complex.

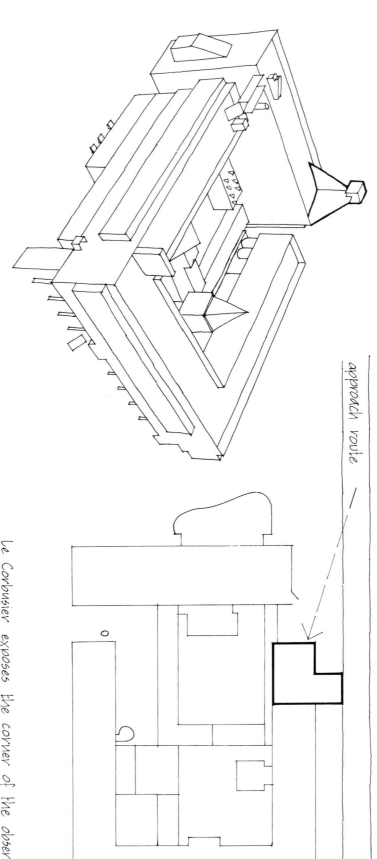

approach route

Le Corbusier exposes the corner of the observation platform so that it becomes visible from the approach route.

CELL CLUSTER

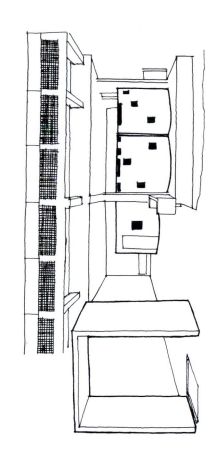

A cluster of interview cells draw the eye towards the entry/ observation platform. These are points of contact with the outside world where visitors may converse with the monks without entering the monastery. The tent-like cluster of cylindrical forms brings the scale down to human dimensions following the powerful north wall of the church. The cylinders are punctuated with small openings which add to the visual interest.

Entry to the monastery is through a gateway across a bridge.

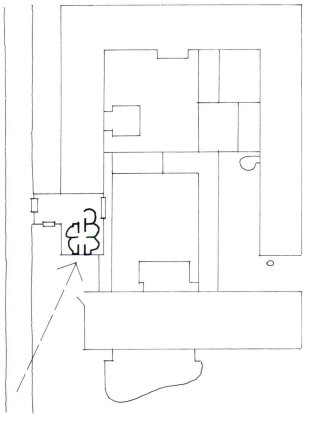

interview cells provide visual focus

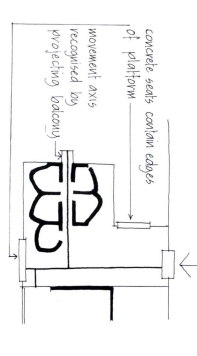

concrete seats contain edges of platform

movement axis recognised by projecting balcony.

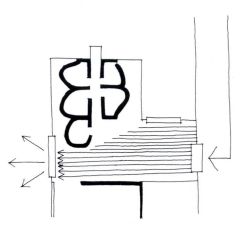

A funnelling process draws the observer towards the court with the main pull provided by the space of the court. The eye is drawn by light.

Movement into the monastery is through the entry 'arch' across the bridge following lines indicated in the floor.

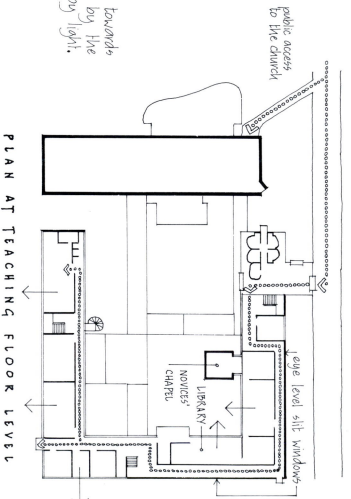

public access to the church

eye level slit windows

LIBRARY

NOVICES' CHAPEL

P L A N   AT   T E A C H I N G   F L O O R   L E V E L

Entry to the monastery is made at the teaching zone immediately below the cells. This route is varied in two ways: 1) by moving both along the inner and outer perimeters of the building. 2) by varying the corridor width. This arrangement gives certain rooms privacy (including the library) while allowing others to take advantage of the view. The floor contains the novices' library, chapel and teaching rooms.

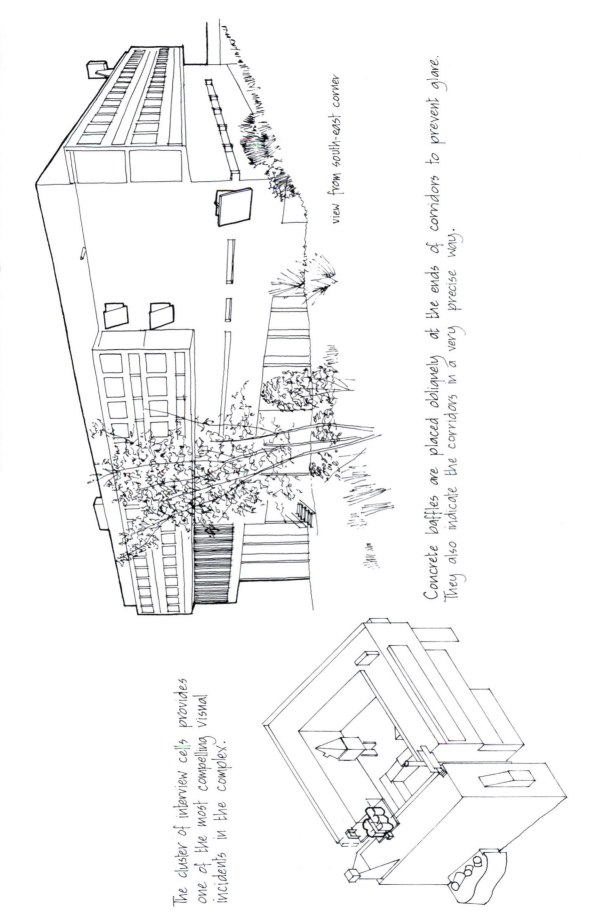

view from south-east corner

Concrete baffles are placed obliquely at the ends of corridors to prevent glare.
They also indicate the corridors in a very precise way.

The cluster of interview cells provides one of the most compelling visual incidents in the complex.

VARIETY AND DRAMA

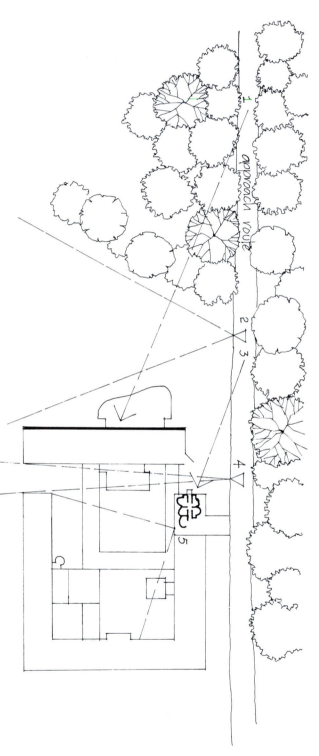

There are five points of visual impact along the approach route. Each provides a different kind of visual experience, being carefully controlled by Le Corbusier.

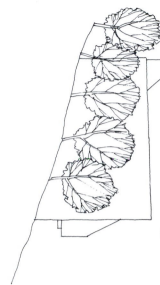

First there is the dramatic impact of the north wall of the church.

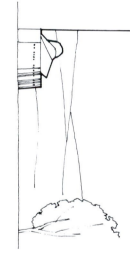

Second, the shock of a distant view after being confined in woodland. Here the sanctuary provides foreground interest.

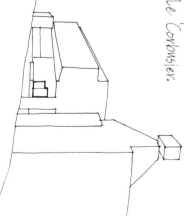

Third, bringing down the scale, the compelling sculptural complexity of the interview cells.

VISUAL SHOCK TACTICS

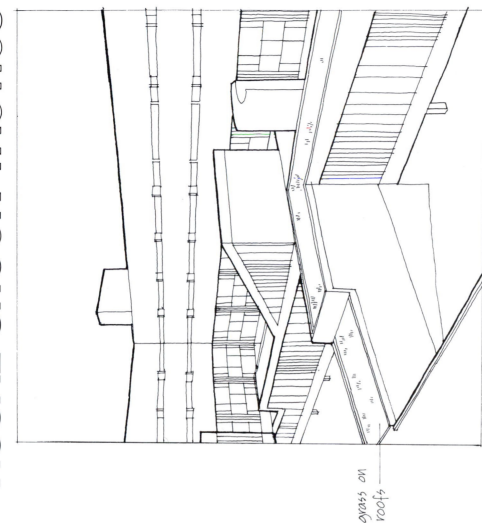

grass on roofs

The final view into the courtyard from the observation platform reveals a variety of forms. These are vigorously deployed with shapes both unfamiliar and unexpected. The direct functional resolution of specific needs of the religious community provides the final tumultuous visual shock.

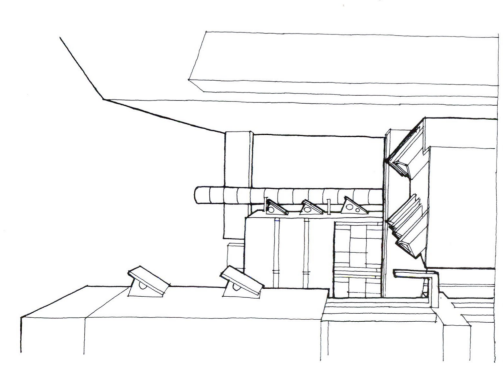

Fourth, at the point of tension between church and remainder of the complex, Le Corbusier provides a particularly potent juxtaposition of verticals, horizontals and obliques, reinforced by rhythms and pattern.

STRUCTURE

The cell blocks are elevated by reinforced concrete pilotis, these supporting a structure of beams on which the floor slabs rest. In general the pilotis are rectilinear with cylindrical columns used in the refectory. The atrium is supported by a series of concrete "fingers".

SECTION THROUGH ATRIUM

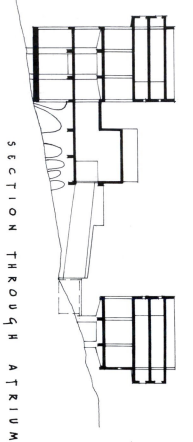

SCHEMATIC STRUCTURAL DIAGRAMS OF WEST BLOCK

SERVICES

REFECTORY

TEACHING

CELLS

THEME

The basic theme is one of contrast between the verticality of the church and the horizontality of the cell blocks. This contrast is furthered by the church resting on the ground, being constructed of poured concrete, whereas the cells 'float' above the ground and are raised on a structural framework. The horizontality of the cell blocks is furthered by the stratified layers below and exemplified by the positive expression of structural edge beams. Each corner of the cell blocks has a planar expression.

Fenestration furthers the vertical/horizontal contrast. Cells provide an insistent regular pattern whereas the accommodation below (excepting corridors) has a relaxed and fluid rhythm. This rhythmic solution is particularly apposite for the cloister in the way movement is suggested.

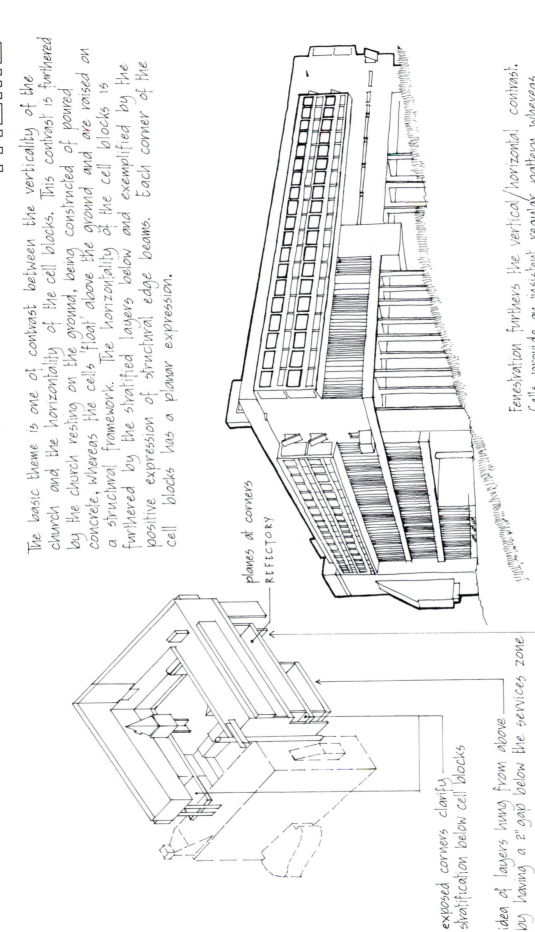

planes at corners
REFECTORY

exposed corners clarify stratification below cell blocks

idea of layers hung from above by having a 2" gap below the services zone

The hung layers are particularly evident in relation to the slope

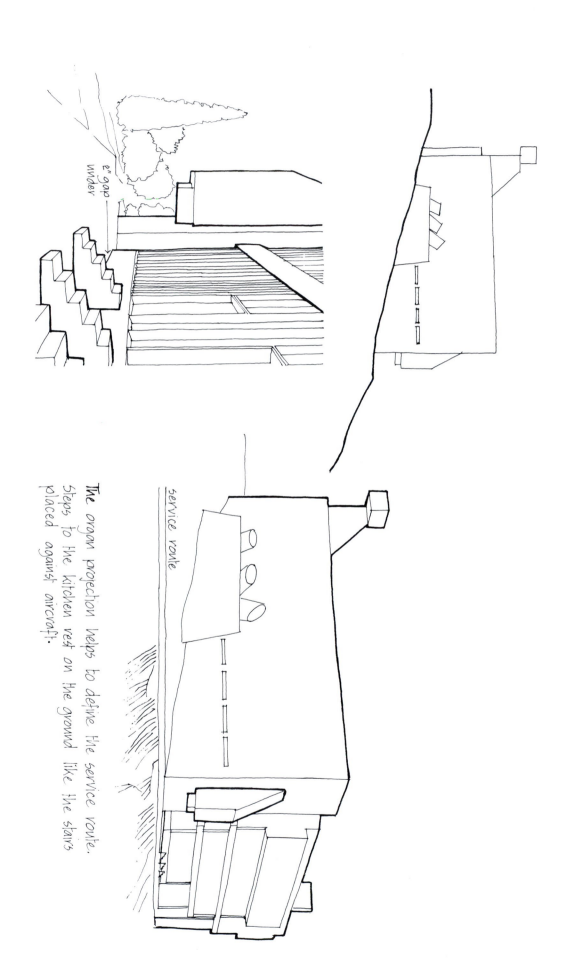

2" gap
under

service route

The organ projection helps to define the service route.
Steps to the kitchen rest on the ground like the stairs
placed against aircraft.

DYNAMISM

The task posed by the monastery and its site gave Le Corbusier an opportunity to explore that relationship between man, nature and the cosmos with which he was constantly preoccupied. The philosophical and metaphysical dimensions of the programme are interpreted through the media of form, space and light.

The intellectual rigour of the organisation of the complex is evident in the clear identification of functional units. These are boldly expressed in taut combinations using the rich sculptural idiom of Le Corbusier's later work.

Programme and site constantly interact, with the slope exploited to telling effect. As in all Le Corbusier's work the articulation system achieves a dynamic state of equilibrium through the juxtaposition of contrasting forms. Although the church is inherently static, the most stable element in the complex, a degree of dynamism is induced by the spatial relationship with the adjacent sanctuary.

The cloister has its own dynamic, with a movement pattern which at one point ascends as the slope descends and at another descends while moving across the contours. The sense of muscular vigour evident in the cloister is echoed throughout the complex, with maximum drama contrived to the west where the serene horizontality of the roof is set against the vertical component at this point on the slope.

The severity of the design reflects the Dominican lifestyle, but the grey concrete surfaces are richly textured and colour is used to telling effect throughout. As generally in Le Corbusier's later work, light transcends form as the main vehicle of emotional expression.

The Villa Shodhan at Ahmedabad was designed as a residence for a Mr. Hutheesing, who was a secretary of the association of Indian cotton mill owners. According to the *Oeuvre complète*,[1] Mr. Hutheesing's requirements were 'personal, complicated and subtle,' but when the plans were completed they were sold to a Mr. Shodhan, who owned a different plot of land, but who was ready to start immediately.

The evolution of the villa can be traced back to the Dom-ino system of reinforced concrete slab and column supports (1914), marking the final stage of Le Corbusier's development of the dwelling as a cubic sculpting of form and space (as opposed to his development of the dwelling as a vaulted structure).

The villa exemplifies Le Corbusier's post-war rejection of the machine age imagery of the 'twenties in favour of an architectural language generated by natural forces. The form of the villa responds directly to the tropical climate of India, with a 'parasol' roof and brise soleil giving shade from the sun and an openness around the perimeter that allows breezes to blow across a series of terraces with hanging gardens.

1 Le Corbusier, *Oeuvre complète 1952-57*, New York, 1957, p. 134.

VILLA SHODHAN 1955-56

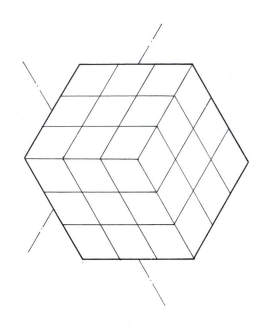

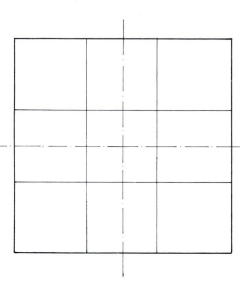

The generic form is a regular cube with equal axes.

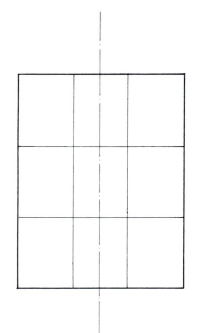

The cube is compressed into a linear configuration with a dominant linear axis.

CIRCULATION SPINE

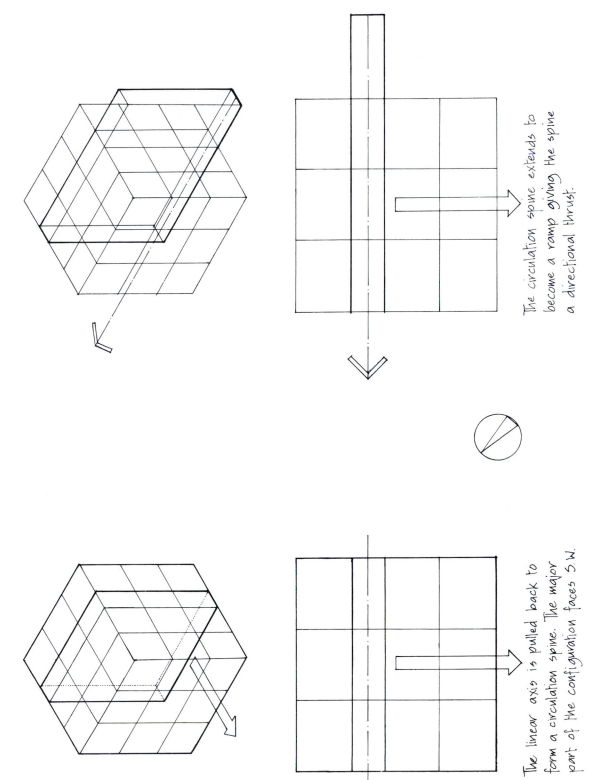

The circulation spine extends to become a ramp giving the spine a directional thrust.

The linear axis is pulled back to form a circulation spine. The major part of the configuration faces S.W.

A major and a minor mass are connected to each other by a plaided grid. The presence of this secondary mass exerts a pull towards it, expressed by the linear thrust of the circulation spine and by the primary reading of one diagonal over the other in the main mass.

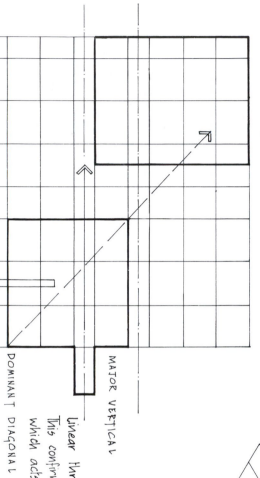

MINOR HORIZONTAL

MAJOR VERTICAL

DOMINANT DIAGONAL

Linear thrust is towards but forward of secondary mass. This confirms the secondary reading of the minor form which acts as a service wing.

Pulling back the secondary mass gives the **north/south** diagonal of the main mass a primary reading.

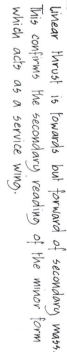

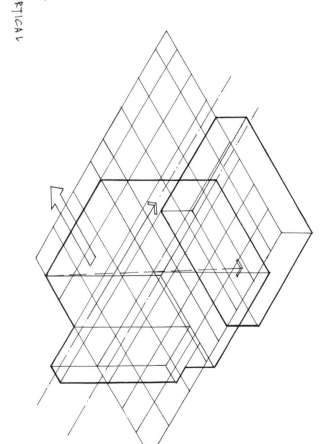

FORMAL DEVELOPMENT

The Villa Shodhan culminates Le Corbusier's development of the dwelling as a cubic, planar expression (as opposed to his development of a vaulted system).

Origins in the Dom-ino diagram embody the freedom inherent in reinforced concrete construction, with horizontal planes and column supports.

Purist dwellings celebrate the machine age in an ambiguous language that can be read as planes or mass. The Villa Stein-de-Monzie strongly emphasises the layering of vertical planes sandwiched between containing sides.

With the Villa at Carthage, Le Corbusier returns to his youthful preoccupation with natural forces. Horizontal floor planes are exposed to cooling breezes with no containing envelope.

Similarly, as a response to the heat of India, Le Corbusier combines the vertical planes of Stein-de-Monzie with the open horizontal systems of Dom-ino and Carthage. The plaided system is fully open in a bold sculptural statement that typifies his late period.

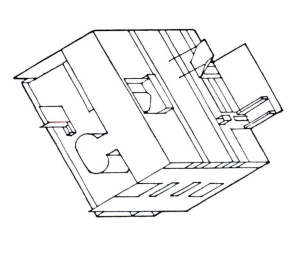

VILLA STEIN-DE-MONZIE 1926-29

VILLA SHODHAN 1955-56

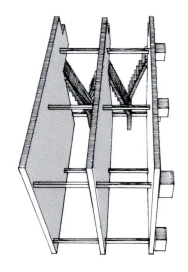

from the diagram in the Oeuvre Complète volume one

DOM-INO DIAGRAM 1914

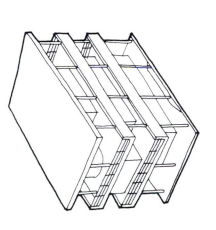

VILLA AT CARTHAGE 1929

317

PLANAR DIAGRAMS

(NOT TO SAME SCALE)

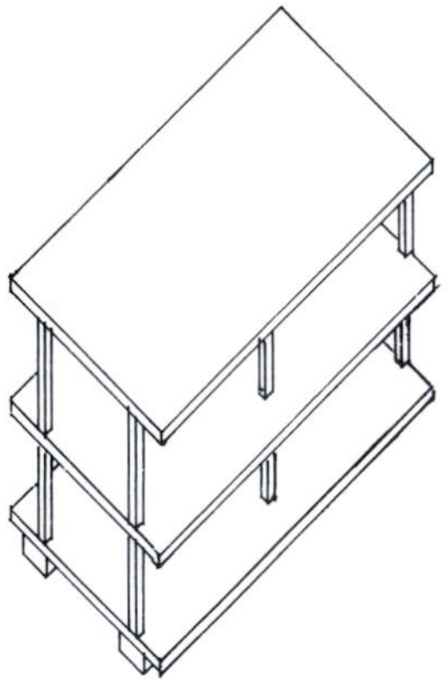

DOM-INO
HORIZONTAL

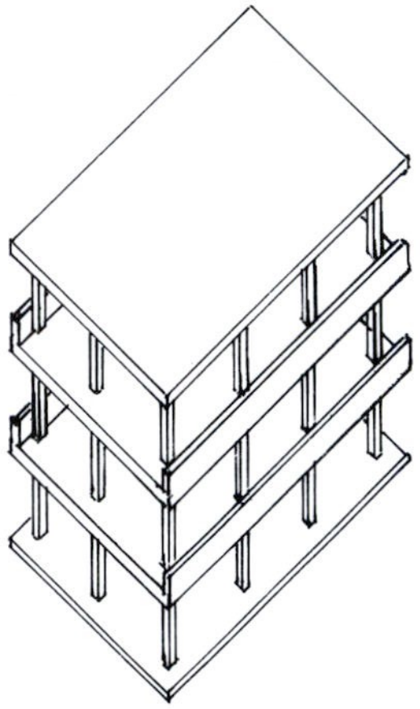

CARTHAGE
HORIZONTAL

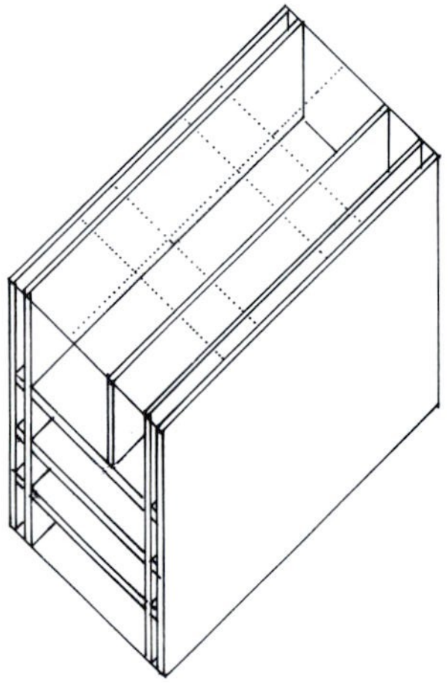

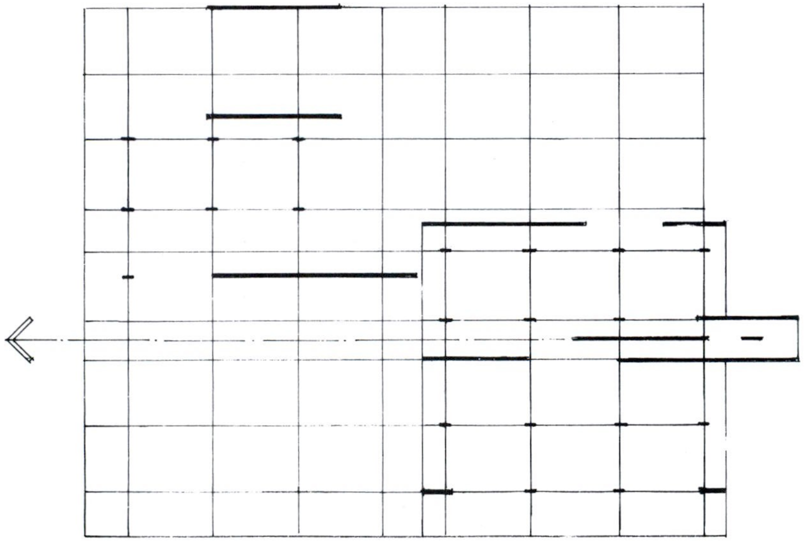

GROUND FLOOR PLAN   LINEAR PLANES
LINEAR COLUMNS

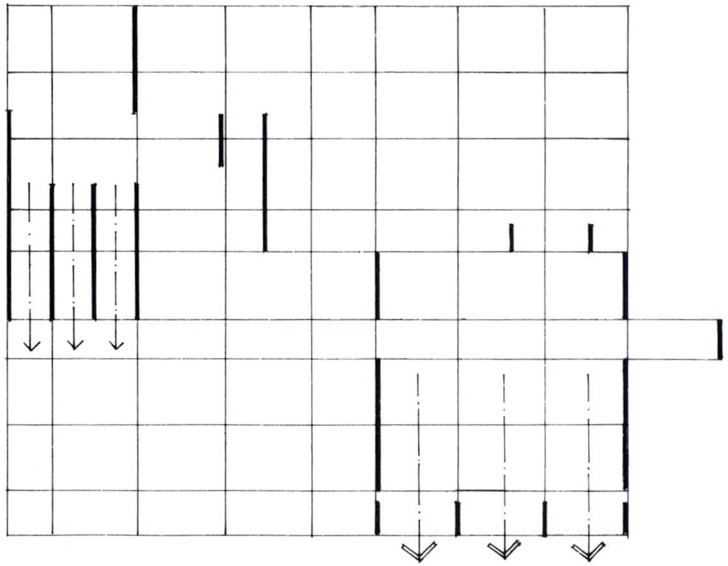

STEIN-DE-MONZIE
VERTICAL / HORIZONTAL

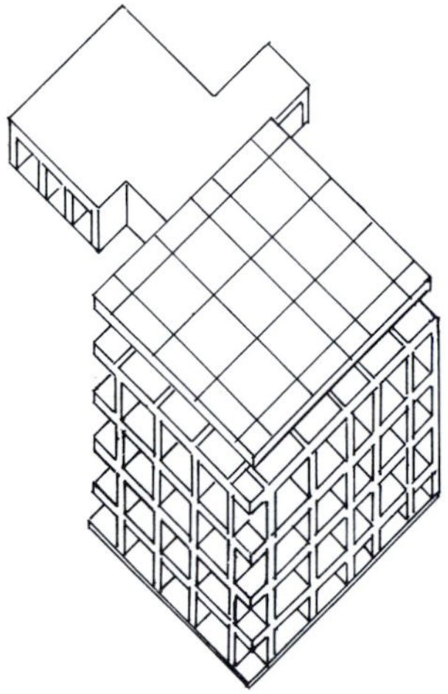

SHODHAN
'MILK CRATE' VERTICAL/HORIZONTAL

GROUND FLOOR PLAN   TRANSVERSE PLANES

GROUND FLOOR PLAN

GARAGE

TOILET

VERANDA

SERVANTS' ROOMS

VERANDAS

PANTRY

KITCHEN

CLOAKS

RECEPTION

OFFICE

RAMP

STAIRS TO CELLAR

LOUNGE

DINING

VERANDA

VERANDA

VERANDA

VERANDA

CONNECTIONS

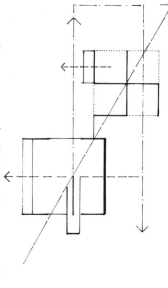

Connections are made between the major and minor forms by the plaided grid and by the geometrical organisation. Each form is centroidal, the major mass being divided into a front and back by the circulation spine. The secondary form has an implied rotational geometry and connections are made by the linear thrust and counter thrust of the ramp and garage and by the oblique thrust that passes through the centre of gravity of each configuration. Entry is clearly defined as it pieces the rear plane.

GROUND LEVEL

REPETITION IN A MINOR KEY

REAR PLANE

SYMMETRICAL FRONTALITY OF THE LOUNGE/DINING

OBLIQUE CONNECTING THRUST

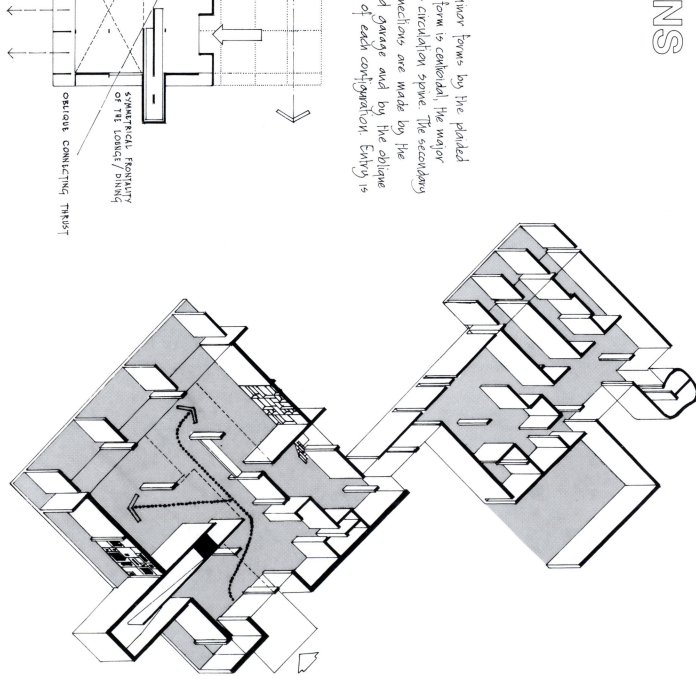

MEZZANINE BRIDGE

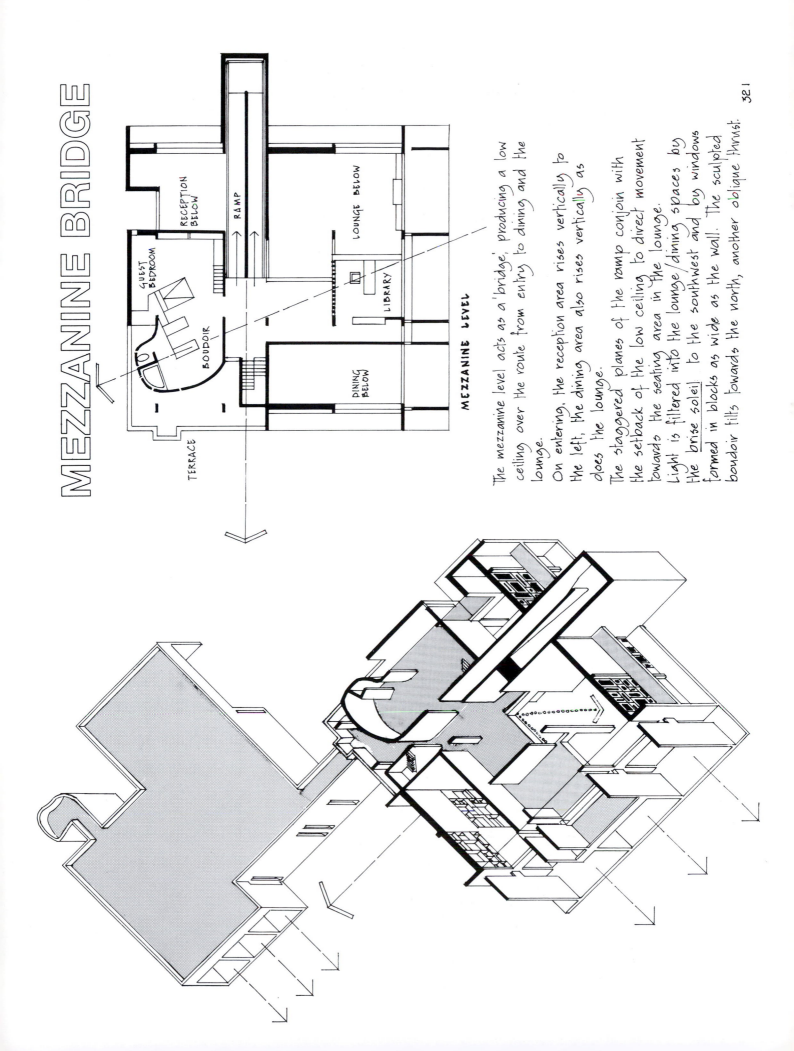

RECEPTION BELOW

RAMP

GUEST BEDROOM

BOUDOIR

TERRACE

DINING BELOW

LOUNGE BELOW

LIBRARY

MEZZANINE LEVEL

The mezzanine level acts as a 'bridge', producing a low ceiling over the route from entry to dining and the lounge.

On entering, the reception area rises vertically to the left, the dining area also rises vertically as does the lounge.

The staggered planes of the ramp conjoin with the setback of the low ceiling to direct movement towards the seating area in the lounge.

Light is filtered into the lounge/dining spaces by the brise soleil to the southwest and by windows formed in blocks as wide as the wall. The sculpted boudoir tilts towards the north, another oblique thrust.

DOMINANT DIAGONAL

At level 2 bedrooms are arranged on the dominant diagonal with a toilet at the core. Between the bedrooms, a south-west facing terrace is open to the roof, three levels above. Each bedroom rises through two levels and stairs lead to terraces and a gallery above.

On the main terrace, four columns support a platform pierced by an opening. The platform defines the space below and acts as a sculptural statement in the large void at the south-west corner of the villa. Alongside the toilet a further opening lets light down to the library.

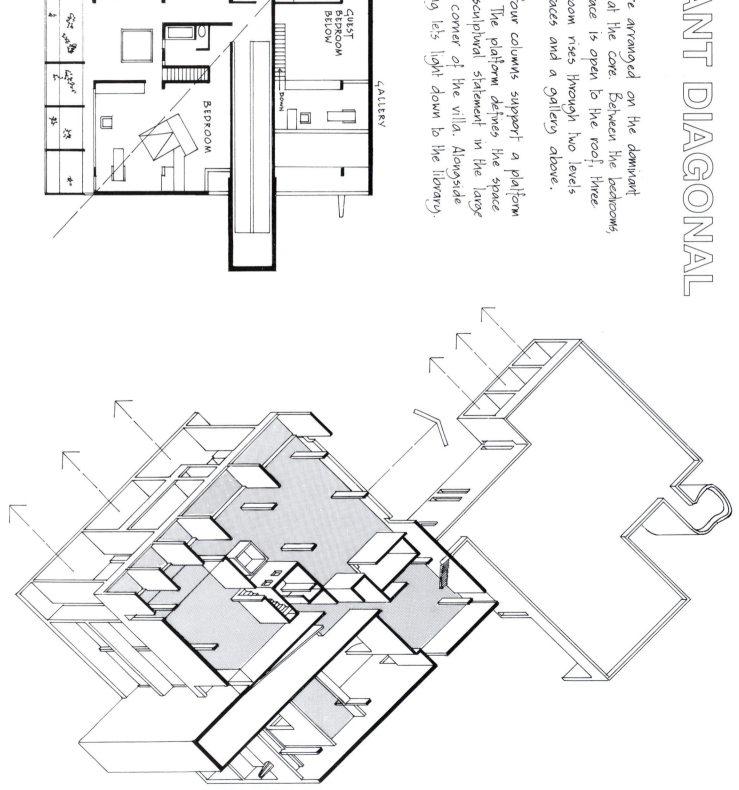

TERRACE

BEDROOM

BEDROOM

GUEST
BEDROOM
BELOW

DOWN

GALLERY

MEZZANINE

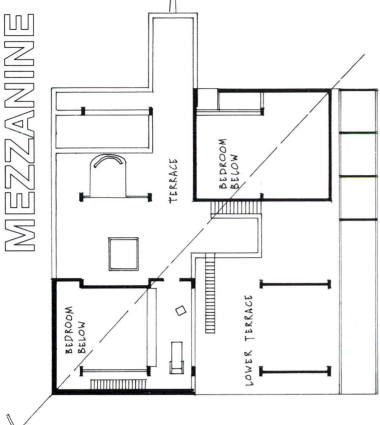

BEDROOM
BELOW

TERRACE

BEDROOM
BELOW

LOWER TERRACE

LEVEL 2 MEZZANINE

The mezzanine contains a terrace with steps down to the main terrace below. There are two 'balconies', one projecting outwards over the ramp, the other overlooking the lower terrace.

Spatially, the major volumes (upper levels of the bedrooms) are on the dominant diagonal whilst the terraces occupy the secondary diagonal.

A long staircase projects outwards and leads from the mezzanine to terraces at level three. This sculpted element, suspended in space, provides a major visual event in relation to the lower terrace.

323

INTERLOCKING CASCADES

At level 3 terraces are again on the dominant diagonal, this directional thrust being marked by a sculpted water tank. Lower terraces cascade down to the south-west and north-east.

The upper terrace locks onto the circulation spine and onto the _brise soleil_ at its south-western edge. Volumes, terraces and the _brise soleil_ lock together in a series of layers compressed within the overall volume.

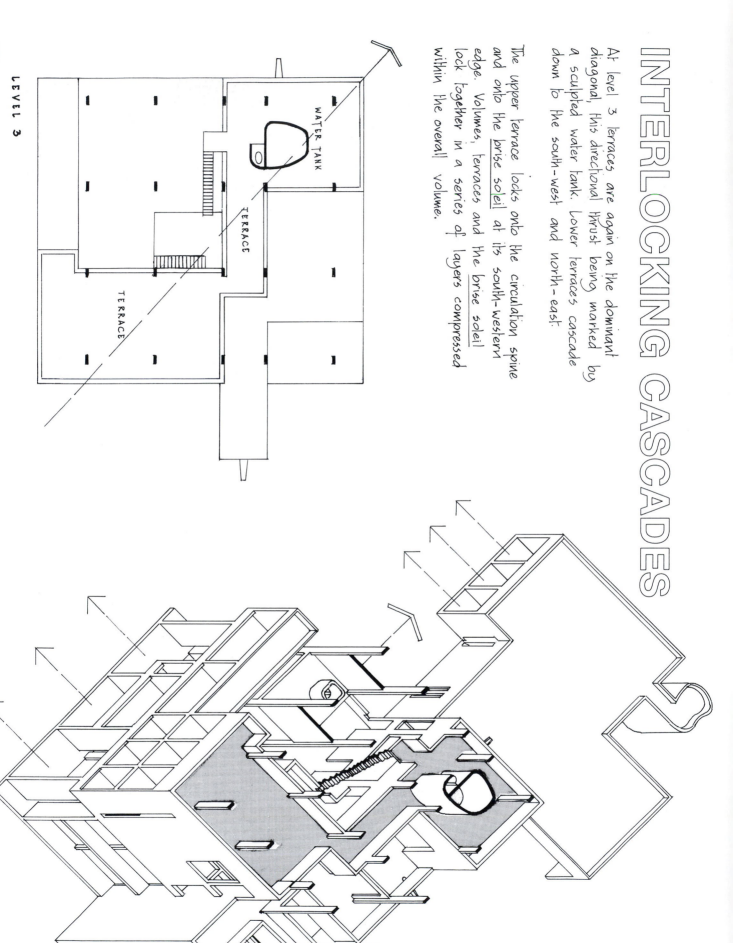

WATER TANK

TERRACE

TERRACE

OPENNESS AND COMPACTION

The sculptural handling of the form recalls Le Corbusier's paintings and tapesteries of the 'fifties and 'sixties with a bold handling of the mass and raw, board-marked concrete instead of the smooth planar finish of the Purist aesthetic.

The objets types of the Purist era, precisely formulated like the parts of a machine are replaced by a relaxed plasticity. The brise soleil replaces the ribbon windows of the Villas Stein-de-Monzie and Savoye, and although the form remains compacted the villa suggests openness and penetrability instead of the closure of the 'twenties decade.

TAPESTRY BY LE CORBUSIER AS A STAGE CURTAIN FOR A TOKYO THEATRE 1956

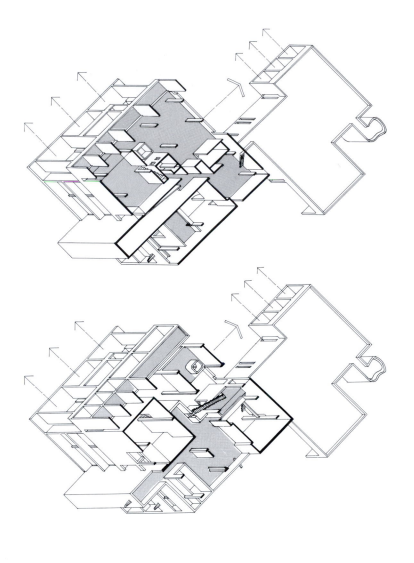

LEVEL 2

MEZZANINE

Like it's precursor in the Villa Savoye, the Shodhan ramp is locked into the ensemble. But whereas the Savoye ramp is contained within a closed external envelope, acting as a central experiential focus, the Shodhan ramp extends out of the form and acts as a divider between the primary and secondary spaces to the south and north.

The ramp slides into the overall form as a closed volume, but its roof participates in the terrace at the level 2 mezzanine. The sense of unity that pervades the Villa Savoye—a harmonious composition held by the central ramp—is denied at the Villa Shodhan, where the vertical progression has an almost Piranesian complexity as we encounter contrasting spaces and volumes.

The movement sequence leads us through a labyrinth that extends vertically at all times, providing unusual experiential diversity. From the closed space of the ramp we emerge with a left turn at level 2 to discover the openness and grandeur of the south-west terrace. Turning left again, a closed stair ascends to the mezzanine with an overlook of the terrace.

DYNAMIC SPACES

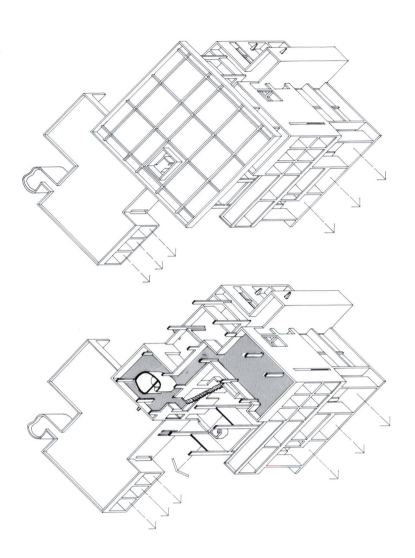

LEVEL 3

The next ascent is by a projecting stair to level 3;
looking out across the south-west terrace. The stair
is a sculptural event that impacts the space. It takes
the eye upwards, finally to the opening in the
roof alongside the stair.

At level 3 there are views out from the villa or
down onto the terraces below, the roof giving shade
and containing the space above the terraces.

The inner spatial and volumetric complexity of the
concept receives externalisation in the south-west
facade, where the brise soleil shifts from the
four-columned symmetry of level one to rhythms
above that reflect internal conditions.

The distinguished Indian architect Charles Correa
describes Le Corbusier's handling of form and space
in the Assembly Building in the government complex at
Chandigarh as 'cunning and sensitive.'[1] In a discussion
equally relevant to the Villa Shodhan, Correa explains
how, like Frank Lloyd Wright, Le Corbusier is 'keenly
aware of the distances that can be seen from any
given point.' He continues:

'By never defining the limits of his vision (the
sections and plans are always co-ordinated so
that the eye can always see beyond and around
the corner), the spaces remain dynamic and un-
contained... creating an overall pattern of
incredible richness.'

1 Charles Correa 'The Assembly, Chandigarh,' Architectural Review
June, 1964, p. 406.

PATTERN

Describing Le Corbusier's use of pattern at Chandigarh, Charles Correa continues:

'The complexity of his architecture is not due to the creation of _one single_ intricate pattern but is rather due to the creation of several different patterns which, through superimposition, generate an indescribable complexity.'[1]

Correa describes the facade of the Secretariat:

'where a complete landscape is created by juxtaposing _brise soleil_ grilles of various patterns and scales. (This technique is often used in the marble grilles of Fatehpur Sikri and the shoji screens of Japan.) This is not to say that Corb could really have calculated all these effects. What he has done is this: he has been shrewd enough to establish a situation where different patterns can interact. The miracles follow of their own accord, and a complete landscape is generated.'[2]

1 Charles Correa, 'The Assembly, Chandigarh,' _Architectural Review,_ June, 1964, p.406

2 Ibid, pp. 406-411.

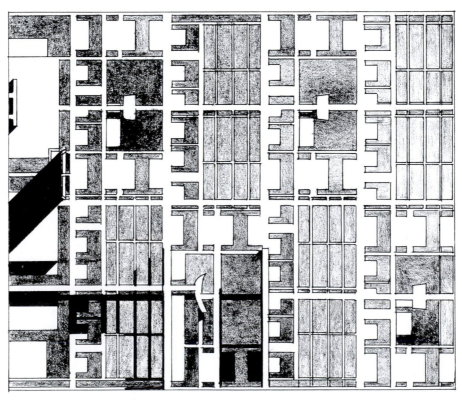

THE SECRÉTARIAT CHANDIGARH 1952-56
PART OF THE BRISE SOLEIL ON THE SOUTHEAST FACADE

LE CORBUSIER AND INDIA

In his late works Le Corbusier rejects any facile interpretation of modernity, and uses the abstract architectural language culled from modern art and technology to represent a centuries old cultural tradition.

As Charles Correa points out, Le Corbusier gave Indian architects a sense of their past 'because in some inexplicable way' he is 'tuned to this country.' Describing the Taj Mahal as the fake India of Hollywood, Correa explains how Le Corbusier evoked a much deeper image. In an unfavourable comparison with the American architect Edward Stone's embassy in Delhi, Correa refers to the integrity of Le Corbusier's work :

'Corb has evoked a much deeper image. His is a more real India, an India of the bazaars, sprawling, cruel, raucous in colour, with a grandeur all its own. His aesthetic evokes our history, and Chandigarh finds echoes in Fatehpur Sikri, in Jaiselmer, in Mandu. Surely, this is why a building of Corb's sits so well on Indian soil, whereas at Harvard it seems an affectation.'[1]

Yet despite all his efforts to design for the Indian climate, with the exception of the Sarabhai house in Ahmedabad, Le Corbusier's buildings in India were poorly ventilated. The _brise soleil_ retained heat that had built up during the day, so that when cooling breezes blew through at night they were warmed by the concrete sun screens.

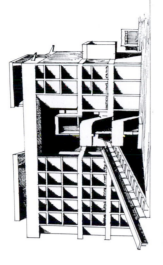

THE MILLOWNERS ASSOCIATION BUILDING, AHMEDABAD INDIA 1954 After Francis D.K Ching

HIGH COURT BUILDING CHANDIGARH 1952-56

[1] Charles Correa, 'The Assembly, Chandigarh,' _Architectural Review_, June, 1964, p.412

The Architect, by his arrangement of forms, realises an order which is a pure creation of his spirit; by forms and shapes he affects our senses to an acute degree... by the relationships which he creates he awakes profound echoes in us, he gives us the measure of an order which we feel to be in accordance with that of our world, he determines the various movements of our heart and of our understanding; it is then that we experience the sense of beauty.

Le Corbusier : Towards a New Architecture, trans. by F. Etchells, Architectural Press, London 1946. p.7.

6

ARTICULATION SYSTEMS IN LE CORBUSIER'S OEUVRE

INTERLOCK

For Le Corbusier, architectural composition posed problems not dissimilar to those he had faced in painting. It was necessary, when putting together the parts of a building, to establish certain guidelines as to how components should be selected and arranged.

Purism and L'Esprit Nouveau were to some extent motivated by the desire to acquire a theory that would lead to a compositional rationale relevant to both painting and architecture, and similarities of technique are apparent in Le Corbusier's work in both fields.

In his architectural work of the twenties Le Corbusier was influenced by his Purist ideals, which reinforced his view that equilibrium was a desirable attribute in works of art or architecture. In his Purist paintings equilibrium was usually attained by balancing a series of elements in compositions which provide a dynamic contrast between verticals and horizontals.

In these paintings there is often a basic contrast between background and foreground incidents, between the curvilinear and rectilinear, and elements are sometimes interlocked as in the way two briar pipes are wrapped around a cylinder as in the morte à la pile d'assiettes.* The interlock is represented as being three dimensional, and in this as in other characteristics the articulation method is similar to that used architecturally by Le Corbusier. Typical examples of interlocking elements occur in the Weissenhof House and in the Chapel at Ronchamp.

* see diagram on page 89

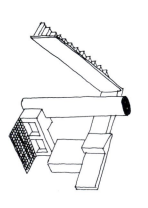

ELEMENTS LOCKED AROUND THE SERVICES STACK IN THE WEISSENHOF HOUSE

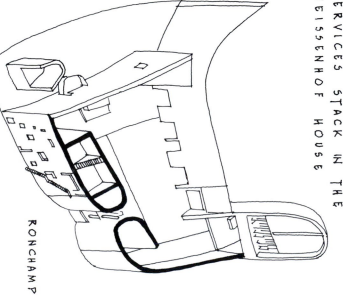

THE REAR CHAPELS ARE LOCKED TOGETHER ABOUT THE SECONDARY ENTRANCE

RONCHAMP

FOUR SYSTEMS

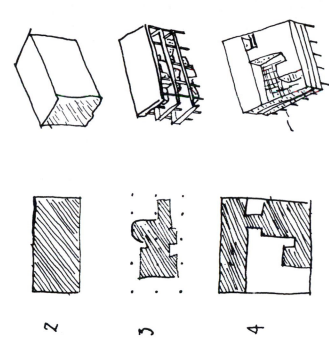

1

2

3

4

In the *Oeuvre Complète*[2] Le Corbusier discusses four basic articulation systems as expressed in four compositions; the La Roche~Jeanneret houses, the Villa at Carthage and the Villa Savoye. These examples demonstrate the different kinds of design problem, each making different demands on the architect.

La Roche~Jeanneret is described as being picturesque, full of incident, not very difficult to handle in that elements may be classified and expressed hierarchically. Garches he explains as posing a difficult problem because in dealing with a simple cubic form it is not easy to provide any 'spiritual' or intellectual satisfaction.

With the Villa at Carthage the problem is simplified by the possibility of linkage with other forms, and the Villa Savoye he explains as being a positive architectural statement allowing a correct disposition of internal functional needs with a compactness that conveniently relates the various parts of the design.

after a drawing by Le Corbusier in the *Oeuvre Complète* 1910-1929 p.189

2 Le Corbusier and Pierre Jeanneret, *Oeuvre Complète 1910-29*, Erlenbach, 1929.

ORTHOGONAL DISCIPLINE

The reinforced concrete frame and slab, symbolised by the Domino System, formed the basis of Le Corbusier's main design approach, and it was within this orthogonal cage that the various 'organs' of a building were accommodated. Frequently the organs themselves were identified by the activities they contained or the purpose they served, as for example when a living area, circulation zone or roof terrace is positively defined.

Le Corbusier's inclination was usually to subdue technology and the expression of structure in order to concentrate on a sculptural statement having sensorial impact. He neither displayed the planes of his buildings as in De Stijl, nor overtly exploited structure as in Constructivist architecture, an exception being the Palace of the Soviets competition project of 1931 in which a giant parabolic arch and series of beams visibly support the roof of the main auditorium.

To Le Corbusier a structural framework gave precise guidelines within which he could compose. As with his Purist paintings this framework was a starting point, providing an underlying discipline that was reassuring :

That is where the triumph lies : in this internal structure... so encouraging because of this harmony, daughter of precision, sensed by everyone. [1]

1 A reference by Le Corbusier to the structure of the Unité d'Habitation at Marseilles, from Le Corbusier, _Modulor 2_, London, 1958, p. 233.

ORTHOGONAL CAGE OF THE VILLA SAVOYE

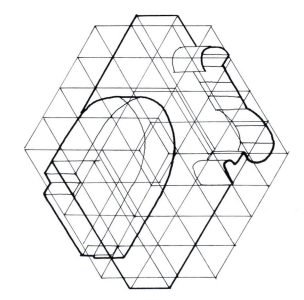

A favourite device during the twenties was the tensioning of curved planes against the orthogonal grid as in the Villa Savoye — also used to good effect in the Maison Cook and Villa at Garches.

These planar techniques contrast with the use of curves as part of the mass in apsidal projections at the Villa Jeanneret-Perret and the Villa Schwob.

STRUCTURAL FRAME

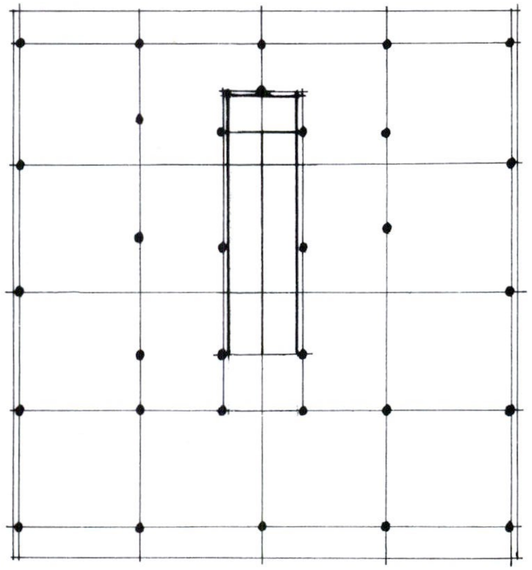

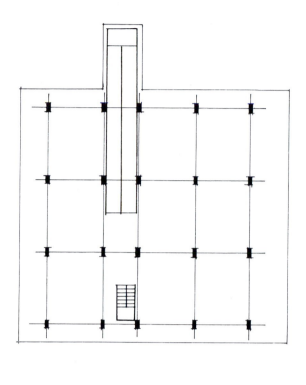

VILLA SHODAN 1952-56

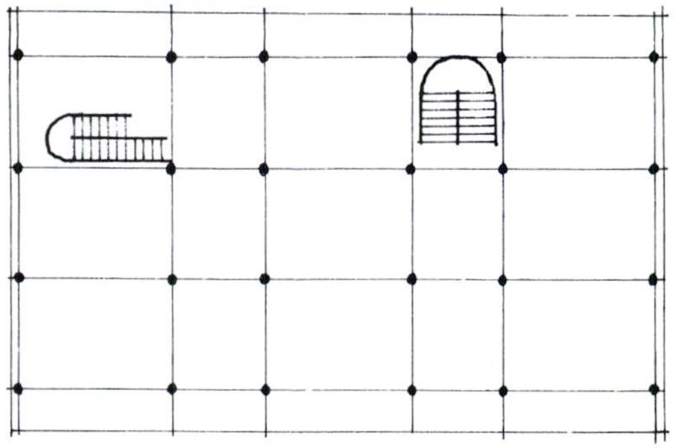

Le Corbusier modulates his structural framework to accommodate circulation elements. In typical villa plans the grid provides an ordering discipline into which ramps or stairs are easily absorbed.

VILLA SAVOYE 1929-31

VILLA AT GARCHES 1927

NATURE AS SOURCE

After 1925 Le Corbusier no longer relied on the *objets types* as subject matter in his paintings, and bones, shells, stones and fruit begin to appear. He called these *objets à reaction poétique* and by 1928 the human figure was introduced, this becoming a dominant theme of canvases painted during the thirties.

This shift of interest, from a limited range of idealised manufactured artefacts towards nature in a broader sense, marks an important change in Le Corbusier's view of the world. On visits to Spain, North Africa and South America he became enchanted with peasant cultures, which he always compared unfavourably with what he regarded as the unsavoury consumerism of western society.

His thirties sketchbooks reveal a consuming interest in 'primitive' cultures, suggesting a growing disenchantment with the machine civilization and the acquisitive attitudes which it encouraged. This perception of the life/nature phenomenon was in a constant state of development, revealed in both sketchbooks and paintings and with inevitable consequences in his architecture.

The paintings clearly indicate changes in attitude and technique, and by 1930 the cool precision and controlled compaction of the early Purist canvases changes to a much looser approach, with diverse subject matter freely composed. The soft curves of the human figure extend the sensuality formerly expressed through the curvilinear profiles of bottles, books or guitars.

In Le Corbusier's architecture, these changes are reflected in the introduction of natural materials around 1930, with the appearance of stone in the curved outer wall of the lower pavilion of the Swiss Students' Hostel at Paris University. A stone wall is also retained in the studio to Le Corbusier's own apartment near the Porte Molitor.

WEEKEND HOUSE 1935

During the thirties the house for M Errazuris in Chile was conceived as being built of timber and stone, with stone walls also used in the villa for Mme. de Mandrot and in the Holiday House at Les Mathes near La Rochelle.
Significantly Le Corbusier returns to the theme first expressed in his vaulted alternative to the Citrohan, the Monol Houses, in the Weekend House in a Paris Suburb (1935). Again stone walls are used, with grass growing on the vaulted roof.

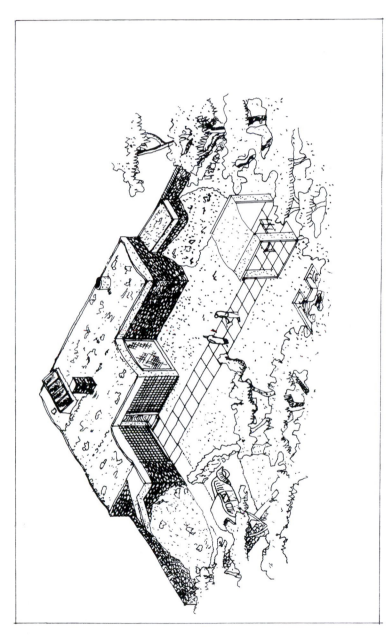

WEEKEND HOUSE IN A PARIS SUBURB (1935) 2nd PROJECT
after drawing No. 9243 in the Le Corbusier Fondation Paris.

If the Villa Savoye represents Le Corbusier's abstract classical ideal, inspired by his Purist ideology, the Weekend House expresses his fascination with vernacular architecture, folk art and the organic. The two strands were to continue in his work, the classical cubic strain leading to the Villa Shodan at Ahmedabad (1952-56) while the Weekend House is the forerunner of the Maisons Jaoul and Villa Sarabhai (1954-56).

Early houses during the twenties such as the Citrohan project and the La Roche-Jeanneret Houses at Auteuil Paris may be read primarily as masses, the forms being sculpted from the solid. This is despite the fact that the solids are composed from an assemblage of planes.

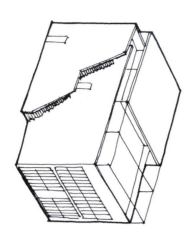

CITROHAN PROJECT 1920

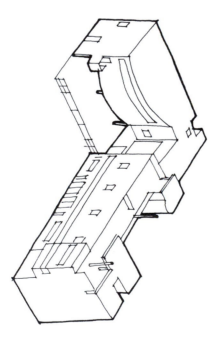

LA ROCHE-JEANNERET HOUSES 1922-23

FRAME AND MEMBRANE

Such mass readings sometimes comprise a membrane stretched over a reinforced concrete frame as in the case of the Weissenhof House and the Villa at Garches, a technique used by Le Corbusier on larger buildings.

These cubic primary forms obey the perceptual laws of Purism. They also put into practice Le Corbusier's five points for the new architecture: 1) columns to raise the building above the ground ; 2) roof gardens ; 3) the free plan; 4) the long window ; 5) the free facade.

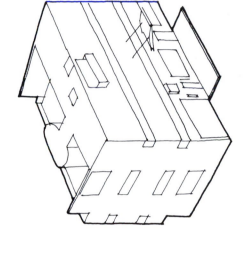

VILLA AT GARCHES 1927

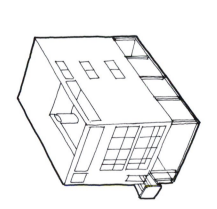

WEISSENHOF HOUSE 1927

MASS PENETRATED

With the Villa Béseult at Carthage Tunisia, for the first time the continuous external membrane is removed entirely, exposing the horizontal floor planes at each end and as well as the 'internal' elements. This statement of columns and slabs reminds us of the structural principles embodied in the Domino system; in this case the overhanging slabs provide shade to interior rooms.

At the Villa Savoye the cubic <u>piano nobile</u> is opened up by cutting out part of the slab exposing the ramp at the upper levels.

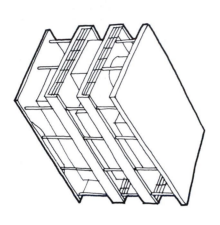

VILLA AT CARTHAGE 1929

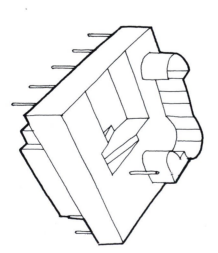

VILLA SAVOYE 1929-31

In 1927 with the Villa at Garches, Le Corbusier had cut away part of the rear of the mass, again to link a terrace to the living zone while exposing the plane at the side of the mass. As with the Villa Savoye the cut-away allows a subtle merging of interior and external space. Again circulation is involved, the terrace extending out and being linked to the garden by a staircase.

Penetrations of the mass made possible by the elimination of the outer membrane at Carthage are realised by the use of the brise soleil in the Villa Shodhan in Ahmedabad India. Use of the brise soleil gives shade from the sun and allows cooling breezes to blow through the building. The Villa Shodhan represents the last significant development in Le Corbusier's domestic architecture in a progression which starts with the Domino idea and takes in the Citrohan prototype and various houses during the twenties and thirties.

VILLA SHODHAN 1952 – 56

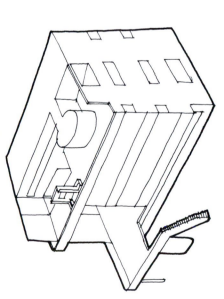

VILLA AT GARCHES 1927

341

Le Corbusier's use of a frame and membrane in which masses are related reached a sophisticated level in buildings such as the Pavillon Suisse and Cité de Refuge. In these residential buildings Le Corbusier places the multi-cellular living accommodation in a large slab block, housing the more varied communal activities in smaller volumes placed next to the main form.

The Swiss Student's Hostel locks the smaller volume into the larger by means of the stair and bathroom segment which adjoins the main block; the composition becomes dynamic by the use of curves, by the oblique alignment of the lower pavilion and stair, and by the way pilotis raise the main block whilst the pavilion remains rooted to the ground.

This technique of contrasting forms rooted in the ground with elevated forms had been used by Le Corbusier in the Villas La Roche-Jeanneret (1923-25) and was to be employed in the monastery of Saint Marie de la Tourette (1957-60).

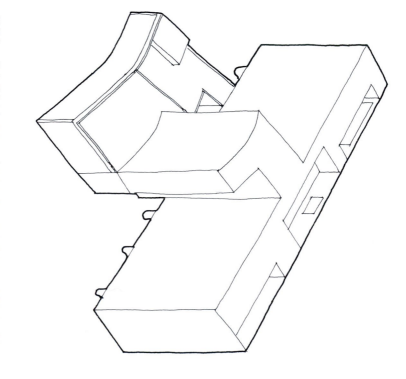

THE PAVILLON SUISSE PARIS 1930-32

VOLUMES AGAINST MEMBRANE

The Cité de Refuge, Salvation Army H.Q. in Paris, having complex organisational requirements, has these identified by a series of volumes placed against the glazed membrane of the main block.

The contrast of the solid primary forms (set against the glazed membrane) with the slab block and with each other, gives a typically positive identification of the various elements. The arrangement also confirms Le Corbusier's belief that the juxtaposition of primary forms plays a key role in the sensory experience of architecture.

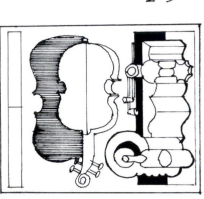

NATURE MORTE AU
VIOLON ROUGE 1920

THE CITÉ DE REFUGE 1932-33

As a composition, the Cité de Refuge has a similar theme to Le Corbusier's Purist painting Nature morte au violon rouge in which a series of objets types act as foreground incidents in contrast with a guitar and its projected shadow.

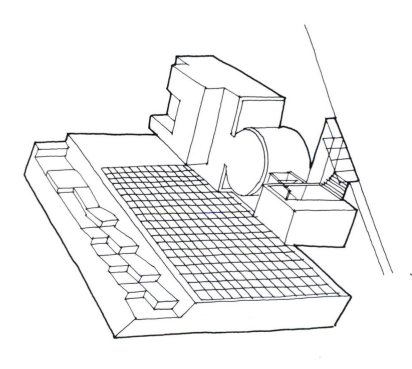

BRISE SOLEIL

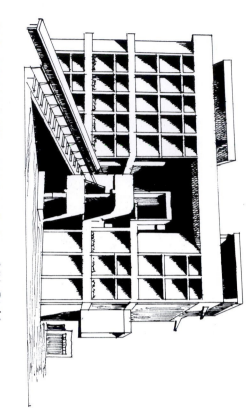

THE MILLOWNERS ASSOCIATION BUILDING
AHMEDABAD INDIA 1954   After Francis D.K. Ching

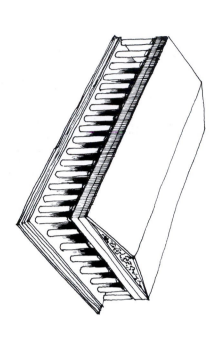

THE PARTHENON ATHENS 447-432 B.C.

Le Corbusier's attitude towards the surface skin of his buildings changed when he realised the kinds of problem caused during the twenties by having a thin membrane with large glazed areas. Many buildings, including his own apartment, suffered from overheating in summer and a loss of heat in winter.

The problem became acute in hot countries and Le Corbusier's solution was the evolution of the form of sunbreaker known as the brise soleil. An example of this occurs with his Ministry of Education building at Rio in 1938 to be followed by his 'Biological' skyscraper for Algiers. Exploitation of the device post-war occurs in the various Unités, the Monastery at La Tourette, the High Court Building, Secretariat and Legislative Assembly at Chandigarh, the Millowners' Association Building at Ahmedabad and the Carpenter Centre for the Visual Arts at Cambridge Massachusetts.

The brise soleil acts as a filter, providing a permeable skin around a building which allows spatial penetration and softens the impact of the form, much as the peristyle of columns around a Greek Temple softens the relationship of the mass to the surrounding space.

The brise soleil destroyed the cubic effect of the earlier houses with a consequent loss of precision in expression. But Le Corbusier used the depth of the device to reveal internal functional elements and with the depth of the 'Biological' skyscraper and in so many post-war buildings the surface treatment gives meaning to the form.

PINWHEEL AND SPIRAL

MUSEUM OF UNLIMITED GROWTH 1939
PROJECT FOR PHILIPPEVILLE ALGERIA

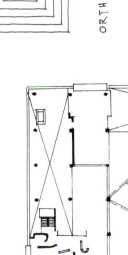

After the twenties Le Corbusier became interested in the organic or 'biological' expression of elements, which he combined with his positive attitude to pedestrian flow. His Museum of Unlimited Growth was inspired by the spiral growth of sea shells. Using a central entry visitors move outwards through the galleries, adapting the spiral principle into an orthogonal system.

With museums at Ahmedabad and Tokyo the elements are pivoted about a fulcrum. A pyramidal rooflight forms part of the fulcrum to the Tokyo museum, its oblique alignment assisting the dynamic. Around this the galleries rotate in a pinwheel configuration.

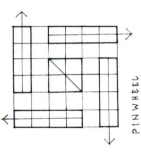

ORTHOGONAL SPIRAL

PINWHEEL

SPIRAL GROWTH OF NAUTILUS SHELL

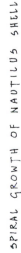

MUSEUM OF WESTERN ART TOKYO 1957-59

DYNAMISM OF THE ROUTE

As components in his buildings, Le Corbusier recognised the value of circulation elements because their role was unambiguous and they afforded such an excellent contrast to the other elements in a composition. Stairs, ramps, bridges and routes of various kinds were used by Le Corbusier to infuse his buildings with dramatic and varied experiences, the precise nature and clear definition of these components conforming to Le Corbusier's articulation requirements because they fitted so easily into his geometric framework.

Another reason why he valued these elements was their capacity to **add a powerful dynamic** content into a design. Although the pursuit of equilibrium was important to Le Corbusier, this balance of forces was usually achieved by setting positive opposing forces against each other. Just as contrasting elements transform a static situation into a dynamic one in his paintings, so too do similar contrasts operate in his architecture, and such elements as ramps, spiral or 'dog leg' stairs, because of their shape and usage, supplied a totally different force characteristic to the other components within a composition. Above all they were animated, containing pedestrian or vehicular flow, as such conveying the very lifeblood, the users of the building, from zone to zone.

Because of this, Le Corbusier uses circulation routes as 'arteries,' linking major 'organs', the route pattern providing a basis for the activity framework of the building.

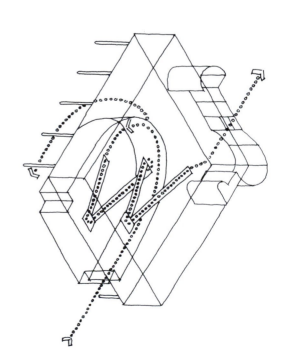

VILLA SAVOYE ANIMATED BY CIRCULATION

PROMENADE ARCHITECTURALE

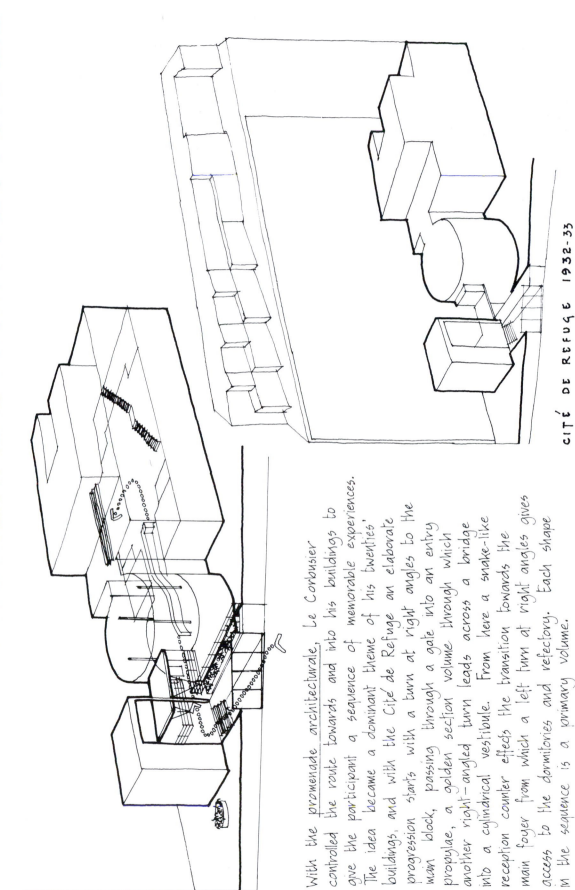

CITÉ DE REFUGE 1932-33

With the promenade architecturale, Le Corbusier controlled the route towards and into his buildings to give the participant a sequence of memorable experiences. The idea became a dominant theme of his twenties' buildings, and with the Cité de Refuge an elaborate progression starts with a turn at right angles to the main block, passing through a gate into an entry propylae, a golden section volume through which another right-angled turn leads across a bridge into a cylindrical vestibule. From here a snake-like reception counter effects the transition towards the main foyer from which a left turn at right angles gives access to the dormitories and refectory. Each shape in the sequence is a primary volume.

By the Thirties, Le Corbusier was fully aware of the way curved surfaces could interact with context and movement towards buildings. This had first been explored in the Villa Favre-Jacot in 1912, and was used in the Villas La Roche-Jeanneret (1923-25) and in the Chapel at Ronchamp (1950-55). The curved planes of the Pavillon Suisse respond to the approach road and turning circle in a gentle termination of views en route towards the Pavillon. The Director's apartment is aligned almost parallel to the Rue Benoist Malon thereby giving a powerful twist to the form.

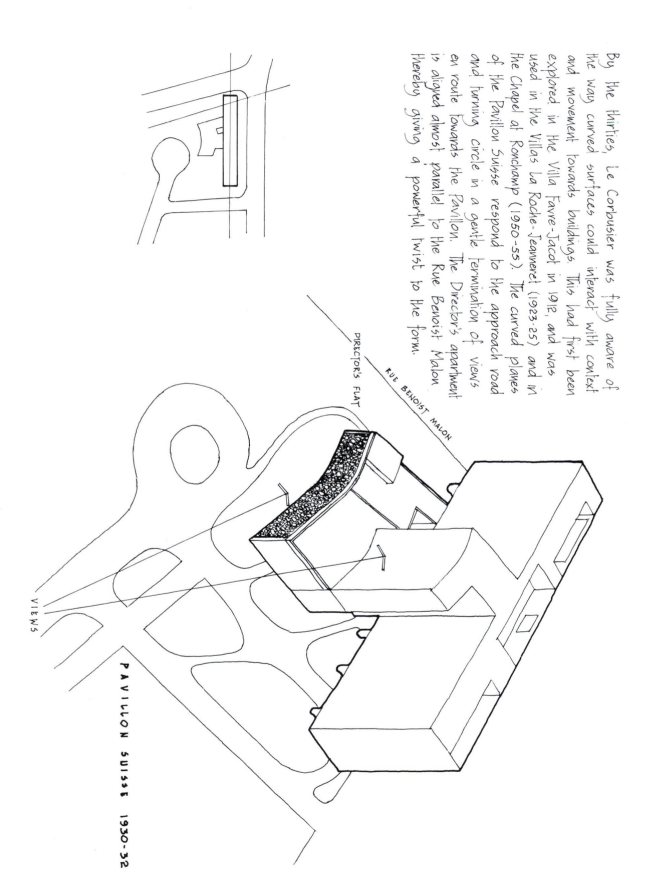

DIRECTOR'S FLAT

RUE BENOIST MALON

VIEWS

PAVILLON SUISSE 1930-32

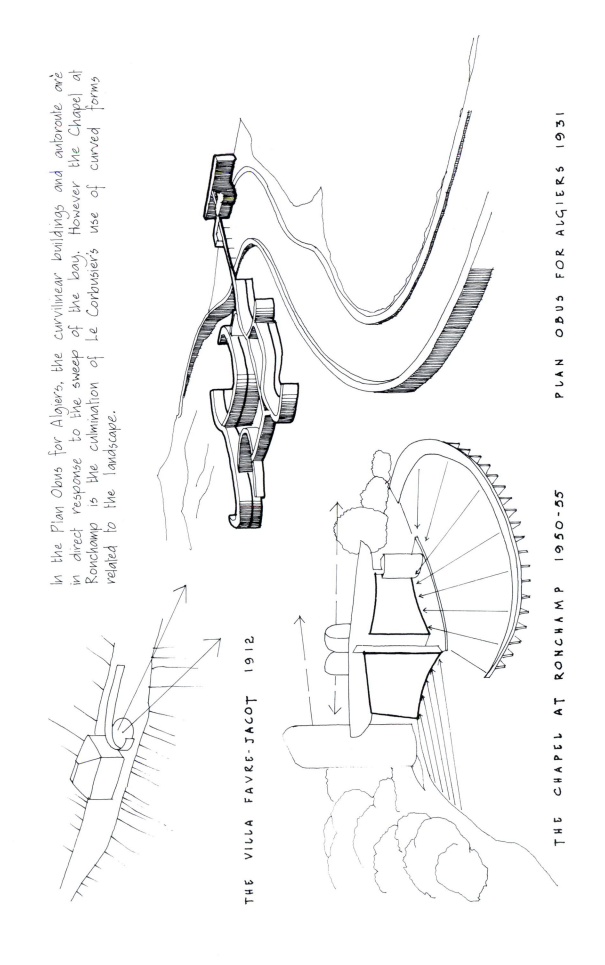

In the Plan Obus for Algiers, the curvilinear buildings and autoroute are in direct response to the sweep of the bay. However the Chapel at Ronchamp is the culmination of Le Corbusier's use of curved forms related to the landscape.

THE VILLA FAVRE-JACOT 1912

PLAN OBUS FOR ALGIERS 1931

THE CHAPEL AT RONCHAMP 1950-55

TENSION

The introduction of tension into a composition is a recurrent theme in Le Corbusier's work. In the Pavillon Suisse the bone-shaped pilotis supporting the main block seem to be pulling outwards like a chest expander, creating a powerful linear axis which intensifies the linearity of the vertical slab. A similar outward pulling action occurs with the twin rear chapels at Ronchamp. At the monastery of La Tourette a tensional relationship occurs between the church and the rest of the complex (see page 284).

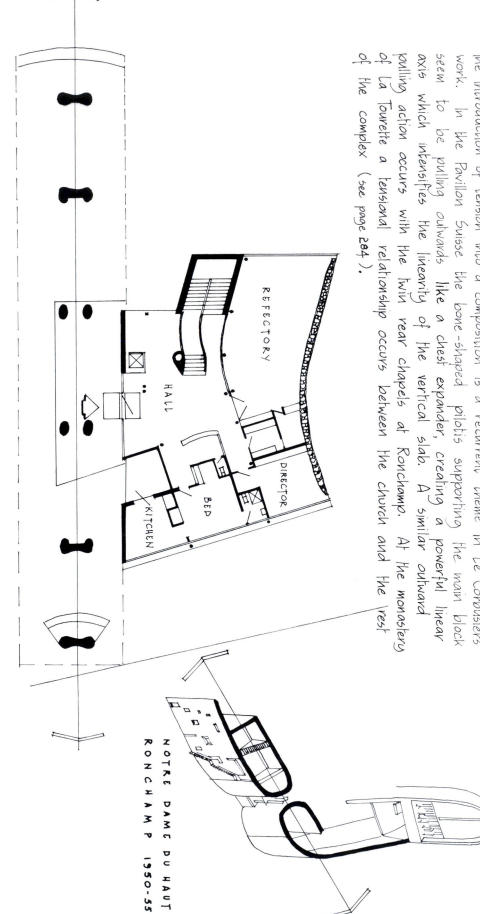

GROUND PLAN PAVILLON SUISSE 1930-32

REFECTORY

HALL

DIRECTOR

BED

KITCHEN

NOTRE DAME DU HAUT
RONCHAMP 1950-55

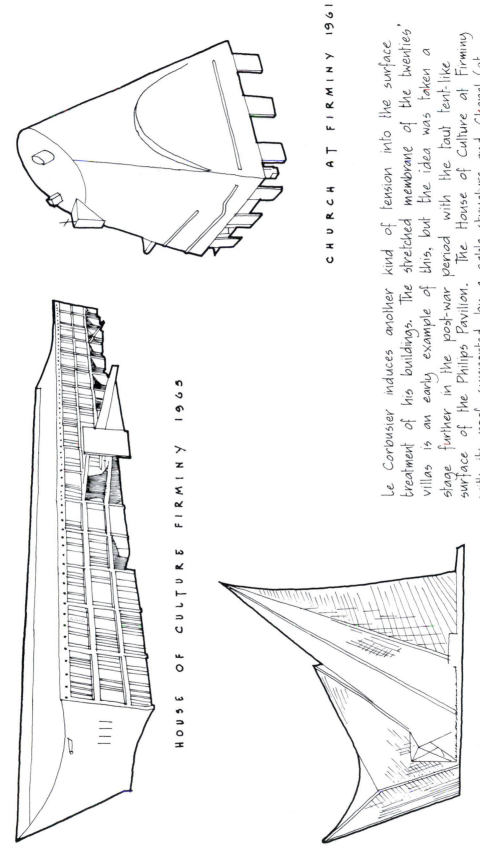

CHURCH AT FIRMINY 1961

HOUSE OF CULTURE FIRMINY 1965

PHILIPS PAVILION BRUSSELS
WORLD FAIR 1958

Le Corbusier induces another kind of tension into the surface treatment of his buildings. The stretched membrane of the twenties' villas is an early example of this, but the idea was taken a stage further in the post-war period with the taut tent-like surface of the Philips Pavilion. The House of Culture at Firminy with its roof supported by a cable structure and Chapel (at Firminy) also explore the dynamism inherent in a stretched skin.

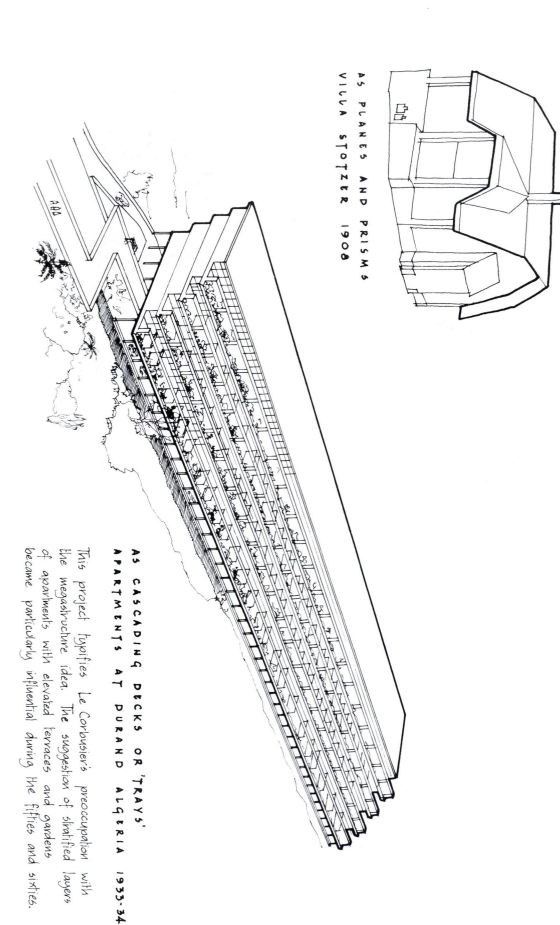

AS PLANES AND PRISMS
VILLA STOTZER 1908

AS CASCADING DECKS OR 'TRAYS'
APARTMENTS AT DURAND ALGERIA 1933-34

This project typifies Le Corbusier's preoccupation with
the megastructure idea. The suggestion of stratified layers
of apartments with elevated terraces and gardens
became particularly influential during the fifties and sixties.

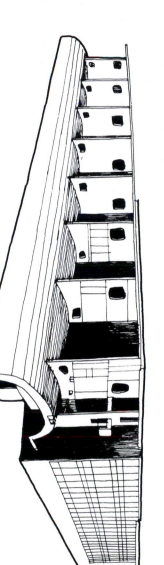

AS UMBRELLA   LEGISLATIVE ASSEMBLY CHANDIGARH 1953-61

These buildings are particularly rich in rhythm pattern and texture, important characteristics of Le Corbusier's post-war architecture.

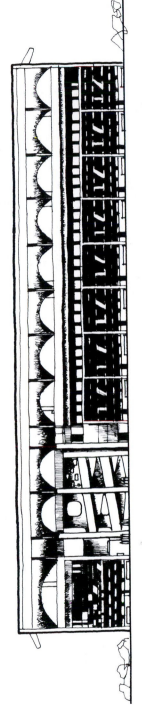

AS UMBRELLA   HIGH COURT BUILDING CHANDIGARH 1952-56

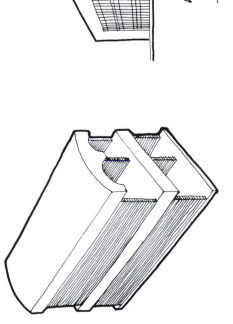

AS CAVE
THE JAOUL HOUSES 1954-56

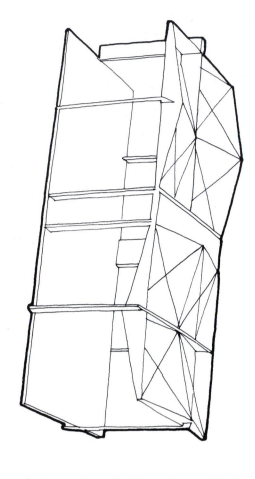

Constructed of steel and therefore untypical of much of his work, the Exhibition Pavilion at Zurich aptly summarises Le Corbusier's technique, encapsulating many of his design principles.

SYMMETRY AND ORTHOGONAL GRID
As with so many of Le Corbusier's projects, the design is based on a bilaterally symmetrical format with an implicit orthogonal grid.

STRUCTURE
The 'umbrella' roof is supported by a series of columns. The structure is evident, supports being provided where necessary with no attempt made to overplay or disguise structural fact and necessity.

COLOUR
Colour is used in a positive way to animate the pavilion (the cubic modules are above enamelled in primary colours).

PERCEPTUAL CLARITY
The form has a simple clear perceptual image.

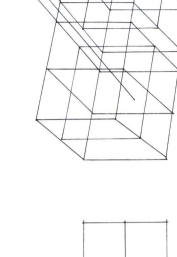

'UMBRELLA' ROOF

ORTHOGONAL GRID

BILATERAL SYMMETRY

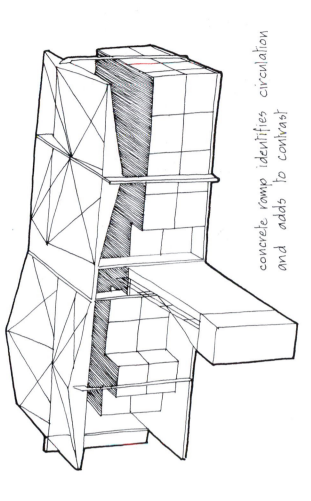

EXHIBITION PAVILION ZURICH 1967

STANDARD SOLUTION

The first ideas for this project can be traced back to 1928, so the pavilion is an example of the evolution of a standard solution, refined over a period of time. Such solutions (Citrohan and the Unités for example) evolve without reference to particular site conditions.

AESTHETIC ECONOMY

Although developed in quite a complex way, the design relies on aesthetic economy, with only three elements; the roof, the cubic pavilion below and the projecting ramp.

FUNCTIONAL IDENTITY AND CONTRAST

The three elements contrast with each other and each function is clearly identified — a protective roof, an enclosing pavilion, with a ramp giving vertical access.

UNITY AND HARMONY

Using the Modulor proportional system and the ordering of the symmetrically organised orthogonal grid, the design is based on unity and a harmonious relationship between all the elements.

concrete ramp identifies circulation and adds to contrast

RHYTHM AND DYNAMISM

The pavilion has a powerful rhythmic content which suggests three different kinds of movement; an undulating wave-like rhythm in the roof; a more regular kind of rhythm in the pavilion below, with a suggestion of lateral movement; a dramatic outward thrust provided by the ramp. Obliques give dynamism to roof and ramp.

SYMBOLISM

The form acknowledges Le Corbusier's interpretation of cosmic forces, with the roof a diagram of the 24 hour daily cycle of the rising and setting of the sun.

CONTRAST

CONTRAST IS THE COMMONEST DEVICE USED BY LE CORBUSIER AS A STARTING POINT FOR DESIGN DEVELOPMENT

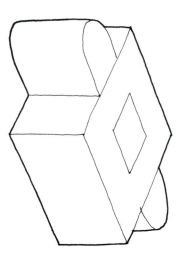

With the Villa Schwob the contrast is between half cylinders and a half cube.

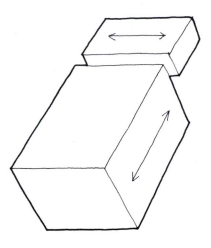

The Villa at Vaucresson has a theme based on contrasting volumes.

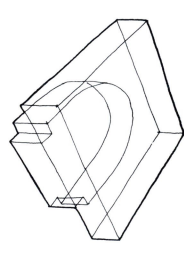

The Villa Savoye contrasts a raised slab with a grounded curvilinear volume.

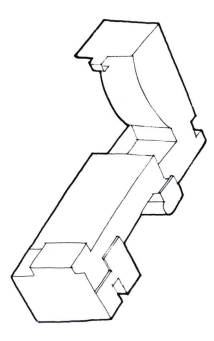

La Roche-Jeanneret has a raised curved volume set against a grounded rectilinear configuration.

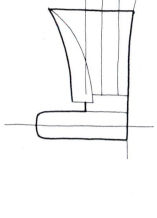

At the Pavillon Suisse a raised slab contrasts with the grounded refectory.

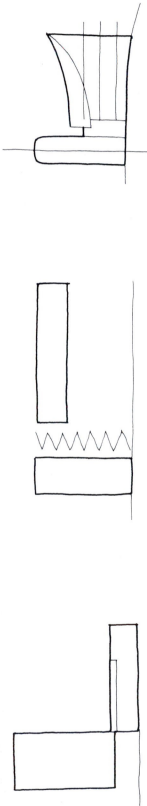

At La Tourette the vertical grounded church contrasts with horizontal raised cells.

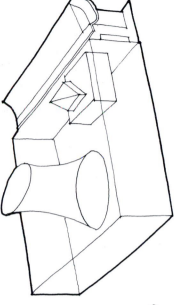

At Ronchamp vertical towers contrast with a horizontal mass.

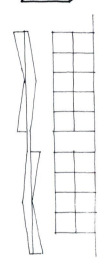

The Zurich Exhibition Pavilion contrasts an oblique roof with the cubic form below.

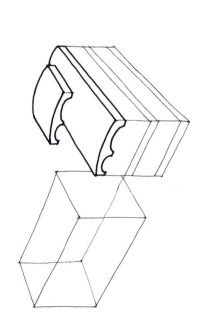

The Legislative Assembly at Chandigarh introduces several contrasting forms into and against the basic slab.

The curved vaults of the Jaoul Houses introduce contrast into the box-like basic form.

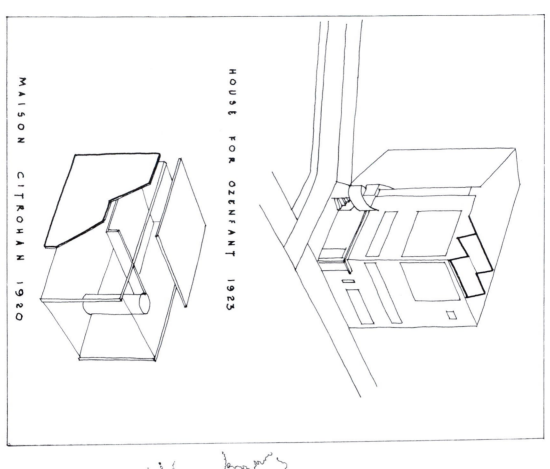

HOUSE FOR OZENFANT 1923

MAISON CITROHAN 1920

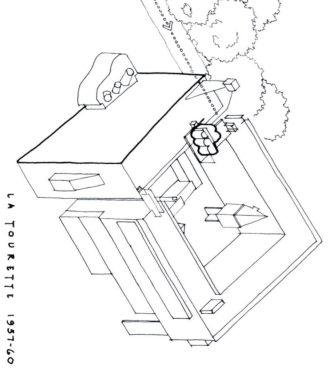

LA TOURETTE 1957-60

The oblique is one of the most potent devices used by Le Corbusier, adding dynamism when in contrast to box-like forms.

Another kind of contrast is provided on the route towards a building as when at La Tourette the large plain north wall of the church is seen immediately before the small cluster of interview cells.

RHYTHM

Rhythm, pattern and texture are important features of all Le Corbusier's work. In the Cité de Refuge the rooftop apartments add a vital rhythmic component while in the Monastery of La Tourette a regular rhythm of cells contrasts with the irregular rhythm of window mullions immediately below.

In his post-war work, particularly in his work in India, the potential of concrete to express pattern and texture is exploited to the full.

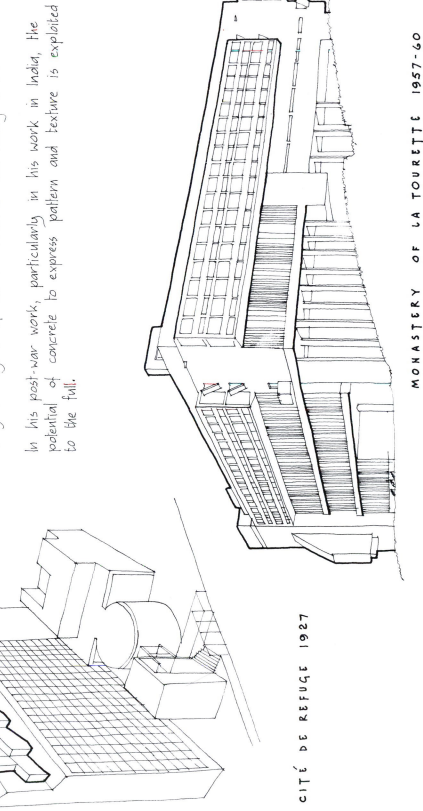

MONASTERY OF LA TOURETTE 1957-60

CITÉ DE REFUGE 1927

MEANING

Le Corbusier uses form to project meaning, and his shapes have a symbolic dimension that cannot be precisely identified and which is open to individual interpretation. During the twenties his imagery suggests the _zeitgeist_, while his later work becomes more abstract following the organic period during the thirties. Curved sculptural shapes are used, partly to relate to the landscape and also to express emotional or metaphysical factors.

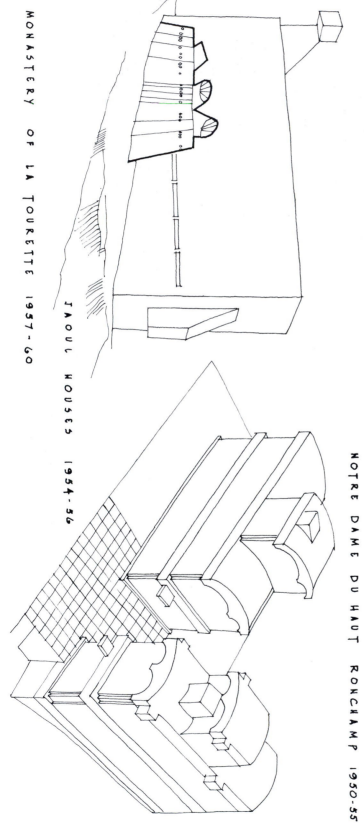

MONASTERY OF LA TOURETTE 1957-60

JAOUL HOUSES 1954-56

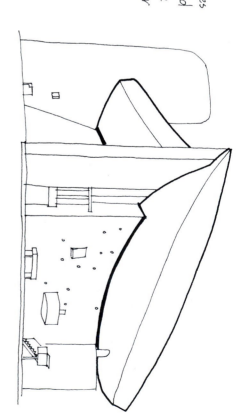

NOTRE DAME DU HAUT RONCHAMP 1950-55

Le Corbusier frequently used the vertical and horizontal slab, seen by him as capable of expressing a noble idea. Such forms were usually handled so that the simple essence of the shape was preserved, thereby adding to the impact made by the slab form. The bold and dramatic handling of slab-like forms is an important feature of Le Corbusier's personal style.

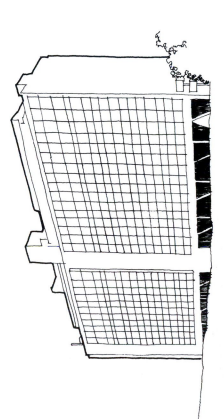

UNITÉ D'HABITATION FIRMINY-VERT 1965-68

In both paintings and architecture, curves in tension against an orthogonal grid are the main expression of lyricism.

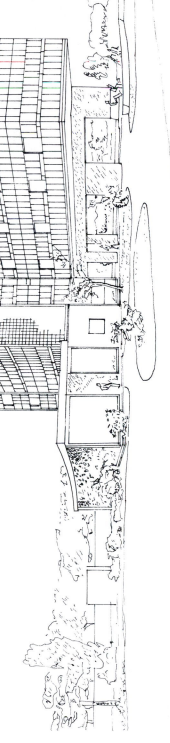

PAVILLON SUISSE PARIS 1930-32

after a drawing by Le Corbusier

AXIAL CONTROL

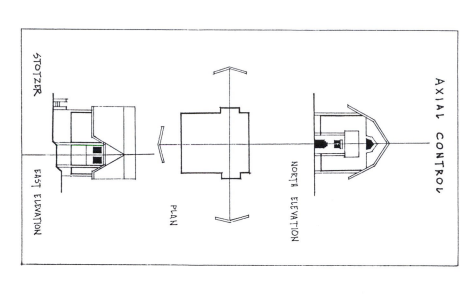

STOTZER

EAST ELEVATION

NORTH ELEVATION

PLAN

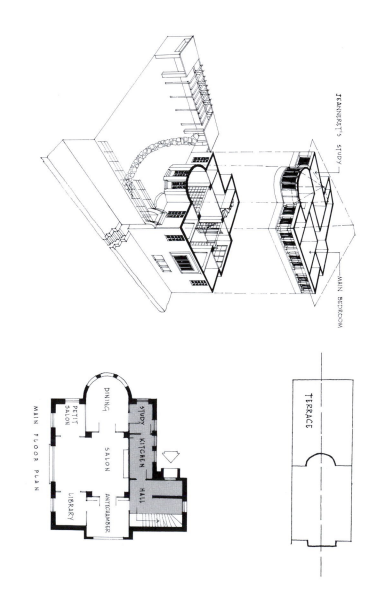

JEANNERET'S STUDY

MAIN BEDROOM

TERRACE

MAIN FLOOR PLAN

PETIT SALON

DINING

SALON

LIBRARY

STUDY

KITCHEN

HALL

ANTECHAMBER

Le Corbusier used axes as a major controlling discipline in his work. This is apparent in his first houses in La Chaux-de-Fonds and continued throughout his career.

Frequently Le Corbusier relates an axis to a curve, this being first used in the Villa Jeanneret-Perret (above). Axes are also related to routes, which in many cases have an implied continuity in that the route terminates in a view. This also occurs first in the Villa Jeanneret-Perret and is repeated in the Villa Schwob.

VILLA SCHWOB

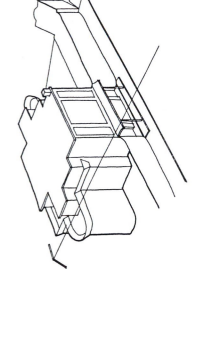

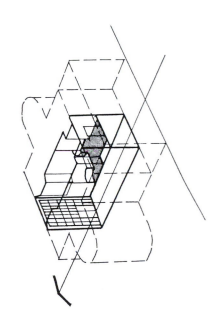

In the Villa Schwob, the lateral axis relates to movement towards a view whilst the longitudinal axis is terminated by curves.

lateral axis developed by double height volume so that movement is towards view

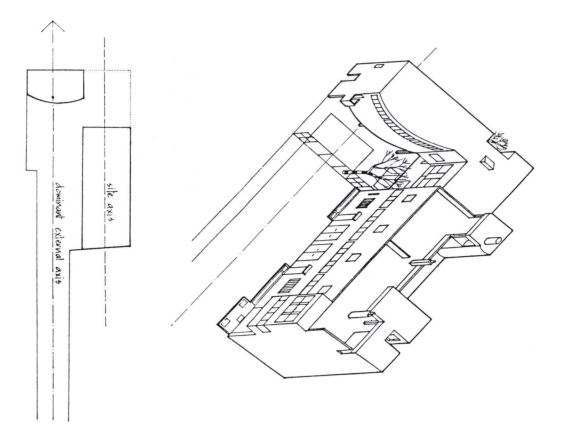

dominant external axis

site axis

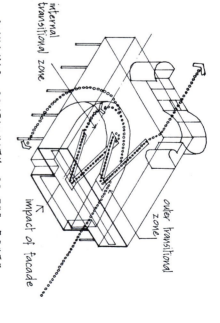

DYNAMIC CONTINUITY OF THE ROUTE

internal transitional zone

impact of façade

outer transitional zone

The La Roche-Jeanneret houses and Villa Savoye each terminate a major axis with a curve, and in each case a route continues beyond the form.

At La Roche the route passes under the raised picture gallery whilst at the Villa Savoye the route 'continues' through an opening in the roof screen.

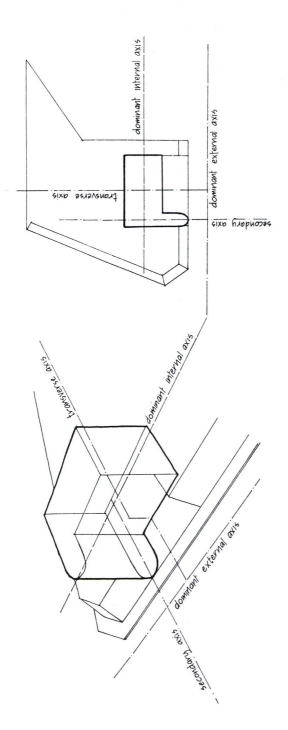

In the Villa at Vaucresson Le Corbusier erroneously terminates a secondary axis with a curved stair.

A balcony projects forward to terminate the stair axis in the Citrohan house (1927). This also extends the movement path from the stair out from the house.

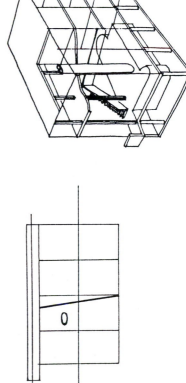

AXES AND CURVES

Axes can be traced in early Purist paintings which run through guitars at the maximum point of curvature.

The roof of the chapel at Ronchamp has its maximum point of curvature on the main axis of the building.

At the Pavillon Suisse, twin axes, equidistant on either side of the lateral axis run through the maximum point of curvature of the outer and inner curved walls.

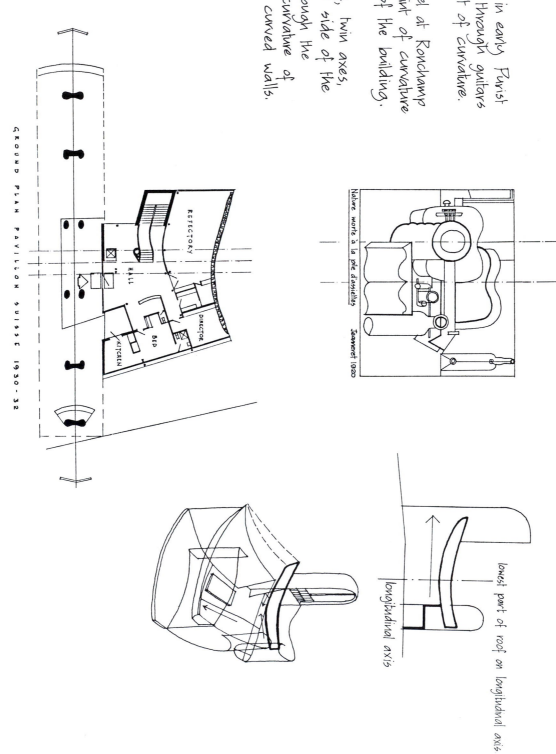

GROUND PLAN PAVILLON SUISSE 1930-32

REFECTORY

HALL

DIRECTOR

BED

KITCHEN

Nature morte à la pile d'assiettes   Jeanneret 1920

lowest part of roof on longitudinal axis

longitudinal axis

AXES AND MOVEMENT

Movement towards the Pavillon Suisse is pulled towards the axis formed by the pilotis. This axis directs movement towards the entry point.

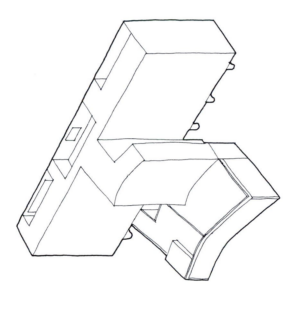

THE PAVILLON SUISSE PARIS 1930-32

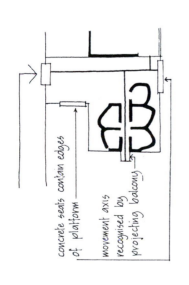

concrete seats contain edges of platform

movement axis recognised by projecting balcony

Axes are used to direct movement on the entry platform at La Tourette.

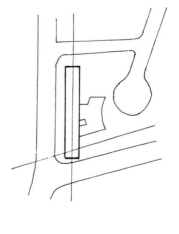

SITE PLAN

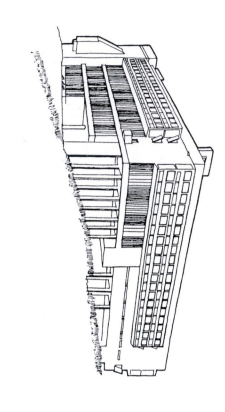

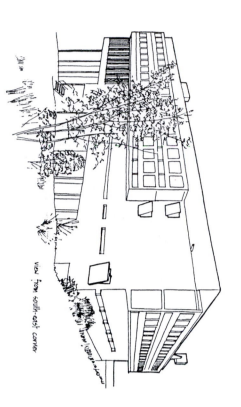

view from south-east corner

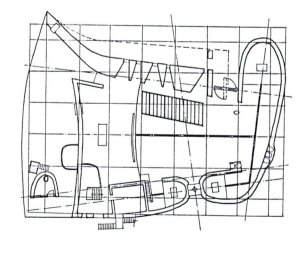

Routes which form the pinwheel circulation system at the monastery of La Tourette 'continue' externally and are deflected by concrete baffles at the ends of the corridors.

In the chapel at Ronchamp internal axes marked on the floor direct movement towards the curved chapels which each contain an altar and towards the main altar placed in front of a curved surface.

ROUTES AND VIEWS

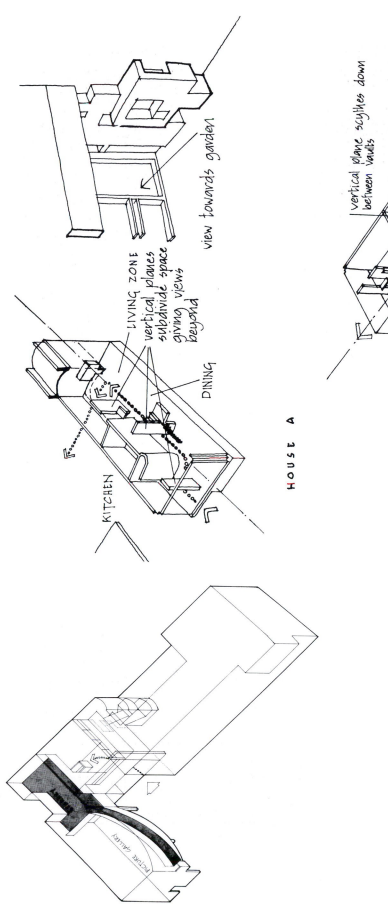

KITCHEN

DINING

LIVING ZONE
vertical planes
subdivide space
giving views
beyond

view towards garden

HOUSE A

PICTURE GALLERY

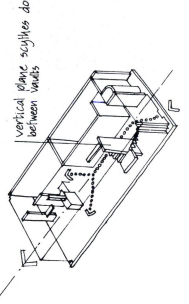

vertical plane scythes down
between vaults

HOUSE B

In the La Roche house the promenade architecturale ends
with a view from the library into the entry volume.

In each of the Jaoul houses the route 'continues' beyond
them into the garden. In House A this occurs with a
right angled turn giving a view towards the garden.
In House B the route along the axis continues towards
a window giving a view into the garden.

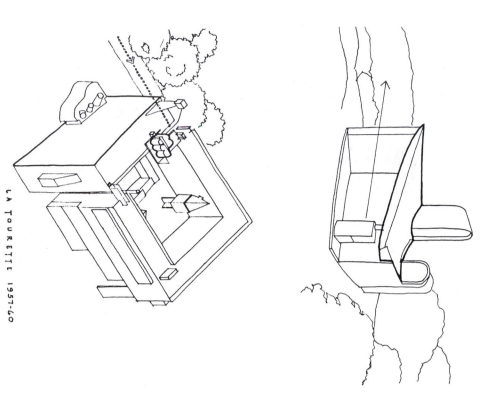

LA TOURETTE 1957-60

A curved form is placed externally on an axis identified by the orthogonal grid in the chapel at Ronchamp.

At the **monastery** of La Tourette the main longitudinal axis of the church is marked externally by the organ housing.

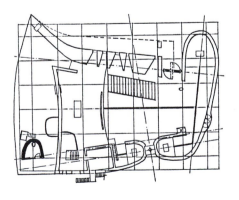

CURVED SCREENS

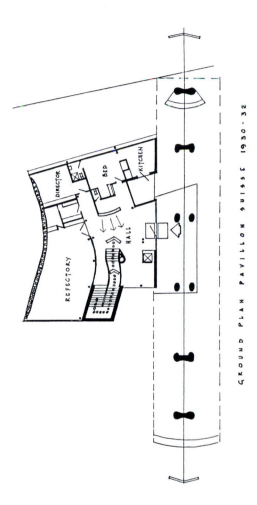

GROUND PLAN PAVILLON SUISSE 1930 - 32

The Villa Stein-de-Monzie and Pavillon Suisse each use a curved surface to blunt a movement path. In the villa the curve is opposite the main entry axis whilst in the Pavillon Suisse the curved screen is opposite the stair.

In each case the curved surface acts as a kind of 'sounding board' from which the movement path is bounced back into the space.

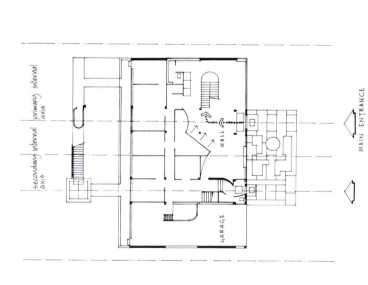

GROUND LEVEL PLAN

REVERSAL

An important consequence of Le Corbusier's continuous re-evaluation of nature as a source for his work, was the introduction of the idea of reversal. Mainly evident in his post-war period, which was itself in many ways philosophically at an opposite pole to his twenties thinking, this consists of the development of opposite readings within the same building or the reversal of roles in elements within a building.

Typical of the attitude which this represents, are sketches in which he portrays several boats beached and lying at different angles with their mooring ropes loosly forming diverse patterns on the sand. Other sketches show the transformation when the tide comes in, resulting in boats and ropes being stretched out uniformly. So nature, in the form of the tide, changes the random into the ordered, reversing the previous state.

Le Corbusier often makes reference to this fundamental principle, manifest in such complimentary opposites as male/female, day/night, whilst inside/outside, open/closed or contraction/expansion have direct architectural connotations.

The principle seems also linked to his preference to operate within an infinitely extending frame of reference in terms of ideas, whilst limiting his expressive range within a compact controlled system in his designs. In that sense his work is simultaneously giving an impression of both expansion and contraction. The Chapel at Ronchamp for example contains a multitude of ideas and cross references, in themselves apparently unlimited in their scope, yet the building concentrates these within a tightly packed organisational framework.

Nor can this be disassociated from Le Corbusier's liking for the paradox, and his later tendency to create simultaneous readings by 'switching' elements reminds us of the double reading given to plates bottles and books in the early Purist paintings by depicting them in plan and the third dimension simultaneously.

AMBIGUITY

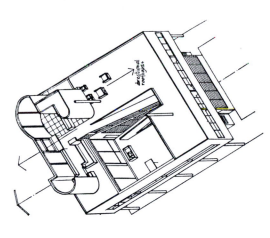

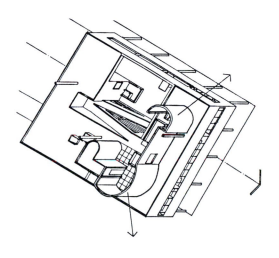

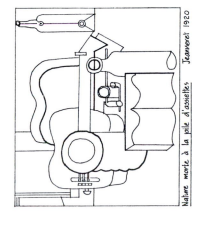

Nature morte à la pile d'assiettes   Jeanneret 1920

A bottle, book and plates are seen simultaneously in plan and in a stylised third dimension. Two guitars are shown, the second ambiguously as if it is a shadow of the first.

The roof screen to the Villa Savoye reads as a solid from one side and as a plane from the other. The screen extends to become the enclosed top of the spiral stair, this enclosure being a solid.

The elevated slab can be read as a solid and also as penetrable where the roof terrace becomes visible through the opening in the ribbon windows.

SOLID · PLANAR   SOLID · PENETRABLE

PLAN · THIRD DIMENSION

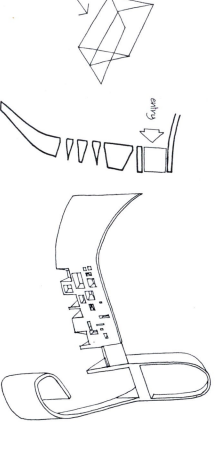

entry

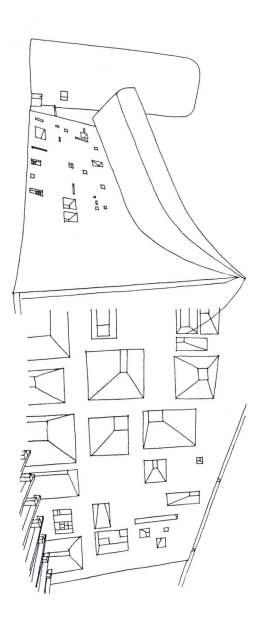

CLOSED · OPEN

The chapel at Ronchamp provides one of the cleavest demonstrations of the idea of reversal.

The south wall is simultaneously open (inside) and closed (outside).

The triangular section of the south wall suggests closure at its upper lip and expansion below. This two dimensional idea assumes richness with the myriad of shapes of the window openings.

CLOSURE · EXPANSION

RONCHAMP

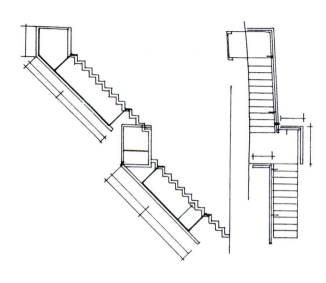

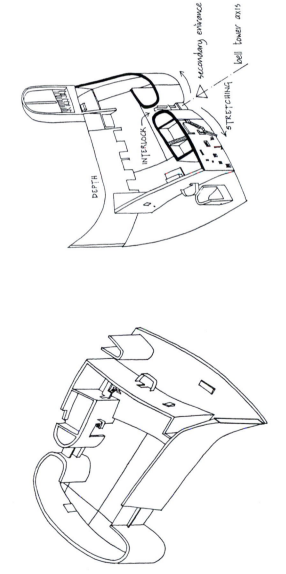

DEPTH

INTERLOCK

secondary entrance

STRETCHING — bell tower axis

The muscular interlock of the twin chapels at the rear reverses the open embrace of the south and east walls.

CLOSED INTERLOCK · OPEN EMBRACE

The stair attached to the north wall is fixed to the wall at the top but shifts outwards away from the wall. The handrail does the opposite, the upper section being on the outside, the lower portion on the inside.

INSIDE · OUTSIDE

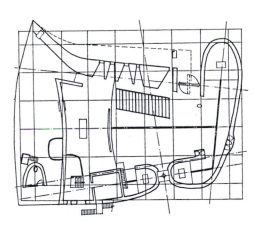

CONCAVE · CONVEX

The interaction of concave/convex forms inside and outside the chapel exemplifies the idea of reversal, with the east wall concave outside and convex inside, the altar rail concave and outer platform edge convex. The three chapels, in being simultaneously convex and concave, proclaim on the exterior but contain on the interior. The roof acts as a protective shelter outside but exerts downward pressure inside. The entire concept of the chapel is generated by the internal/external dialogue suggested by the brief.

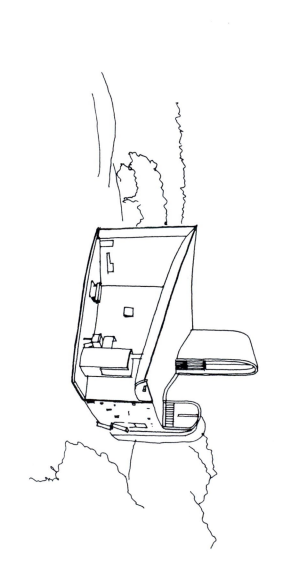

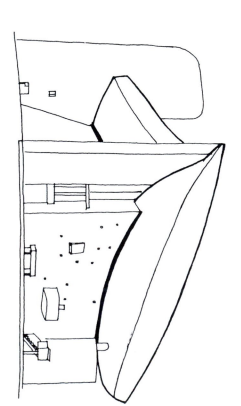

LA TOURETTE

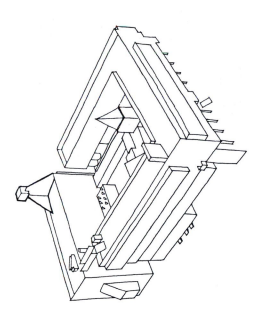

SOLID · PLANAR

The bell tower at the monastery of La Tourette is solid when seen from one side and appears as part of the solid mass of the church. When seen from the other side it reads as two planes.

REGULAR · ORGANIC

The main places for prayer, church and sanctuary are opposites as forms. The church is a regular rectangle, its horizontal floor raised above the slope. The sanctuary is a contorted organic shape with its floor descending down the hill. The close juxtaposition of these forms intensifies the differences between them.

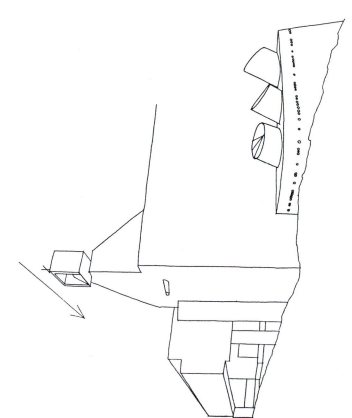

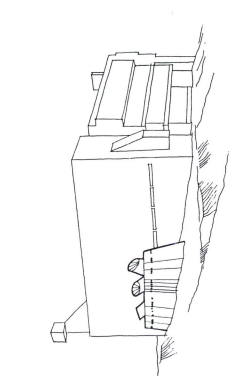

OPPOSITES

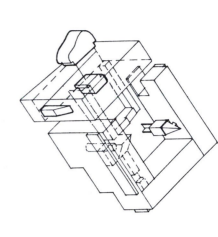

STABILITY · MOTION

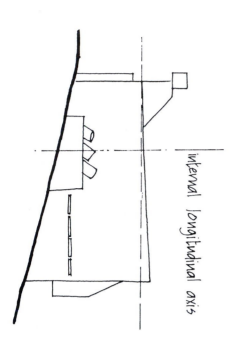

internal longitudinal axis

The stability of the church is in opposition to the dynamic sense of motion induced by the pinwheel around the court.

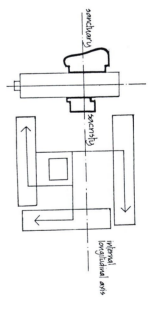

sanctuary

sacristy

internal longitudinal axis

UP · DOWN

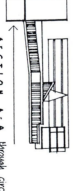

SECTION A·A through circulation spine

As the slope descends the church roof is tilted up. Within the court, the route from the novices block to the circulation spine moves upwards as the slope moves downwards. The circulation spine runs along the slope. Its top remains horizontal but the floor and ceiling slope down to give access to the church.

LA TOURETTE

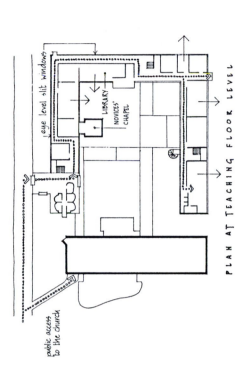

public access
to the church

eye level slit windows

LIBRARY
NOVICES'
CHAPEL

PLAN AT TEACHING FLOOR LEVEL

The route around the teaching floor starts
inside the court, moves outside along a
corridor before turning at right angles
along a narrow corridor. On reaching
the central circulation spine the route
moves inside, continuing around the
court.

INSIDE · OUTSIDE · INSIDE

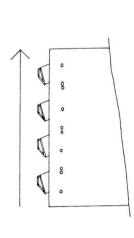

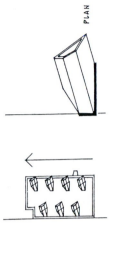

PLAN

The light sources participate in the pinwheel.

Light sources to the sacristy appear to
be 'moving' in the direction of the pinwheel
around the court. They point in the direction
of the pinwheel and are at an oblique
angle. Yet they are securely held by a
right angle at their base. They appear to
be 'moving', yet are held.

MOBILE · STATIC

REVERSAL

The vaults on the Jaoul houses are reversed on each house, minor then major in house A, major then minor in house B. They are also concealed in the lower slabs and expressed in the upper. The juxtaposition of the two blocks at right angles to one another results in the pairs of vaults facing different directions, yet they are locked together by the access zone.

MAJOR · MINOR · MINOR MAJOR
CONCEALMENT · EXPOSURE
NORTH EAST · SOUTH WEST · SOUTH EAST · NORTH WEST
INTERLOCK

As with the deployment of the Jaoul houses the towers at Ronchamp face different and opposite directions yet are locked together within the ensemble.

EAST WEST · NORTH
INTERLOCK

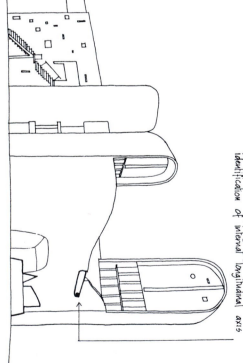
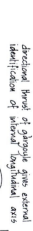

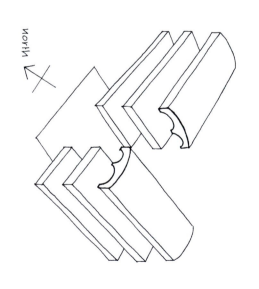

north

directional thrust of gargoyle gives external identification of internal longitudinal axis

JAOUL HOUSES

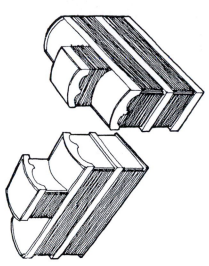

The ends of house B are 'open', the ends
of house A are closed

OPEN · CLOSED

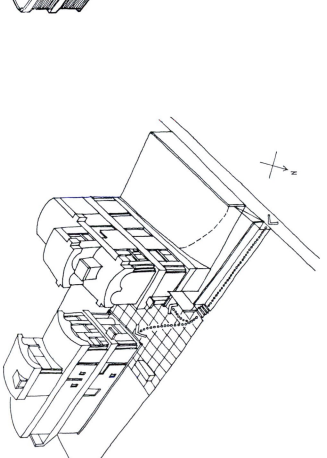

N

To add to the controlled and compacted reversals
in the Jaoul houses the ramps go up for pedestrians
and down for cars.

UP · DOWN

SYMMETRY · ASYMMETRY
ROOF UP · ROOF DOWN
INTERLOCK

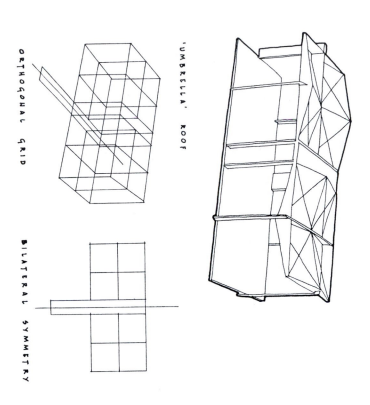

'UMBRELLA' ROOF

ORTHOGONAL GRID

BILATERAL SYMMETRY

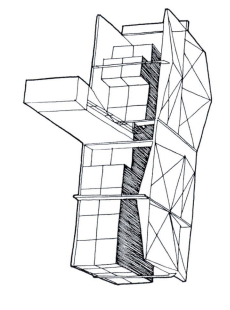

The Zurich Exhibition Pavilion is by implication linked to Le Corbusier's diagram of the 24 hour rhythm of the day in which the sun rises and sets in a continuous rising and falling curve. This is reflected in the ascending descending profile of the edge of the roof. This inversion of the roof reverses the deployment of structural members and roof panels on either side of center.

Underneath the roof umbrella, in a bi-laterally symmetrical format, Le Corbusier arranges the exhibition space asymmetrically. The twin roofs are locked together about the ramp.

OPPOSITES

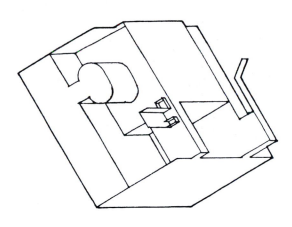

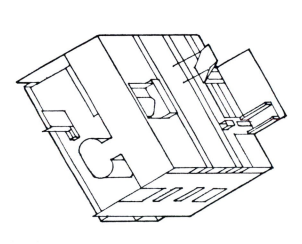

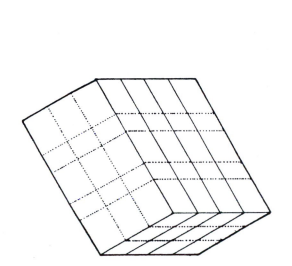

BI-LATERAL SYMMETRY

CLOSED FACADE · ASYMMETRY   **OPEN FACADE · ASYMMETRY**

Within the bi-laterally symmetrical format of the Villa Stein-
de-Monzie, Le Corbusier develops open and closed facades
each of which is asymmetrical yet controlled by symmetry.

BUILDINGS BY LE CORBUSIER IN AND AROUND PARIS

1 Villa at Vaucresson.....................................1922..........85, boulevarde de la République, Vaucresson (very much changed)
2 Studio Apartment for Ozenfant......................1922.........53, avenue Reille, Paris 14th district
3 La Roche Jeanneret houses..........................1923........10, square du Dr Blanche, Paris 16th district (Fondation Le Corbusier) Tel. 288 41 53
4 Houses Lipchitz and Miejschaninoff..............1924........9, allée des Pins, Boulogne
5 Maison Cook..1926........6, rue Denfert-Rochereau, Boulogne sur Seine.
6 Dortoir du Palais du Peuple........................1926........29, rue Cordières, Paris 13th district
7 Villa Stein-de-Monzie.................................1927........17, rue du Dr Pauchet, Vaucresson
8 Maison Planex..1927........26, bis boulevarde Masséna, Paris 13th district
9 Maison Church..1928........rue Bourbon. Ville d'Avray
10 Asile flottant...1929........Pont d'Austerlitz, Paris 5th district
11 * Villa Savoye...1929........Chemin de Villiers, Poissy
12 Pavillon Suisse..1930........Cité Universitaire, boulevarde Jourdan, Paris
13 Apartment for M. Beistegui..........................1930........Champs Elysées at the corner of the rue Balzac Paris
14 Cité de Refuge..1932........12, rue Cantagrel, Paris 13th district
15 Apartments..1933........24, rue Nungesser-et-Coli, Paris 16th district
16 Residence at la Celle St Cloud.....................1935........49, avenue du Chesnay (residence La Chataigneraie at the corner of the boulevarde de la République)
17 Maisons Jaoul..1954........81, rue de Longchamp, Neuilly Paris
18 Maison du Brésil...1959........Cité Universitaire, boulevarde Jourdan, Paris

Most of the above are private residences; those marked with an asterisk are open to visitors at certain times. Buildings marked with a circle can be visited by arrangement.

The Monastery of La Tourette is located at Eveux sur l'Arbresle near Lyon. Ronchamp is near the Swiss border, about 15 km from Belfort and about 70 km from La Chaux-de-Fonds.

LOCATION PLAN

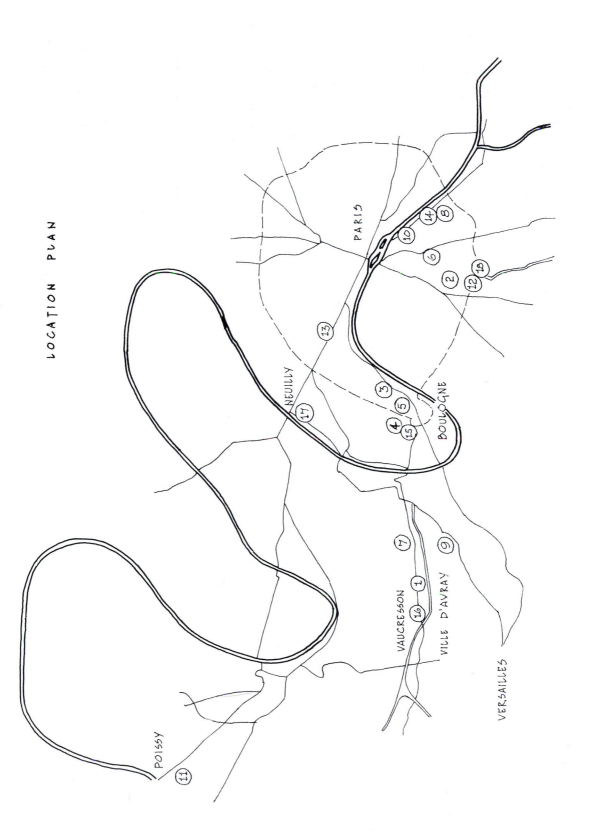